Institutions, Production, and Working Life

Institutions, Production, and Working Life

Edited by
Geoffrey Wood and Phil James

OXFORD
UNIVERSITY PRESS

This book has been printed digitally and produced in a standard specification in order to ensure its continuing availability

OXFORD
UNIVERSITY PRESS

Great Clarendon Street, Oxford OX2 6DP

Oxford University Press is a department of the University of Oxford.
It furthers the University's objective of excellence in research, scholarship, and education by publishing worldwide in

Oxford New York

Auckland Cape Town Dar es Salaam Hong Kong Karachi
Kuala Lumpur Madrid Melbourne Mexico City Nairobi
New Delhi Shanghai Taipei Toronto

With offices in

Argentina Austria Brazil Chile Czech Republic France Greece
Guatemala Hungary Italy Japan South Korea Poland Portugal
Singapore Switzerland Thailand Turkey Ukraine Vietnam

Oxford is a registered trade mark of Oxford University Press in the UK and in certain other countries

Published in the United States
by Oxford University Press Inc., New York

Reprinted 2010

ISBN 978-0-19-929177-9

Contents

List of Figures

List of Tables

List of Contributors

Peter Bain is Senior Lecturer in Human Resource Management, Department of Human Resource Management, University of Strathclyde.

Chris Baldry is Professor and Director of the Centre for Human Resource Management in the Department of Management and Organization at the University of Stirling.

Robert Boyer is Senior Researcher (Directeur de Recherche) at National Center for Scientific Research (CNRS) (www.cnrs.fr), Head of the Research Unit (URA 922 : 'Régulation, Human Ressources et Public Choice') Associated to CNRS, Economist at CNRS, and Professor (Directeur d'Etudes) at l'EHESS.

Chris Brewster is Professor of Human Resource Management at Henley Management College.

Mick Brookes is Senior Lecturer in Economics, Middlesex University Business School, Middlesex University.

Rachel Dwyer is Assistant Professor in the Department of Sociology, Ohio State University.

John Grahl is Professor of European Integration at Middlesex University Business School, Middlesex University.

Damian Grimshaw is Reader in Employment Studies and Director, European Work and Employment Research Centre (EWERC) at Manchester Business School, University of Manchester.

Mark Harcourt is Professor of Strategy and Human Resource Management in the Department of Strategic Management, Waikato University, New Zealand.

J. Rogers Hollingsworth is Professor in the Departments of Sociology and History at the University of Wisconsin (Madison), Visiting Fellow, Neurosciences Institute (La Jolla, California), Visiting Scholar, Institute for Nonlinear Science, University of California, San Diego.

Ray Hudson is Professor of Geography in the Department of Geography at Durham University.

Jeff Hyman is Professor of Management at the University of Aberdeen Business School.

Phil James is Professor of Employment Relations at Oxford Brookes University Business School, Oxford Brookes University.

Jim Kitay is Associate Professor and Chair of the Work & Organisational Studies discipline in the School of Business at the University of Sydney.

Russell Lansbury is the Associate Dean (Research) in the Faculty of Economics and Business and Professor of Work and Organisational Studies in the School of Business at the University of Sydney.

Mick Marchington is Professor of Human Resource Management at Manchester Business School, University of Manchester.

Jamie Peck is Professor of Geography at the University of Wisconsin, Madison.

Ian Roper is Principal Lecturer in Human Resource Management, Middlesex University Business School, Middlesex University.

Jill Rubery is Professor of Comparative Employment Systems and Co-Director of European Work and Employment Research Centre (EWERC) at Manchester Business School, University of Manchester.

Andrew Sayer is Professor of social theory and Political Economy in the Department of Sociology at Lancaster University.

Phil Taylor is Professor of Work and Organisation, Department of Human Resource Management, University of Strathclyde.

Nick Wailes is Lecturer in Work and Organisational Studies, School of Business, at the University of Sydney.

Geoffrey Wood is Professor of Human Resource Management in the School of Management at the University of Sheffield, and Overseas Associate of the University of Witwatersrand.

Erik Olin Wright is Vilas Distinguished Professor of Sociology in the Department of Sociology at the University of Wisconsin, Madison.

1

Introduction
Institutions, Regulation, and Practice: Traditions and Modes of Understanding

Phil James and Geoffrey Wood

It is a truism to say that the past two decades or more have witnessed significant changes occurring in the world of work, both in developed and emerging economies. In the case of the former, for example, one only needs to take heed of the widespread decline that has occurred in trade union membership and power, the rise in importance of employment in small- and medium-sized enterprises, the growth that has taken place in various 'nonstandard' forms of employment, the shifts that have occurred in the occupational and sectoral composition of employment, and the way in which technological developments have stimulated not only major changes to work tasks and processes, but whole new industries and occupational groupings.

That these developments, and others of equal importance, notably the way in which employers have sought to reform work processes and broader aspects of their employment regimes, have been occurring is, unsurprisingly, given the ample evidence available to support them, widely accepted. It is also similarly accepted that their occurrence has been supported, at the micro-, macro-, and supranational levels, by neoliberal policy agendas aimed at freeing up labor markets and, more generally, enhancing the discretionary power of employers. The nature and coherence of these agendas, and the reasons why they have come to occupy their current levels of predominance, however, all remain issues of uncertainty and debate. For example, the role played by the process of globalization remains an issue of contention, with different commentators adopting very different positions with regard to the extent to which it is acting to reform product markets and hence the degree to which it is serving as a material, as opposed to ideological, force for change.

A similar situation is also apparent if attention turns to the connections that exist between, on the one hand, the broad aims of this underlying neoliberalism and, on the other, the way in which they are in practice pursued within individual nation-states and organizations. For the available evidence indicates that wide differences exist at both of these levels in terms of the way in which the desire to reduce labor market constraints and reform systems of organizational governance has, in reality, been operationalized. For example, there would seem marked variations in the extent and nature of reform between Anglo-Saxon and the coordinated type economies found in Western Europe. Similarly, within individual countries significant differences can be discerned with regard to how employers have changed their employment strategies in response to the changed environments confronting them. At the same time, there is far from universal agreement as to the causes of these variations and differences, and there seems a need for them to be the subject of further exploration, both theoretically and empirically.

These important points of debate exist, in turn, alongside two more, inevitably related, organizationally focused ones. The first of these concerns how the changes occurring in working life are impacting on the emotional and material experiences of workers. Here an important point of debate remains the question of whether 'things are getting better or worse', with three very different positions being identifiable in the literature, which can, in short-hand terms, be usefully labeled the optimistic, pessimistic, and bifurcated.

The first of these, commonly articulated by proponents of 'high performance work systems', suggests that the current trend is toward the creation of empowered systems of workplace governance marked by developmental- and justice-based supports which act to engender greater levels of worker satisfaction, motivation, and commitment. The second, in contrast, questions the extensiveness of use of these systems, in other than a rhetorical way, and instead embodies the view that the predominant trajectory involves the utilization of 'lean and mean' ones that encompass increases in work intensity and managerial surveillance and control. Finally, the third embodies the view that there is no overwhelmingly predominant trend but rather a growing variation in the practices of employing organizations, even across the same sector, as well as a tendency for greater variation in how different occupational groupings are treated within them.

Meanwhile, debates continue to rage in respect of the relationship that exists between economic performance and modes of employment regulation. Two main important strands to these debates can be discerned. One, which is very much linked to the alleged superiority of high performance work systems, concerns the way in which the performance of organizations is related to how they go about managing those that they employ. The other focuses attention on the extent to which the relative economic performance of countries reflects variations between them in the national institutional frameworks and the informal regulations that shape the nature of employer—worker relationships, both collectively and individually; with an important focus of interest here being on whether higher or lower levels of state regulation are conducive to better such performance over specific time periods.

The relationship between formal and informal regulation and performance outcomes, furthermore, serves to raise another important issue, namely the desirability or otherwise of the increasing reliance that has come to be placed, perhaps, particularly, in the United States and Great Britain, on 'networked' forms of production and service delivery which, by definition, support the development of more fragmented and diffused patterns of employment; whether this be through the in-house use of agency staff or the externalization of previously internally based work activities. To date this question has received little theoretical and empirical attention. Yet, it has obvious potential implications for the way in which workers are managed, and their levels of motivation and commitment.

This last point of debate, in turn, highlights graphically that the development of a more rounded and better understanding of the various issues raised above is not just a matter of theoretical importance. For the positions adopted in relation to them also have potentially important policy implications. If, for example, the forces of globalization are less than commonly claimed, the freedom of nation states to set their own policy agendas is correspondingly greater and the need for them to mimic those utilized elsewhere is correspondingly less. In a similar vein, if empowered systems of governance are supportive of better economic performance, then this clearly raises the issue of whether their establishment should be supported by government and the question of whether this support is best provided through legal or nonlegal means.

Rationale for This Volume

The above points of debate essentially provided the impetus behind the preparation of this book. For it struck the editors that a volume which drew together a group of leading international scholars to provide rigorous examinations of a number of key issues central to them would do much to enrich and facilitate their discussion and identify ways in which they can be taken forward, while also, simultaneously, providing academic colleagues, policymakers, and students with a valuable reference source.

At the same time, it was recognized that careful thought needed to be given to the type of contributions that could best be brought together to meet these objectives. In the event, it was decided that this selection should be informed by three, initial, and main considerations; all of which were seen as important to ensuring that the book could live up to the editors' expectations for it. These were the needs to ensure the inclusion of analyses encompassing the comparative international, national, and subnational and workplace levels, the provision of both purely theoretical and more empirically based pieces and studies that paid substantial attention to the dynamics of the interrelationships that exist between employing organizations and their wider institutional contexts.

In combination, these considerations, particularly the first, subsequently led on to a fourth criterion that, ultimately, exerted an important influence over the final shape of the book. This was the perceived desirability of bringing together contributions which reflected two of the most important strands of current scholarship regarding the examination of the nature and causes of recent organizational-level change, namely the essentially macro-orientated analyses offered by regulation theorists and the more micro-based, and empirically based, ones that have been such an important feature of the work of researchers in the field of employment relations and the labor process and related traditions.

Regulation theory represents a heterodox approach to socioeconomics that highlights the inherently unstable nature of capital accumulation and the rules and practices that provide—always on a spatially and temporarily confined basis—macroeconomic stability and growth (Aglietta 1979; Boyer 1990; Jessop 2001*a*: xi). In other words, it is an approach that considers the historicity of institutions and specific practices which explain the causes underlying periods of prosperity and instability (Amable 2003: 75–6). In particular, regulation theorists have highlighted the relatively positive mix of social (equity and mobility) and economic outcomes (stable growth) that at various times have characterized cooperative varieties of capitalism (Amable 2003: 76).

In some respects, regulation theory parallels the varieties of capitalism literature (see Whitley 1999; Hall and Soskice 2001), which has accorded particular attention to the defining features of differing extant varieties of capitalism. It has, however, devoted more attention to the process of evolution and rupture. For example, the relatively strong (albeit volatile) performance of the US economy in the early 2000s vis-à-vis cooperative alternatives has led leading writers in the regulationist tradition to reemphasize the centrality of evolution and rupture to the understanding of the chronic instability that characterizes capitalist development and to correspondingly question the capacity of simple benchmarking and/or emulation of existing rules and practices to cope with it in particular time and space. Thus, in the face of the instability—and, indeed, underlying brutality—of neoliberalism, regulation theorists do not simply hearken to the past, but, rather, examine the process of institutional coherence and change, the pathologies of the present, and the circumstances under which more progressive forms of institutional mediation are likely to emerge (cf. Hollingsworth 2004).

In contrast, to this macro-level analysis of regulationists, the labor process tradition has been distinguished by a focus on changes in the nature of work organization as a means of securing continued capital accumulation, with much of the focus being on workplace based studies. Following on Braverman's dissection (1974) of managerial control over the labor process and latter developments and critiques (cf. Piore and Sabel 1984), the annual *Labour Process Conferences* have resulted in the production of a series of books looking at specific changes in work organization.

Early works in this series, including those of Knights, Willmott, and Collinson (1985) and Knights and Willmott (1986*a*, 1986*b*), focused on issues such as job redesign, gender at work, and the changing role of management and encompassed a strong critical and theoretical orientation. However, while some later volumes retained such an orientation, this was often marked by an infusion of postmodernist tools and concepts (e.g. Knights and Willmott 1989), and, by the early 1990s, an increasing emphasis on the nature and effects of the transformation of production regimes, with attention being paid in this regard to new managerial strategies, like Total Quality Management (Wilkinson and Willmott 1994), and the scope that existed to emulate seemingly successful paradigms from abroad, including 'Japanization' (Elger and Smith 1994). More recently, the trend has been toward an even more applied focus, dealing with issues such as knowledge management (Prichard et al. 2000), critical perspectives on customer service (Sturdy, Grugulis, and Willmott 2001), and skills development (Warhurst, Keep, and Grugulis 2004).

Closely related to such accounts are those critical empirical works that are overtly or tacitly located within—or in close dialog with—the broad political tradition. Similarly, distinguished by a focus on plant-level issues, this very sociological tradition is characterized both by a strong emphasis on methodological and analytical rigor and by a certain pragmatism; theory is deployed, where necessary, as a means of elucidation and explanation, but the primary focus is on the recording of practices and their practical implications, and has encompassed issues ranging from industrial relations to recruitment and planning, while recognizing the need to understand social phenomena beyond 'outward appearances' and expected outcomes (Jessop 2001*a*: xii). Some recent examples of such work includes Edwards and Collinson (2002), Belanger, Edwards, and Wright (2003), Marchington and Speakman (2004), and Frobel and Marchington (2005).

It was, of course, recognized from the outset that these two strands of analyses are not mutually exclusive. In particular, due recognition was accorded to the fact that while the work undertaken within this last strand of scholarship has varied in terms of the attention paid to the way in which workplace- and organizational-level practices and developments have been shaped by wider institutional factors, they have invariably eschewed the use of analytical frameworks which see them as being impermeable to outside influence. Nevertheless, it was felt that there was much to be gained from combining the accounts emerging from this work with the more theoretically sophisticated explanations of the relationship between institutional configurations and firm-level practices that are to be found in the regulation theory–inspired literature. Particularly given that both sets of literature share common ground in emphasizing the fragile and unstable nature of capitalist accumulation and the need that employers have, at the workplace and societal levels, for mechanisms which enable them to both exert control over workers and gain consent from them.

Indeed, it was hoped that this underlying common ground would, when combined together with the differing theoretical and empirical foci of these two traditions of scholarship, provide a platform for a volume that could make an important contribution to furthering our understanding of the 'what' and 'why' of the changing world of world and the directions that future analyses could most productively take.

Volume Structure and Content

Fortunately for the editors a range of internationally respected scholars expressed a willingness to participate in our proposed volume. As a result, they found it remarkably, and surprisingly, easy to produce a collection in line with the above thinking.

The contributions provided embody, as intended, a rich and varied collection of analyses that differ widely in terms of their level, subject focus, and intellectual and methodological approaches. They also, inevitably, contain lines of analysis which overlap to a greater or lesser degree. Nevertheless, an attempt has been made to group them thematically in order to assist the reader in comparing and contrasting their analyses. Four such themes have been identified.

The first, *Rethinking Institutions, Society, and Firm-Level Practices*, contains five chapters which, as its title suggests, provide important, but differing, explorations of the way in which practices at the organizational level are influenced by wider societal and institutional forces. The first of these, by Robert Boyer, provides new insights into the process of institutional coherence and change, and the second, by Rogers Hollingsworth, examines how the process of developing more effective institutions of governance is hindered by a growing lack of understanding of the surrounding social world, draws on the pathbreaking work of Niels Bohr to identify some of the key factors that contribute to this lack of understanding, and suggests actions that could be taken to partially address it. The broad-based and wide-ranging contributions of these authors are then supplemented by three more narrowly focused and empirically orientated ones. Thus, that of Russell Lansbury, Jim Kitay, and Nick Wailes examines how far forces of globalization have led to similar processes of reform in the auto and banking sectors in two very different national settings, South Korea and Australia, that of Ray Hudson focuses attention on the way in which the interaction between successive governments and the changing priorities and composition of local business interests have influenced regional industrial policies in the North-East of England and that of John Grahl analyzes the implications of recent changes in financial markets for aspects of European employment relations.

These six chapters are followed by a further three that provide important insights into the factors shaping *Continuity and Change in Working Life*, the balance that exists between these two processes and the way in which recent reforms have impacted workers. The first of these, by Damian Grimshaw, Mick Marchington, and Jill Rubery, draws on detailed case study work to examine the rationales underlying the rise of interorganizational contracting, and its associated deverticalization, and the implications of such contracting for employment relations and employers. The second, coauthored by Mark Harcourt, Ian Roper, and Geoffrey Wood, considers, against the backcloth of widespread international pressures to reduce employment security rights as a means of facilitating greater numerical flexibility, the relationship that exists between such protection and employment stability, working hours, and functional task flexibility and productivity. There then follows a chapter, by Jeff Hyman that uses new and existing research evidence to investigate how far developments in respect of worker empowerment, in both the 'old' and 'knowledge' economies, have served to increase worker discretion and control and another by Andrew Sayer which explores how the balance between the instrumentalism of employing organizations and the interests, needs, and concerns of those that they employ may either help or impede the realization of their goals. Finally, a contribution by Phil James pays attention to how recent economic and political developments have acted to change the level of workplace risks faced by workers and their propensity to suffer injury and ill health, another by Chris Baldry, Phil Taylor, and Peter Bain examines the implications of call center work for workers' health and the factors that shape them and one from Chris Brewster, Geoffrey Wood, and Mick Brookes explores the extent to which several distinct and viable varieties of firm may coexist within specific varieties of capitalism, and whether specific varieties of capitalism are associated with a greater or lesser degree of diversity in firm-level practices.

The third and last substantive part of the book, entitled *Changing Labor Market and the New Outsiders*, contains two further chapters. The first of these, written by Erik Olin Wright and Rachel Dwyer, investigates the changing nature of job formation in the United States; they point to the increasing polarization of work and employment, trends which are increasingly apparent in many other national economies. Meanwhile, the second, by Jamie Peck, discusses the nature and origins of workfare programs, and considers their ramifications for recipients, as well as wider labor markets.

Finally, in a concluding chapter, the editors, drawing on the findings of the preceding chapters, highlight some of the central issues and contestations surrounding the nature of regulation, macroeconomic growth, and firm-level practices in the neoliberal age.

References

Aglietta, M. (1979). *A Theory of Capitalist Regulation*. London: New Left.

Amable, B. (2003). *The Diversity of Modern Capitalism*. Oxford: Oxford University Press.

Belanger, J., Edwards, P., and Wright, M. (2003). 'Commitment at Work and Independence from Management: A Study of Advanced Teamwork,' *Work and Occupations*, 30: 234–52.

Boyer, R. (1990). *Regulation Theory: A Critical Introduction*. New York: Columbia University Press.

Braverman, H. (1974). *Labor and Monopoly Capital*. New York: Monthly Review Press.

Edwards, P. and Collinson, M. (2002). 'Empowerment and Managerial Labor Strategies: Pragmatism Regained,' *Work and Occupations*, 29: 272–99.

Elger, T. and Smith, C. (eds.) (1994). *Global Japanisation*. London: Routledge.

Frobel, P. and Marchington, M. (2005). 'Teamworking Structures and Worker Perceptions,' *International Journal of Human Resource Management*, 16(2): 256–76.

Hall, P. and Soskice, D. (2001). 'An Introduction to the Varieties of Capitalism,' in P. Hall and D. Soskice (eds.), *Varieties of Capitalism: The Institutional Basis of Competitive Advantage*. Oxford: Oxford University Press.

Hollingsworth, R. (2004). 'The Impact of New Knowledge and World Affairs on Socio-Economics.' Address to the Annual Conference for the Advancement of Socio-Economics, George Washington University, Washington D.C.

Jessop, B. (2001*a*). 'Series Preface,' in B. Jessop (ed.), *Regulationist Perspectives on Fordism and Post Fordism—Regulation Theory and the Crisis of Capitalism Volume 3*. London: Edward Elgar.

—— (2001*b*). 'Introduction,' in B. Jessop (ed.), *Regulationist Perspectives on Fordism and Post Fordism—Regulation Theory and the Crisis of Capitalism Volume 3*. London: Edward Elgar.

Knights, D. and Willmott, H. (eds.) (1986*a*). *Gender and the Labour Process*. London: Gower.

—— —— (eds.) (1986*b*). *Managing the Labour Process*. London: Gower.

—— —— (eds.) (1989). *Labour Process Theory*. London: Macmillan.

——, ——, and Collinson, D. (eds.) (1985). *Job Redesign: Critical Perspectives on the Labour Process*. London: Gower.

Marchington, M. and Speakman, S. (2004). 'The Bounded Workplace,' *Industrial Relations Journal*, 35(2): 122–38.

Piore, M. and Sabel, C. (1984). *The Second Industrial Divide*. New York: Basic Books.

Prichard, C., Hull, R., Chumer, M., and Willmott, H. (eds.) (2000). *Managing Knowledge: Critical Investigations of Work and Learning*. London: Macmillan.

Sturdy, A., Grugulis, I., and Willmott, H. (eds.) (2001). *Customer Service: Empowerment and Entrapment*. London: Palgrave.

Warhurst, C., Keep, E., and Grugulis, I. (eds.) (2004). *The Skills That Matter*. London: Palgrave.

Whitley, R. (1999). *Divergent Capitalisms*. Oxford: Oxford University Press.

Wilkinson, A. and Willmott, H. (eds.) (1994). *Making Quality Critical*. London: Routledge.

Part I

Rethinking Institutions, Society, and Firm-level Practices

2

How Do Institutions Cohere and Change? The Institutional Complementarity Hypothesis and Its Extension

Robert Boyer

Introduction: An Emerging Research Agenda

Traditionally, economic theory has focused on the allocation of scarce resources by pure market mechanisms and therefore the role of economic institutions was only referred within descriptive historical studies or comparative system of analyses. During the last two decades, economists have rediscovered with Coase (1937) that firms do play a major role in the allocation of resources and might be more efficient than markets when transaction costs are introduced on top of production costs. This hypothesis has triggered a new interest in the institutions of capitalism that previously was a quite neglected domain of research (Williamson 1985). More fundamentally, modern neoclassical microeconomic theory has recognized that market mechanisms cannot cope with public goods, externalities, innovations, and social justice concerns (Ingrao and Israel 1990), and these market failures call for alternative coordinating mechanisms such as quality standards, law, conventions, norms, and even State interventions at the macroeconomic level (Stiglitz 1987).

Starting from a quite different point of view, some social scientists have shown that markets, firms, and the state are not the only institutional arrangements enabling economic coordination (Hollingsworth and Boyer 1997) since the private organization, the network, the joint venture, and the community may play a significant role in the organization and viability of modern economies. Furthermore, it can be shown that markets are not the best allocating mechanism in all circumstances, since each coordinating mechanism calls for specific requisites and displays both strengths and weaknesses (Boyer

1997). The viability of an institutional configuration is consequently closely related to the ability to compensate the weakness of some coordinating mechanisms by the strength of others.

Two major events contributed to the renewed interest of economists in institutions. First, the deregulation policies initiated by the conservative governments in the Unites States and the UK have not always delivered the expected results. For instance, privatization of public utilities without clear contractual obligations has led to a deterioration of the quality of service. Thus, policymakers as well as theoreticians have had to recognize that market economies require sophisticated regulations and institutions governing the functioning of each market. Second, the collapse of the Soviet Union and the subsequent difficulties in implementing markets as well as democracy have triggered a string of research about previously neglected issues. What are the basic institutions of a market economy? How to build such institutions? Is there a single brand of capitalism, that is, a liberal type, or can a significant variety of capitalisms (VOC) coexist, even in the long run?

These issues tend to converge toward two quite central but difficult research agenda. First, what are the forces and mechanisms that coalesce a series of economic institutions into a viable system? Second, how do the institutional configurations of capitalism change and evolve in the long run? The answers drastically differ from one research program to another.

Standard neoclassical theory considers that economic calculus in terms of costs and benefits can be applied to the choice among alternative institutional forms. Basically, they emerge out of the interaction of individual agents and this process is assumed to deliver a *smooth evolution* and a continuous adjustment to external shocks that are translated into relative price movements. If some inertia or irrationality prevails, public authorities should use *benchmarking* in order to convince individuals to adopt superior economic institutions.

Transaction costs theory assumes that organizational forms should be selected in order to minimize these costs. This framework has mainly been applied to industrial organization in order to distinguish between subcontracting, vertical integration, franchising, and so on.... Some authors, such as Williamson (1985), have proposed to extend transaction costs to the analysis of capitalism systems. Given the sunk costs associated with any investment into a given organization and institution, these systems should display inertia, *path dependency*, and in some cases *suboptimality*, but in the long-run institutions should evolve according to the factors that govern transaction costs. This research program is now addressing the issue of economic and institutional change and this implies a significant redesign of the basic concepts and tools of New Institutional Economics (NIE) (North 2005).

Evolutionary theory is built on the hypothesis that heterogeneous organizations and institutions are selected by the equivalent of a fitness criterion, and/or they can also evolve via a process of trial and error and learning.

A general feature of these models is to exhibit nonergodicity, path dependency, potential irreversibility, and *ex post* suboptimality. Therefore, the results that have been obtained for technologies exhibiting increasing returns to scale (Arthur 1989) can be extended to institutions, scientific paradigms, and conventions. Consequently, the very process of evolution is able to deliver contrasted industrial, technological and economic structures, even when national economies are open to trade (Dosi et al. 1993). Capitalist economies are seen as systems of *coevolving* technologies, organizations, institutions, and conventions.

A branch of the NIE stresses that the constitutional and legal processes are crucial in the definition of economic rights, among them property rights, and consequently various national economies differ due to their constitutional order (North 1990). Paradoxically, this vision is not far away from the older conception that considers that economic transactions are embedded into a dense web of social relations (Polanyi 1944; Granovetter 1985, 1992). Therefore, the institutions of capitalism are not necessarily selected according to their economic efficiency since their role is to define the rules of the game, to deal collectively with uncertainty and to help solve the conflicts, disequilibria, and crises that are typical of any market economy.

Each of these hypotheses captures a part of the stylized facts concerning the evolution of institutions in contemporary capitalisms. The present chapter proposes another string of analyses that start from the hypotheses of *institutional complementarity* and extends this notion to related concepts. This hypothesis originates from scholars that try to comprehend the persisting institutional diversity between the United States and Japan and still more between economies in transition (Aoki 1988, 1994, 2000, 2001), or between the United States and Germany and other continental European countries (Amable 2000, 2003; Boyer 2001; Hall and Soskice 2001). A variant of this hypothesis considers that some complementarities derive from the impact of one institution over another and that this feature, that is, *institutional hierarchy*, may have been a major ingredient in the coherence of economic systems (Ebizuka, Uemura, and Isogai 1997; Boyer 2000).

Broadly speaking, the Institutional Complementarity Hypothesis (ICH) is able to explain many stylized facts about the evolution and diversity of institutional architectures. First, comparative analyses do show a *limited number of varieties of capitalism* (Amable, Barré, and Boyer 1997*a*, 1997*b*), far fewer to that which would result from a pure combinatory process (Amable 2003). Second, ICH explains why most *benchmarking experiments* do not deliver the expected results when applied to capitalism, since the same factors do not shape capitalist institutions and business internal organizations. There is a good example of the methodological weakness of benchmarking: the rather mixed (Zeitlin and Trubeck 2003) or poor results (Kok 2004) of the open method of cooperation put forward by the European Commission under the name of the Lisbon strategy that was supposed to bring Continental Europe to the technological frontier, simply by mimicking the best practices observed in the world. Third, ICH also provides an explanation of the difficulties experienced by the former socialist East European countries when they tried to adopt and adapt to market mechanisms: the Web of past interdependency between labor institutions, credit management, and State interventions hindered the adoption of the new market-oriented institutions (Delorme 1996; Chavance and alii 1999). More generally, the existing institutional complementarities, inherited from the Golden Age, explain the *painful process of institutional reform* in many Continental European countries (Boyer 2004*d*).

Nevertheless, ICH is not such a simple notion. Thus this chapter intends to discuss various *methodological issues* and then apply the major findings to one major issue: have not the 1990s been a watershed in terms of the variety of capitalism? A tentative answer to this question will build on research about the institutional prerequisites for the successful implementation of a knowledge-based growth regime (Boyer 2004*c*). A twin paper (Crouch et al. 2005) has investigated a related issue: are nonliberal capitalisms, such as Germany or Japan, de facto converging toward a market-oriented configuration similar to the Anglo-American one (Yamamura and Streeck 2003)? In order to deal with these issues, the chapter is organized as follows.

First of all, one should distinguish carefully between proximate but actually *different concepts* that try to capture the interaction between two or more institutions or organizational devices: supermodularity, complementarity, compatibility, hierarchy, coherence, isomorphism, clustering, and coevolution deserve precise definitions and explicit comparisons of their contents and implications (Part I). Second, this string of concepts brings to the forefront a series of methodological issues. How to detect institutional complementarities or more generally the factors of coherence of an institutional configuration? It is important also to recognize the large *variety of mechanisms* that may generate the equivalent of institutional complementarity: clearly, a purely technological complementarity is only a highly specific conception of the mechanisms that explain the clustering of institutions or alternatively of organizations. A third methodological issue relates to the level at which the complementarity hypothesis is relevant: the arguments used to explain the diversity of *internal organizations of firms* are not the same as those that are invoked for the *diversity of capitalisms* in spite of the efforts of the VOC literature to relate one with another. Institutions are generally conceived as constraints that are detrimental to economic performance. By contrast, a branch of the literature proposes that institutional constraints might be beneficial and complementarity plays an important role in promoting better outcomes. Another important question deals with the issue of complementarity by *ex ante design* or by *ex post discovery*. Put differently, it is important to make a clear distinction between the retrospective analysis of the social scientists and the vision and interpretation of the actors themselves acting on the spot (Part II).

These advances in the analysis of economic institutions helps then in understanding why the diversity of capitalist brands may originate in the coexistence of contrasted complementarities between the basic institutions of these economic systems. The limited number of these configurations explains why we do not observe as many brands of capitalism as countries. It is then important to respond to a frequent objection: institutional diversity is a legacy of the past and will vanish along with the process of globalization. This general framework is mobilized in order to detect the diverse configurations that were associated to the so-called 'new economy' of the 1990s, now transformed into a knowledge-based economy (Part III). The use of the concept of complementarity is rather static since it is argued that it introduces a large institutional inertia. Nevertheless, this vision can be challenged and quite to the contrary the shift from one type of complementarity (or hierarchy) to another may explain the transformation of an institutional architecture. It is an invitation to survey the various approaches of institutional change. First, softening of the hypothesis of strict complementarity entitles to explain the sequence of emergence, maturation and crisis of a given configuration. Second, making explicit the conflicts of interest helps a lot in understanding the process of institutional change. Third, comparative historical analyses propose a series of mechanisms in order to explain why a series of marginal institutional innovations may finally deliver a totally different institutional configuration (Part IV). Finally, it is argued, along with *Régulation* theory (RT), that institutions do shape macroeconomic adjustments and that specific processes govern the evolution of '*régulation* modes'. The shift from one institutional hierarchy to another, as well as hybridization, endometabolism, and the dynamic interactions between the economic and political spheres, defines many mechanisms for macroinstitutional change (Part V).

Part I: The Factors that Govern the Coherence of Institutional Configurations

There is a risk of confusing complementarity with seemingly similar but distinct concepts. The emergence of this term has been associated with some implicit hypotheses that have to be spelled out. (Boyer 2003*a*)

Supermodularity

Two elements E and E' are said to be supermodular if the performance R of the conjunction of E and E' is superior to any other mix of elements, that is

$$R(E, E') > R(E, A)\ \forall A \neq E' \quad \text{and} \quad R(E, E') > R(B, E')\ \forall B \neq E$$

This precise definition puts strong limits on the use of the notion of supermodularity. First, the analyst has to posit a criterion of performance that is not clearly evident (profit maximization for the firm, but what should be the relevant criterion for a capitalist economy: average profit rate, rate of growth, total factor productivity, level of employment and activity, equalitarian distribution of income, wealth, . . . ?). Second, the concept is clearly associated with the idea of optimum and maximization, a core trend of economic analysis but not necessarily in sociology, law, history, and so on. Basically, only sophisticated models (see, e.g. Amable, Ernst, and Palombarini 2001, 2002) are able to prove such a supermodularity. But how to diagnose supermodularity by direct observation without the construction of a formal model engendering a series of fictitious worlds?

A good example of possible supermodularity relates to productive models. It has been argued that just in time, total quality control and highly skilled workers define a genuine productive model at odds with the previous Fordist model whereby mass production of standardized goods required less competence from the workers and less demanding consumers in terms of quality. The very concept of supermodularity has been used to show that a continuous and marginal adjustment of managerial tools was not able to promote the transition from the old to the new productive model (Milgrom and Roberts 1990).

Complementarity

Two elements E and E' are said to be complementary if the performance R of the conjunction of E and E' is superior to the performance of each element considered separately, that is

$$R(E, E') > R(E) \text{ and } R(E, E') > R(E')$$

The concept of complementarity is less demanding than supermodularity, since it only requires that the conjunction of two elements is Pareto-improving with respect to the existence of only one of the two entities. Nevertheless, both complementarity and supermodularity require the choice of a performance criterion R and the ability to compare various systems in order to check the basic property. Either by using formal modeling or by observing a hierarchy in the ranking of systems composed respectively of only E, only E' or both E and E'.

Some examples of possible complementarity might be useful to help grasp the nature of this concept. According to many authors, a financial regime governed by direct finance is complementary with weak unions and the domination of short-term strategies and conversely, a patient financial regime built on bank credit is complementary to a strong union, with both involved in long-term strategies. Another example associates as complementary an accommodating monetary policy and flexible labor markets, a typical

American configuration, whereas the monetary regime associated with a conservative central banker is seen as complementary to rigid labor markets that are supposed to explain European unemployment.

Compatibility

This third notion is frequently confused with the second one ... but it should not be! Actually E and E' are compatible if they can be jointly observed in existing economies and societies, that is

$$\text{There exists an economy such that: } E \cap E' \neq \emptyset$$

An interesting example is provided by Höpner (2001, 2003*a*, 2003*b*) when he investigates the links between the dual management board system and employees' codetermination in Germany. The proponents of a strong variant of VOC would regard these institutions as complementary—having observed the good 'performance' of the German economy until the early 1990s—whereas the observation only says that they are compatible. The proof of complementarity would call for a theoretical model adding up and/or subtracting a complete series of institutions and assessing the related impact on an agreed measure of performance.

Hierarchy

This third notion implies a form of causality between two entities E and E'. Basically, the idea is that in order to be sustainable or viable the entity E absolutely needs the presence of another entity E' out of a complete series E', E'', E''. Formally, this means:

If $\exists E$, then among a complete set (E', E', ..., E''), there is only one E' such that $E \cap E' \neq \emptyset$ and $E \cap E' = \emptyset, \ldots, E \cap E'' = \emptyset$.

In a sense, this criterion is more demanding than both pure compatibility and complementarity. The very existence of one entity cannot be observed without the presence of a single other one. Just to give *an example* for some monetarists and free marketers, an efficient monetary policy absolutely requires totally flexible employment and wage adjustments. This is a strengthening of the concept of complementarity and involves introducing an *asymmetry* between institutions: E requires E', but E' could be compatible with many other entities.

Coherence

This is still another notion. Two institutions are declared coherent if they can easily coexist, that is if $E \cap E' \neq \emptyset$ is likely for structural, theoretical reasons, for example. This is more than compatibility since it means that the fitness of each institution is improved by the existence of the other, but it is less than complementarity since this does not imply that the mix between E and E' gives the best result among any possible association of alternative institutions. Here is the ranking of the various concepts according to an increasing fitness of the two institutions:

Compatibility $\prec$ coherence $\prec$ complementarity $\prec$ supermodularity $\prec$ hierarchy

The empirical observation of the coexistence of two entities may hint that they are coherent, whereas in order to declare that they are supermodular, one must select a performance criterion and show by theoretical and abstract reasoning—a model—that the precise mix of two entities gives the best results among a whole spectrum of entities. It is easier to show that two entities are complementary, whereas coherence defines an intermediate concept between compatibility and complementarity.

Isomorphism

In a sense, this is a specification of the case of coherence. Given the fact that organizations and institutions have interfaces, the constraint on communication and mutual understanding implies some common principles that may come from one of the composing organizations and institutions (DiMaggio and Powell 1991). Formally, two entities are said to be isomorphic if they are equivalent according to a general common principle P which defines a relation of equivalence R so that,

$$E R./P E'$$

This *ex post* symmetry might well be the unintended outcome of the imposition by element E of its logic to element E'. Thus, it is a form of coherence and may appear as the consequence of hierarchy. Sociological research on institutions gives many examples of institutional architectures generated by isomorphism. For instance, the rise of a Weberian public bureaucracy may impact on the internal organization of large corporations. Conversely, the triumph of a free market ideology may induce a redesign of the same large corporations in order to mimic quasi-market competition among profit centers. The concept of an industrial and military complex is a third example of the consequence of isomorphism, even if the explanation of its emergence is up to a political economy analysis. Therefore, in a sense, isomorphism is a specification of a mechanism able to produce some form of coherence.

Just to summarize: Isomorphism $\in$ Coherence

Hierarchy $\Rightarrow$ Isomorphism

[Note that this implication is not general, since hierarchy may be associated with contrasted logic, i.e. flexibility for E' but rigidity for E.]

Clustering

This concept simply describes the fact that two or several institutions are frequently observed simultaneously when some systematic comparisons are carried out. The concept is therefore purely descriptive and does not imply at all any idea that such a grouping of institutions necessarily implies better performance. Formally, this can be described by the existence of a significant correlation across various case studies ($i = 1, 2, \ldots, N$)

For a sufficiently large N, correlation $(E_i, E_i') > A$: a set according to a given significance threshold.

Clustering and coherence are twin concepts, but they should not be confused. The first one relies on empirical and statistical observations, the second one calls for theoretical reasons that might explain the grouping of two entities. Ideally, these two approaches, inductive and deductive, respectively, could converge and come close to the concept of complementarity.

Nevertheless, a distinction has to be made between clustering/coherence and complementarity. Implicitly at least, competition is not perceived to be a strong selective mechanism that would destroy any inefficient clustering. Furthermore, there is no natural efficiency criterion for a given institution that may fulfill simultaneously various objectives in different fields. Last but not least, evolutionary theories suggest that the fitness is relative to a given context, be it ecological, economical, social or political (Dosi et al. 1993). The relations of clustering with related concepts are the following:

Clustering = high frequency of compatibility

Clustering + Coherence = presumption of complementarity

Isomorphism = a possible source of coherence and clustering

Again, an example might be useful. When German multinationals go abroad, they rarely, or do not, export codetermination nor do they export the dual training system. This would mean that these two institutions are clustering within the context of the German economy, but that they are not necessarily complementary at the level of the firm. The coherence of two institutions could well be context related. This means that institutions may exhibit triadic and not only dyadic relations, a quite important feature indeed (see Figure 2.10, infra § 11).

Coevolution

Most if not all the previous concepts were mostly static. By contrast, the notion of coevolution implies that the observation of the joint occurrence of two institutions or organizations might be the unintended outcome of a selection process or a learning mechanism operating via the succession of stochastic shocks and possibly major events such as crises. This concept is central to contemporary evolutionary research that was first designed in order to understand technological innovation, but it can be extended to social norms, managerial tools, or even economic institutions. A formal definition could be the following:

When $t \to T$ correlation $(E_t, E'_t) \to 1$ with t time variable, T sufficiently large

Again, the German trajectory is an interesting example. In a sense, the contemporary vision of a built-in complementarity between industrial relations and corporate governance might well be the unintended outcome of a highly unpredictable historical process made of class struggle, institutional innovations, and trial and error processes at various levels (Streeck 1997*a*). The observation of the resilience of a mix of institutions implies only that they fit one with another without any idea of superiority in terms of efficiency. The example of technologies with increasing return to scale clearly shows that the result of the evolutionary process does not necessarily deliver the most efficient technological system (Arthur 1989). Hence the following relations with the previous concepts:

Complementarity = *ex post* and sometimes false presumption of efficiency for the outcome of an evolutionary process that is the origin of the coevolution of institutions

Clustering = evidence that the outcome of a series of coevolution processes might be less idiosyncratic than expected, i.e. more than compatibility

Part II: Some Major Methodological Issues

A first problem arises: how to distinguish among these various concepts? One is facing severe methodological problems but is not the only one: what is the origin of these links? Are the institutions pure constraints to individual optimization or does the constraint they impose have an impact upon the performance? Does the coherence of an institutional configuration come exclusively from complementarity between component institutions or can it derive from isomorphism? Why is it useful to distinguish between institutional complementarity and institutional hierarchy?

How to Detect Complementarity? Various Alternative but Imperfect Methods

A priori various methods are available in order to test ICH. Of course, the first step is to define a performance criterion and this is not evident at all since each brand of capitalism has its own criteria: rate of growth, total factor productivity, and profit rate for market-led capitalism but improvement and homogeneity of standards of living for social democratic capitalism ... and so on. Once this choice has been made, the economists may first build a theoretical model and formalize how economic agents react to various institutional environments and what are finally the global performance indexes. Contemporary microtheory and game theory have thus been used in order to assess the possible complementarity of various institutions that result from the interaction of agents within the given institutional context. For instance, some models show that employment stability and the main bank were complementary for the Japanese economy in the 1980s (Aoki 1988). Or alternatively a highly mobile and competent work force was complementary with venture capitalists in the Silicon Valley of the 1990s (Aoki 2001). Similarly, strong unions and financing by bank intermediation have been proved to be complementary under some conditions (Amable, Ernst, and Palombarini 2002) and this helps to understand the European configurations.

These models are highly abstract and theoretical. They basically discuss the conditions under which the mix of two institutions delivers a superior performance and the related thresholds are confronted with some stylized facts drawn from historical analyses or international comparisons. Therefore, a direct test of the relevance of a given complementarity has to be carried through different approaches, that is, rather sophisticated econometric studies, generally combining cross section along with time series. Two institutions are analyzed as complementary with respect to growth, if the term built by multiplying a representative index of each institution has a positive and significant impact on growth (Ernst 2001). Such a strategy has been popularized by the empirical research on corporate governance. For the time being, few results seem to be robust enough and to fit with the teaching of the theoretical models.

Other methods can capture the rather different concept of clustering. Among them, the qualitative comparative analysis (QCA) (Ragin 1987, 1994) is interesting since it removes the issue of optimization of performance just to try to reveal the various mixes of institutions that deliver a given qualitative outcome. Such a method has been used in order to detect what institutional architectures can cope with the use of information and communication technology (ICT) and one of its merits is to leave open the nature and the number of institutions that can be associated with good performance (Boyer 2004*a*). Similarly, it can be enlightening in the interpretation of the success of business models to directly test the de facto complementarity between managerial devices, often obscured by the rhetoric and the marketing of these models (Kogut et al. 2002).

But such methods miss a crucial point: the evolutionary aspect of complementarity, clustering, and still more coevolution. In order to address this issue, a first method, available and frequently used by institutional research, consists in digging up national or regional economic history in order to check if the circumstances of the creation of an institution are really the same as the reasons that may explain its persistence and viability. In this respect, most of the institutions that are today perceived as complementary were in fact created for distinct purposes and only the succession of crises, experiments, and sequential innovations finally delivered the complementarity that is recognized at the end of a rather long historical process. But of course it is difficult to drive general results out of a series of singular case studies. QCA was invented precisely in order to extract some general hypotheses from the juxtaposition of case studies. But economists generally do not use this method since they dream of generating a counterfactual history and thus they prefer to build models in order to simulate various dynamic processes under different institutional and stochastic hypotheses. This is precisely the aim of evolutionary models, the last generation of which has stressed the importance of coevolution: what static neoclassical theory explains as complementarity might be the outcome of distinct selection and learning processes that are nevertheless related in terms of outcomes (Dosi et al. 1993).

Thus one observes a rough correspondence between the nature of the links among institutions and the tools that are required in order to check the existence of these links (Table 2.1). Alas none of these strategies is self-sufficient. Consequently, facing a given issue, research should ideally try and use each method that can possibly deliver a piece of the puzzle.

Diverse Origins of Complementarity Matter

The contemporary research displays a clear temptation to derive some major institutional complementarity for purely technical constraints. Just two examples: Milgrom and Roberts (1995) use the concept of supermodularity in order to make explicit a strong complementarity between just in time, total quality control and team work. This hypothesis is reminiscent of the hypothesis of a strict complementarity between capital and labor in growth theory. Actually, it is far from evident to see managerial tools as basic inputs as that can be dealt with the equivalent of a production function with complementary between factors. In the literature on the VOC, the resilience of coordinated market economies is attributed to the organizational complementarity that exists at the firm level between skilled and high-paid workers. This complementarity is extended to economic institutions by the equivalent of an isomorphism between private organizations and national institutions. One may challenge this supremacy of technical complementarity and propose a complete spectrum of origins for institutional complementarity:

Natural complementarity derives from scientific laws about nature. For instance, the chemical industry is a good example of production functions

Table 2.1 What tools for what type of relationships between institutions?

Tools Notions	Economic Reasoning	Economic Modeling/ Game Theory	Qualitative Comparative Analysis	Automatic Data Analysis	Econometric Analysis with nonlinear term	Historical Analysis	Evolutionary models
Supermodularity	*	**					
Complementarity	*	**	*		**		
Compatibility			*			*	*
Hierarchy		**				**	*
Coherence	*			*		*	*
Isomorphism				*	*	*	
Clustering			**	**	*		**
Coevolution		*				**	**

with strong complementarity due to the property of atoms and molecules. This constraint deriving from science may of course exert some influence on the organization of the industry. But please note that technical complementarity is strict indeed (only the right mix of inputs gives the desired molecules) and nevertheless one could observe a significant variability in the organizations and institutions governing the same industry across countries.

Technical complementarity is a proximate concept of natural complementarity but the difference is about the origin of the efficiency associated with the conjunction of two inputs. Most of these complementarities are man made and not deriving from natural laws. For instance, in the computer industry the hardware and the software are complementary and not only coherent, since they derived from a coordinated design. Similarly, the combustion engine creates a complementarity between car production and use on one side, and oil consumption and production on the other. De facto, social systems of innovation exhibit a series of complementarity or at least compatibility between various techniques and products.

Complementarity by design could be a better description of these complementarities. A good example is the invention of the assembly line that creates intentionally a complementarity between the mechanical speed of the assembly line and the intensity of work, as well as between the equipment and the volume and skill composition of manpower. A complementarity that seems to be embedded into materials and techniques is actually the result of a choice and a strategy of social control and economic efficiency. At a more macrolevel, the independent central bank needs as a corollary a sufficiently flexible labor market and a strong control over deficit spending. Such a complementarity is rarely observed de facto since it requires a strategy in order to transform the industrial relations inherited from the Golden Age. This form of complementarity is not at all a constraint but a transformational project.

Ex post discovered complementarity is a fourth configuration: it is not an intrinsic property of organization or institutions but it results from the observation of the properties of an emerging regime that can be better understood after a long period of trials, errors, and learning. Paradoxically, such a discovery of complementarity comes at the very moment when an aging system is entering into a decline or even crisis. A well-known example is the recognition of Fordism, as the synergy between mass production and mass consumption, at the very moment when this macroregime entered into a structural crisis. Let us add two contemporary examples. Information and communication technologies (ICT) do not deliver automatically more productivity, unless they are associated with a significant reorganization of the firms (Askenazy 2002), a condition that was not at all evident in the early 1990s. Similarly, ICT and profit optimization are seen as complementary but in the case of the air travel industry it took more than a decade to perceive that the sophisticated information flow that was created by the computerization of air travel reservation could be used in order to develop a real time yield management via continuous price adjustments (Bresnahan 2002). For this author the emerging complementarity between technology and a managerial model is the outcome of a coevolution process made of trials and errors that are erroneously interpreted in retrospect as a typical and well-known static model built upon clear complementarities.

Functional complementarity is still another origin for the clustering of institutions. This is specially important for social scientists: for sociology the social roles complement each other since the duty of an individual is the right of another one; for the economists, the credit given to a firm is the strict counterpart of the obligation to reimburse to the bank, as supply and demand do have to fit one with another. Since functionalism has been severely criticized, functional complementarity has been somehow neglected in understanding the viability of socioeconomic systems. For instance, are not property rights, the existence of a strong and independent justice, and the enforcement of law the joint requisites for any capitalist system? This basic finding was neglected when the Soviet-type economies collapsed and some mainstream economists thought that the market would endogenously emerge out of the self-interest of individuals.

It would be thus interesting to survey the numerous researches on institutional complementarity and specially the case studies, in order to clarify the nature of the mechanisms involved. In the absence of such a survey, one may fear that the concept of complementarity degenerates into a buzz word and a misleading fad.

Institutional Complementarity as Synergy Between Two Beneficial Constraints

A second issue is about the conception of institutions as pure constraints that are detrimental to economic efficiency because they block the free adjustments of preferences and production constraints via price formation. For Douglass North (1990) they are also enablers for the strategy of individuals, in dealing with uncertainty, coordination, and the interpretation of information. Thus, contrary to the Chicago School's conceptions, some mix of institutions may deliver better economic and/or social outcomes than a pure market economy. This conception considers that some constraints restricting economic opportunism, and short-termism (ST) or allowing the supply of some public goods, are quite essential to the competitiveness of firms and thus they may have a beneficial impact on economic and social outcomes (Streeck 1997*b*).

THE ORIGIN OF A PARADOX

In the Walrasian tradition, the equilibrium prices make compatible preferences and technological constraints. This feature can be captured by the following equation, which expresses the idea that excess demand for each product and factor market is equal to zero.

$$Z = f(p, \quad P, \quad T) = 0 \Longrightarrow [p^w \quad C^w, \quad N^w]$$

Z		$f(p,$	$P,$	$T)$		$[p^w$	$C^w,$	$N^w]$
Net excess Employment demand		Price	Preferences	Technology		Equilibrium price	Consumption	Walrasian equilibrium

Unfortunately, the Walrasian auctioneer, that is, the global market maker, does not exist and has to be replaced by a series of institutions: a monetary regime (I_1), a competition law, and labor market institutions (I_2). Therefore, individuals now not only react to the price signals but also according to the existing institutions that shape the formation of prices. A priori this institution-rich economy displays a different equilibrium.

$$Z = g \quad (p, \quad I_1, \quad I_2) = 0 \Longrightarrow [p^i \quad C^i, \quad N^i]$$

Z		g	$(p,$	$I_1,$	$I_2)$		$[p^i$	$C^i,$	$N^i]$
Net excess demand			Price	Institutions	Institutional equilibrium		Equilibrium price	Consumption	Employment

For most economists, the name of the game is to compare the outcome of a totally abstract economy, the Walrasian one, for which any market equilibrium is Pareto-optimum, with a more realistic economy with various institutions but still an auctioneer. It is easy to understand then that any institution can only deteriorate the fit between preferences and technological possibilities. But if really existing decentralized imperfect markets are introduced, the various institutions might help in reaching a satisfactory equilibrium. Ideally, the various institutional settings should be compared according to their economic and social outcomes. But this requires the equivalent of a social welfare function in order to derive a single index out of the distribution of economic outcomes among individuals. Concerning the issue of complementarity, this very simple formalization might help in understanding the difference between compatibility and complementarity.

Compatibility among institutions is observed when there exists a set of equilibrium prices, consumption, and employment. Such a property is not necessarily fulfilled and thus this is a discriminating criterion in the assessment of the viability of alternative institutional architectures.

I_1 and I_2 are compatible if there exists an equilibrium such that $E(I_1, I_2) \neq \emptyset$.

Complementarity is a much more demanding criterion. First, the analyst has to compute an equilibrium with only the first institution I_1, that is, $E(I_1)$ and repeat the same operation for institution I_2. Second, one adds the second institution and has to compute the new equilibrium $E(I_1, I_2)$. Third, and this is still more difficult, the economist has to adopt a welfare function in order to compare the two equilibria. Finally, the institutions I_1 and I_2 will be said to be complementary if their joint presence delivers a better outcome than each of the separate institutions. It can be captured by the two following conditions:

$$I_1 \text{ and } I_2 \text{ are complementary if } E(I_1, I_2) \succ E(I_1) \quad \text{and} \quad E(I_1, I_2) \succ E(I_2)$$

A RATHER FREQUENT CONFIGURATION: FOUR EXAMPLES

If one sticks to general equilibrium theory, one could introduce two discrepancies with respect to the conditions that deliver an equilibrium. First, increasing returns to scale (H_1), second, imperfect competition or, more precisely, oligopolistic pricing (H_2). Whereas a pure competition (H_0) equilibrium does not exist with (H_1), the existence of imperfect competition entitles the existence of an equilibrium, that is,

$$E(H_1, H_2) \succ E(H_1, H_0)$$

Recent research about institutional complementarity (Amable, Ernst, and Palombarini 2002) shows by formal modeling that strong unions (SU) and patient capital (PC) provided by bank credit may deliver better macroeconomic outcomes than competitive labor (CL) markets and ST capital markets, i.e.

$$E(\text{SU, PC}) \succ E(\text{CL, PC}) \quad \text{and} \quad E(\text{SU, PC}) \succ E(\text{SU, ST})$$

Similarly, theoretical and empirical investigations exhibit a rather surprising complementarity (Amable 2000, 2003). Traditionally, economists consider that product market deregulation (PMD) and labor market flexibility (LMF) strategies are to be undertaken simultaneously, because they complement one with another. But empirical analysis shows that a second configuration is built on the complementarity between product market regulation (PMR) and a significant institutionalization of labor mobility (ILM). By contrast, the intermediate configurations (deregulation of one market, but strong regulation of the other one) display less satisfactory outcomes in terms of growth and employment.

$$E(\text{PMD, LMF}) \approx E(\text{PMR, ILM}) \quad \text{and} \quad E(\text{PMD, ILM}) \prec E(\text{PMD, LMF});$$

$$E(\text{PMR, LMF}) \prec E(\text{PMR, ILM})$$

The viability of a banking system is threatened by periodic bank runs especially when free banking (FB) and fierce competition (FC) prevail. This has triggered the efforts of economists to find out regulations that could prevent such dramatic episodes. After nearly two centuries of recurring banking crises, practitioners and analysts finally find out the complementarity of two corrective devices. On one side a deposit insurance (DI) reduces the probability of bank runs but it simultaneously might induce banks to take more risk for their credit activities. Thus, on the other side, prudential ratios

(PR) have been imposed in proportion to the risk taken for each category of credit (Borio 2003). We find again that this institutional equilibrium is better than the constraints free equilibrium:

$$E(\text{DI, PR}) \succ E(\text{DI, FB}) \quad \text{and} \quad E(\text{DI, PR}) \succ E(\text{FC, PR})$$

This leads to two general proposals expressing the same idea. First, two imperfections might be better than a single one, since they correct each other's potential imbalances. Second, two constraints might be beneficial to the quality of economic equilibrium and social outcomes, provided they adequately interact with each other.

Two Forms of Coherence: Are Similarity and Complementarity Substitutes or Complements?

The challenge is then to try to disentangle between two general hypotheses about the coherence and viability of institutional systems: do they stick by complementarity or do they coalesce by the similarity and generality of the same principles? By the way, in many taxonomies of capitalisms, authors tend to emphasize a common feature, be it market or nonmarket coordination (Hall and Soskice 2001) or more disaggregated approaches: market-led, social-democrat, meso-corporatist, State-led (Amable, Barré, and Boyer 1997; Amable 2003). This suggests that the relative importance of the two mechanisms may vary according to the level of analysis.

COMPLEMENTARITY OF INSTITUTIONAL ARRANGEMENTS AT THE MICROLEVEL

If one agrees with the taxonomy of the institutional arrangements and their ability to coordinate strategies and behaviors (Hollingsworth and Boyer 1997; Crouch 2004), it is rather clear that no single institutional arrangement can function in isolation (Figure 2.1).

- Conceptual analysis and empirical research inspired by economic sociology confirm that market adjustments can only operate within an exogenous enforcement of the rule of the game, either via an association or a public authority in charge to monitor the fairness and transparency of the market.
- Similarly, most research programs in institutional analysis now agree that States and markets are more complementary than complete substitutes. It is so even for the international organizations that used to defend and diffuse the so-called Washington consensus (World Bank 2001).

The transaction cost theory tends to oppose organization to market since they describe their relative share in coordinating economic activity as the result of an equilibrium of costs and benefits. A deeper analysis (e.g. Chandler

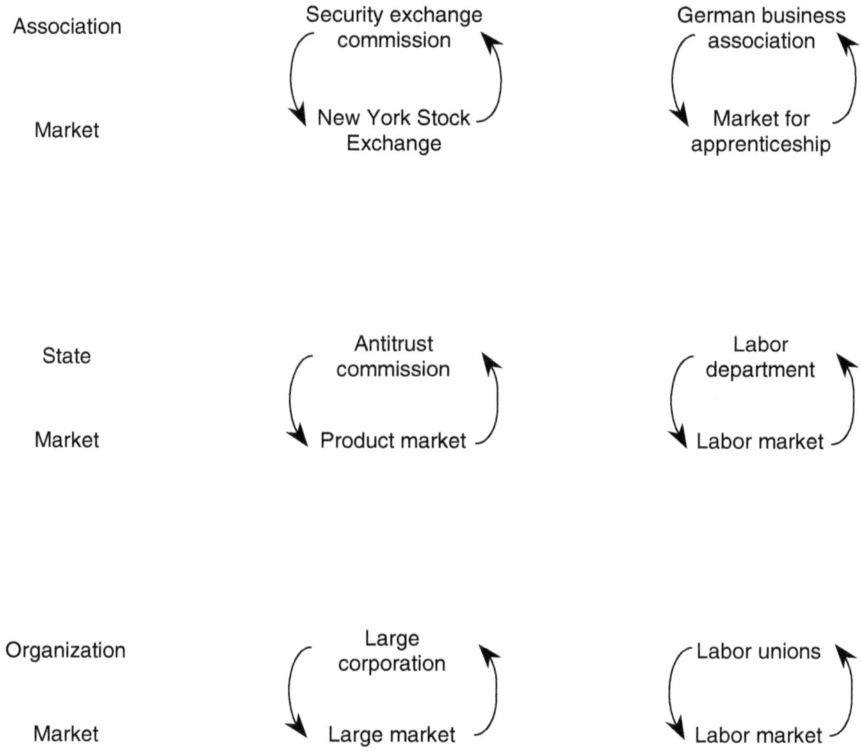

Figure 2.1. Complementarity of institutional arrangements as dissimilarity.

1977, 1990) shows that the emergence and viability of the large corporation cannot be disentangled from the constitution of a large integrated product market. Similarly, the functioning of labor markets is deeply influenced by the structuring organization and objectives of labor unions, that is, another type of interdependence between a market and organization.

SIMILARITY AND HOMOLOGY ARE QUITE PRESENT AT THE SYSTEM LEVEL

The previous arrangements combining two institutions generally do not work in isolation since they are related by competition on the markets, common legislation, the influence of the same power structure (Amable and Palombarini 2005) and more or less binding social norms. A priori these are some of the factors that may introduce some common features, across various local institutional and organizational architectures.

It is clear that this feature is conceptually different from complementarity, but it contributes simultaneously to the coherence or/and the intelligibility

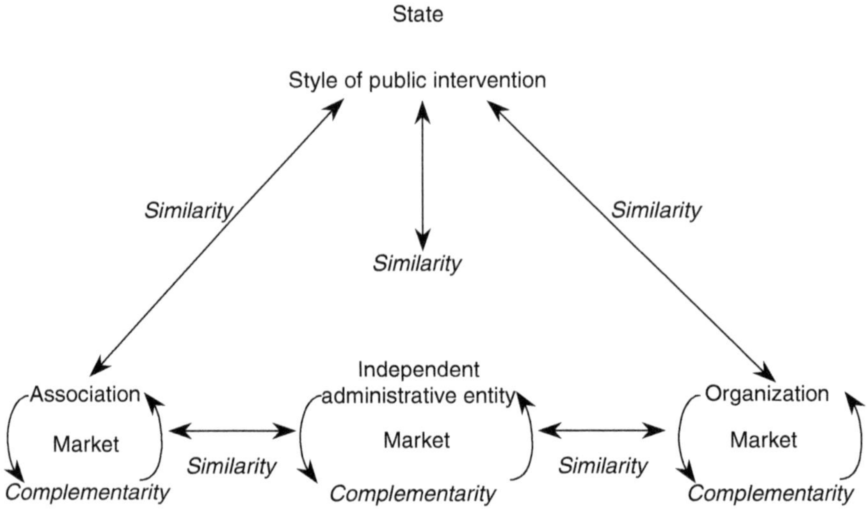

Figure 2.2. Complementarity at the local level, similarity at the system level.

of the systems for actors. Taking some of the same institutional entities as Figure 2.1, Figure 2.2 builds some links among them. It is important to note that in this representation the similarity may derive from quite different areas:

- Competition within one market may spillover into another type of market, therefore creating interdependence between domains that would be a priori disconnected. For instance, a strong competition on the product market has definite consequence for the internal or external mobility of labor and thus on the labor market (Amable, Ernst, and Palombarini 2001, 2002).
- The style of collective interventions (by delegation to nonprofit associations, by the implementation of substantive rules by the State, or by procedural ones) may permeate from one domain to another and give a definite flavor to the institutional architecture within a given political space.

Contrasting Institutional Hierarchy with Institutional Complementarity

The notion of complementarity implicitly assumes an equal role for every institution or organization entering into this relation. According to evolutionary theorizing, the process of coevolution is a possible mechanism according to which largely unexpected complementarity may emerge (Streeck 2003). Nevertheless, within each historical period and for a given society, some institutional forms might be more important than others (Boyer and Saillard 2002). A first definition of hierarchy stresses that the internal organization of institution B is designed in order to be compatible with the requirements

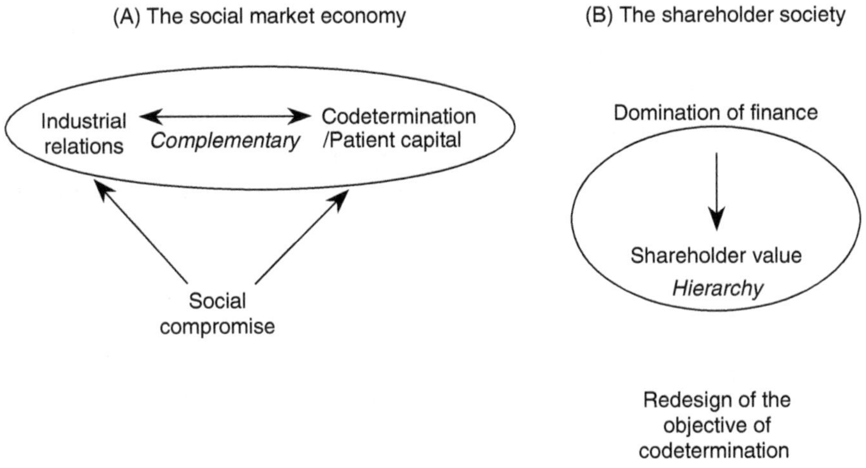

Figure 2.3. A shift in institutional hierarchy?

of another institution A: A is then defined as hierarchically superior to B. A second definition considers that A is hierarchically superior to B if the evolution of A triggers an endogenous restructuring of B in a direction which benefits the purpose of A.

According to this distinction, another interpretation of the coexistence of codetermination with shareholder value can be given and it is quite different from the interpretation in terms of mere compatibility (see, p. 5, supra) (Figure 2.3). In the social market economy, of which Germany is supposed to be the emblematic example, the institutional architecture seems to have been designed in order to introduce a series of checks and balances between various entities pursuing different objectives (Labrousse and Weisz 2001). Even if the success was not at all warranted *ex ante* (Streeck 1997*a*), this innovation turned out to be quite favorable to economic performance and the reduction of social conflicts. By contrast, in a finance-led configuration the international financial regime has the leading role in inducing the redesign of the domestic monetary regime, the nature of competition, the style of economic policy, and even the wage–labor nexus (Boyer 2000*a*, 2000*b*). Shareholder value may then be interpreted as a strategy in order to promote the hierarchical superiority of the financial regime over any other economic institutions. Consequently, the objective and the process of codetermination could well be significantly redesigned according to the new imperative of shareholder value. In a sense, the compatibility observed until 2000 (Höpner 2001) would only be transitory since the long-term configuration that will emerge from a complete domination of shareholder value is likely to be quite different from the present one. In a sense, a snap shot could not represent the course of action that will result from the unfolding of the full scenario of financialization (Figure 2.3).

The Links Between Micro- and Macrocomplementarities

The recent trend of research has been to work out the microfoundations for macroregularities and therefore to try to derive institutional complementarities from complementarities observed at the level of the firm. The VOC approach is a good example of such a strategy (Hall and Soskice 2001).

Hence it is theoretically possible to generate a VOC based on a combination of two hypotheses: first a technological or organizational type of complementarity between work, equipment, and product; second an isomorphism between companies' organization and society-wide economic institutions. The reasoning can be captured by the following equation:

$$\begin{aligned}(\text{Hall–Soskice [2001]}) = {} & (\text{Milgrom–Roberts [1990]}) \\ & + (\text{DiMaggio–Powell [1991]})\end{aligned}$$

or in more theoretical terms:

$$\begin{aligned}\text{VOC} = {} & \text{theory of supermodularity} \\ & + \text{isomorphism between organization/institution}\end{aligned}$$

A careful examination of the reasoning and design of Figures 2.3 and 2.4 (Hall and Soskice 2001: 28, 32) demonstrates that the complementarities also relate to society-wide institutions which in turn shape, constrain, or provoke appropriate management mechanisms and routines within firms. The causality is therefore twofold: on one side, it goes from the macrolevel to the microlevel, and on the other side, the macroeconomic dynamic is of course never more than the result of a conjunction of the different firms' strategies. Yet these macroeconomic properties have absolutely no reason to be the direct expression of the constraints that the representative firms face.

Thus, the distance between the VOC's reality and results and an alternative macroorientation—such as RT—is made explicit. The aim of RT is to develop macroinstitutional foundations for a series of microbehaviors. Figuratively, we could postulate a second equation that is representative of the latest RT developments, but, in a sense, of the VOC as well:

$$\begin{aligned}\text{RT Microeconomics} = {} & \text{institutional complementarity} \\ & + \text{institution/organization isomorphism}\end{aligned}$$

This paves the way for a vast but difficult field of research, where we would examine the extent to which these two conceptions constitute alternatives (Figure 2.4) or inversely can be combined in practice, if only because technology, companies' organization, and economic institutions seemingly coevolve over the long run.

The previous sector is an invitation to apply the concepts to two major problems: first the diversity of institutional configuration (Part III), second the factors that shape their evolution (Part IV).

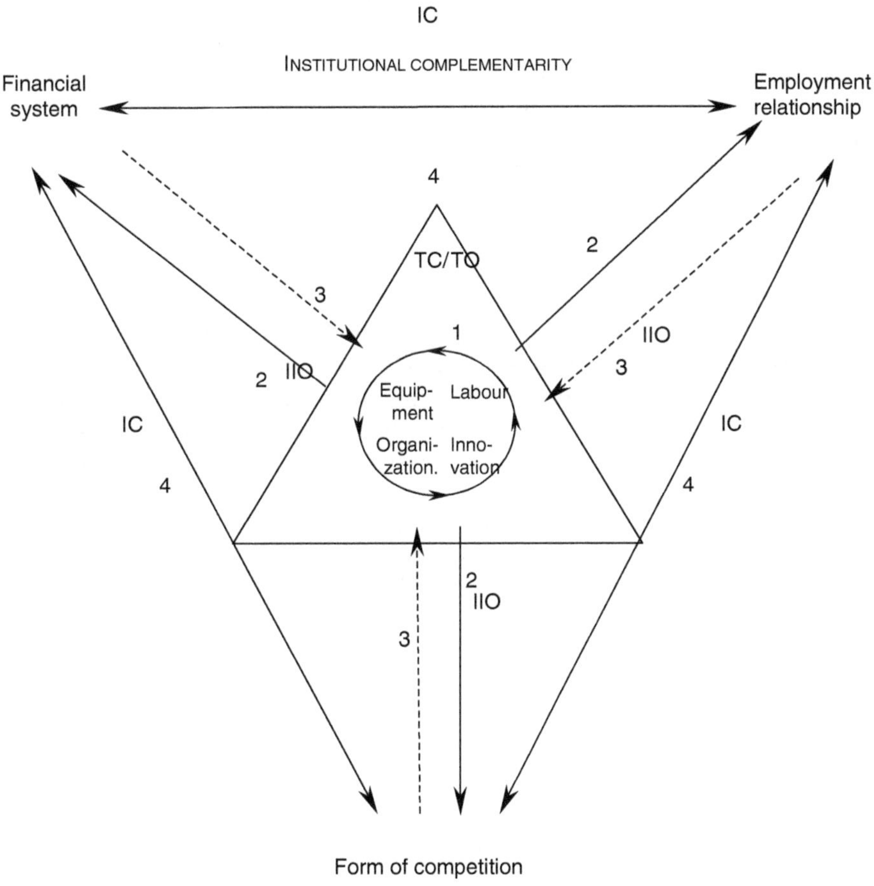

1 TC/TO Technological/organization complementarity
(Example: Just-in-time, total quality, polyvalence)

2 IIO Isomorphism between institutions and organizations
3 *(Example: Just-in-time, industrial district polyvalence, training system)*

4 IC Institutional complementarity
(Example: industrial district, stable employment, patient financial market)

Figure 2.4. Links between organizational complementarity,organizational/institutional isomorphism, and institutional complementarity.

Part III: The Diversity of Capitalism Revisited

The VOC debate is an invitation to revisit the large and increasing literature that starts from the seminal analysis by Albert (1991). It generated a large interest during the 1990s when the collapse of the Soviet-type regime suggested to many analysts that all economies will converge toward a single brand of capitalism. The objective is not to provide new evidence but simply to review how the previous concepts help to understand the issue of convergence/divergence of contemporary capitalism.

Away from Binomial Oppositions: A More Ambitious Taxonomy

Basically, both notions (complementarity and isomorphism) describe bilateral relations between institutions, and this is a serious limitation already mentioned when the German case was briefly discussed. In many cases, the stability of a given configuration can only be understood by considering three interrelated institutions and not only two of them. This is a quite general feature. When notions are introduced and defined, the analysis can be restricted to two institutions (Figure 2.5), but when the issue is about the congruence of a configuration, a multiplicity of institutions ($n > 2$) is necessarily introduced and makes the picture much more complex (Figure 2.5, supra). But then, a difficult methodological issue pops out: how to analyze the compatibility of such a complex mix of institutions? The methodology proposed by Colin Crouch suggests that, for the time being, the approach should be quite eclectic and rather impressionistic. One can use alternatively pure logical principles, hypotheses derived from case studies, international comparisons, or historical analyses, some derivations from Weberian or organization theory with some inspiration from chemistry (Crouch 2005).

This remark points out a crucial difficulty in the understanding of institutional configuration. Of course, any relevant theory recognizes the presence of at least two institutional arrangements, for instance, State and market in the literature on market failures, coordination, and externalities. On the other hand, transaction cost theory investigates the choice between market and organization, whereas the research on rules and norms may enlighten the relative strengths of organization and civil society. Finally, game theory investigates under which conditions cooperation and trust may emerge even within market relations.

Casual observation suggests that all of these institutional arrangements are present in most contemporary societies and that they probably play some role in the viability of the related institutional configurations (Figure 2.5, supra). But we have *few methods* in order to disentangle among the huge variety of combinations of each specific institutional arrangement. Therefore, however attractive might seem QCA 'à la Ragin', we need one form or another of theoretical modeling, as economists usually do. Thus, one may investigate the outcome associated with the interaction of at least three basic institutions. For instance, in Italy, State, business association, and workers' union are the relevant institutions (Palombarini 2001). Alternatively, macromodeling

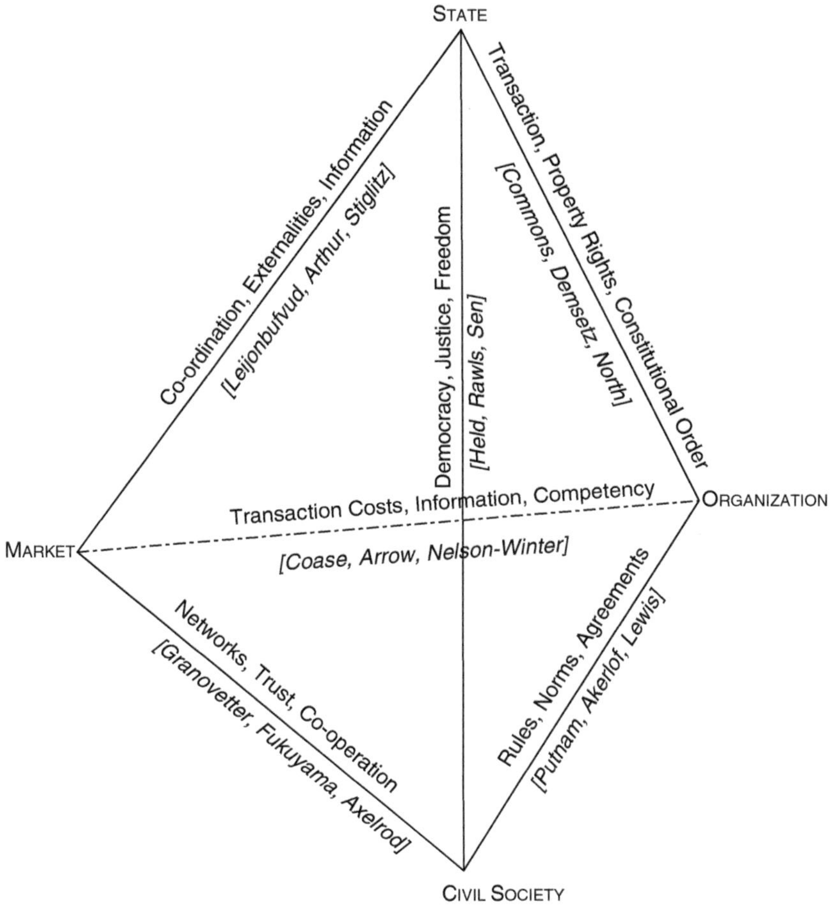

Figure 2.5. The multidimensional space of institutional economics.

delivers some results about the compatibility between a form of industrial relations, the access to credit or finance, and the style of innovation (Amable, Ernst, and Palombarini 2001).

The Limits of a Pure Combinatory Method: The Example of Variety of Capitalisms

Since much research has been done on the source of institutional diversity in contemporary capitalism, it could be useful to try to work out a synthesis about the explanatory factors that seem the most relevant. But again, most theoreticians are fond of black and white pictures (Figure 2.6).

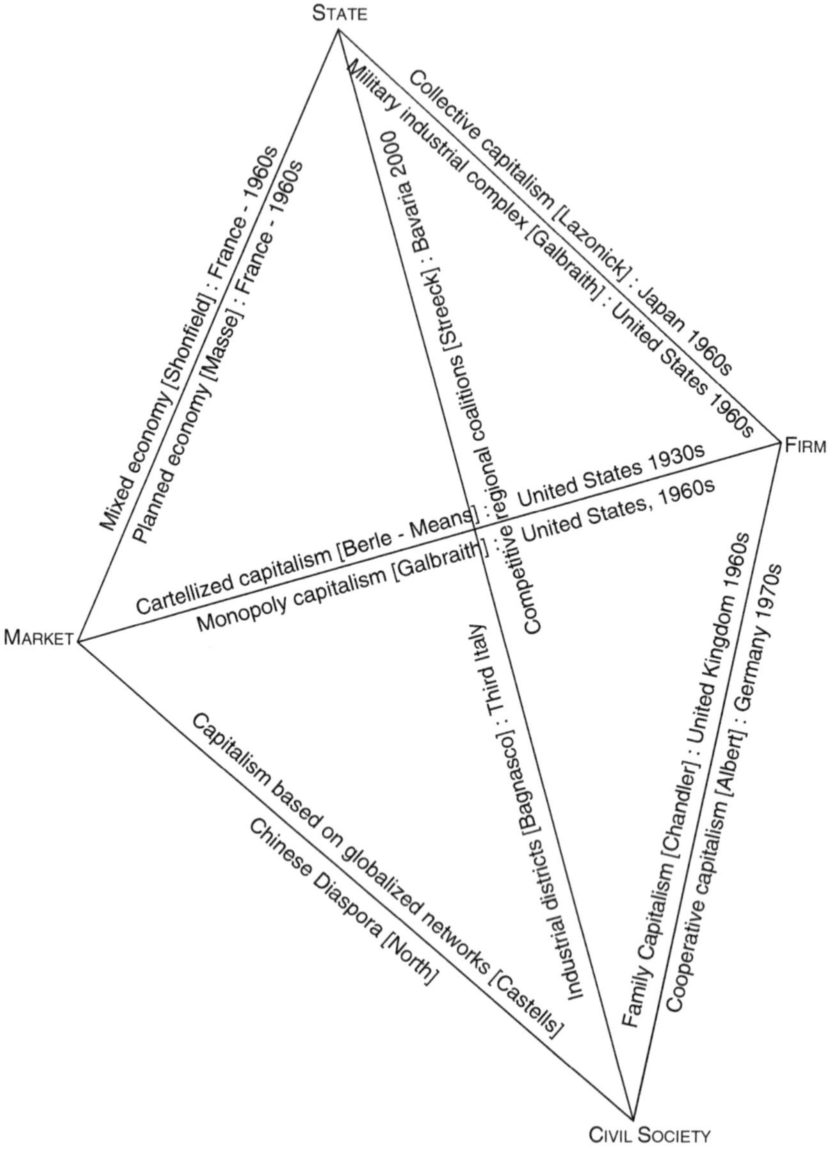

Figure 2.6. Analysis of the variety of capitalisms as the expression of a combination of the four main principles of coordination.

- One typical dichotomy concerns the degree of State interventions in market mechanisms: between a totally planned economy and a pure market led one, there is a whole spectrum of mixed economies.
- Transaction cost theory helps in understanding the dividing line between

markets and firms, with a series of intermediate cases (subcontracting, vertical integration, franchising, and networking).

- Some social scientists think that the trust in market relations must be embedded into another form of network built on extra economic ties (family, religion, and political party).

Clearly, all of these ingredients are present in any viable economy but we do not have the equivalent of a Mendelief table that details all the possible mix between institutional arrangements. The reference to chemistry is interesting ... but alas, social sciences do not exhibit the same ability to explain the stability of their objects, by strict analogy with the explanation of molecules by atom theory. A tentative proposal should be twofold. First, the method could be inductive, since a survey of existing literature could deliver a quite complete list of observed forms of capitalist configurations. Second, the deductive method may elaborate theoretical models built on a minimalist set of core hypotheses derived from the inductive approach.

The first method has been quite useful in pointing out the alternative institutional configurations supporting the ICT paradigm.

Still the Diversity of Capitalisms: No Single Configuration for the Institutions of the Knowledge Based Economy

The 1990s have propagated the practices of *benchmarking*, and the ideas that both corporate governance and capitalist institutions should *converge* toward the most efficient configuration. This vision can be tested (Boyer 2004*a*, 2004*b*). First, a performance criterion has to be selected: let us define a successful economy as experiencing simultaneously an increase in total factor productivity, fast growth, and job creation. Second, quantitative as well as qualitative indexes of institutional forms have to be built, in order to characterize each institutional configuration. Third, in order to leave open the number of successful configurations, it is convenient to use the QCA method.

The results are interesting since they confirm the plurality of successful institutional architectures, but they do not cope with conventional opposition between two brands of capitalism (Figure 2.7).

The typical knowledge economy relies on the complementarity between the high general educational levels that permit intensive job training and institutionalized cooperation between, on the one hand, the academic system and the research centers, and, on the other, business. On average, a large proportion of total output is devoted to education, software, and other vehicles for the transmission of knowledge. Information and communication technologies are intensively used, but they are simply a channel that favors *widespread socialization* of knowledge by means of collective investments. This model is basically different from the so-called 'New Economy', and its leading

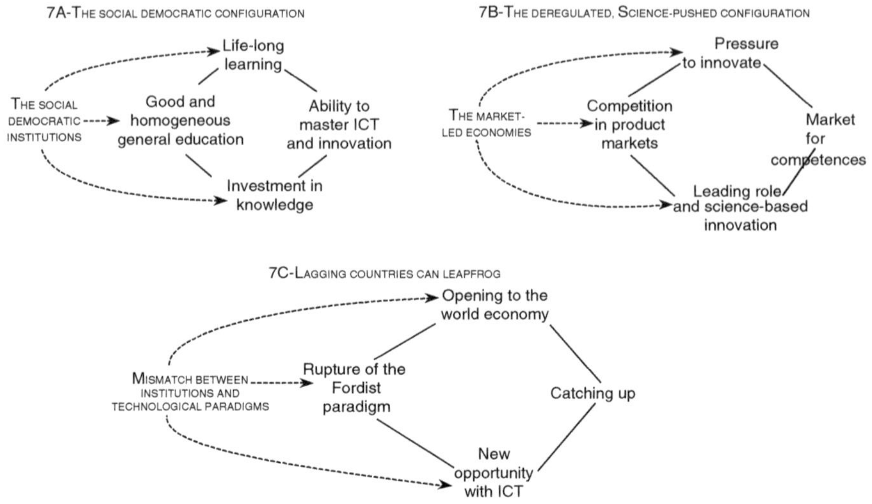

Figure 2.7. The successful contemporary capitalisms: three distinctive complementarities.

firms such as Intel and Microsoft, since Linux may well become the emblem of this type of knowledge economy. Here the market is not the dominant form of coordination—instead *cooperation* is, in this instance, institutionalized and organized on a national basis. Thus this configuration does not bring major inequalities since the rather even distribution of education endows individuals with good skills. Sweden, Finland, and Denmark (Lundvall 2002) belong to this configuration. This feature is good both on the production side, with the dynamism of innovation, and on the demand side, for diffusion of new products with a large informational content.

The deregulated economy on the other hand allows for a *private appropriation* of advances in knowledge inasmuch as patents and the defense of intellectual property rights become the tools that enable those who have the highest diplomas and/or the major talent to keep most of the innovation rents for themselves. A very active external labor market is given the task of evaluating at all times how much everyone is to be remunerated, depending on his/her competency and on the demands of the market. This capture of the rents associated with innovation is mitigated by the fact that competition in the product markets tends to cause a considerable drop in the price of information goods, allowing consumers to benefit ultimately from innovation-driven advances. In this configuration, the unequal distribution of competences is a key ingredient of the very dynamism of growth. Not only the United States but also most English-speaking countries explore this trajectory.

The accelerated catch-up model is made possible by a shift in the technological paradigm. This is another configuration that is capable of triggering a virtuous circle, despite, or maybe because of, the initial lag that the countries in question (Ireland, Portugal) were experiencing during the old Fordist mass production period. A *heavily protected labor force* does not impede membership of this regime—unlike the second configuration, which is typical of countries featuring a significant confidence in market mechanisms. The complementarity between institutional arrangements is not so clear but the structural changes in the international economy and innovation systems play a role since they remove the barriers to development that previously existed.

This method finally exhibits the complementarities or at least compatibilities between various institutional arrangements (Amable, Ernst, and Palombarini 2002). Nevertheless, they do not derive from a canonical supermodularity originating in technology (Milgrom and Roberts 1990): just-in-time and total quality control are not considered here. Furthermore, these configurations differ from the ones previously investigated. Comparative institutional analysis (Aoki, 2001) contrasts the hierarchical and vertically integrated mass-production firm with the flexibility associated with modular production and the mobility of competences typical of Silicon Valley. The VOC theory stresses a dichotomy between noncoordinated and coordinated market economies, with the United States on one side, and Germany on that of a social market economy (Hall and Soskice 2001). In fact, different configurations emerge when the analysis focuses on complementarity/compatibility issues.

Part IV: Forces and Patterns of Institutional Change

Can the same concepts explain the changes in institutions and institutional configurations? The ICH, as well as its various related concepts, has definite consequences about the nature and the pattern of institutional change. But the time dimension of institutions calls for an extension of the previous framework in various directions. Are the full information hypothesis and the substantive rationality principle able to analyze institutional change? Is the building of an institutional configuration a permanent feature or does it undergo a specific time profile? Are cognitive problems and therefore learning, the core determinants in the evolution of institutions?

A major ambition of contemporary research is to investigate some of these factors that govern institutional changes (Pierson 2004; Crouch 2005; North 2005). It is especially important to investigate these issues in order to understand under which conditions governments succeed in promoting institutional reforms (Boyer 2004*c*). First, one should not yield to the illusion of a retrospective analysis according to which a successful innovation has been the direct outcome of an *ex ante* rational and full assessment. Or conversely, to be tempted to conclude that an innovation that is now incompatible with existing institutional configuration will necessarily fail. Second, by contrast, tinkering is very frequent and finally may deliver a system that was thought as impossible by contemporary actors. Third, whereas rational choice theory suggests that homogeneity is a necessary property of a single one best way, in many cases heterogeneity is required for generating new institutional combinations. Fourth, the degree of openness or closeness plays some role in the ability to innovate and in the speed of diffusion of an innovation. From a theoretical point of view, innovation can be explained by a series of factors.

- The logic of action: *tinkering* much more than a theory of *substantive rationality*.
- *Heterogeneity* of institutional arrangements more than a trend toward *homogeneity* via the synchronization of all institutions.
- The *separability* of some subsystems and the slack in institutional complementarity help in nurturing a search process for new configurations. That may be better than a *full connectivity* of a totally coherent system.
- Is innovation a matter of *pure cognitive problems* solving or/and does it imply some bargaining and compromise between *conflicting interests*?

Tinkering More Than Full Information and Substantive Rationality

Some theoreticians think themselves to be forward-looking and clever enough to detect *ex ante* complementarity (Milgrom and Roberts 1990). Actually, they probably are simply struggling in order to capture in their models the logic of the clustering of institutions that has been developed by a highly complex and unintended process. Even *ex post* 'the fact that one institution complements another is fundamentally uncertain' (Streeck 2003). Furthermore, the institutions that are supposed to be complementary by institutional design, rarely end up so. A good example of such a retrospective illusion relates to the methods that have been invented to prevent bank runs.

Many such episodes took place in history before theoreticians in sociology (Robert Merton) or economists (Diamond and Dybvig 1983) proposed explanations for them. For Robert Merton, the key interpretation was in terms of self-fulfilling prophecies, whereas Diamond and Dybvig are interested in the issue of the preservation of liquidity in response to a lower than expected rate of return on the credit offered by a bank. Furthermore, the contemporary mix of insurance deposit and prudential ratios was not initially perceived as THE solution to bank runs. Various experts proposed the creation of a money-clearing market among private banks, while others thought that the central bank should be the lender of last resort and thus stop bank runs. This is not to speak about the proponents of a pure currency principle according to which banks should only manage the payment system, without managing any

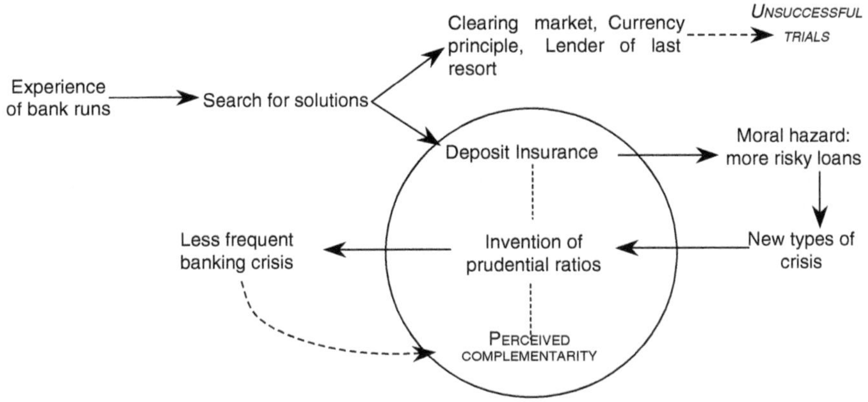

Figure 2.8. How deposit insurance and prudential ratios became to be preceived as complementary.

credit. This means that the complementarity between (DI) and (PR) was not at all evident even two decades ago, not to speak of one century ago! (Figure 2.8).

Clearly, this was the result of a largely unintended process that is *ex post* summarized by the hypothesis of complementarity. A priori, many solutions were available from the more backward-looking (interdiction of monetary creation by private banks) to the most innovative and unconventional ones such as the supply of an unlimited amount of liquidity to banks suffering from liquidity and even solvency problems. Private insurance companies were supposed to provide the liquidity help required during banking crises, and various forms of bank deposits (with or without insurance) could have been proposed to customers and have diffused the cost of banking crises. But the trial and error process has converged toward the idea that a compulsory public insurance should cover individuals' bank accounts, up to some thresholds. But then, bankers may become more risk prone since they are sure to be bailed out in the case of liquidity shortage. Therefore, the type of banking crisis has changed and calls for new countervailing mechanisms. It took several decades to invent the prudential ratios elaborated by the Bank of International Settlements (BIS) and for this device to be propagated all over the world. Observing that, at least for financially developed economies, banking crises had become less frequent, many economists were induced to conclude that there exists an intrinsic complementarity between (DI) and (PR).

Yet this was not at all the end of the history of banking management and this nice complementarity has in turn encountered some limits (Borio 2003). For instance, when prudential ratios were introduced into the ailing Japanese banking system after the bursting of the 1980s bubble, the direct impact was to exacerbate a credit crunch and a contraction of investment. Thus,

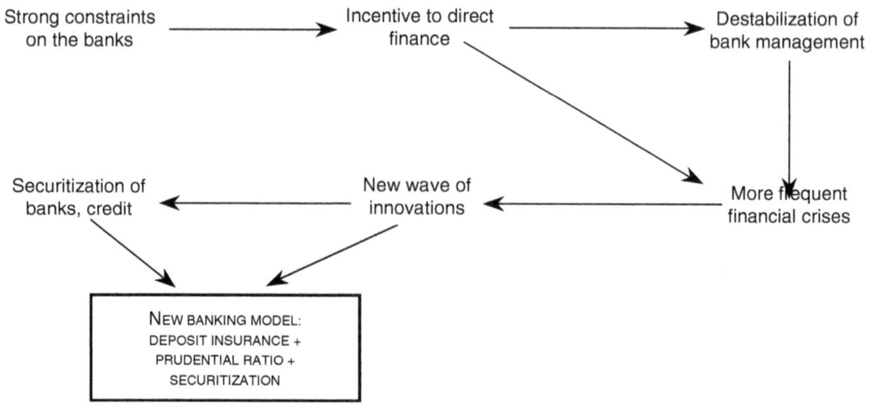

Figure 2.9. The rise of direct finance puts pressure on previous complementarities.

depressing the level of economic activity, the introduction of prudential ratios has created a new wave of nonperforming loans. Given a complete deposit insurance, no bank run took place in Japan. Nevertheless, the conjunction of deposit insurance and prudential ratios has not been sufficient to restore the confidence of customers about the soundness of the banking system and the recovery of the Japanese economy. In a sense, the complementarity between two institutions has a variable impact according to the general context in which such a complementarity is embedded.

And there is another reason to put in historical perspective such a complementarity by looking at the American trajectory. Since the early 1980s, financial innovations have been promoting direct finance to the detriment of banking intermediation. Consequently, the competitive situation of banks has been deteriorating and has pushed them to take more risks. But to compensate for the different risks linked to default of payment and interest rate variations, the banks have benefited from the new trend toward securitization: by grouping some of their credits and converting them into securities, the banks could spread out the risk that traditionally was concentrating into the credit system. Thus appears a new complementarity of ID and PR with the strategy of securitizations (Figure 2.9). Now ID, PR, and S exhibit a triadic complementarity.

From the Building of a Complementarity to Its Demise

In reality, the theoreticians and model builders drastically simplify the issue of institutional complementarity in removing most of the uncertainty that is at the origin of the emergence of most, if not all, the observed clustering of institutions. Serendipity is more frequent than rational economic calculation as far as the emergence of institutional complementarity is concerned. The very recognition by the actors of a complementarity may trigger destabilizing strategies and innovations that erode the beneficial role of this complementarity that then may enter into a crisis. The degree of coupling of institutions might first be rather weak but increases through time by the recognition process according to which actors try to exploit this perceived complementarity (Streeck 2005). The success of the complementarity between two institutions is context dependent, that is, it has to be compatible with the social and economic global ordering.

The evolution of the institutional architecture of most OECD countries after-World War II gives a good example of such a pattern. In the early 1950s, new rules of the game are implemented, especially in the domain of industrial relations: the nominal wage tends to be indexed both on productivity increases and inflation. After a while, most economic actors perceive the positive consequence of this device that organizes the complementarity between wage and profit and therefore stabilizes the growth regime. Given its success, all actors therefore ask for the indexing of their incomes along with the consumer price index, and this triggers both an acceleration of inflation in response to income distribution conflicts and more rigidity into the economic adjustment process (Boyer and Mistral 1982). Endogenously, the economy progressively shifts from a stable to an unstable regime that can be revealed by any external shocks such as energy price increases.

Thus, the perception by most of the actors of a complementarity could well be the early warning that the system may enter a crisis due to the exploitation by a larger and larger fraction of the population of the benefits of this complementarity (Figure 2.10). More generally, these remarks put some emphasis upon the time dimension of complementarity, that is, a quite essential feature in order to understand institutional change. Some contemporary political scientists do converge toward the same challenge: how to introduce historical time in theories dealing quite exclusively with a stationary world (Pierson 2004).

Conflicts of Interest as Sources of Institutional Change

A first answer consists in taking into account the role of interest and the fact that the transformation of a governance regime might be triggered by insider rewards for powerful interests (Crouch 2005). The notion of institutional entrepreneurs is interesting because it removes the naive idea of neoclassical institutional economics that the search for systemic performance and efficiency is at the origin of institutional transformation. The related developments strongly remind of the framework elaborated by Bourdieu (2000) in order to understand the processes according to which innovation and change can take place within a given field (Boyer 2003*b*). They can be summarized by

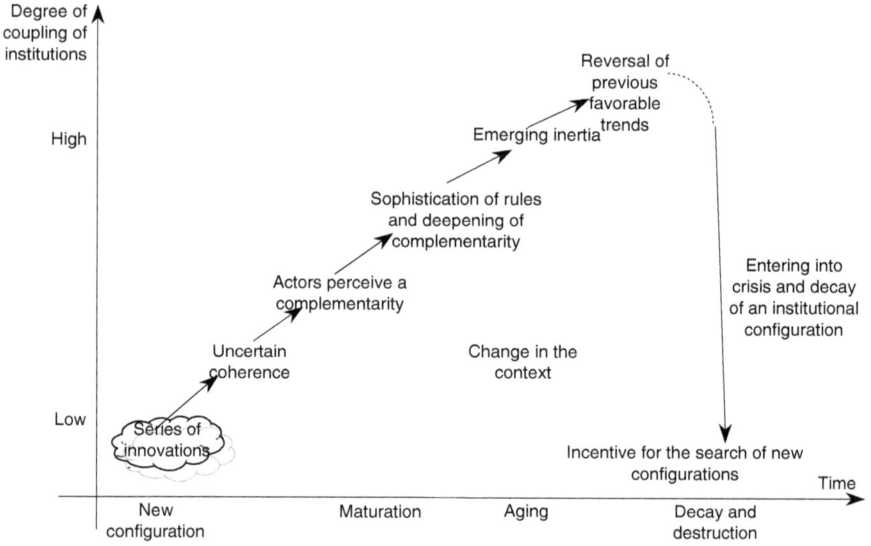

Figure 2.10. The process of emergence of institutional complementarity: a synoptic view.

the following figure (Figure 2.11). Basically, five factors may set into motion an institutional change:

- First it is the interest of the leading and more powerful actors in a given field (*les dominants* in French) to innovate in order to keep their superiority. Thus the institutional entrepreneurs would mainly be the *incumbent actors* and the principal benefactors of innovation. 'Innovate in order to preserve the existing distribution of power' that would be the motto associated with this first factor.
- A second process of change clearly comes from the *entry of new actors* into a given field, be it by a generation change or by a changing architecture among fields. In a sense it is a parallel with the Schumpeterian vision of entrepreneurs, once extended from, technology and organization to institutions.
- The internal struggles within a field may *spill over* into proximate ones and then trigger a process of global institutional change. The shifting of frontiers between fields would be a third factor of innovation. Again, it is a well-known factor in the literature about technological paradigm shift. The internationalization of trade and investment is a good example; it is the result of struggles internal to the economy, but it affects law and jurisprudence and promotes the shift from a Roman conception to common law.

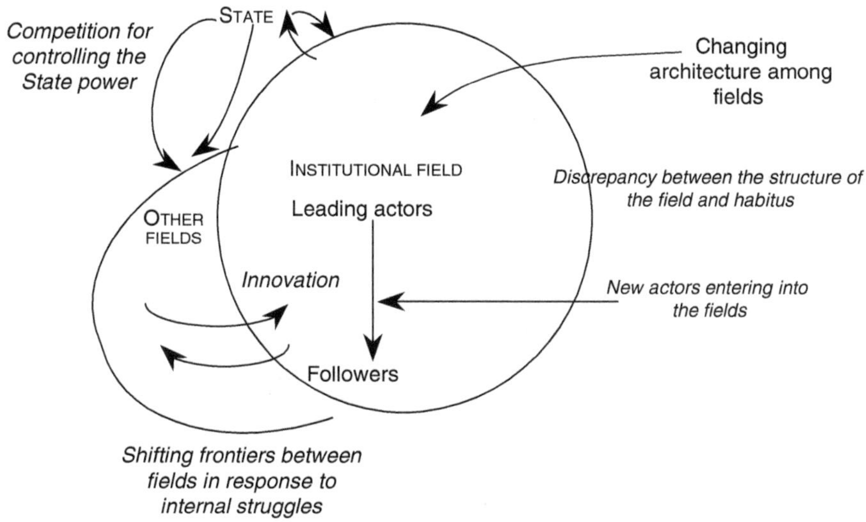

Figure 2.11. The strategic interactions that may trigger institutional change.

- When the distribution of power does not enable the emergence of a clear and stable configuration, the actors may *call for the intervention of State power* in order to establish rules of the game within their field in order to consolidate or set up their power as leading actors.
- Finally, a changing structure of one field, imposed by a large and overarching transformation in society, may make apparent a major discrepancy between the transformation of the field and the permanence of strategies generated according to the previous *habitus*. This *desynchronization between a field and the related habitus* can be at the origin of major crises.

All these factors share the same concern for the role of conflicting interests and power struggles in the evolution of the structuring of any field. This may define the elementary unit of analysis but this does not exhaust the analysis of systemic institutional change that is implicitly the issue most institutionalists would like to investigate.

Reconfiguring Institutions: Conversion, Sedimentation, and Recombination

When the issue shifts from the evolution of a single institution to the analysis of the transformation of a whole institutional configuration, other mechanisms have to be introduced. The process of *bricolage* is quite important since 'in a kind of institutional bricolage to produce new combinations that bring together the apparently incompatible function . . .' (Crouch 2005). Another

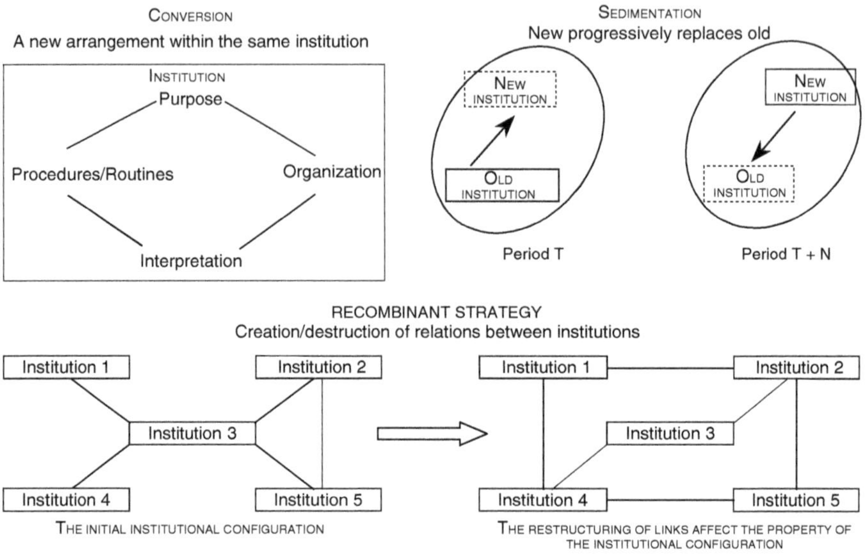

Figure 2.12. A summary of some of the mechanisms at the origin of institutional change.

promising avenue for research is opened by the framework elaborated by Thelen (2003, 2004) and Stark (1997). Combining their proposals, one gets a quite complete set of mechanisms at the origin of institutional change (Figure 2.12).

- First we have to open the *black box of institution,* as other social scientists did for the firm or the organization. An institution is defined by an objective that is implicitly or explicitly pursued, a series of routines and procedures, an organization, and finally a permanent interpretation by actors of the objectives, and procedures of the institutions (Reynaud 2002). Hence, a part of institutional change may come from a change of either objectives or routines in the same institution. This might be called a *conversion.*
- *Adding new institutions to old ones* progressively alter the role of an institution within the whole system. This process can be called *sedimentation* and is quite frequent in history. Institutions are rarely destroyed except during wars and major crises, since they are complemented by new ones and then the equivalent of a selection process operates. This reminds of evolutionary theory but the selecting mechanism is not the competition in markets but a much more complex social, political, and economic process.

- Given an institutional system with a lot of redundancies, by *redesigning the strong/weak links among existing institutions,* it is possible to drastically change the functioning of the whole system. This is *recombination* that is frequently the outcome of explicit strategies from leading actors (Stark 1997). Under the same label (e.g. codetermination in Germany) may operate a different mechanism if this device is embedded into a different context (strong national industrial relations or under the pressure of shareholder value) (Höpner 2003*a*, 2003*b*).

Some Alternatives to Rational Choice Theory

Combining these three mechanisms (conversion, sedimentation, and recombination) opens a lot of opportunities for institutional change. They share the same basic hypothesis that the redundancy/looseness of an institutional configuration is an important factor to be taken into account. This is a strong contrast with the neoclassical approach to institutional change (Table 2.2).

A first tension opposes the homogeneity hypothesis adopted by most neoclassical approaches to the heterogeneity that some institutional analyses take into account. A second issue questions the respective role of cognition, interest, morale/justice, and polity. This opens a large avenue for further researches (Table 2.3).

Table 2.2 Two analyses of innovation and institutional change

	Rational choice	Bricolage
Logic of action	Full rationality	Learning and interacting
Nature of the field	Homogeneous Rather simple	Heterogeneous Complex
Ideal type	One best way	Tinkering
Performance	Static efficiency	Flexibility
Problem to be solved	Cognitive	Composition of interests

Table 2.3 A typology of alternative analyses of institutions

	Cognition	Interest	Morale/Justice	Polity
Homogeneous system	Rational expectation models	Neoclassical economic models	Economies of convention	Median voter political economy models
Heterogeneity	Evolutionary models	Game theory	Rawls procedural conception of justice	Machiavel's theory

Section V: When Institutional Change Affects Macroeconomic Realities: Regulation Theory

The concept of complementarity was not present in the earlier RT, since this research program relied on the notions of accumulation regime, *régulation* mode, architecture of institutional forms, and exogenously driven and endogenously generated crises (Boyer and Saillard 2002). Nevertheless, the inner development of this research agenda has shown the usefulness of two concepts in order to understand the coherence of a set of institutions: those of institutional complementarity and hierarchy. But the major emphasis of RT is about structural transformation and endogenous coevolution of institutional forms. Thus, this approach has proposed three other mechanisms: hybridization and endometabolism of institutional configurations as well as the joint dynamics of political and economic forces.

The Coherence of a Régulation Mode: From Complementarity to Hierarchy

Basically, a coherent régulation mode is only the *post factum* outcome of a series of innovations and adjustments. Quite all institutional forms result from social compromises that are then embedded into law, jurisprudence, social norms, and conventions. Each of these institutional forms induces some specific behavior, for firms, wage earners, banks, and so on. At the economy wide level, there is no automatic mechanism that would warrant the compatibility of the behaviors associated with the different institutional forms that have contrasted origins, purposes, and outcomes. Thus, institutional forms are continuously adjusting one to another and coevolving. The coevolution is the process of trial and error through which a series of institutional forms that are initially disconnected and formally independent (since they result from institutionalized compromises among diverse agents in different fields) adjust to one another until a viable institutional configuration emerges. The economic adjustments then become part of a mode of régulation and retrospectively this mode appears as coherent. Thus, RT extends to institutional analysis a concept developed by neo-Schumpeterian theories in relation to the joint evolution of technologies and organizations. However, the mechanisms at work may differ: for technologies, market selection is crucial, while for institutional forms political processes play a determining role.

In retrospect, in order to capture the core of a régulation mode, it may be useful to invoke the concept of *institutional complementarity*. More precisely, the complementarity of institutional forms describes a configuration in which the viability of an institutional form is strongly or entirely conditioned by the existence of several other institutional forms in such a manner that their conjunction offers greater resilience and possibly better performance compared to alternative configurations. It has already been mentioned how the Fordist wage–labor nexus and a credit-based monetary regime appeared to be complementary, as were the competitive wage–labor nexus and the gold standard regime. The same idea is emphasized by the 'Comparative Institutional Analysis' with respect to the complementarity of keiretsu, employment stability and the main bank in Japan (Aoki 2001). The notion of institutional complementarity seemingly transposes at the macroeconomic level the theory of supermodularity (Milgrom and Roberts 1990), but the underlying mechanisms are rather different: the institutional complementarity is only observed *ex post* and does not derive from any organizational or technological complementarity observed at the firm level.

Institutional Change: From One Hierarchy to Another

The observation of the transformations of industrialized countries during the last two decades has shown the interest of a third notion that of *hierarchy* of institutional forms. This describes a configuration in which, for any given era and society, particular institutional forms impose their logic on the institutional architecture as a whole, lending its dominant style to the mode of régulation. Whereas the notion of institutional complementarity implies at least implicitly symmetry between two or more institutions, the hypothesis of institutional hierarchy stresses the asymmetry among these institutions. Thus, RT adopts two definitions, one static, the other dynamic.

Institutional hierarchy by design means that during the conception of some institutional form, the constraints of another central, and hence superior, institutional form, are explicitly or implicitly taken into account. For instance, if nominal wage becomes the equivalent of a labor standard, the objective and the tools of monetary policy have to be redesigned (Hicks 1955) and this means that collective bargaining on wages has a primacy over the (Keynesian) monetary regime, and thus that there is a hierarchy from labor market institutions to the monetary regime. Similarly, the monetary regime put forward by a conservative Central banker implies flexible labor market adjustments and the absence of any structural public deficit by governments. This is *an inversion* with respect to the previous institutional hierarchy.

According to a second interpretation, *the transformation of an institutional form guides the development of one* or several other institutional forms. Under Fordism, the wage–labor nexus played this role, because of the founding compromise from which it originates and its transformations finally permeated nearly all other institutional forms (Figure 2.13). With the opening of domestic economies and the financialization of corporate governance, the form of competition and the financial regime have progressively shaped quite

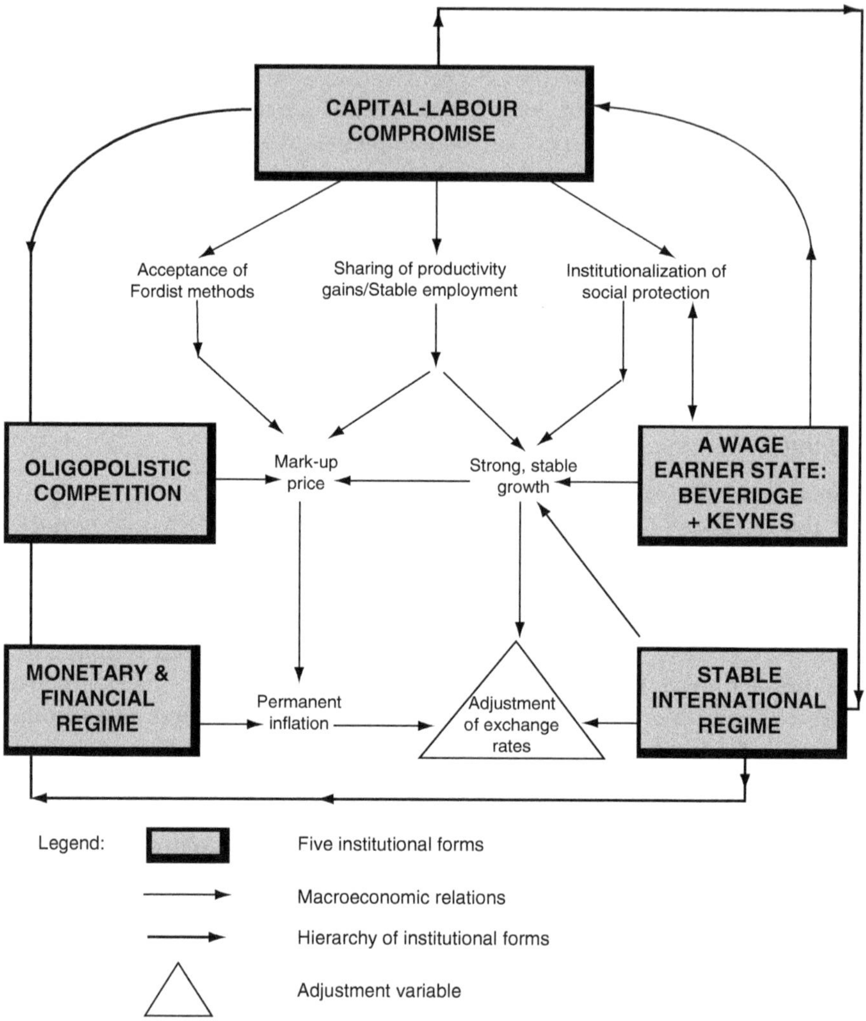

Figure 2.13. Hierarchical position of the wage–labor nexus during the Fordist Golden Age.

important transformations into the inner organization of the wage–labor nexus (Figure 2.14).

Ex post, the two definitions converge but when analyzing the process of institutional change, the second definition is more operative than the first one. This remark brings an important issue about *the time horizon* of institutional hierarchy. Both concepts may give the impression of a completely static and deterministic system, without any uncertainty, slack, or time dimension.

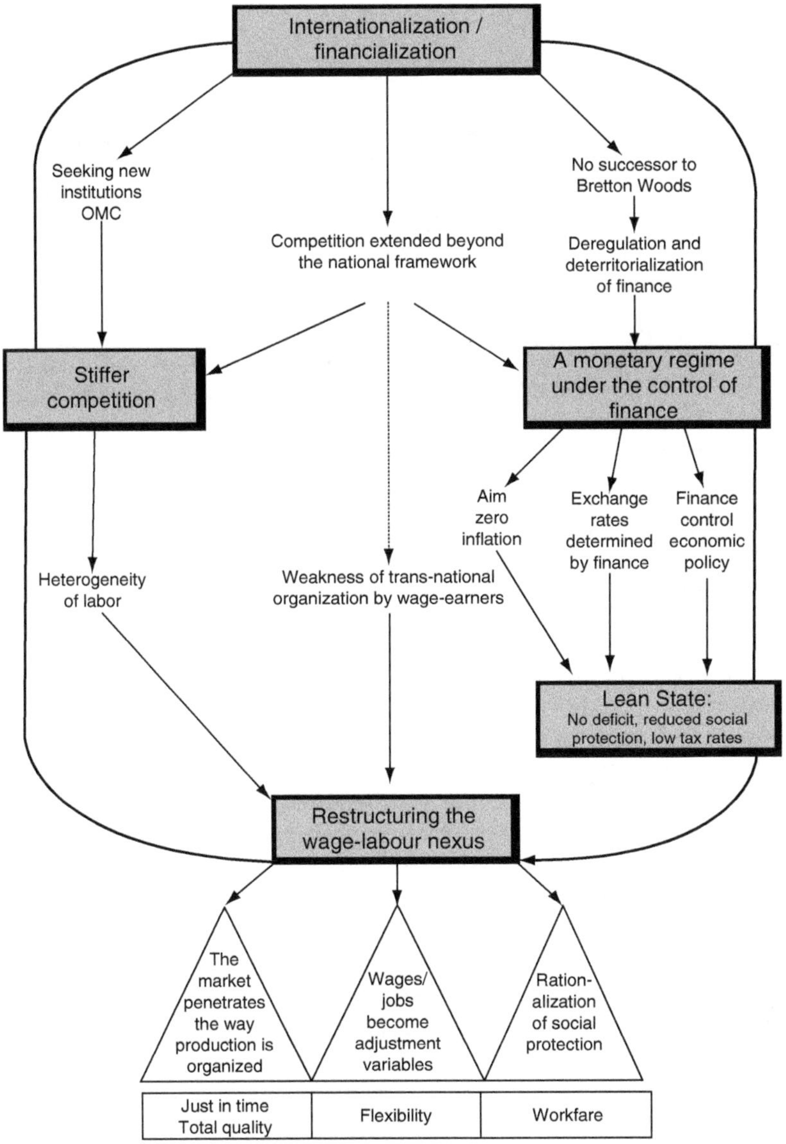

Figure 2.14. Internationalization and financialization: The new hierarchy since the 1990s.

Actually, the issue of time and space in institutional analysis is central for RT, since the cross-national comparison of régulation modes has shown that the fit of various institutions was far from perfect and that it varies in the long run in response to three major mechanisms.

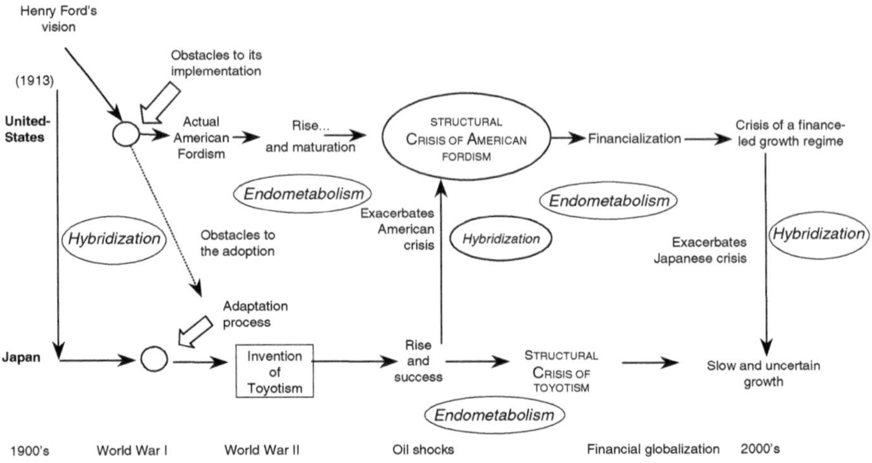

Figure 2.15. Hybridization and endometabolism, two factors of institutional change: The joint evolution of American and Japanese trajectories.

The Transfers of Institutions From One Space to Another

Hybridization describes the process through which tentatively imported institutions or organizations are transformed via their interaction with domestic institutional forms (Boyer et al. 1999). This means that there are some degrees of freedom within each general institutional form. This mechanism of hybridization is a major factor in order to explain the evolution of institutions and the diversity in institutional architectures. Hybridization also plays a major role in the evolution of productive models (Boyer and Freyssenet 2002). For instance, it may explain why the adaptation of Fordism to Japan has finally delivered a quite original productive model: Toyotism (Shimizu 2000). Thus, the respective institutional architectures of the American and Japanese capitalisms can be fruitfully interpreted as the results of their interactions, including by hybridization, over nearly a century (Boyer and Yamada 2000) (Figure 2.15).

The Endogenous Destabilization of a Regime

Endometabolism, that is, the inner development of tensions within a given architecture, is a second source of evolution of institutional architectures. In a sense, the mechanism described by Figure 2.10 above is one example of such a dynamic analysis of the emergence, maturation, and crisis of a regime. The recognition that the fit among institutions is always partial and transitory brings to the forefront the mechanisms diagnosed by comparative historical analysis: layering and conversion are powerful mechanisms of evolution (Thelen 2003) as well as the recombination of institutions (Stark 1997). Again this implies a 'softening' or at least a careful use of the concepts of complementarity and hierarchy.

The Joint Dynamics of Polity and Economy

Most new institutional theories assume that the self-interest of economic actors is the major source in the creation of institutions as well as a factor in their self-enforcement thus delivering a long-run equilibrium. Actually, these three hypotheses do not fit with the stylized facts derived from historical case studies and contemporary international comparisons. For RT, institutional forms are the outcomes of social struggles, once mediated by the political process and the elaboration of law. Only the experience sets whether the related innovations simultaneously define a coherent adjustment process and allow the persistence of a political coalition that entitled their emergence. There is a priori no reason for the corresponding institutional configuration to be coherent. The tension between the evolution in the two spheres, the

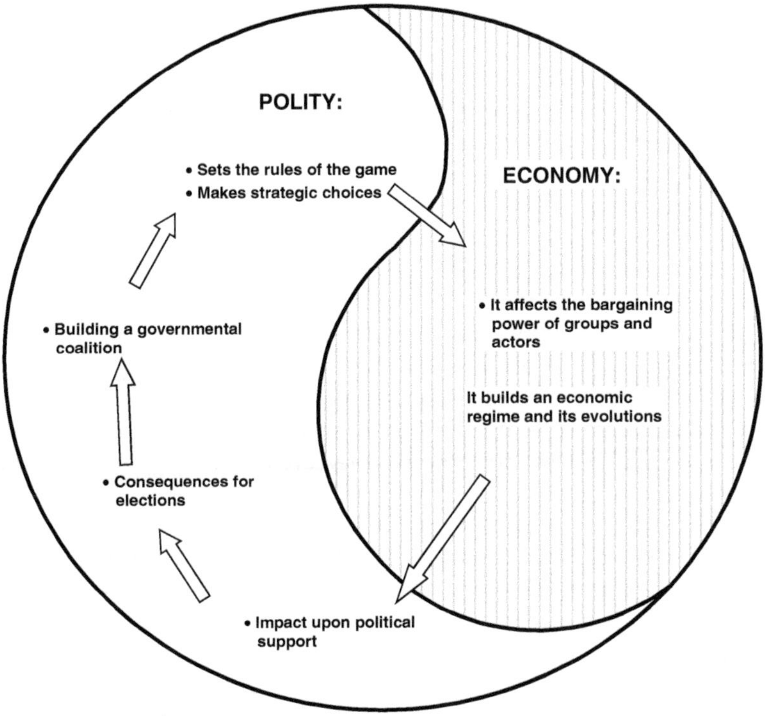

Figure 2.16. Emergence of institutions by political processes, their destabilization by endometabolism.

polity and the economy, is a major source of transformations of the institutions (Figure 2.16). It can explain too why some economic crises are closely associated with the breaking down of political coalitions (Palombarini 2001).

It is not an easy task to calibrate the relevance of these various mechanisms. Clearly, the analysis of institutional change is still an infant industry: many new theoretical developments and empirical studies are required in order to dare to provide any clear prognosis. By chance, it is a very active field of research (Djelic and Quack 2003; Thelen 2004). Nevertheless, it is interesting to test these notions, tools, and hypotheses against some contemporary evolution. Ideally the background could be the large literature about the diversity of capitalisms and evolutions (Hancké 1999; Fligstein 2001; Jessop ed. 2001; Coates ed. 2002; Whitley 2002; Amable 2003).

Conclusion

The Institutional Complementarity Hypothesis ICH opens a rather promising research program that could help understanding the nature and evolution of institutional configurations. First, complementarity is one of the forces that stick institutional forms one with another. Second, there is not a single form of complementarity but a significant variety. Third, this explains why benchmarking is not necessarily successful and why institutional reforms are so difficult: as soon as two different institutions are complementary they should be changed simultaneously, whereas reformers tend to divide and segment the issues at stake.

From a methodological standpoint, ICH has to make clear some major issues. First, complementarity should not be confused with more or less close notions such as compatibility, coevolution, or clustering. Second, various methods have to be combined in order to test ICH. Among them, QCA and nonlinear econometric methods seem rather promising for a general social science approach, whereas formal modeling is an avenue more easy to explore for economists than for other disciplines. Third, if complementarity is not only dyadic but triadic, empirical research becomes more difficult but probably more relevant.

From a theoretical point of view, three major findings emerge concerning respectively the origin of complementarity, the time horizon that governs complementarity, and finally the level at which it operates. First, economists often refer to technical complementarities in order to derive the related complementarities between institutions. Of course, they might exist but they describe only a part of the large set of complementarities. Some of them derive from pure institutional factors: for instance, the liquidity of the commercial bank calls for deposit insurance, then prudential ratio, and finally a lender of last resort. Second, historical studies exhibit a form of paradox:

when a majority of actors discover and opportunistically use the benefits of a given institutional complementarity, this complementarity tends to decay, to vanish, and the institutional system enters into a crisis. Third, the ICH is not sufficient to bridge the gap between micro- and macroanalyses of institutional complementarities. Nevertheless, the notions of isomorphism, and to a certain extent of hierarchy, do provide some cohesive factors between firms, organizational configuration, and the overall institutional architecture.

When applied to the issue of capitalism diversity and evolution, ICH suggests quite interesting hints. First, complementarity is one of the factors that provide the glue that holds together an overall institutional architecture. Second, even in the era of globalization, financialization, and knowledge-based competitiveness, national economies still exhibit contrasting institutional configurations. Nevertheless, the number of these configurations is quite limited compared with what should result from a purely combinatory approach. Third, capitalism diversity is not a pure matter of historical legacy, inertia, or irrationality since at least three mechanisms permanently drive institutional change both in terms of the destruction of obsolete configurations and the creation of new institutions: endometabolism, hybridization and the dynamic principle that opposes the objectives and the time scale of the two domains of polity and economy.

The present chapter points out a challenging research agenda. What are the patterns of institutional evolution and what are the forces and factors that shape these patterns? The ICH explains some typical patterns: emergence, diffusion, maturation, sophistication, lack of reactivity, and finally erosion and crisis. Nevertheless, case studies and comparative analyses suggest that other and quite complex patterns are observable. A priori, a creative use of the various notions of compatibility, coevolution, clustering, and of course complementarity and hierarchy may probably explain the diversity of these patterns in institutional change. This could help in the design of institutional reforms that have proved to be so difficult during the 1990s and the early 2000 in most OECD countries.

References

Akerlof, G. (1984). *An Economic Theorist's Book of Tales*. Cambridge: Cambridge University Press.

Albert, M. (1991). *Capitalisme contre capitalisme*. Paris: Le Seuil.

Amable, B. (2000). 'Institutional Complementarity and Diversity of Social Systems of Innovation and Production,' *Review of International Political Economy*, 7(4): 645–87.

——(2003). *The Diversity of Modern Capitalism*. Oxford: Oxford University Press.

——, Barré, R., and Boyer, R. (1997*a*). *Les systèmes d'innovation à l'ère de la globalisation*. Paris: Economica.

Amable, B., Barré, R., and Boyer, R. (1997*b*). 'Diversity, Coherence and Transformations of Innovation Systems,' in R. Barré, M. Gibbons, Sir John Maddox, B. Martin, and P. Papon (eds.), *Science in Tomorrow's Europe*. Paris: Economica International, pp. 33–49.

——, Ernst, E., and Palombarini, S. (2001). 'Institutional Complementarities: An Overview of the Main Issues,' Roneotypé Cepremap, Seminaire sur 'Institutional Complementarities and Dynamics of Economic Systems,' Paris, Cepremap-Ens, april 5–6.

——, ——, —— (2002). 'Comment les marchés financiers peuvent-ils affecter les relations industrielles? Une approche par la complémentarité institutionnelle,' *L'Année de la régulation* 2002, Vol. 6, Paris, éditions de Sciences-Po, 271–88.

Amable, B. and Palombarini, S. (2005). L'économie politique n'est pas une science morale, Collection Raison d'agir. Paris: Seuil.

Aoki, M. (1988). *Information, Incentives and Bargaining in the Japanese Economy*. New York: Cambridge University Press.

——(1994). 'The Contingent Governance of Teams: Analysis of Institutional Complementarity,' *International Economic Review*, 35: 657–76.

——(2000). *Information, Corporate Governance, and Institutional Diversity. Competitiveness in Japan, the USA, and the Transitional Economies*. Oxford: Oxford University Press.

——(2001). *Toward A Comparative Institutional Analysis*. Cambridge, MA: MIT Press.

Arthur, B. (1989). 'Competing Technologies, Increasing Returns And Lock-In By Historical Events,' *Economic Journal*, 99: 116–31.

Askenazy, P. (2002). *La croissance moderne: Organisation innovante du travail*. Paris: Economica.

Borio, C. (2003). 'Towards a Macroprudential Framework for Financial Supervision and Regulation?,' BIS Working Paper, no. 128, February, Bank for International Settlements, Basel, Switzerland.

Bourdieu, P. (2000). *Les structures sociales de l'économie*. Paris: Seuil.

Boyer, R. (1997). 'The Variety of Unequal Performance of Really Existing Markets: Farewell to Doctor Pangloss?,' in J. R. Hollingsworth and R. Boyer (eds.), *Contemporary Capitalism: The Embeddedness of Institutions*. Cambridge: Cambridge University Press, pp. 55–93.

——(2000). 'The Political in the Era of Globalization and Finance; Focus on Some Régulation School Research,' *International Journal of Urban and Regional Research*, 24(2): 274–322.

——(2000*a*). 'Is a Finance-led Growth Regime a Viable Alternative to Fordism? A Preliminary Analysis,' *Economy and Society*, 29(1): 111–45.

——(2001). 'The Diversity and Future of Capitalisms: A Régulationist Analysis,' in M. Hodgson Geoffrey, Itoh Makoto, and Yokokawa Nobuharu (eds.), *Capitalism in Evolution*. Cheltenham, UK: Edward Elgar.

——(2003). 'L'anthropologie économique de Pierre Bourdieu,' *Actes de la recherche en sciences sociales*, 150: 65–78.

——(2004*a*). 'New Growth Regimes, but Still Institutional Diversity,' *Socio-Economic Review*, 2(1): 1–32.

——(2004*b*). *The Future of Economic Growth. As New Becomes Old*. Cheltenham, UK: Edward Elgar.

Boyer, R. (2004*c*). 'A quelles conditions les réformes institutionnelles réussissent-elles?,' Roneotypé CEPREMAP, Contribution au contrat finalisé Commissariat Général du Plan—CEPREMAP 2003–2004.
——, Charron, E., Jürgens, U., and Tolliday, S. (eds.) (1999). *Between Imitation and Innovation*. Oxford: Oxford University Press.
——and Freyssenet, M. (2002). *The Productive Models*. Gerpisa: Palgrave MacMillan.
Boyer, R. and Mistral, J. (1982). *Accumulation, Inflation, Crises*. Paris: PUF.
——and Saillard, Y. (eds.) (2002). *Régulation Theory. The State of the Art*. London: Routledge.
——and Yamada, T. (eds.) (2000). *Japanese Capitalism in Crisis*. London: Routledge.
Bresnahan, T. (2002). 'La contribution des technologies de l'information à la croissance économique,' in J.-P. Touffut (ed.), *Institutions et innovation: de la recherche aux systèmes sociaux d'innovation*. Paris: Albin Michel, pp. 287–323.
Castells, M. (2000). *The Information Age: Economy, Society, and Culture*. Oxford: Blackwell (revised edition).
Chandler, A. (1977). *The Visible Hand: The Managerial Revolution in American Business*. Cambridge, MA: Harvard University Press.
——(1990). *Scale and Scope: The Dynamics of Industrial Capitalism*. Cambridge: Harvard University Press.
Chavance, B., Magnin E., Matamed-nejad R. and Sapir, J. (eds.) (1999). *Capitalisme et Socialisme Enperspective*. Paris: La Découverte.
Coase, R. (1937). 'The Nature of the Firm,' *Economica*, 4.
Coates, D. (ed.) (2002). *Models of Capitalism: Debating Strengths and Weaknesses*—Vol. III. Cheltenham, UK: Edward Elgar.
Crouch, C. (2004). 'Complementarity and Innovation,' Discussion paper at second meeting of Complementarities Group, Cologne, March 26–27.
——(2005). *New Advances in Institutional Change*. Oxford: Oxford University Press.
——, Streeck, W., Boyer, R., Amable, B., Hall, P., and Jackson, G. (2005). 'Dialogue on Institutional Complementarity and Political Economy,' *Socio-Economic Review*, 3: 361–84.
Delorme, R. (ed.) (1996). *A l'est, du nouveau. Changement institutionnel et transformations économiques*. Paris: L'Harmattan.
DiMaggio, P. J. and Powell, W. (eds.) (1991). *The New Institutionalism in Organizational Analysis*. Chicago, IL: Chicago University Press.
Diamond, D. and Dybvig, P. (1983). 'Bank Runs, Deposit Insurance, and Liquidity,' *Journal of Political Economy*, 91: 401–19.
Djelic, M.-L. and Quack, S. (2003). *Globalization and Institutions. Redefining the Rules of the Economic Game*. Cheltenham, UK: Edward Elgar.
Dosi, G., Fabiani, S., Freeman, C., and Aversi, R. (1993). 'On the Process on Economic Development,' WP C.C.C. no 93–2, University of California at Berkeley, January.
Ebizuka, A., Uemura, H., and Isogai, A. (1997). 'L'hypothèse de " la relation hiérarchisée marché-firme " et l'économie japonaise d'après-guerre,' *l'Année de la régulation*, 1, La Découverte, Paris: 297–317.
Ernst, E. (2001). 'Complémentarités institutionnelles et croissance économique à long terme,' Thèse EHESS, Mars.

Fligstein, N. (2001). *The Architecture of Markets. An Economic Sociology of Twenty-First-Century Capitalist Societies*. Princeton, NJ: Princeton University Press.

Granovetter, M. (1985). 'Economic Action and Social Structures: The Problem of Embeddedness,' *American Journal of Sociology*, 91: 481–510.

——(1992). 'Economic Institutions as Social Constructions: A Framework of Analysis,' *Acta Sociologica*, 35: 3–12.

Hall, P. and Soskice, D. (eds.) (2001). *Varieties of Capitalism: The Institutional Foundations of Comparative Advantage*. Oxford: Oxford University Press.

Hancké, B. (1999). 'Varieties of Capitalism Revisited: Globalisation and Comparative Institutional Advantage,' *La Lettre de la régulation*, 30: 1–4.

Hicks, J. R. (1955). 'Economic Foundations of Wage Policy,' *The Economic Journal*, (September): 389–404.

Hollingsworth, R. and Boyer, R. (eds.) (1997). *Contemporary Capitalism: The Embeddedness of Institutions*. Cambridge: Cambridge University Press.

Höpner, M. (2001). 'Corporate Governance in Transition: Ten Empirical Findings on Shareholder Value and Industrial Relations in Germany,' MPIfG Discussion Paper 2001-5, Cologne, Max Planck Institute for the Study of Societies.

——(2003*a*). 'What Connects Industrial Relations with Corporate Governance? A review on complementarity,' Mimeograph Max Plank Institute, Cologne.

——(2003*b*). 'Wer beherrscht die Unternehmen? Shareholder Value, Managerherrschaft und Mitbestimmung in Deutschland,' Frankfurt and New York, Campus.

Ingrao, B. and Israel, G. (1990). *The Invisible Hand. Economic Equilibrium in the History of Science*. Cambridge, MA: MIT Press.

Jessop, B. (ed.) (2001). *Regulation Theory and the Crisis of Capitalism. Country Studies*—Vol. 4. Cheltenham, UK: Edward Elgar.

Kogut, B., Macduffie, J. and Ragin, C. (1999). Prototypes and fuzzy work practices. Assigning causal credit for performance. Working paper, Wharton School, August.

Kok, W. (2004). 'Relever le défi. La stratégie de Lisbonne pour la croissance et l'emploi, Rapport du groupe de Haut niveau' (préside par) http://www.europa.eu.int

Labrousse, A. and Weisz, J.-D. (eds.) (2001). *Institutional Economics in France and Germany: German Ordoliberalism versus the French Regulation School*. Berlin: Springer.

Lundvall, B. A. (2002). *Innovation, Growth and Social Cohesion. The Danish Model*. Cheltenham, UK: Edward Elgar.

Milgrom, P. and Roberts, J. (1990). 'The Economics of Modern Manufacturing: Technology, Strategy, and Organization,' *American Economic Review*, 80(3): 511–28.

North, D. (1990). *Institutions, Institutional Change and Economic Performance*. Cambridge: Cambridge University Press.

——(2005). *Understanding the Process of Economic Change*. Princeton, NJ: Princeton University Press.

Palombarini, S. (2001). *La rupture du compromis social italien*. Paris: Editions du CNRS.

Pierson, P. (2004). *Politics and Time. History, Institutions, and Social Analysis*. Princeton, NJ: Princeton University Press.

Polanyi, K. (1944). *The Great Transformation: The Political and Economic Origins of Our Time*. Boston, MA: Beacon Press.

Ragin, C. H. (1987). *The Comparative Method*. Berkeley, CA: University of California Press.

——(1994). *Constructing Social Research, Pine Forges Press*. Thousand Oaks, CA: Sage.

Reynaud, B. (2002). *Operating Rules in Organizations: Macroeconomic and Microeconomic Analyses*. New York: Palgrave.

Shimizu, K. (2000). *Le Toyotisme, Repères*. Paris: La Découverte.

Stark, D. (1997). 'Recombinant Property in East European Capitalism,' in G. Grabher and D. Stark (eds.), *Restructuring Networks in Post-Socialism: Legacies Linkages and Localities*. Oxford: Oxford University Press, pp. 35–69.

Stiglitz, J. (1987). 'Dependence of Quality on Price,' *Journal of Economic Literature*, 25: 1–48.

Streeck, W. (1997*a*). 'German Capitalism: Does It Exist? Can It Survive?,' in C. Crouch and W. Streeck (eds.), *Political Economy of Modern Capitalism: Mapping Convergence & Diversity*. London: Sage.

——(1997*b*). 'Beneficial Constraints: On the Economic Limits of Rational Voluntarism,' in R. Hollingsworth and R. Boyer (eds.), *Contemporary Capitalism: The Embeddedness of Institutions*. Cambridge: Cambridge University Press, pp. 197–219.

——(2003). 'Taking Uncertainty Seriously: Complementarity as a Moving Target,' Mimeograph Max Plank Institute, Cologne.

——(2005). 'Conversation on Institutional Complementarity,' *Socio-Economic Review*, 2(1): 1–32.

Thelen, K. (2003). 'How Institutions Evolve: Insights from Comparative Historical Analysis,' in J. Mahoney and D. Rueschenmeyer (eds.), *Comparative Historical Analysis in the Social Sciences*. New York: Cambridge University Press, pp. 208–40.

——(2004). *How Institutions Evolve. The Political Economy of Skills in Germany, Britain, The United States, and Japan*. Cambridge: Cambridge University Press.

Whitley, R. (ed.) (2002). *Competing Capitalisms: Institutions and Economies*. Cheltenham, UK: Edward Elgar.

Williamson, O. (1985). *The Economic Institutions of Capitalism*. New York: Free Press.

World Bank (2001). *World Development Report 2002. Building Institutions for Markets*. Washington, DC.

Yamamura, K. and Streeck, W. (eds.) (2003). *The End of Diversity? Prospects for German and Japanese Capitalism*. Ithaca, NY: Cornell University Press.

Zeitlin, J. and Trubeck, D. M. (eds.) (2003). *Governing Work and Welfare in a New Economy. European and American Experiments*. Oxford: Oxford University Press.

3

Advancing Our Understanding of Capitalism with Niels Bohr's Thinking About Complementarity

J. Rogers Hollingsworth

Introduction

This chapter is structured around several basic perspectives. First, we live in an age in which our understanding of the world is ever more limited. It is not clear that we have any idea of how to develop a more coherent view of the world and more effective institutions for governing the world. Second, the essay identifies some of the key factors which interfere with our understanding, and suggests a few important steps for improving the situation. These are only very modest steps, as most of us are still profoundly ignorant of the universe around us, despite substantial advances in knowledge over the last century and the vast resources which our societies invest in education, research, and information technology.

Disjuncture Between Development and Diffusion of Information and Ability to Understand the Social World Over the Last Century

The pace of social change over the past century has been far more rapid than in any other period of human history. Of course, all societies are always changing, but in many periods of history, there have been long periods of institutional stability. In such periods societies may develop comprehensive worldviews, not necessarily consistent or correct. During the past century, the rate of change—technologically, demographically, economically, politically—has been so great that even the best educated individuals have had a very limited ability to develop a coherent view of the world. Even the most informed policymakers have all too often behaved as though they were in a fog, with limited perspective on where they are in the context of history and where they are moving. The past century has been a period of unprecedented turbulence and chaos, and it seems to me that we are in a global miasma as we blindly tap our way into the third millennium. Part of our problems result from the fact that never in human history have people had so much information almost instantaneously available from the entire globe. As information has become more and more specialized and differentiated, our societies lack the capacity to integrate this information. Because we understand little of the information bombarding us, we need better navigational tools to understand where we are and where we are drifting.

Reexamining Our Conceptualization of the Social World

One of the main tenets of this chapter is that most social scientists have long had an overly simplistic view of the social world. Partly for that reason, social scientists have often had an excessively optimistic view of their capacity to change the world. And even if certain aspects of the social world are susceptible to change, there has been poor understanding of what can be manipulated and what cannot. It is no wonder that those in the seats of power in Berlin, London, Paris, and Washington and those who control the mass media have long had an overly simplistic view of the world. The root of the problem is the conceptualizations we have employed for our analysis. Essentially, the world of social science has been shaped by two dominant paradigmatic perspectives, one with long historical antecedents and the other of more recent origin.

For several hundred years, much of Western natural and social sciences has been very much influenced by Descartes' metaphor of a machine as put forth in Part IV of his *Discourse on Method*. While his metaphor was originally presented as a way of understanding living things, over time it has been generalized to be a view about the entire world. Descartes' metaphor has been interpreted not only as a description of how the world operates but as a prescription for how to study the world. Adopting his mechanistic view, the scholarly community has developed strategies for manipulating and predicting world events, and in the process it has all too often adopted an overly simplified view of the world, the relation of parts to wholes, and causes to effects (Lewontin 2000). Adopting the machine metaphor, scholars have extended the metaphor to that of an engineer and designer. Many scientists and policymakers have assumed that they can redesign the course of history or nature. Such a mentality suggests that we can understand the interaction of variables and that only a few variables need be manipulated in order to change nature or a society's history. There is a widely shared view that we can easily design new institutions, even transfer them to various practices from one society to another. Practitioners talk about genetic engineering; planners draw up five-year plans for altering national economies. In the United States, and to a lesser extent in the UK, policymakers draw up plans for the democratization and transformation of whole regions of the world.

Even though the visions are often grand, the mentality is that of the engineer with an emphasis on efficiency and redundancy: design the project as simply as possible and keep interactions among the necessary parts to a minimum. When the mentality of the engineer shapes policy or designs a project, logic is expected to prevail, but for fail-safe purposes, designers usually include in their plans a modest degree of redundancy (i.e. the performance of the same function by similar elements). Whether the project is built from the ground up or whether there is a great deal of bricolage or incrementalism, the mentality of the design is to keep the components or plan as uncomplicated as possible. In very complex and sophisticated projects, there is some feedback modeling or other elements from control theory. Each part is designed to complement the next. The engineering model is not a totally incorrect characterization of the world, as with it, we are able to understand some of the world, and can indeed alter parts of the world.

In modern Western history, the physical sciences evolved with a heavy emphasis on equilibrium states, from the shoulders of Newton and Descartes to the statistical mechanics of James Clerk Maxwell and Ludwig Boltzmann and nineteenth-century physics of thermodynamics. Similarly, there is a long tradition in social thought from Thomas Hobbes through Adolphe Quetelet, Adam Smith to twentieth-century academic economists who attempted to develop a science of society which operated according to a self-regulating steady-state type of equilibrium. But it was the French mathematical economist Léon Walrus who placed the concept of market equilibrium on a formal footing, which in turn gave rise to general equilibrium theory which dominated neoclassical economic thinking throughout the twentieth century. In the economics of market equilibrium, from the writings of Adam Smith to those of Vilfredo Pareto and Walrus, things were viewed as being in a steady state. Markets would always clear, as long as a society did not interfere with their proper working, thus resulting in little waste and goods being distributed to the greatest benefit. In this form of thinking, a deregulated 'market' economy was perceived as the most effective way to maintain a healthy society and to stimulate economic growth and wealth (Ball 2004: 236–7).

One might think that economists would understand that they had painted themselves into a corner by restricting their view of the economic world to being one always in equilibrium. After all, most everyone could recognize that economies are always changing. Of course, neoclassical economists acknowledge that change occurs, but so extremely slowly that it cannot be observed. It is as though one can examine a system and see nothing happening—as though everything is in a continuous state of equilibrium. According to

Philip Ball, an economic system operates somewhat analogously to a series of interconnected water reservoirs. 'It is like drilling the tiniest of tiny holes into the bank of the reservoir so that the trickle then fills it drip by drip, but at any moment both the higher and lower reservoirs appear to be in stable equilibrium states' (2004: 126, also 258). Increasingly, twentieth-century neoclassical economists began to construct highly elegant and abstract mathematical models, devoid of the messiness and complexity of the real world. And in this process, the human element was squeezed from the discipline, as representing little more than 'noise.' Before long, according to Princeton economist Paul Krugman, the area of academic economics that attracted the most attention was that which permitted 'a clever but not very original young man' to demonstrate his skills in presenting complex equations (Krugman 1994: xi).

Just as economists borrowed the tools of physicists in thermodynamics for their conceptualization of the economic world, similarly many sociologists and political scientists—especially in America—became fascinated with statistical models which also incorporated little perspective on social change. In these fields as well, human actors and contingency were not to be found in statistical models. As the thinking of economists diffused to other social sciences, an emphasis on static analysis—with a conservative bias—became the dominant tone in the major journals of several American social science disciplines in the latter half of the twentieth century.

Such static research strategies relied heavily on statistical models which emphasized how variation on one variable—holding others constant—impacted on a dependent variable. Over time, of course, nonlinear models also became part of the strategy. But the game was to identify the relative efficacy of key variables to shape a dependent variable. As long as this strategy prevailed, the enormous complexity of the world was minimized and thus poorly understood, and there was relatively little concern with long-term social change. Many who were interested in change over time would do cross-sectional analysis at multiple time points, but most of the statistical models were nevertheless relatively static in nature (Aydelotte, Bogue, and Fogel 1972; McCloskey 1985).

In contrast to the Newtonian–Descartian tradition of thinking about the world, an alternative conceptualization has been emerging in recent years, one for want of a better label I call a coevolutionary perspective. Whereas the Descartian paradigm emerged from the natural sciences, the more recent coevolutionary perspective has more varied and complex roots. Many social scientists—particularly those of a Marxist or various socialist persuasions—had long contended that the world was quite dynamic, with complex interactions. But the more recent community of scholars sharing a coevolutionary perspective is much more heterogeneous in nature, and among their main tenets has been the view that the world does not change with inherent order.

Systems have a fundamental nonlinear dynamic quality to them. The games in which actors are engaged are everchanging, and even in the same game, the rules keep evolving. Even though there is a great deal of stability in the world, there is also an enormous amount of randomness and chance in a continuously evolving world. In short, there is a great deal of coevolution, and chance events involving very small changes which often have major long-term consequences (Arthur, Durlauf, and Lane 1997).

The coevolutionary perspective is clearly not an engineering one. Rather, it is primarily concerned with an effort to comprehend the world retrospectively. Whereas the worldview shaped by Newton and Descartes was comparatively tidy and predictable, the coevolutionary perspective emphasizes the complexity and chaotic view of the world, one open to many more possibilities than have been previously realized. If this perspective has a hero, it is Charles Darwin, the greatest historian of all time, whose strategy was to understand the biological world with retrospective analysis. The latest versions of a coevolutionary perspective became much more widespread and gained considerable legitimacy after physicists and computer scientists began to demonstrate in the 1960s and 1970s that even simple equations can produce surprising results which are essentially unpredictable. Subsequently, advances in genetics and neurosciences have led to an acceleration of a conception of science which increasingly emphasizes the important role of chance and randomness in explaining events (Edelman and Gally 2001). In the words of the economist Brian Arthur, more and more scientists have come to realize 'that logic and philosophy are messy, that language is messy, that chemical kinetics is messy, that physics is messy, and finally that our efforts to understand the economy and the entire social world are messy' (quoted in Waldrop 1992: 329, for similar views, see Lewin 1993). Over the past two decades, specialists in discipline after discipline have followed the lead of physicists and computer scientists and have increasingly recognized that the world is far more complex than previously thought. The most recent coevolutionary perspectives are now rapidly diffusing across academic disciplines, both the natural and social sciences.

With the Newtonian-Descartes perspective, social scientists have long tended to assume that the same functions are continuously performed by identical structures, in a machinelike fashion. A particular independent variable had an effect on a dependent variable. With this perspective, it could be believed that a social system with a particular kind of structure would be quite egalitarian while those with opposite structures would be inegalitarian. In contrast, the more recent coevolutionary perspective has demonstrated that systems which have very different structures may have the same output. In short, fundamentally different structures often have similar consequences. In addition, more and more social scientists are recognizing that at different moments in a particular society, the same type of structure can be associated with completely different outputs or performances. Meantime, cross-national studies reveal that countries with quite different structures may be associated with the same output or performance.

It is important to note that in the history of Western scientific thought the same large conceptual frameworks are often shared by natural and social scientists. Hence, it is not surprising that social scientists are increasingly recognizing that biologists are making significant advances in understanding the natural world with their observations that fundamentally different structures often have similar consequences (Tononi, Sporns, and Edelman 1999; Edelman and Gally 2001), and that these same perspectives are increasingly having an impact on the social sciences (Hollingsworth and Gear 2004).

A Historical Example of Interdisciplinary Thinking for Advancing a Contemporary Social Sciences Agenda: The Concept of Complementarity

I hardly need to urge the reader of this volume to be interdisciplinary, but we should reflect on whether the range of our interdisciplinarity is broad enough. Might we enhance our insights for research if we broadened our disciplinary perspectives and attempted to understand how concepts useful for our work have been used by scientists in other more distant fields? My recent opportunity to spend several years in the company of some of the world's leading physicists, biologists, and chemists has enhanced my understanding of the social world. Many social scientists and natural scientists share common views of the world and are wrestling with similar kinds of problems, but generally in very different venues and with little awareness of their common interests.

Rather than despairing over the fact that we have two dominant ways of conceptualizing the world, we may find that this is a blessing in disguise. To get some insight as to how the scholarly community might respond when confronted with two broad views of the world, it is instructive to turn once more to the natural sciences for some perspective—to the career of the Danish physicist and Nobel laureate Niels Bohr and his views on complementarity. While I draw on Bohr's philosophy, I deliberately oversimplify his views because of the constraints of space (Bohr 1963; Rosenfeld 1963, 1967; Favrholdt 1976; Folse 1985; Jones 1985; Rasmussen 1987; Pais 1991; Held 1994).

In Bohr's thinking, complementarity was originally framed as an epistemological or explanatory principle in which two formally incompatible modes of description are used to understand the same phenomenon. In Bohr's earliest formulations, complementarity existed when two very different aspects of a description are necessary for a full understanding of what is being described.

For Bohr, paradoxical thinking became the key to complementary thinking. Complementarity as a scientific concept first emerged in the late 1920s as physicists were encountering great difficulties in reconciling two contradictory theories about light: physicists were in strong disagreement as to whether light was to be explained as waves or as particles. By the 1920s, various physicists could demonstrate experimentally that both theories were correct. Bohr's position was that the two descriptions of light had a 'complementarity relationship' with each other—meaning that although they were incompatible or irreconcilable, each was indispensable for a full understanding of light. The recognition that there could be different but at the same time valid observations of the same phenomenon formed the basis for the kind of paradoxical thinking which later became the core of Bohr's philosophy for understanding reality. Before long, scholars from other disciplines also became quite intrigued by the fact that different methods and tools of observation of the same phenomenon could lead to contradictory but complementary findings. This perspective had enormous implications not only for Bohr and his colleagues but also for the dominant paradigms in Western thought as well as for how we might proceed in shaping a research agenda not only in the social sciences but in other fields of science as well.

Historically, Western thinkers have given high priority to unity and consistency as criteria for theoretical explanations, with the view that two different explanations of the same phenomenon are unacceptable (Pattee 1978; Kothari 1985; Collins 1998). Most scholars assume that the recognition of a paradox or contradictory observations suggests the need to resolve contradictions, that when confronted with two competing interpretations, one must be better than the other. Faced with paradox, Western scholars have often attempted to integrate competing claims, to propose a synthesis of competing perspectives, or to take a broader view. But as Bohr began applying his thinking to other fields, he realized that complementarity contained two critical features: competing perspectives might be mutually exclusive but together they could provide for a fuller understanding of the objects being studied. The challenge for Bohr was consistently to search for observations which could not be resolved. For him, the presence of irreconcilable points of view was not disturbing; rather, bringing contradictory perspectives to bear was often illuminating, and enhanced understanding of the world. He developed the argument that many areas of science could be advanced by searching for problems where the findings appeared to be complementary but in contradiction with each other.

A study of Bohr's thinking about physics and about contradictory perspectives on many other phenomena is highly relevant to those of us who are pursuing an agenda for understanding the social world. A Bohrian perspective would have us realize that there are different answers to the same problem depending on how the problem gets posed: whether one pursues a micro- or undertakes a macroperspective; whether one examines only a part or the whole of a system; whether one focuses on variation of the same phenomenon among many different observations at one point in time; or whether one focuses on the origin of a phenomenon and analyzes how its component parts evolve over a long period of time. Obviously, one could mention many other conditions which lead to different perspectives of the same phenomenon. What was essential for Bohr was that those who had fundamentally different perspectives on the same phenomenon would be in frequent—perhaps daily-contact with one another. Thus, in a Bohrian world, there would be frequent communication among those who do micro- and macro-analysis, those who do cross-sectional and historical analysis, those who do aggregate, comparative, or case studies, those who undertake a Descartian or coevolutionary approach to studying the world.

Descartian and Coevolutionary Perspectives on the Literature of Varieties of Capitalism and Institutional Change

As we confront these two large conceptual views of the world, we might reflect on how they have recently influenced our study of capitalism in the contemporary world. Much of the varieties of capitalism literature reflects a strong bias toward static analysis, an *ahistorical* perspective, though at the same time most of those doing these studies paid lip service to the necessity of undertaking historical analysis, to understanding the origins of systems as well as institutions (Hollingsworth 1997; Hall and Soskice 2001; Streeck and Yamamura 2001; Crouch et al. 2005). Significantly, a number of authors of the varieties of capitalism literature incorporated the concept 'complementarity' into their work, apparently being totally unaware that the concept had a long and rich history in physics beginning with Bohr. Later, the concept became a dominant concept in chemistry and biology. For many of the authors in the varieties of capitalism literature, their perspective has been distinctly Descartian in nature. They have conceptualized capitalist systems in very broad terms and have characterized them as operating in a somewhat mechanistic manner—maybe not like the metaphorical clock in the Descartian tradition—but nevertheless with a variety of parts which contributed to the coherence and functioning of an entire system: a society's system of education and training, its industrial relations system, the banking and system of finance, the nature of the state. All of these subsystems were perceived as being complementary and mutually reinforcing to each other and were usually described as being necessary for how the system performed in the global economy. I think it is now time to stand back and engage in some deep reflections on the strengths and weaknesses of this literature. Because of the constraints of space, I focus herein primarily on some of the shortcomings. As I have been a frequent contributor to these three bodies of literature, any criticisms I make, I indict myself foremost—all in the spirit of moving forward in order to attain a richer understanding of the social world.

Some of the most visible literature emphasized the distinction between the structure, behavior, and performance of liberal and nonliberal capitalist societies—focusing for the most part on these two types during the 1970s and early 1980s. Germany and Japan were generally characterized as the arch-type of a nonliberal system while the UK and the United States were portrayed as the prime examples of liberal capitalism. In general, the liberal systems were portrayed as 'strong market-type economies', having lower rates of growth and productivity and higher levels of unemployment than less market coordinated economies such as Germany and Japan. By the mid- to late 1990s and continuing to the present, however, the performances of all these countries had been reversed, though they still had the same institutional arrangements as when they were performing exceedingly well. For some years, the nonliberal economies of France, Germany, and Japan have had lower rates of growth and productivity and higher levels of unemployment, while the performance of the economies labeled 'liberal' have now been reversed from the situation of the 1980s.

These are examples of how over time in the same society similar structures can yield different outcomes. How can this be? Unfortunately, we do not have good answers. In the 1980s and 1990s the scholarly community was engaged in cross-sectional statistical and/or Boolean algebra type analyses to understand how structural variables are associated with outcomes and performance. But it is interesting that the results of the analyses tended to vary, depending on the time period at which the cross-sectional analysis was done.

As suggested above, we now need to engage in a deep reassessment of this literature. Fortunately, this type of critique is getting underway (Herrigel 2005; O'Sullivan 2005; Pempel 2005). Indirectly, Boyer's paper in this volume might be understood in this vein. As scholars engage in an evaluation of this literature, several criticisms, along with suggestions for future work have arisen. The most important critique of the varieties of capitalism has been that it has not been adequately theorized, that the arguments have been overly simplistic, somewhat static and mechanistic in nature (O'Sullivan 2005). Herrigel (2005) argues that the nonliberal models—particularly of Germany and Japan—were never as coherent, with parts interconnected and complementary, as the literature suggests. The German and Japanese systems were much more incoherent, nonunitary, and provisional (p. 565). Moreover, the coherent and unitary characteristics of the Anglo-American liberal models were greatly overstated. For example, the changes brought about by the Thatcher government resulted in a much more state-collectivized system of higher education in Britain, with resources allocated to universities based on a production model—reminding one of the old Soviet method of coordinating and allocating resources based on performance criteria determined in an autocratic manner by state officials (Adams 2002). In short, none of these systems were ever as coherent as the varieties of capitalism literature have portrayed them.

This is especially true of the very heterogeneous type of capitalism which exists in the United States. Following World War II, the different parts of the American political economy were never so tightly linked, coherent, and unitary as the 'liberal model' in the variety of capitalism literature suggested. Some of the most dynamic areas of the American economy over the past four decades were due to the important role of the state in coordinating various sectors: aerospace, aircraft, jet engines, new technologies derived from materials science and metallurgy, the semiconductor industry, the Internet, biotechnology, and pharmaceutical industries. It is certainly a gross oversimplification to characterize the American dairy industry and its medical system as driven and coordinated by some vague conceptualization of 'the market' (Hollingsworth 1986; Young, Lindberg, and Hollingsworth 1989; Young 1991).

In retrospect, perhaps the most serious shortcoming of the varieties of capitalism literature is its inherent neo-Descartian static bias. This concern immediately raises a number of considerations. Why did the performance of the two types of systems (liberal versus nonliberal) become so reversed by the end of the twentieth century? Were the typologies of liberal and nonliberal varieties of capitalism expected to perform well only at a certain moment in history but not at other moments? And if so, what are the characteristics of the periods when they were expected to perform well and perform poorly? And if these 'types' of capitalism are time specific in nature, this consideration should be an integral part of the typology. Even for the contemporary world, perhaps there are many more varieties of capitalism beyond the types developed in the rather influential book by Hall and Soskice, *Varieties of Capitalism* (2001). Streeck (2005: 579) suggests that the Hall and Soskice volume reads as though all the world is evolving toward two varieties of capitalism (liberal and nonliberal), and eventually every capitalist system must locate itself into one of the two camps.

Rather than viewing societies as having systems that are in some type of equilibrium, with the parts somehow highly congealed, we should conceptualize systems and societies as in a continuous state of flux. As Streeck (2005: 580) observes, systems of capitalism are 'the temporary idiosyncratic products of fleeting configurations of competing causal forces entering an unending permutation of local compromises with one another.' Indeed, the two systems which many who have written about in the varieties of capitalism literature were already coming apart at the very time that the analysts had discovered them—leading O'Sullivan (2005) to question whether the analysts had actually developed real typologies or simply ideologies about different forms of capitalism.

Serious reflections on the shortcomings of the static nature and lack of coherence in the types of capitalism described in the varieties of capitalism literature suggest that perhaps we should shift gears and study capitalism with a more coevolutionary perspective—a more Schumpeterian view of capitalism as economics systems which are inherently unstable, constantly changing, with parts never congealed in particular moments of history (as suggested in the varieties of capitalism literature).

Significantly, some of those who were central in developing the varieties of capitalism literature have already shifted to a more evolutionary perspective, moving way from the effort to construct 'types' of systems. This change in emphasis is essentially an acknowledgment that the development of typologies generally results in characterizing a system as being somewhat static. Thus, the emphasis is now shifting to a study of long- and short-term institutional change within and across capitalist societies (Stark and Bruszt 1998; Mahoney 2000; Pierson 2000, 2004; Manow 2001; Hollingsworth, Müller, and Hollingsworth 2002; Thelen 2003; Streeck 2005; Streeck and Thelen 2005; Boyer's chapter in this volume).

In order to comprehend long-term historical change, the scholarly community is confronted with a dilemma. Only historians are adequately trained to study all the factors which lead to short- and long-term institutional changes, but with few exceptions (Braudel 1972; Tilly 1984; Skocpol 2003), historians tend not to be interested in developing strong theoretical perspectives. Hence, the social science community interested in developing theoretical perspectives about institutional change are dependent on historical studies which were written and conceived for purposes quite different from those shaping the social scientist's agenda. Thus, most of those social scientists doing some of the most interesting work in writing about long-term institutional change in capitalist economies generally lack the understanding of the societal complexity in which institutional change occurs.

Those who do 'armchair' theorizing about long-term institutional change should note that in the last 150 years the scholars most influential in shaping our thinking about long-term change were social scientists thoroughly involved with historical data: Fernand Braudel, Alfred Chandler, Robert Fogel, Alexander Gerschenkron, Charles Kindleberger, Simon Kuznets, David Landes, Gerhard Lehmbruch, Karl Marx, Douglass North, Stein Rokkan, Nathan Rosenberg, Theda Skocpol, Charles Tilly, Max Weber.

This of course brings us back to the Bohrian type perspective for developing a richer understanding of reality. To advance our understanding of institutional change, we need for historians and social scientists who are interested in institutional change to work in continuous interaction with each other. But until we develop this type of 'Bohrian cooperation', we must make the best use of the knowledge we now have about institutional change, as we attempt to understand the emergence of different forms of capitalism.

The following are a few of the more astute perspectives to emerge in the literature by those who are attempting to develop theoretical perspectives about long-term institutional change.

1. The factors responsible for an institution are generally very different from those which sustain it over time (Mahoney 2000: 515).
2. Institutions are both constraints on choices by actors at particular time points and strategic resources to be drawn upon as actors respond to changes in their social environments (Haydu 1998).
3. Institutions often outlive the uses which brought them into being in the first place but continue to persist and are often then used for quite different purposes (Skocpol 1992; Campbell 1997; Stark and Bruszt 1998; Manow 2001; Thelen 2003).
4. Institutional change involves a great deal of chance, contingency, and unpredictability; early events are often much more important than later events in institutional persistence (Mahoney 2003). Though the behaviors of actors are not strictly determined by their institutional environment, actors nevertheless adopt strategies which utilize the institutions prevailing at any given time (Levi 1997; Pierson 2000, 2004; Hollingsworth, Müller, and Hollingsworth 2002).
5. In studying institutional change, we must engage in multilevel analysis. Institutions operating at one level often influence institutions and events occurring at other levels (Boyer and Hollingsworth 1997; Hollingsworth 2006).
6. Much of the literature on the development of institutions has borrowed a punctuated equilibrium model—emphasizing the abrupt and discontinuous nature of institutions. Some of the best studies of institutional change, however, have demonstrated that most long-term change is quite incremental and nuanced. Moreover, several recent studies suggest that most change is not due to exogenous forces or shocks but is endogenous in nature and 'in some cases is produced by the very behavior an institution itself generates' (Pierson 2004; Streeck and Thelen 2005: 19).
7. In contrast to much of the varieties of capitalism literature, the framework of institutions in any given society is rarely highly coherent. Even if there are dominant sets of institutions, they generally exist in proximity—often in contradiction—to other institutional arrangements (Orren and Skowronek 2004). Quite often, institutions have been highly dormant but persistent in a society only to be revitalized and rediscovered when needed. Because they were part of the historical baggage in a society, they can often be legitimately revived and utilized (Piore and Sabel 1984; Herrigel 2000).

8. Scholars studying institutional change in capitalist societies tend to reject the strong functionalist bias inherent in the varieties of capitalism literature, which suggests that specific capitalist configurations emerged because of the need to address specific problems. In contrast to this view, there is the literature on institutional change which incorporates a much more contingent view of outcomes, describes actors as constantly coping to solve particular problems and facing a high degree of uncertainty as they attempt to address a world of enormous complexity (Beck 2005; Streeck 2005).
9. In explaining institutional change, analysts usually employ post hoc explanations—which are all too easy to invent and can quickly be discarded (Scharpf 1997: 29). When we study the past, we always have a problem of what to search for. Hopefully, if we have a set of common problems to explain, if we work with scholars from a variety of disciplines, and if we have intense and frequent interactions with one another, we can assist one another to avoid traveling down blind alleys.
10. When biologists began to discover that the same structures within systems could lead to different outcomes, they realized that they had to turn to Darwinian explanations and biological history to explain how and why structures with similar consequences emerged. However, this type of analysis required highly skilled scientists with specialized training who could engage in the study of the slow development and decay of specific structures. Similarly, in the social sciences, as we are learning from the varieties of capitalism literature, to understand why different structures have similar consequences, we too must turn to the historical evolution of specific structures. It is in this context that we are observing a strong emphasis on evolutionary models as we also study institutional change (Hodgson 1999).

The Importance of Multilevel Analysis in Understanding a Complex World

Most scholars study institutions at only one level of reality. In the social sciences, many focus on firms or other organizations, business associations, trade unions, financial organizations. Others focus on local or regional governments as institutions. In the varieties of capitalism literature, much of the analysis was at the level of nation-state. Other scholars concentrate their attention on institutions at the transnational regional level (e.g. the European Union), and most recently others are focusing on institutional change at the global level. Indeed, globalization has become a kind of buzzword during the past decade, but with few exceptions, few scholars have a systematic strategy for doing analysis at the global level (Wallerstein 1974; Chase-Dunn and Hall 1997).

Again, if social scientists will reflect on what is occurring in the biological sciences, they will not only observe that biologists face a similar set of concerns, but the two fields could probably benefit by interacting with one another. In biology, some researchers work at the level of atoms, others at the molecular, others at the cellular, tissue, or the entire organism, while others work on entire ecosystems. The task in both the social and the biological sciences is to understand how processes at one level influence or are influenced by processes at every other level. Indeed, one of the most critical problems facing a number of scientific fields is to understand how processes at multiple levels are interacting.

Some years ago, my colleague Robert Boyer helped to advance my thinking on these processes in the contemporary social world as we wrote a jointly authored paper (Boyer and Hollingsworth 1997). We argued that increasingly major institutions of coordination/governance are intertwined at all levels of the world—at the subnational region, nation-state, transnational region, and the global level. As a result, no single authority has the power to monitor and regulate all economic activities in such a complex system. And as a consequence, very much in contrast to the varieties of capitalism literature, coherence in economic coordination is becoming increasingly difficult to discern at any single level.

Clearly, the most important social functions do not occur at the same level. Coordination of money and finance (e.g. the rate of interest, the value of currencies) is increasingly regulated at levels beyond the nation-state, whereas taxation, welfare functions, education, and training tend to take place within national boundaries. Business firms express rhetorical preferences for market freedom, while the rhetoric of other groups demands protection from the nation-state against the effects of the logic of markets. Thus, the complexity of nestedness makes coherent economic policy and institutional planning more difficult than ever. Market-type forces tend to regulate exchange and interest rates at the global level, while nation-states struggle with other institutional arrangements to address the welfare, health, education, and training of their citizens.

As societies experience a shift from a national embeddedness of social institutions to those nested within a multilevel global system, it has become increasingly difficult for societies to adjust their industrial relations systems, levels of skills, and system of innovation to external forms of competition. Within advanced industrial societies, this difficulty of adjusting to a complex, multilevel world is increasingly leading to shrill debates between labor and capital within nation-states as various actors attempt to cope with a rapidly changing world which is poorly understood.

We now realize that the institutional arrangements that at one time were viewed as being congruent at the level of the nation-state have actually diffused to multiple spatial levels. This means that impressive economic performance requires that economic actors be well coordinated at all spatial levels simultaneously—a task that rarely occurs in the contemporary world.

Of course, coordination of economic actors at the level of the nation-state has not completely disappeared. However, the future of any given society's system of production remains highly uncertain. So many contradictory forces are operating that it is quite difficult to gauge the direction of the global economy and its constituent parts. The future is very much open, with very few actors having a clear perspective of where their societies are drifting. Actors at best can make only short-term, incremental, and marginal choices about the future. As our institutions are increasingly nested in a world of subnational regions, nation-states, transnational regions, and global regimes, actors are faced with the perplexing problem of how effectively to govern themselves. Clearly, one of the great challenges of our time is to create a new theory of democracy for coordinating institutions nested in a world of unprecedented complexity, one in which subnational regions, nation-states, and continental and global regimes are all intricately linked. It is no exaggeration to suggest that our seventeenth- and eighteenth-century theories of democracy, even twentieth-century neocorporatist conceptions of democracy, have become increasingly anachronistic.

Concluding Observations: A Complementarity Perspective on How We Might Better Understand the World

Once more, I remind the reader of the disjuncture between the amazing amount of information we have about the world and our incapacity to understand it. Among the factors responsible for this problem, there are at least two which deserve our serious attention. The first is ideological. We have been so captivated by the Newtonian-Descartian perspective that we can solve any problem—social or technological—that we risk losing our perspective on how complex the world is, and that we lack capacity to solve most problems. It would be in our self-interest if we were a bit more humble and became more realistic about our incapacity to redesign the world anew, both technologically and socially.

A second factor which limits our capacity to understand much of the information with which we are bombarded is the structure of the modern university. Our universities have become fragmented into large numbers of disciplines, and within each discipline we have numerous subspecialties. But there is relatively little communication across subspecialties within disciplines, and of course, there is relatively little meaningful communication across disciplines. Indeed, the intense fragmentation and specialization pose serious problems for having a better understanding of the age in which we live.

For some years I have been engaged in a large-scale research project—a project about research organizations: universities, research institutes, etc. The research problem has been to understand how the institutional and organizational environments of research organizations either hamper or facilitate their capacity to make major discoveries in basic biomedical science. This is a four-nation project (involving the countries of Britain, France, Germany, and the United States) which attempts to understand the organizational context in which approximately 291 discoveries occurred throughout the twentieth century. My colleagues and I have conducted in-depth case studies of each, and Figure 3.1 is a brief summary of our key findings. The more frequent and intense the communication among scientists with diverse perspectives within a particular organizational context, the greater the likelihood of having a major discovery. These findings have important implications for our ability to enhance our understanding of the social world. Picking up on the perspective of Niels Bohr, ideally we want to have rich interactions with those who have different perspectives from our own. In Bohrian terms, the greater the complementarity among different perspectives about the same phenomenon, the greater our capacity to understand the world, as actors with diverse views have intense interactions with one another (for a similar view, see Pierson 2004).

There are potentially high costs for our permitting the modern university to become ever more fragmented and specialized. There are several consequences which are likely to follow if we do not restructure our universities in order to promote more effective communication among scholars in different fields.

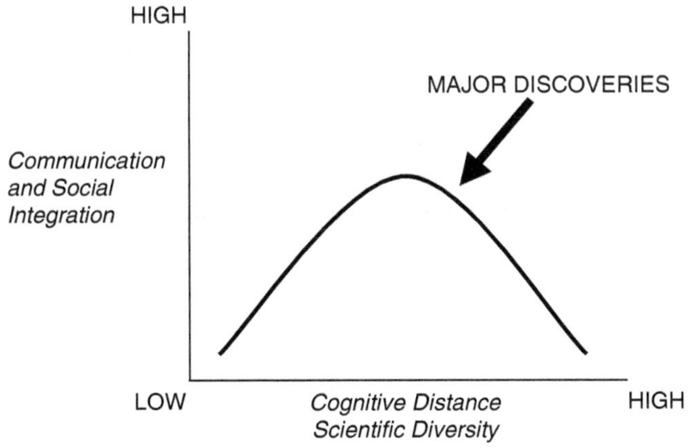

Figure 3.1. The impact of communication and cognitive distance on major discoveries.

"Sources: Hollingsworth and Hollingsworth (2000), Hollingsworth (2004), and Hollingsworth, Hollingsworth, and Hage (2006)."

First, as our universities become more and more fragmented and specialized they run the risk of becoming less relevant to our societies.

Second, our societies are problem oriented, while our universities are discipline based and oriented toward greater specialization. This tension is healthy, but unless the universities can better unify the rapidly fragmenting knowledge, they risk being charged by an increasing number of citizens as irrelevant to the needs of society.

Third, and perhaps most importantly, the cost of continuing with our present university structure lies in what it does to the way society thinks about its problems. The increasing specialization of knowledge is contributing to an authoritarian mentality in American society. Scientific and technical knowledge have become so vast and complex that no person can authoritatively know more than a minute fraction of all that can be known. Scholars tend to opt for their own specialties—areas they can know well, to avoid being labeled scientific dilettantes. Thus, the only way of knowing something outside of one's specialty is to accept the word of an authority in a specialized field. To counteract this trend, our universities should adopt a set of structures that will facilitate meaningful communication within and across academic disciplines. It is important to restructure our universities so that we can better comprehend the relationships among different branches of knowledge before the rigidities of specialization begin to kill our curiosity about a complex world (Hollingsworth 1984).

As social scientists, if we study institutions with a micro- and a macro perspective, at a single point in time or multiple points in time, at one or at multiple levels of reality we probably will emerge with different perspectives of reality. However, from a Bohrian perspective of complementarity, we will have a more complete understanding of reality if we work closely together in an effort to resolve the paradoxes and contradictions in our perspectives.

If we as social scientists wish to have an even richer understanding of reality from a Bohrian perspective, we should even interact with our colleagues in the biological and other sciences, for they too are engaging in micro and macro, cross-sectional and dynamic, and multilevel analysis. They too are attempting to understand why similar and dissimilar phenomena are attracted to, or repelled from, each other. In a very real sense, both the biological and social science research communities are engaged in similar kinds of activities and from both a Newtonian-Descartes and a neoevolutionary type perspective. Neither the Newtonian-Descartian nor the neoevolutionary perspective has a monopoly on the way to understand the world. We need both, for they are complementary. But one without the other provides a distorted view of reality. If we apply the Bohrian complementarity principle to our research strategies and begin to interact with our colleagues in other fields who are interested in the same kind of problems, we should substantially advance our understanding of reality. Moreover, we could contribute to narrowing the cultural divide between the natural sciences and the rest of the world which C. P. Snow and others have found so frustrating during the last half-century.[1]

Acknowledgments

Somewhat different and earlier versions of this paper were presented before the Society for the Advancement of Socio-Economics in Washington, D.C. and the Karl Polanyi Institute of Political Economy in Montreal. I am extremely grateful to Roger Krohn and Margie Mendell of Montreal and to Karl Müller of Vienna for useful comments on earlier drafts. I was first able to develop some of my broader views on complementarity at the Workshop on Complementarity at the Max-Planck-Institut für Gesellschaftsforschung in Cologne. My colleague David Gear at the University of Wisconsin has been very helpful in working with me on Bohr's views on complementarity. He and Ellen Jane Hollingsworth have been of inestimable help in developing all aspects of the paper. Any of the merits of the paper are due very much to them.

References

Adams, J. (2002). 'Research Assessment in the UK', *Science*, 296: 805.

Arthur, W. B., Durlauf, S. N., and Lane, D. A. (eds.) (1997). *The Economy as an Evolving Complex System II: Proceedings Volume XXVII, Santa Fe Institute Studies in the Sciences of Complexity*. Reading, MA: Addison–Wesley.

Aydelotte, W. O., Bogue, A. G., and Fogel, R. W. (eds.) (1972). *The Dimensions of Quantitative Research in History*. Princeton, NJ: Princeton University Press.

Ball, P. (2004). *Critical Mass: How One Thing Leads to Another*. London: Arrow Books.

Beck, U. (2005). *Power in the Global Age: A New Global Political Economy*. Cambridge: Polity Press.

Bohr, N. (1963). *Essays 1958–1962 on Atomic Physics and Human Knowledge*. New York: John Wiley & Sons.

Boyer, R. and Hollingsworth, J. R. (1997). 'From National Embeddedness to Spatial and Institutional Nestedness', in J. R. Hollingsworth and R. Boyer (eds.), *Contemporary Capitalism: The Embeddedness of Institutions*. Cambridge and New York: Cambridge University Press.

Braudel, F. (1972). *The Mediterranean and the Mediterranean World in the Age of Philip II*. New York: Harper & Row.

Campbell, J. (1997). 'Mechanisms of Evolutionary Change in Economic Governance: Interaction, Interpretation and Bricolage', in L. Magnusson and J. Ottosson (eds.), *Evolutionary Economics and Path Dependence*. Cheltenham, UK: Edward Elgar.

Chase-Dunn, C. and Hall, T. D. (1997). *Rise and Demise: Comparing World-Systems*. Boulder, CO: Westview Press.

Collins, R. (1998). *The Sociology of Philosophies: A Global Theory of Intellectual Change*. Cambridge, MA: Belknap Press of Harvard University Press.

Crouch, C., Streeck, W., Boyer, R., Amable, B., Hall, P. A., and Jackson, G. (2005). 'Dialogue on "Institutional Complementarity and Political Economy"', *Socio-Economic Review*, 3(2): 359–82.

Edelman, G. M. and Gally, J. A. (2001). 'Degeneracy and Complexity in Biological Systems', *Proceedings of the National Academy of Sciences USA*, 98(24): 13763–8.

Favrholdt, D. (1976). 'Niels Bohr and Danish Philosophy', *Danish Yearbook of Philosophy*, 13: 206–20.

Folse, H. J. (1985). *The Philosophy of Niels Bohr: The Framework of Complementarity*. Amsterdam: Elsevier.

Hall, P. and Soskice, D. (eds.) (2001). *Varieties of Capitalism: The Institutional Foundations of Comparative Advantage*. Oxford and New York: Oxford University Press.

Haydu, J. (1998). 'Making Use of the Past: Time Periods as Cases to Compare and as Sequences of Problem-Solving', *American Journal of Sociology*, 104: 339–71.

Held, C. (1994). 'The Meaning of Complementarity', *Studies in History and Philosophy of Science*, 25(6): 871–93.

Herrigel, G. (2000). 'Large Firms and Industrial Districts in Europe: Deregionalization, Re-regionalization, and the Transformation of Manufacturing Flexibility', in J. H. Dunning (ed.), *Regions, Globalization, and the Knowledge-Based Economy*. Oxford: Oxford University Press.

—— (2005). 'Institutionalists at the Limits of Institutionalism: A Constructivist Critique of Two Edited Volumes from Wolfgang Streeck and Kozo Yamamura', *Socio-Economic Review*, 3(3): 559–67.

Hodgson, G. M. (1999). *Evolution and Institutions: On Evolutionary Economics and the Evolution of Economics*. Cheltenham, UK: Edward Elgar.

Hollingsworth, J. R. (1984). 'The Snare of Specialization', *Bulletin of Atomic Scientists*, 40(June): 34–7.

—— (1986). *A Political Economy of Medicine: Great Britain and the United States*. Baltimore, MD: Johns Hopkins University Press.

—— (1997). 'Continuities and Changes in Social Systems of Production: The Cases of Japan, Germany, and the United States', in J. R. Hollingsworth and R. Boyer (eds.), *Contemporary Capitalism: The Embeddedness of Institutions*. Cambridge and New York: Cambridge University Press.

—— (2004). 'Institutionalizing Excellence in Biomedical Research: The Case of The Rockefeller University', in D. H. Stapleton (ed.), *Creating a Tradition of Biomedical Research: Contributions to the History of The Rockefeller University*. New York: Rockefeller University Press.

—— (2006). 'A Path Dependent Perspective on Institutional and Organizational Factors Shaping Major Scientific Discoveries', in J. Hage and M. Meeus (eds.), *Innovation, Science, and Institutional Change: A Research Handbook*. Oxford: Oxford University Press.

—— and Gear, D. (2004). 'The "Paradoxical Nature" of Complementarity in the Quest for a Research Agenda on Institutional Analysis', Paper prepared for Workshop on Complementarity, Max Plank Institute for Study of Societies, Cologne, Germany, 26–27.3.04.

Hollingsworth, J. R. and Hollingsworth, E. J. (2000). 'Major Discoveries and Biomedical Research Organizations: Perspectives on Interdisciplinarity, Nurturing Leadership, and Integrated Structure and Cultures', in P. Weingart and N. Stehr (eds.), *Practising Interdisciplinarity*. Toronto, CA: University of Toronto Press.

—— —— and Hage, J. (2006, forthcoming). *The Search for Excellence: Organizations, Institutions, and Major Discoveries in Biomedical Science*. New York: Cambridge University Press.

—— Müller, K. H., and Hollingsworth, E. J. (2002). *Advancing Socio-Economics: An Institutionalist Perspective*. Lanham, MD: Rowman & Littlefield.

Jones, R. V. (1985). 'Complementarity as a Way of Life', in A. P. French and P. J. Kennedy (eds.), *Niels Bohr: A Centenary Volume*. Cambridge: Harvard University Press.

Kothari, D. S. (1985). 'The Complementarity Principle and Eastern Philosophy', in A. P. French and P. J. Kennedy (eds.), *Niels Bohr: A Centenary Volume*. Cambridge, MA: Harvard University Press.

Krugman, P. (1994). *Peddling Prosperity*. New York: W.W. Norton.

Levi, M. (1997). 'A Model, a Method, and a Map: Rational Choice in Comparative and Historical Analysis', in M. I. Lichbach and A. S. Zuckerman (eds.), *Comparative Politics: Rationality, Culture, and Structure*. New York: Cambridge University Press.

Lewin, R. (1993). *Complexity*. Phoenix, AZ: Orion Books.

Lewontin, R. (2000). *The Triple Helix: Gene, Organism, and Environment*. Cambridge, MA: Harvard University Press.

Mahoney, J. (2000). 'Path Dependence in Historical Sociology', *Theory and Society*, 29: 507–48.

——(2003). 'Long-Run Development and the Legacy of Colonialism in Spanish America', *American Journal of Sociology*, 109(1): 50–106.

Manow, P. (2001). 'Social Protection, Capitalist Production: The Bismarckian Welfare State and the German Political Economy from the 1880s to the 1990s', Habilitationsschrift, University of Konstanz, Konstanz.

McCloskey, D. (1985). *The Rhetoric of Economics*. Madison, WI: University of Wisconsin Press.

O'Sullivan, M. (2005). 'Typologies, Ideologies and Realities of Capitalism', *Socio-Economic Review*, 3(3): 547–58.

Orren, K. and Skowronek, S. (2004). *The Search for American Political Development*. Cambridge: Cambridge University Press.

Pais, A. (1991). *Niels Bohr's Times, in Physics, Philosophy, and Polity*. Oxford: Oxford University Press.

Pattee, H. H. (1978). 'The Complementarity Principle in Biological and Social Structures', *Journal of Social and Biological Structures*, 1: 191–200.

Pempel, T. J. (2005). 'Alternative Capitalisms Confront New Pressures to Conform', *Socio-Economic Review*, 3(3): 569–75.

Pierson, P. (2000). 'Increasing Returns, Path Dependence, and the Study of Politics', *American Political Science Review*, 94: 251–68.

—— (2004). *Politics in Time: History, Institutions, and Social Analysis*. Princeton: Princeton University Press.

Piore, M. and Sabel, C. (1984). *The Second Industrial Divide, Possibilities for Prosperity*. New York: Basic Books.
Rasmussen, E. (1987). *Complementarity and Political Science: An Essay on Fundamentals of Political Science Theory and Research Strategy*. Odense, Denmark: Odense University Press.
Rosenfeld, L. (1963). 'Niels Bohr's Contribution to Epistemology', *Physics Today*, 16: 47–54.
—— (1967). 'Niels Bohr in the Thirties: Consolidation and Extension of the Conception of Complementarity', in S. Rozental (ed.), *Niels Bohr: His Life and Work as Seen by His Friends and Colleagues*. Amsterdam: North-Holland.
Scharpf, F. W. (1997). *Games Real Actors Play: Actor-Centered Institutionalism in Policy Research*. Boulder, CO: Westview Press.
Skocpol, T. (1992). *Protecting Soldiers and Mothers: The Political Origins of Social Policy in the United States*. Cambridge, MA: Belknap.
—— (2003). 'Doubly Engaged Social Science: The Promise of Comparative Historical Analysis', in J. Mahoney and D. Rueschemeyer (eds.), *Comparative Historical Analysis in the Social Sciences*. Cambridge and New York: Cambridge University Press.
Stark, D. and Bruszt, L. (1998). *Postsocialist Pathways: Transforming Politics and Property in East Central Europe*. New York: Cambridge University Press.
Streeck, W. (2005). 'Rejoinder: On Terminology, Functionalism, (Historical) Institutionalism and Liberalization', *Socio-Economic Review*, 3(3): 577–87.
—— and Thelen, K. (2005). *Beyond Continuity: Institutional Change in Advanced Political Economies*. New York: Oxford University Press.
—— and Yamamura, K. (eds.) (2001). *The Origins of Nonliberal Capitalism: Germany and Japan in Comparison*. Ithaca, NY: Cornell University Press.
Thelen, K. (2003). 'How Institutions Evolve; Insights from Comparative Historical Analysis', in J. Mahoney and D. Rueschemeyer (eds.), *Comparative Historical Analysis in the Social Sciences*. Cambridge: Cambridge University Press.
Tilly, C. (1984). *Big Structures, Large Processes, Huge Comparisons*. New York: Russell Sage Foundation.
Tononi, G., Sporns, O., and Edelman, G. M. (1999). 'Measures of Degeneracy and Redundancy in Biological Networks', *Proceedings of the National Academy of Sciences USA*, 96: 3257–62.
Young, B. (1991). 'The Dairy Industry: From Yeomanry to the Institutionalization of Multilateral Governance', in J. L. Campbell, J. R. Hollingsworth, and L. N. Lindberg (eds.), *Governance of the American Economy*. Cambridge: Cambridge University Press.
—— Lindberg, L. N., and Hollingsworth, J. R. (1989). 'The Governance of the American Dairy Industry: From Regional Dominance to Regional Cleavage', in W. D. Coleman and H. J. Jacek (eds.), *Regionalism, Business Interests and Public Policy*. London and Beverly Hills: Sage.
Waldrop, M. M. (1992). *Complexity: The Emerging Science at the Edge of Order and Chaos*. New York: Simon & Schuster.
Wallerstein, I. (1974). 'The Rise and Future Demise of the World Capitalist System: Concepts for Comparative Analysis', *Comparative Studies in Society and History*, 16(4): 387–415.

4

Globalization and Working Life: A Comparative Analysis of the Automobile and Banking Sectors in Australia and Korea

Russell D. Lansbury, Jim Kitay, and Nick Wailes

Introduction

Since the early 1990s, Ohmae (1995) and others have argued that changes in the international economy, captured by the rubric of globalization, have created the conditions under which national differences will steadily erode. For many concerned with labor and working life, this has been taken as a prediction that increased competition in factor and product markets, coupled with the increased locational mobility of capital, have created the conditions for a universal 'race to the bottom' in labor standards and convergence in national patterns of working life (see, e.g. Tilly 1995). Despite these predictions, empirical studies of working life and employment relations during the 1990s provide evidence of continued cross-national diversity in national patterns of working life in the face of globalization. These studies explain the continuing differences by stressing the importance of national institutional arrangements in refracting the pressures associated with globalization and their impact on working life.

This *institutionalist* approach provides an important counter to the *simple globalization* argument and points to the ongoing significance of national level institutional arrangements in shaping working life outcomes. To this extent, it is consistent with those who have argued that globalization has not eroded the importance of the nation-state (see, e.g. Evans 1997; Weiss 1998). Nevertheless, there are a number of limitations associated with the institutionalist approach. In particular, the institutionalist approach finds it difficult to explain similarities in changes in working life across countries with different institutional arrangements. It also has difficulty explaining changes in institutions themselves. We argue that this is because institutionalist arguments privilege the explanatory role of institutions and, as a result, tend to downplay the potential significance of material interests in shaping working life outcomes. This chapter uses the comparison of changes in employment relations in the auto assembly and retail banking sectors in two very different countries, South Korea and Australia, during the 1990s to argue for an *integrated* approach to globalization and working life. This approach accepts the importance of institutions, but at the same time acknowledges the role that material interests may play in shaping working life outcomes in the context of globalization.

The chapter is structured as follows. The first section briefly reviews debates about globalization and working life, notes some of the limitations of the institutionalist approach, and outlines the case for an integrated approach to globalization and working life. The second section argues that a 'most different' case research design focusing on Australia and Korea provides an excellent framework within which to test competing claims about globalization and working life. Sections three and four provide an overview of changes in employment relations in the Australian and Korean auto and banking sectors. The chapter concludes by arguing that changes in employment relations in autos and banking in Australia and Korea during the 1990s cannot be explained adequately by either a simple globalization argument or by an institutionalist approach. These findings suggest the need to rethink the relationship between globalization and working life and point to the fact that an integrated approach may provide a better framework within which to understand this relationship.

Globalization and Working Life: Recent Debates

Globalization and its implications for all aspects of economic, social, and political life, including working life, has been one of the most widely debated topics in the social sciences since the beginning of the 1990s. One of the implications of the arguments put forward by Ohmae and others is that globalization produces pressures for the convergence of employment relations practices and working life conditions across countries. However, empirical studies during the 1990s provided little evidence of a simple and universal convergence of employment relations practices. Rather comparative employment relations scholars have stressed the extent to which there was continuing, or even increasing, diversity in national patterns of working life and employment relations (see, e.g. Ferner and Hyman 1992, 1998; Wever and Turner 1995; Locke and Kochan 1996; Visser 1996).

In line with the growing focus on the explanatory role of institutional arrangements across a number of social sciences (see Goodin 1996), explanations for this pattern of continued diversity in national patterns of employment relations have focused on the role played by national and even subnational institutional arrangements in shaping national patterns of employment relations. Indeed, as Hyman (2001: 211) argues, 'if there is a dominant analytical premise in recent Anglo-American research it is the principle that institutions matter'. Thus, for example, in summarizing the findings of a major international survey of employment relations in developed market economies, Locke and Kochan (1996: 365) argue that while international economic forces have created uniform pressures for increased labor market flexibility, 'different institutional arrangements filter these common pressures differently so that the valence of particular issues and changes in practices are quite varied in national contexts'. Similarly, in a recent major study of labor market arrangements and outcomes in developed economies, Traxler, Blaschke and Kittle (2001) note that there is little evidence to support the notion of convergence and suggest that, across a range of variables, national patterns of employment relations and working life arrangements are characterized by path dependency. They attribute these outcomes to 'the fact that market pressures affect labor relations institutions indirectly, in that they are processed and filtered by institutions' (Traxler, Blaschke, and Kittle 2001: 289).

As these examples suggest, the institutionalist approach to globalization and working life argues that even though globalization has created common pressures across national economies, differences in national institutional arrangements refract these common pressures in different ways and produce different outcomes which may persist over time. This reflects the influence of two key theoretical insights associated with the new institutionalism, and especially historical institutionalism in comparative politics (see Thelen and Steinmo 1992; Pierson and Skocpol 2001). The first is that national and even subnational institutional arrangements develop over time and tend to persist. The second is that institutions not only provide a context for decision-making but also play a role in shaping the interests of social actors (Immegrut 1998). Indeed some have argued that preference formation may be endogenous to institutional context (see Hall and Taylor 1996). There are also close connections between these institutionalist arguments and the increasingly influential *varieties of capitalism* approach (see Thelen 2001).

This institutionalist approach represents an important corrective to the simple globalization argument. It provides an explanation for the diversity of national patterns of working life and draws attention to the continued significance of nation-states and politics in helping to determine working life practices and outcomes. Ironically, however, while the institutionalist approach strongly criticizes the implications of the simple globalization argument, it largely accepts the view that globalization has created an integrated international market, and that competitive pressures are the same everywhere (Radice 2000). However, the view that globalization creates a uniform economic pressure has been widely criticized. Globalization 'skeptics' like Hirst and Thompson (1996) and Wade (1996) dispute the notion of a fully integrated international market and argue that while the international economy is more internationalized, it is still highly differentiated. Even those who accept the idea that there has been a substantial change in the configuration of the international economy reject the notion that globalization has created uniform pressures for change in all sectors and across all economies (Held et al. 1999).

This suggests that globalization has differential effects on the interests of employers, workers, and governments in particular working life arrangements, irrespective of institutional arrangements. A framework that incorporates interests as well as institutions may overcome the tendency of the institutional approach to exaggerate differences between cases and provide an explanation for similar change across different cases (Pontusson 1995; Smith and Meiskins 1995). It would also provide a means of explaining why even institutions themselves change (Remmer 1997; Gorges 2001).

There are a number of different ways in which such an approach can be developed. In one recent example, Wailes, Ramia, and Lansbury (2003) use the international political economy literature to develop what they call an integrated approach to help explain similarities and differences in working life outcomes in Australia and New Zealand during the 1980s and 1990s. They demonstrate that the policy divergence that developed between the two countries during the 1980s was a product of both differences in institutional arrangements and the configuration of material interests that underpinned these institutions. Wailes, Ramia, and Lansbury (2003) argue that as differences in the coalition of material interests subsided, there was notable policy convergence despite continued institutional differences between the countries.

Australia and Korea as Most Different Cases

As the previous section outlined, there are a number of competing hypotheses about the relationship between globalization and working life. This chapter uses the comparison between Australia and Korea during the 1990s to test these competing hypotheses. In social science research it is often difficult to control for sources of variation and isolate causal factors, particularly where the variation of a number of dependent variables is explained by more than one set of independent variables. A number of leading scholars have argued that it is possible to overcome some of these problems through comparative research using carefully selected cases (see Skocpol and Somers 1980; Strauss 1998). As Skocpol and Somers (1980) note, this can take the form of comparing countries which are similar in a number of important respects or by comparing countries which differ in important respects. Both approaches, they argue, make it possible to isolate sources of variation and to isolate causally significant factors while at the same time situating these causal explanations in a rich description of context. There has been considerable growth in comparative literature that uses closely matched pairs of countries as the basis for *most similar* comparisons (see, e.g. Bray and Walsh (1998) on Australia and New Zealand and Taras (1997) on Canada and the United States). Less attention has been paid to the use of *most different* comparisons in the employment relations literature, even though this has long been recommended as an equally important approach to the testing of theory in the social sciences (Przeworski and Teune 1970).

A most different case research design is particularly well suited to testing the competing hypotheses about the relationship between globalization and employment relations outlined above. The simple globalization hypothesis suggests that globalization is producing a convergence in employment relations policies across all countries. If this hypothesis is correct, then it should be possible to identify common developments in even the most dissimilar countries. The institutionalist hypothesis suggests that the greater the differences between countries, in terms of their national institutional frameworks, the greater the divergence is likely to be. If, however, these countries show some signs of convergence then there will be grounds for questioning the validity of the institutionalist hypothesis. Finally, evidence of both similarities and differences between most different comparators would imply that the relationship between globalization and employment relations is best explained by an integrated approach.

There are a number of reasons to suggest that Korea and Australia are good examples of most different cases. Employment relations patterns are likely to be affected by a number of factors including culture, the timing and nature of economic development, the structure of the economy, firm size and orientation, and the political and institutional traditions of the country. Australia and Korea show significant differences along these five dimensions. First, there are a number of obvious differences in the cultural traditions of the two countries. Second, both countries developed at different times and in different ways. Australia experienced rapid economic development in the second half of the nineteenth century and was based primarily on the export of wool. Economic development in Korea began in the 1960s and was based mainly on the export of manufactured goods. These differences in timing have resulted in significant differences in the economic structure of the two countries and particularly the structure of manufacturing—a third point of comparison. Korea has a large export-oriented manufacturing sector, while Australia's manufacturing industry is relatively small and largely focused on the domestic market. A fourth major difference between the countries relates to firm size and orientation. The Korean economy is dominated by large family-owned organizations called *chaebol*, which have high levels of diversification but whose main operations are in export-orientated manufacturing. Unlike Korea, where there are low levels of foreign direct investment (FDI), many of the large firms in Australia are subsidiaries of multinational corporations. Australian-owned manufacturing firms tend to be much smaller and more domestically focused than is the case in Korea (Lansbury, Kitay, and Wailes 2003).

There are also significant differences in the political and institutional traditions of Australia and Korea. In political terms, Australia has a long unbroken tradition of democratic government built on the British traditions of its colonial past. Political arrangements in Korea have been much more turbulent during the twentieth century. These include Japanese colonization, American occupation, civil war, and United Nations military intervention which resulted in the division of the Korean peninsula at the 38th parallel. This was followed by a period of authoritarian rule which lasted until 1987 when President Roh Tae Woo was forced to announce free presidential elections in response to widespread social protests. The political system in Korea is also characterized by significant fluidity in its party structure, the existence of strong regional divisions in political loyalties, and the absence of a genuine workers' class party aligned to the trade union movement, and can be contrasted with Australia on this basis (Lansbury, Kitay, and Wailes 2003).

There are also major differences in employment relations traditions in the two countries. Australia has traditionally relied on a system of wage determination and dispute resolution known as arbitration, introduced at the end of the nineteenth century, which encouraged the formation of trade unions and led to the development of industrial awards which regulated wages and conditions across industries. During the 1980s and 1990s, there was significant decentralization of the arbitration system as governments sought to improve the flexibility of the Australian labor market. Much of this decentralization began during a social pact between the peak council of trade unions, the ACTU, and the Labor Federal government (known as the Accord), which lasted from 1983 until Labor lost the 1996 election. Since 1996, the conservative Liberal–National Coalition government has eschewed corporatist arrangements and continued to introduce changes aimed at further eroding arbitration (Lansbury and Wailes 2004*a*). Starting with the Japanese colonial administration, independent trade unionism has been traditionally suppressed by the state in Korea. State and employer suppression of independent trade unionism remained a common feature of Korean industrial relations until the democratization announcement in 1987. In the aftermath of this announcement there was a massive strike wave and independent unions were formed in key sectors of the economy including retail banking and automobile manufacturing. Since the late 1980s, Korean industrial relations have been characterized by high levels of industrial conflict. During the 1990s there have been a number of legislative attempts to reform the Korean industrial relations system, in an effort to reduce these levels of conflict. In the aftermath of the 1997 Asian financial crisis, reforms were introduced to allow employers to lay off workers in return for some legal recognition of the independent trade unions. This corporatist arrangement proved to be highly unstable and industrial relations in Korean remains highly conflictual (Lansbury and Wailes 2004*b*; Park and Leggett 2004).

This study focuses on changes in employment relations in two industries, autos and banking in the two countries since the mid-1990s. Data for the study were gathered by teams of Australian and Korean researchers between 2001 and 2005. In each country the research teams visited two leading companies in each sector at least twice over this period and conducted semistructured interviews with managers, union officials, and workers. These interview data were supplemented in some cases by company documentation. The auto assembly and retail banking industries were chosen for a number of reasons. In both Korea and Australia, auto manufacturing is one of the largest employers of blue-collar workers and is integrated with a vast network of component suppliers, while retail banking is one of the main sources of white-collar employment. A focus on these two industries thus makes it possible to compare and contrast developments in manufacturing and services. Both industries are highly unionized, and their unions have played a major role in shaping industrial relations in each country. Globalization has had a major impact on each industry in recent years and caused extensive restructuring as companies have been increasingly exposed to international competition. In both industries there are strong convergence pressures associated with increased competition. In autos this has translated into the growing use of lean production systems (Kochan, Lansbury, and MacDuffie 1997). In retail banking there has been increasing diffusion of a standard business model which employs technology to reduce costs (Regini 1999). There have also been important differences in the experience of the two industries. In Australia, the auto industry has been focused mainly on the domestic market and has not faced global market pressures until recently. By contrast, the auto industry in Korea is highly export oriented. Banks in Korea have also been a major victim (and contributor) to that country's economic crisis, whereas banks in Australia have been gradually adapting to financial deregulation and external competition over a longer period of time.

The Banking Industry in Australia and Korea

The retail banking industry in Australia and Korea has undergone significant restructuring, with important implications for employment relations, although the effects have been more substantial in Korea following the 1997 financial crisis. In both countries, the financial services sector remains a significant employer of labor despite restructuring and some downsizing. Retail banking is a particularly interesting area of employment because it combines labor-intensive work with extensive use of technology, and is both customer-facing and knowledge intensive.

There were fifty-two licensed banks in Australia in September 2004. The industry is concentrated, with five domestic banks controlling 69 percent of resident assets. The thirty-eight locally incorporated foreign banks or foreign bank branches control under 17 percent of resident assets, with the remainder controlled by domestic regional banks (APRA 2005: 16).

In Australia, three main background factors underlie the changes taking place in retail banking. First, a process of financial sector deregulation, which began in earnest under a Labor federal government in 1983, increased the competitive pressures on what was previously a highly protected industry. As controls were loosened on capital movements and exchange and interest rates, banks changed from rationing money to selling it. As well, deregulation increased the number of institutions undertaking banking activities and reduced the barriers between different segments of the industry. This began a shift toward a *bancassurance* model, in which the customers of financial sector organizations can find banking, insurance, and investment services under one roof. At the same time, however, new entrants to the industry established low-cost operations without branch structures in lucrative niche markets such as home mortgages, which placed considerable pressure on the traditional full service banks to cut costs.

Second, privatization increased competitive pressures by increasing the number of banks operating on a commercial basis. Australia has gone from having a significant proportion of its financial services enterprises (both banking and insurance) within the public sector, with distinctive employment relations practices, to virtually none. Competition increased not only in the retail product market for personal and business customers, but also for favorable ratings on the share market. However, while governments withdrew from commercial banking activities, they continued to influence the industry by an active compliance and competition enforcement role. Most notably, there is little doubt that there would be mergers among the four largest banks, with wide ranging staff reductions and branch closures, if not for the very public refusal of both Labor and Conservative federal governments to permit this in the face of a long running campaign by bank CEOs and other corporate leaders to allow it.

Third, new technology has enabled significant changes to take place in business strategy, organizational structure, and employment relations practices. Technological change has affected where, when, and how banking takes place. Among the many changes associated with new technology, the two most important have been a change in the location of processing work from the 'back office' of branches to centralized locations and the diversification of service channels away from a reliance on 'bricks and mortar' branches.

Korean banks were typically smaller than most major foreign banks, but some have recently increased in size through government-encouraged mergers. Unlike Australian banks, until recently they maintained a strategy of growth based on the expansion of branches, which had a negative effect on their profitability. This applies not only to domestic business but also at the international level.

Many serious problems became apparent in Korean banks during the IMF crisis, including poor asset quality, inadequate provisioning, lack of transparency in decision-making, and lack of competitiveness. Part of the government's response to the crisis was to pressure the banks strongly to undertake structural reforms, which resulted in mergers and acquisitions, privatization, and workforce reductions. The bank crisis in Korea (like the financial crisis overall) was caused mainly by corporate misbehavior. Banks borrowed too much money from both the internal and external financial institutions, and their assets included loans to too many doubtful enterprises within and outside Korea. Not only was there a failure of risk management on the part of the banks, but also a failure on the part of the government to provide adequate regulation. The government had played the role—often implicit—of promoter and guarantor of the financial services sector, rather than rule-maker, regulator, and supervisor, as a result of which most financial institutions failed to monitor and manage their risks adequately and assumed that the government would protect them from any serious debt crisis. The magnitude of the crisis made this approach unsustainable.

The postcrisis restructuring process involved the recapitalization of financial institutions with public funds, the outcome of which was the de facto nationalization of a number of Korean banks. After expending some $60 billion worth of public funds, the 'first round' of Korea's banking restructuring ended with the closure of some small regional banks and the realignment of larger retail banks through government-promoted mergers. As a result, numerous bank branches were closed and the number of bank employees was reduced by about one-third. However, despite the measures in the initial round of restructuring, bank profitability remained tenuous. The turmoil at Daewoo, the nation's second largest industrial conglomerate, created havoc in the Korean banking industry, and subsequent problems in major chaebol groups, including Hyundai, exacerbated the difficulties in Korea's financial sector.

Almost all of the retail banks have reduced their exposure to corporate lending for fear of further defaults, while expanding their asset base in the private household market. Telephone banking and Internet banking, which had been slow to develop in Korean banks, expanded rapidly after the financial crisis because of the need to recruit individual customers.

Employment practices have changed considerably in both countries in the context of this background. In Australia, one of the most significant changes has been the demise of the 'rounded career banker'. This process took over ten years to evolve, commencing in the mid-1980s. In the traditional model, Australian banks were characterized by strong internal labor markets (ILMs) and 'jobs for life', though this applied more to men than women. Employees were typically recruited directly from high school into bottom rung positions in branches and moved slowly through a career structure with a limited number of pathways but a tall career ladder, with a reasonable expectation on the part of most male employees that they would ascend to a position of at least minor responsibility. Indeed, until the 1990s, the path to CEO in Australian banks invariably began in branch back offices licking stamps and making cups of coffee!

Because of long career ladders, skills were learned gradually. There were both formal training programs for those expected to move to new functions within the branch, as well as a great deal of informal 'learning by doing', such as staff learning new skills by 'helping out' during quiet periods. A seniority-based compensation system operated until the late 1980s. Major banks were highly unionized, with 70 percent union density or higher, and the personnel function was both centralized and powerful. Industrial relations were adversarial but relatively peaceful. Negotiations in banking were centralized at industry level, with a common award which flowed on, with some variations, to the public sector banks.

A range of changes occurred during the past twenty-five years, particularly since deregulation. First, work organization changed considerably. Back office processing functions were gradually removed from branches and centralized, and call centers were introduced for enquiries. The number of branches fell considerably, and they were increasingly located in shopping malls rather than the 'high street'. Hours of branch operations increased as well, with the introduction of limited weekend banking in some locations. More significantly, new low-cost distribution channels were introduced and customers were encouraged to use them rather than attend a branch by the introduction of differential fee structures for transactions. Access to many banking services increased to 24/7 over the Internet and in some banks to 24/7 in call centers. Branches were reconfigured as 'sales outlets', and performance targets for sales and referrals were introduced for frontline staff in branches and call centers.

Second, staffing practices have changed. Branch employment changed from primarily full time to a large complement of part time staff. The great majority of part time workers are female, particularly women with school-age children. The staffing profile of branches became leaner as banks applied complex formulae to match the peaks and troughs in demand. As a result, many long-serving employees reported an increase in work intensity. The concept of lifetime jobs disappeared, as banks sought to cut costs by slashing their branch networks and back-office operations. Much of the reduction was by attrition and voluntary redundancy, but retrenchments began to occur in the early 1990s, in some cases involving thousands of employees. This reached a height in three of the major banks in the early to mid-1990s in response to a combination of mergers and poor financial performance, but has continued since then with periodic rounds of highly publicized staffing reductions. Noncore functions such as IT were outsourced, and even some previously core processing functions have been outsourced as well. The drive to minimize costs has led the banks to explore joint bank office operations, which reportedly has only been precluded by the threat of action by government anticompetition regulators.

Third, the range of skills learned by bank employees was reduced with the separation of front- and back-office tasks. In a general sense, this undoubtedly constitutes deskilling because few retail bank employees recruited since the early 1990s have the comprehensive understanding of the full range banking activities that most experienced employees would have had previously. However, at a detailed level the skills required of branch staff today is difficult to compare to prederegulation branches because the nature of branch work has changed considerably. In particular, the skills necessary for much front-office work expanded to include a sales focus which requires a distinctive set of competencies that were not previously needed, and the variety of products available to retail customers has greatly expanded. Whether this constitutes deskilling or a deepening of a narrower range of skills is open to interpretation. Training practices have varied over time. The training offered to branch staff, both at induction and ongoing, diminished in the major banks in the 1990s. However, this trend reversed by the early 2000s, in part due to significant increases in compliance requirements imposed by the federal government. Compliance also affected work organization. While there were some variations in the range of tasks undertaken by customer-facing staff in branches and call centers in different banks in the 1990s, the banks have found it expedient to converge on a model in which a distinction between transaction and sales staff is enforced.

Fourth, the seniority pay framework was abandoned in the major banks in the late 1980s, replaced by a combination of job evaluation and performance appraisal. The generous nonsalary benefits of working in a bank, for example, low cost loans, remain but are being wound back. The amount of performance pay available at lower levels varies, but it is seldom large—often under 10 percent—for most retail staff. An exception arose in the early 1990s with the introduction of 'mobile lenders', which were unequivocally sales positions. They did not have 'normal' hours of work, and in some banks a considerable amount of their income was commission based. However, the performance component of compensation for these positions has been wound back as the greater willingness to accept risk inherent in this model became apparent. More recently, the major banks have become heavily involved in wealth management, and have employed substantial numbers of financial planners. Many financial planners in banks—like some call center employees—identify more with their occupation than their employing organization. The compensation practices in financial planning typically involve far greater opportunities to gain incentive-based payments than in retail banking, and in order to retain staff in this area the banks have adjusted their practices accordingly.

The nature of employment relations has also changed in Australia. The system of industrial relations has become increasingly decentralized. This has occurred through the introduction of enterprise awards and agreements as well as by agreements at the business unit or, in some cases, at the site level. Two of the major banks have introduced individual employment agreements to lower management levels, with considerable union opposition. In general, the variations between banks have not been great, though they differ in details such as the application of industrial agreements to managers. The level of disputation in banking has increased, typically involving eruptions of industrial action around Enterprise Bargaining Agreement negotiations. However, unlike the 1970s and 1980s, when the industry was in a growth phase and the unions were expanding, recent years have witnessed not only a decline in employment but also a shrinking unionized workforce and a decline in bargaining strength. Management–union relations within the industry now differ considerably. In the major banks, relations between management and the Finance Sector Union (FSU) range from cordial to openly hostile. The privatized Commonwealth Bank, for example, moved from a very close relationship with its enterprise-based union as recently as the 1980s to an aggressive anti-union stance by the late 1990s. Even those banks that have maintained a good working relationship with the FSU are seeking to limit the areas in which unions are involved in decision-making and to develop a more direct relationship with employees. There has been a considerable decline in union density in the major banks.

In Korea, the nature of employment in the industry has undergone more radical change than in Australia. Since the economic crisis in late 1997, the number and proportion of nonstandard workers in the Korean banking sector have increased rapidly. This coincided with the massive layoffs of regular workers within banks. In 1998, just after the IMF bailout, regular workers in the banking sector declined by 34 percent, while nonstandard workers increased by 74 percent. In 1999, 90 percent of new recruits in some banks were nonstandard workers. Nonstandard workers are overwhelmingly female.

In many cases, nonstandard workers had previously been employed in banks as regular workers, and are doing the same or similar work within the same bank. They were frequently pressured by management to resign from their previous positions, and re-entered the banks as nonstandard workers because they could not find alternative jobs. However, as a consequence their wage levels were reduced by as much as 50 percent. Due to the labor reductions widely adopted by most banks after the onset of the financial crisis, the industry has experienced a reduction of workers per branch of approximately 20 percent and an increase in the average hours of work.

Like Australia, Korean banks have removed many back-office and information provision tasks from branches to processing centers and call centers respectively, and branches are increasingly seen as sales outlets. As the banks involved in merger activity have begun to consolidate their activities, a consequence has been the beginning of a trend of branch rationalization. The use of alternative forms of service delivery such as ATMs has grown considerably since the crisis.

The opportunities for career advancement have declined even more in Korean banks than their Australian counterparts. A widely recognized distinction between 'general' and 'ordinary' career paths existed, with only the former providing access to management positions. While nominally open to the choice of individual employees, the family commitments of women generally led them to opt for the restricted opportunities of 'ordinary' careers. However, even men now find their careers restricted, as employment levels have dropped considerably and organizational structures have flattened. While seniority continues to play a role in promotion, performance is increasingly a criterion.

Almost all of retail banks in Korea are unionized. Workers below the manager level are entitled to be union members. Virtually all regular workers are union members. By contrast, nonstandard workers cannot legally be union members. Before the financial crisis, company unions of individual banks bargained separately with their management. However, faced with the financial crisis and wave of downsizing, bank workers increasingly responded at an industry level, and bank unions have been reorganized as one united Finance Industry Union. In July 2000, the Finance Industry Union mobilized workers across many banks for their first general strike, mainly against structural reforms initiated by the government.

The increasing market pressures from the foreign banks in Korea and other financial institutions have forced the major retail banks to reduce the margins on interest rates and concentrate on high value-added sales. This has resulted in pressures to contain costs, which has also been a condition of gaining financial support from the government. Despite ongoing conflict between the banks, the government, and the unions over cost reductions, the banks have nevertheless toed the government line by undertaking massive layoffs and replacing regular with nonstandard workers. Employment stability and career development plans associated with the traditional ILMs have disappeared. By following this 'low road' path, the banks are finding it difficult to change to a profit-centered and high-quality sales culture. Most large retail banks are continuing to centralize back-office jobs, establish call centers, and introduce Internet transactions, while simplifying teller roles. They are also analyzing information about their customers more intensively with a view to more accurately identifying sales opportunities. Accordingly, investments on IT have increased dramatically, and this is one of the major reasons which the larger banks have given for embarking on further mergers and acquisitions.

The Auto Industry in Australia and Korea

The auto industry in each country exhibit both similarities and differences. In both countries the industry developed with significant government assistance and protection, but now faces increasing global competition. There are four assemblers of passenger motor vehicles in Australia: Ford, General Motors Holden, Mitsubishi, and Toyota, and approximately 400 component suppliers. All four assemblers are foreign-owned and controlled, as are many of the major component producers. The scale of production of the assemblers in Australia is small by world standards. Overall, the Australian auto industry accounts for less than 1 percent of the world auto production and consumption.

During the past two decades, there has been considerable reform and restructuring of the industry in Australia, yet there remain many questions concerning its long-term survival. For many years, the auto manufacturing industry in Australia operated behind high levels of tariff protection. From 1985 to 2005, tariff levels were lowered from 57 percent to 15 percent. As a consequence, local manufacturers faced increasing competition from imported vehicles and this has heightened the need for higher levels of productivity, quality and far-reaching changes in the industry. Most assemblers improved their export performance and many component manufacturers became more internationally competitive. Yet there remained considerable variation in the performance levels of both component producers and domestic assemblers, some of which are marginal operators with an uncertain future.

Although there was some improvement from the second half of the 1990s to 2005, the Australian auto industry has experienced relatively low levels of profitability for a number of years. A report by Standard and Poors in 1996 awarded the auto industry in Australia a 'D' rating (fourth lowest on a five-point scale) and questioned whether it could remain viable unless it was more integrated into global components sourcing and developed its own niche export markets. Standard and Poors commented that 'the profit performance of Australia's automotive industry remains patchy.... Historically, a lack of progress with structural inefficiencies, cyclical markets, low volumes and slow progress with microeconomic reform have contributed to low returns on capital employed' (1996:15). Not a great deal changed during the subsequent decade.

The auto industry in Korea is one of the key industries that has substantially contributed to the country's sustained economic growth and export increases during the last thirty years. Among newly industrializing economies, Korea is one of the few countries in which the auto sector has possessed independent R & D capability and massive manufacturing capacity. By the mid-1990s, Korea was positioned as the fifth country worldwide in terms of the volume of auto production, and was regarded as one of the key competitors as well as a sizable auto market in the international auto industry.

However, the Korean auto industry was confronted with unprecedented hardship during the serious economic slump and foreign currency exchange crisis which took place in the period of 1997–8. Kia went bankrupt in the Summer of 1997, whereas Samsung, Ssangyong, and Daewoo fell into deep financial crisis in 1999. The auto industry has since been undergoing reconstruction: Kia and its affiliate, Asia Motor, merged with Hyundai, and Samsung was acquired by Renault. Both Daewoo and Ssangyong were placed under the control of creditor banks as well as the government, which provided public funds to them. In addition, most automakers took a series of actions to restructure business units and downsize employment during the period 1997–2000. A number of auto parts manufacturers were taken over by foreign multinational companies.

The Australian and Korean auto industries have both faced the need to undertake significant reforms in order to adjust to the increasingly globalized product market. This has had important implications for labor–management relations. As in Korea, the Australian industry has become increasingly integrated into the global marketplace. Both the assemblers and many of the component manufacturers are subject to the direction of foreign parent companies. Typically, all four major auto manufacturers use common basic designs (platforms) for vehicles produced at different locations around the world. Many assemblers have rationalized their international sources of components. This has encouraged a move to larger component suppliers, which also have production facilities around the world. The effect of this aspect of globalization has been to provide the major vehicle producers with a greater choice as to where they source suppliers of components and models. In some cases, the Australian industry has benefited from these developments, through their access to the world's major markets, but it has also meant a greater pressure on price, quality, and productivity. Global production and marketing strategies are developed by parent companies, which pay little heed to local considerations in other countries. Furthermore, there is excess production capacity worldwide and the Australian industry faces competition from lower-cost, newly industrializing countries which are eager to enter the market as assemblers and component suppliers. Hence, while the industry in each country has faced similar problems, the responses by the individual companies have varied.

Industrial relations have been another point of contrast between the Australian and Korean industries. Although the auto industry in Australia was regarded as highly strike prone in the past, there has been a marked reduction in industrial disputes in the industry. The number of working days lost per thousand employees in the automotive industry was very low in the 1990s, well below the levels which were experienced in the industry during the 1980s and before. Recent disputes have been mainly concerned with negotiations over enterprise-level workplace bargaining as employers have begun to push for greater flexibility and productivity improvement. There were also disputes related to changes in industrial relations legislation which were general issues and not specific to the automotive industry. A rise in the number of working days lost, combined with a fall in the number of workers involved, shows that the remaining industrial action has been localized—which may also reflect the processes involved in enterprise bargaining. For example, there was a significant strike at Toyota in 1996 during the negotiation of a new enterprise agreement, which resulted in an abnormally high number of working days lost. However, this should be seen in the context of the parties adjusting to the new enterprise-based bargaining system and particular circumstances at the new Toyota plant. Consequently, the automotive sector lost relatively more working days per thousand employees in 1996 than the total manufacturing sector. This was the worst result recorded for the sector since 1989 when issues such as the national wage case award restructuring were the issues involved in the industrial disputes.

Employment relations in the Korean auto industry have shown a tendency toward centralization, in contrast to the decentralizing trends in Australia. Following Hyundai's acquisition of Kia, as well as the mergers of business operations taking place in most auto producers, the auto unions carried out the organizational integration with other unions representing merged business units and established a more centralized bargaining framework. Moreover, the unions have forged common policies over issues such as production standards, the use of irregular workforce, and the deployment/transfer of union members in the process of the recent restructuring. If all the auto unions join the industrial confederation, it is expected that the centralizing tendency in union activities and bargaining will continue.

The key aspects of the evolution of employment relations in major auto firms (Hyundai, Kia, and Daewoo) during recent years have been as follows. Following the economic crisis period of the late 1990s, workforce reductions were the key employment relations issue in the auto industry. Massive downsizing, including permanent layoffs which were implemented by management under financial pressures, produced very intense disputes, especially in Hyundai (1998) and Daewoo (2001). All the unions that experienced job losses put particular emphasis on the employment security of union members and made great efforts to impose restrictions on management's discretion over employment adjustment. The management's actions to downsize through layoffs and early retirements ended the myth of 'lifetime employment' and created deep distrust toward their companies.

Management's stance toward the unions at the three major Korean auto companies has changed over the years. Hyundai management's hard-line position between 1997 and 1998 caused severe confrontation with the union. A new top management team, which was appointed in early 1999, took a more proactive approach toward the union, thereby contributing to stabilizing the labor–management relations. Management at Daewoo tried to build cooperative relations with their union in order to overcome the company's financial crisis, while the new management at Daewoo, assigned by the creditor banks, adopted a firm approach to enforcing business restructuring and massive downsizing. This resulted in a major dispute with the union in early 2001. In the case of Kia, management had maintained an antiunion policy prior to 1997, yet formed a collaborative partnership with their union in an attempt to secure the company's survival, when confronted with bankruptcy in mid-1997.

Changes in work organization, in response to globalization and the restructuring of the auto industry, have also taken different paths in the two countries. In Australia, there has been movement away from rigid job distinctions and demarcations toward multi-skilling, job rotation, and job enlargement. Skill development continues to be important, although it is now less coordinated at a national level with more emphasis on enterprise-based, on-the-job training. Job security is a major issue for employees as companies rationalize and reduce their workforce numbers. This is particularly the case within the component supplier sector which is subject to fierce price competition from other countries such as China, where labor and materials are cheaper. Performance-related pay is confined mainly to managerial levels, although it is now an issue in enterprise bargaining agendas for production workers.

While the adoption of fully fledged lean production has been only gradual in the Australian auto industry, there are signs that this may change with new greenfield investment and new supplier arrangements at GM Holden, and innovations at Toyota and Ford. The union maintains an optimistic view of the future of the industry, but there is also a more pessimistic alternative, which would see the demise of vehicle manufacturing in Australia if tariff protection and other forms of government assistance ceased and the market was opened up to full international competition.

By contrast, work organization and wage schemes for production workers in the Korean auto industry have hardly changed in the face of extensive restructuring. Because the companies still rely on a mass production system to produce mainly lower-priced cars in a labor-intensive fashion, their managements have shown only moderate interest in moving away from the traditional supervision-driven work system toward a high-involvement production model. Furthermore, management in the auto sector has largely failed in attempts to introduce more flexible wage schemes such as performance-linked pay and skill-based pay, partly due to strong opposition from the unions and an unwillingness of management to compromise their positions.

Conclusions

There are a number of conclusions that can be drawn from the comparison of employment relations changes in autos and banking in Australia and Korea during the 1990s. First, there is little evidence to support the simple globalization hypothesis. As we noted in Section 2, Korea and Australia represent excellent examples of 'most different' cases. If the globalization hypothesis was to be supported, we would expect to find evidence of convergence between the cases and evidence that national differences between the cases did not matter. While there are some common developments in employment relations in the two industries, such as changes in work organization, there are still important differences in relation to issues like bargaining structure. Nevertheless, the evidence provided in this chapter does not provide unambiguous support for an institutionalist approach. While national level institutional arrangements which impact on the level and type of bargaining and the nature of labor representation are clearly important in both cases, and have played a role in shaping working life, they are not the only factors that matter. The comparison of the banking and auto-assembly industries reveals that working life arrangements are the product of complex interaction between competitive market conditions, organizational strategy, patterns of interest representation, and government regulation. Hence, interests and institutions are important in explaining the relationship between globalization and working life.

Perhaps the clearest issue to emerge from the comparison is that globalization has had differential effects on working life in the two countries. Thus, while Australia has experienced a series of gradual changes in employment relations since the mid-1980s, in Korea there have been a series of dramatic changes in response to the Asian financial crisis. This has produced some similar outcomes in Korea as in Australia. In retail banking, for example, while important differences remain, changes in working life arrangements in Korean banks in the late 1990s are similar to those patterns that began to emerge in Australia more than a decade earlier. Yet it seems clear that national political and institutional differences between the two countries, as well as differences in the market conditions faced by organizations, are not likely to produce a common pattern of employment relations in them.

These results suggest not only the continuing importance of examining the role of both interests and institutions in shaping working life outcomes but also the need to rethink arguments about convergence and divergence in contemporary debates about globalization and working life. As Boyer (1996) argues, globalization theorists move quickly from the argument that globalization creates a series of pressures to the assumption that these pressures will force firms to adopt a single best practice model. Similarly, it can be argued that the institutionalists move from stressing the importance of national institutional arrangements, to a position which downplays the possibilities of globalization producing pressures for convergence. This dichotomy is too simplistic to capture the complexities of the relationship between globalization and working life. Katz and Darbishire (2000) have provided evidence that there is considerable convergence in a number of aspects of employment relations across a range of countries although this process is uneven. Hence, employment relations practices have become more similar in some respects and more differentiated in others. The evidence provided in this chapter is consistent with this finding and suggests that the impact of globalization on working life is the result of complex interrelationships between interests and institutions.

References

Australian Prudential Regulation Authority (APRA) (2005). *Insight.* Quarter 1.

Boyer, R. (1996). 'The Convergence Hypothesis Revisited: Globalisation but Still the Century of Nations?', in S. Berger and R. Dore (eds.), *National Diversity and Global Capitalism.* Ithaca, NY: Cornell University Press.

Bray, M. and Walsh, P. (1998). 'Differing Paths to Neo-liberalism? Comparing Australia and New Zealand', *Industrial Relations,* 37(3): 358–87.

Evans, P. (1997). 'The Eclipse of the State? Reflections on Stateness in an Era of Globalisation', *World Politics,* 50(1): 62–87.

Ferner, A. and Hyman, R. (1992). 'Introduction, Industrial Relations in Europe: Seventeen Types of Ambiguity', in A. Ferner and R. Hyman (eds.), *Industrial Relations in the New Europe.* Oxford: Blackwell.

——(1998). 'Introduction: Towards European Industrial Relations?', in A. Ferner and R. Hyman (eds.), *Changing Industrial Relations in Europe.* London: Blackwell.

Goodin, R. (1996). 'Institutions and Their Design', in R. Goodin (eds.), *The Theory of Institutional Design.* New York: Cambridge University Press.

Gorges, M. (2001). 'The New Institutionalism and the Study of the European Union: The Case of the Social Dialogue', *West European Politics,* 24(4): 152–68.

Hall, P. and Taylor, R. (1996). 'Political Science and the Three New Institutionalisms', *Political Studies,* 44(5): 936–57.

Held, D., McGrew, A., Goldblatt, D., and Perraton, J. (1999). *Global Transformations: Politics, Economics and Culture.* Cambridge: Polity Press.

Hirst, P. and Thompson, G. (1996). *Globalisation in Question: The International Economy and the Possibilities of Governance*. Cambridge: Polity Press.

Hyman, R. (2001). 'Trade Unions Research and Cross National Comparison', *European Journal of Industrial Relations*, 7(1): 203–32.

Immegrut, E. (1998). 'The Theoretical Core of the New Institutionalism', *Politics and Society*, 26(1): 5–34.

Katz, H. and Darbishire, O. (2000). *Converging Divergences: Worldwide Change in Employment Systems*. Ithaca, NY: ILR Press/Cornell University Press.

Kochan, T. A., Lansbury, R. D., and MacDuffie, J. P. (1997). *After Lean Production: Evolving Employment Practices in the World Auto Industry*. Ithaca, NY: ILR Press.

Lansbury, R. D. and Wailes, N. (2004*a*). 'Employment Relations in Australia', in G. Bamber, R. D. Lansbury, and N. Wailes (eds.), *International and Comparative Employment Relations: Globalisation and the Developed Market Economies*. Sydney: Allen and Unwin.

——(2004*b*). 'Current Trends in Korean Industrial Relations: An External Perspective', *Korean Journal of Industrial Relations*, 14(2): 1–22.

—Kitay, J., and Wailes, N. (2003). 'The Impact of Globalisation on Employment Relations: Some Research Propositions', *Asia Pacific Journal of Human Resources*, 41(1): 62–74.

Locke, R. and Kochan, T. (1996). 'Conclusion: The Transformation of Industrial Relations? A Cross National Review of Evidence', in R. Locke, T. Kochan, and M. Piore (eds.), *Employment Relations in a Changing World Economy*. Cambridge, MA: MIT Press.

Ohmae, K. (1995). *The End of the Nation-State: The Rise of Regional Economies*. London: Harper Collins.

Park, Y. and Leggett, C. (2004). 'Employment Relations in Korea', in G. Bamber, R. Lansbury, and N. Wailes (eds.), *International and Comparative Employment Relations: Globalisation and the Developed Market Economies*. Sydney: Allen and Unwin.

Pierson, P. and Skocpol, T. (2001). 'Historical Institutionalism in Contemporary Political Science', in I. Katznelson and H. Milner (eds.), *Political Science: The State of the Discipline*. New York: W. W. Norton.

Pontusson, J. (1995). 'From Comparative Public Policy to Political Economy: Putting Political Institutions in their Place and Taking Interests Seriously', *Comparative Political Studies*, 28(1): 117–48.

Przeworski, A. and Teune, H. (1970). *The Logic of Comparative Social Inquiry*. New York: John Wiley & Sons.

Radice, H. (2000). 'Responses to Globalisation: A Critique of Progressive Nationalism', *New Political Economy*, 5(1): 5–19.

Regini, M. (1999). 'Comparing Banks in Advanced Economies: The Role of Markets, Technology, and Institutions in Employment Relations', in M. Regini, J. Kitay, and M. Baethge (eds.), *From Tellers to Sellers: Changing Employment Relations in Banks*. Cambridge, MA: MIT Press.

Remmer, K. (1997). 'Theoretical Development and Theoretical Decay: The Resurgence of Institutional Analysis', *World Politics*, 50: 34–61.

Skocpol, T. and Somers, M. (1980). 'The Uses of Comparative History in Macro-Social Inquiry', *Comparative Studies in History and Society*, 22(2): 174–92.

Smith, C. and Meiskins, P. (1995). 'System, Society and Dominance Effects in Cross-National Organisational Analysis', *Work, Employment and Society*, 9(2): 241–67.

Standard and Poors (1996). *Industry Profiles: Automotive Australia*, Melbourne: Standard and Poors.

Strauss, G. (1998). 'Comparative International Industrial Relations', in K. Whitfield and G. Strauss (eds.), *Researching the World of Work: Strategies and Methods in Studying Industrial Relations*. Ithaca, NY: ILR Press/Cornell University Press.

Taras, D. (1997). 'Collective Bargaining Regulation in Canada and the United States: Divergent Cultures, Divergent Outcomes', in B. Kaufman (ed.), *Government Regulation of the Employment Relationship*. Washington: IRRA.

Thelen, K. (2001). 'Varieties of Labour Politics in the Developed Democracies', in P. Hall and D. Sosicke (eds.), *Varieties of Capitalism: The Institutional Foundations of Comparative Advantage*. New York: Oxford University Press.

——and Steinmo, S. (1992). 'Historical Institutionalism in Comparative Politics', in K. Thelen, S. Steinmo, and F. Longstreth (eds.), *Structuring Politics: Historical Institutionalism in Comparative Perspective*. New York: Cambridge University Press.

Tilly, C. (1995). 'Globalisation Threatens Labour's Rights', *International Labour and Working Class History*, 47: 1–23.

Traxler, F., Blaschke, S., and Kittel, B. (2001). *National Labour Relations in Internationalised Markets: A Comparative Study of Institutions, Change and Performance*. Oxford: Oxford University Press.

Visser, J. (1996). 'Traditions and Transitions in Industrial Relations: A European View', in J. Van Ruysseveldt and J. Visser (eds.), *Industrial Relations in Europe: Transitions and Traditions*. London: Sage.

Wade, R. (1996). 'Globalisation and its Limits: Reports of the Death of the National Economy Are Greatly Exaggerated', in S. Berger and R. Dore (eds.), *National Diversity and Global Capitalism*. Ithaca, NY: Cornell University Press.

Wailes, N., Ramia, G., and Lansbury, R. D. (2003). 'Interests, Institutions and Industrial Relations', *British Journal of Industrial Relations*, 41(4): 617–37.

Weiss, L. (1998). *The Myth of the Powerless State: Governing the Economy in a Global Era*. Cambridge: Polity Press.

Wever, K. and Turner, L. (1995). 'A Wide Angle Lens for a Global Marketplace', in K. Wever and L. Turner (eds.), *The Comparative Political Economy of Industrial Relations*. Madison, WI: Industrial Relations Research Association.

5

The Production of Institutional Complementarity? The Case of North East England

Ray Hudson

Introduction

In this chapter, I explore the use of some of the concepts elaborated by Boyer (Chapter 2) to help account for the coevolution of the institutions of the state and private sector companies in the north east of England. The north east of England has formed a 'laboratory' in which experiments in institutional innovation have formed part of attempts to develop new forms of public policy in and far the region over a period of some seventy to eighty years. Boyer elaborates a range of concepts relating to varying forms of institutional relationships, ranging from strong concepts of supermodality and complementarity to weaker concepts of compatibility, hierarchy, coherence and complementarity, and related concepts of isomorphism, clustering, and coevolution that are helpful in understanding these successive institutional innovations.

For Boyer, supermodality is a very strong notion, defined by a state in which the performance resulting from a particular conjunction of institutions is superior to that of any other such conjunction. As such, it carries strong normative connotations of optimization and maximization and the approach of mainstream orthodox economics but as such raises questions as to the sorts of behavior and performance that are sensibly conceptualized in these terms. It also raises the issue of how to identify supermodality by direct observation, without constructing a formal model engendering a series of fictitious worlds—for many social scientists, this is a methodologically dubious strategy. For these reasons, I will not consider it further here. Complementarity is a weaker, but nonetheless strong, concept. Complementarity requires that the performance of two elements together is superior to the performance of each considered separately. Thus it is superior performance as a result of conjunction that is the key defining criterion. Hierarchy requires that one entity absolutely requires the presence of another and this requirement of necessary causality makes this quite a strong concept. Compatibility is a weaker condition, defined by the presence of two sets of institutions in two existing economies and societies. It implies correlation but not necessarily causation. Coherence is a still weaker notion. Two institutions can be said to be coherent if they can easily coexist or interact due to identical or common principles.

Isomorphism can be thought of as a specification of a mechanism able to produce some form of coherence between institutions. This may originate from one of the institutions and become the basis of forging links between it and other institutions. Clustering simply refers to the frequent observation of two or more institutions in the same time or space. It is no more than a descriptive concept. In contrast to those discussed so far, coevolution introduces a sense of change and time. Moreover, the notion of coevolution implies that the joint occurrence of two institutions might be the unintended outcome of a trial-and-error learning process, stimulated by a variety of random shocks of various magnitudes.

In the remainder of this chapter, I explore the applicability and relevance of these concepts in understanding the development of institutions within north east England in three time periods, characterized by particular sets of issues relating to institutional relationships and the dominance of some institutions over others and which demonstrate the extent to which institutions have coevolved over the last eighty or so years, typically managed and controlled by a small political and economic elite. The first of these periods, the 1920s and 1930s, was characterized by institutional innovation driven by major capitalist interests in the region as they sought to redefine relations between economy and state to protect their private interests. Recognizing the threat to private capital posed by free markets as the key institution shaping developmental trajectories, new state institutions became mechanisms for protecting private sector interests. This process culminated in the war economy of 1939–45. The second period, from 1945 to the mid-1970s, was one in which the institutions of the state, especially the nationalized industries, became the key institutions steering the trajectory of economic development in a state-managed region. The succeeding third period—still ongoing—saw a resurgence of the market as the key institution reshaping the regional economy within a resurgent neoliberal globalization. After some fifty or sixty years of experiments with a variety of state institutions that sought to strongly shape, or even replace, markets as steering mechanism, once again the notion of the free or 'lightly regulated' (in terms of limits on capital and protection to labor) market became the dominant institution shaping economy and society in north east England.

Institutions have a variety of cognitive, discursive, and material effects on economies and societies and their developmental trajectories. A key aspect of institutions is that they both 'parametize' and 'constrain', while in any one given environment they also shape the visions of the world, the interaction networks, the behavioral patterns and, ultimately, the very identity of the agents. The key aspect of coevolution is that what happens in each partly autonomous domain of the system (e.g. institutional structures) shapes and constrains what is going to happen in the other ones. Hence, the overall system dynamics are determined not only by the ways each domain evolves but also by the ways in which the various domains are coupled with each other (Coriat and Dosi 2002: 96–7 and 115). The case of north east England exemplifies this clearly.

The Origins of Regional Policy Institutions: Private Capital Seeking a Route Out of Crisis in the 1920s and 1930s

Over a period of less than twenty years, capitalist interests in north east England succeeded in bringing about two critical and related developments: the definition of the north east as a region, and as a particular sort of 'problem region', and the shaping of emergent institutional state forms to address those problems which embodied the transition from a liberal to interventionist mode of regulation as an integral part of creating a new governmentality regarding relationships between capital and the state and the objects of state policy (Carney and Hudson 1978; Hudson 1989; Hudson 2006). Major firms based in the region devised clear political strategies to create and seek to administer new institutional arrangements and forms of state policy to underpin their interests and to enroll other key social forces in the region—notably major trade unions—into a hegemonic project that was represented as being in the regional interest, as serving the interests of all people resident in the region rather than simply specific private interests. Thus, the region was to become institutionalized in a particular way. Furthermore, this was a shift in the dominant conception of governmentality that was to have wider consequences as regions became the objects of specific central government regional policies.

The dominant mode of regulation in the north east in the four decades from the 1870s was firmly grounded in liberal politics that gave primacy to the market as the key insitution steering the trajectory of economic development in the region, restricting the role of the state to the establishment, maintenance, and regulation of markets (Moore 1974). However, these arrangements came under pressure from the mid-1880s. Increasingly, the existing mode of regulation became untenable, as the practices of governmentality in which it was grounded became fragile and contested. These pressures intensified in the depression of the 1920s.

The economy of the Great Northern Coalfield was dominated by interlocking coal combines, capital groupings that had the bulk of their capital 'fixed' within the region and that were interconnected via varied forms of interfirm and intra-regional collaboration (Carney, Hudson, and Lewis 1977; Hudson 1989).[2] These locational ties profoundly restricted their attempts to cope with the slump and depression of the interwar period. From 1921, the boom conditions that had prevailed for several years suddenly evaporated, especially in key sectors of the regional economy dependent upon export markets, such as coal, steel, and shipbuilding, affecting all the main companies in the region. Locked into a liberal governmentality, the majority of combine interests perceived the problem as the distortion of 'normal trade' by the war. Consequently, they saw the solution as cutting wages and raising the number of hours worked and reasserting the role of markets as the key institution steering the regional economy. This policy was relentlessly implemented, resulting in chronic mass unemployment. In the Liberal world this could only happen because the cuts were not severe enough. Thus, the failure of the policy in practice resulted in its intensification.

However, these failures were accompanied by an active search for solutions and institutional arrangements more appropriate to the new conditions, especially after the general strike of 1926 when the dangers to social stability of singleminded wage cutting were amply demonstrated (especially to noncoal combine capitalist interests: Gilbert 1976, chapters 10 and 11). A variety of institutional and policy innovations was explored but, in practice, made things worse. Influential members of combines in the north east were appalled at the damage done to their interests (economic and political) by the inadequacies of the existing and alternative institutional arrangements and the resultant politics of reaction that were set in motion in the 1920s.

By the early 1930s the liberal mode of regulation and the conception of governmentality in which it was embedded, predicated on the institutional primacy of the market as a steering mechanism, were shattered but it was unclear as to what might replace them. By the mid-1930s, however, there was evidence of an emergent alternative governmentality and a considerable commitment in the north east to search for a new mode of regulation, encompassing new institutions and policies, to explore the possibilities for capital in selective state intervention and protectionism to defend 'regional interests'. From an early stage, Chambers of Commerce had begun to explore policy options that prefigured a change in the dominant mode of regulation in the region (and beyond), seeking to attract inward investment to the area and seeing increased state involvement as part of the solution rather than as a problem. Since the capital represented in the Chambers was mainly tied up *within the region*, they realized the possibilities of representing *their* problems as a *regional* problem and seeking to resolve them as such. The companies comprising the combines could argue the need to ensure that conditions for continued capital accumulation in the region were reproduced, while representing this as in the regional interest. Consequently, they sought to construct a new governmentality, incorporating fresh institutions and an interventionist mode of regulation that would redefine the relationship between capital and state, define the region as an object of regional policy, accord a central role to the state in attracting new industries, and install the representatives of the combines as key actors in the new institutional arrangements and organizations that would administer the new regional policies.

By the mid-1930s, therefore, combine and allied interests had successfully prosecuted a political strategy that made the case for radically different institutional arrangements and policies and new organizations at national and regional levels to implement the latter. The establishment of a Commissioner for the Special Areas in England and Wales in 1934 signaled that national government accepted the need for a major policy shift, defining and representing 'Special Areas' as objects of state policy. Within the region, the formation in 1935 of the North East Development Board (NEDB) was an equally significant organizational innovation as the institutional architecture of the region was redrawn. The initial aim of the organization was to allow '. . . the exchange of opinions and concerted action on nonparty lines by representatives of a great variety of interests who have no other common meeting ground.' As such, the Board sought to broaden the class basis of support for the new regional development policies and construct it on a regionalist basis. By 1938, its membership included several Labour Members of Parliament, many local authority representatives and several trade unionists and members of the Industrial Advisory Council as the NEDB claimed the right to speak for the region and promote its interests.

The policy tentatively adopted by the NEDB was elaborated in 1943 by the Northern Industrial Group (NIG)—composed of essentially the same industrial interests and employers that had formed the NEDB, together with some major trade unionists. The Group was formed to discuss the problems that would arise on the 'reconversion' from a war-time to a peace-time economy in the region. The NIG's 1943 publication *Considerations Affecting Post-War Employment in the North East* set out an elaborate program that assumed that state intervention would be necessary for the short-period reconversion of the regional economy to peace-time production. Indeed, it assumed that such intervention *ought* to occur and be instrumental in achieving economic and social ends, not least by attracting inward investment to diversify the economy and help guarantee 'full employment' in the region and help stem out-migration from it. The Group also had a clear view as to the form that such state intervention ought to take, based upon the wartime experience of its members who had held positions of executive power in the state apparatus. These experiences further increased support for the transition to an interventionist mode of regulation of the economic and social life in the region. This remarkable shift from the old 'Liberal' fear of state intervention, with capital calling for new institutional arrangements and a new interventionist mode of regulation, reflected the confidence of its private sector proponents that they could shape the activities of the state to their own requirements while representing these as in the general regional interest.

The NIG elaborated its position in its November 1944 *Memorandum on the Government White Paper on Employment Policy*, setting out its policy as to how the proposed 'Development Areas' should be administered. The White Paper suggested that in Development Areas there would be regionally organized branches of central government departments concerned with industrial location policy. The Group *Memorandum* responded to these proposals as follows: 'We would like to emphasize strongly that success depends upon quick decision and that this will not be obtained unless the various Government Departments in Whitehall delegate full authority to their regional representatives . . . '. However, this administrative decentralization would be ineffective unless other changes were made. The Group considered it 'to be of vital importance that the Government regional organization should have effective executive responsibility' and that such an organization should

> '. . . maintain close contact with and be advised by a parallel group representing employers, employees and other interests in the area. The NIG and the North East Development Association *because of their widely representative character* and the work which they are already carrying out, can advise in many ways any Government regional organization which may be established'.
>
> (NIG 1944: 11, emphasis added)

This self-interestedly proposed that the NIG and NEDA became key organizations in the new institutional order and in implementing and administering the new regional policies.

This remarkable change in the conception of the most appropriate governmentality clearly reflected the perception by the NIG that it had successfully prosecuted political strategies that secured the interests of private capital in the north east, and, in doing so, had succeeded in defining these as synonymous with the general regional interest. The enrollment of trade union leaders and Labour Members of Parliament into the coalition reflected their perception, grounded in a reformist Labourist politics, that this offered the best (or perhaps more accurately least bad and only possible) option of securing employment for their members and constituents. Seeking to create a sense of a shared regional interest involved attempting to ensure that the 'spatial reaches' of economic, political, and cultural processes coalesced to form the boundaries of the region—or at least were widely perceived to do so—conferring a distinctive and shared north-eastern identity to those that lived within these common boundaries. Moreover, this establishment of a cross-class regionalist project had an enduring effect over the next sixty years on development policies in and for the region. It can be seen as the predecessor of a succession of regional plans and development strategies, grounded in a cross-class consensus as to what was 'good for the region', and administered by the 'usual suspects' within the state, private sector companies, and organizations and the trade unions, typically male and middle aged (e.g. see Hudson 1989; Robinson et al. 2000).

Crucially, however, these remained regionalizations of central government policies and initiatives, an administrative devolution rather than one that devolved the power to act, the power to decide on policy, and commensurate resources to enable regional organizations to implement *their* policy choices (see Hadjimichalis and Hudson 2003). Insofar as business concerns in the region felt that they were able to secure their interests via these institutional arrangements, they were happy to rest with administrative devolution, as were those in the local political elites and dominant strata, who were content with these arrangements—not least as they helped secure their own power and influence within the region. However, the lack of political devolution and meaningful transfer of powers and resources to make policy and decisions within the region continued to rankle with other regional politicians and fractions of political strata in the region.

Nationalized Industries as Dominant Regional Institutions from 1940s to 1980s

I have argued elsewhere that for some three decades from the mid-1940s the north east of England can be understood as a quintessentially state-managed region, with an unprecedentedly high degree of involvement of the institution of the state in regulating economic and social life in the region, linked to a particular—weak and indicative—conception of planning (Hudson 1989). The nationalized industries were pivotal organizations in these institutional arrangements as the uneven impacts of a national industrial policy shaped the trajectory of the region's economy, although the timings and specific motives for nationalization varied among industries (Hudson 1986). Above all, the National Coal Board (NCB) became *the* dominant and decisive institution shaping economy, labor and housing markets, and civil society over much of the region. Not least, this was because of the political significance of the National Union of Mineworkers in the politics of Labourism, as well as the economic and labor market significance of coal mining in the region.

Soon after its formation in 1947, the NCB began work on a long-term plan, to be based on detailed surveys of production possibilities in each coalfield and a careful examination of individual projects for colliery modernization and expansion. By 1949 the final task of allocating investment and fixing a long-term production target for each coalfield was well-advanced. This was confirmed in relation to the northeast coalfield in the coal industry forecasts put forward in *The North East Development Area (NEDA) Plan* (Pepler and MacFarlane 1949). Although the NCB did not wish it to be known even to the restricted audience that would have access to this plan, these forecasts were clearly taken from its own forecasting documents, prepared in 1948. The NCB distinguished three phases in the projected reorganization of the industry:

(a) 'An immediate very short-term policy of labour recruitment to expand production before increased output through reorganization [could] begin to be effective.'

(b) 'A middle phase of intensive reorganization' to raise output per man shift to 30 cwt.

(c) 'A long-term phase ... during which much of the remaining coal reserves in the older mining areas [might] become exhausted.'

Probable future changes in different parts of the northeast coalfield were also indicated in the NEDA Plan, again taken directly from NCB policy documents. For example, coal mining employment in Durham was forecast to decline by 21,000, with losses mainly concentrated in North West Durham. In the longer term (to 1978), the NCB estimated that employment in West Durham would fall by a further 7,500 and in East Durham by 2,500, with 'comparatively stable conditions' expected in Northumberland (p. 54). These changes were disaggregated to the level of individual collieries—information that the NCB was already denying and was subsequently systematically to deny to county councils in their role as planning authorities: for example, to Durham County Council. Thus, in 1946, Durham County Council Planning Department recognized serious defects in the system through which the NCB released information to local authorities and raised this matter with the regional controller of the Ministry of Fuel and Power (DCCPC, u, 29.10.46, item 7).

The 1948 forecasts and investment intentions of the NCB thus implied that coalfield areas could more or less unproblematically be classified either as 'stable long-life' areas or as 'declining' areas. This dual classification relied heavily upon the magnitude of physical reserves, then considered an appropriate criterion for a resource such as coal, in accord with a national priority to maximize coal output. However, it failed to consider possible changes in the energy market, falling demand for coal, and a switch to 'economic' rather than 'physical' criteria to determine the life of a colliery. Nevertheless, this classification was of great significance. As well as being adopted in *NEDA Plan,* by the Northern Region Distribution of Industry Panel, it was also incorporated in the county development plans devised by the planning authorities in the coalfield areas (see Durham County Council 1951; Northumberland County Council 1951). Thus, the colliery classification system became incorporated as

an *assumption* upon which other planning policies were based. This, coupled with the priority given to maximizing coal output, had profound implications for the northeast coalfield (and for others).
The NEDA Plan argued that:

> ...from the national point of view, with coal the most precious and urgently needed of industrial raw materials, *to introduce into mining areas, without surplus male labour, male employing industries housed in up-to-date factories and able to offer pleasant work at good wages, would inevitably attract men away from the mines with disastrous consequences for coal production.* (p56, emphasis added).

Accordingly the Plan was based:

> ...on the assumption that no appreciable volume of alternative male employment should be deliberately introduced into stable long-life mining districts which are unlikely to possess much surplus male labour.

It is virtually certain that this assumption was adopted at the insistence both of the NCB and the Ministry of Fuel and Power, the dominant organizations within the institution of the state in relation to the fate of the coal industry and the coalfields. Clearly, the NCB had a strong interest in controlling the introduction of new industries, even into areas where a future contraction of employment was anticipated. The Board wanted to retain existing labor forces in all parts of the coalfield until demand could be met from reconstructed collieries. In the final analysis, the Labour Government also had to support the NCB's approach as the only route to guaranteeing coal output. It was impossible substantially to raise the wages of miners or to improve working conditions and labor productivity through investment in new production technologies, since these would have clashed with other Government economic policy objectives.

Equally, at local level within the coalfields with county councils, usually controlled by the Labour Party, considerable support for policies of maximizing coal output was generally assured. As early as 1946, for example, the prioritization of coal production had been accepted by Durham County Council Planning Committee and by the Planning Department. A report to the Committee (DCCPC, 29.10.46, item 7, emphasis added) pointed out that as long as there was a shortage of mining labor

> Government policy indicates that industries which are mainly male employing will be brought only into those areas with a definite need for immediate male employment *as distinct from diversification only.*

The point that competitive industries should not be encouraged in mining areas to such an extent as to create a shortage of male labor in the mines was periodically reiterated in Planning Committee discussions, reports, and Minutes. For example, in the context of the draft town map for

Houghton-Ie-Spring, an area considered to be a 'stable long-life' part of the coalfield, it was argued as follows:

> It has frequently been said that the main weakness of an area such as [Houghton-le-Spring] lies in the almost complete dependence upon one industry-coalmining. However, the National Coal Board has made it clear that as far as can be foreseen, the employment level in coal mining in the area should not fall much below its present level. In some senses, therefore, this high degree of reliance on coalmining does not present a real problem....
>
> *In view of the importance of the coal mining industry to the nation as a whole it might be considered dangerous to propose any major diversification as this would almost certainly mean the attraction away from the mines of the young recruits so vitally necessary to the industry.*
>
> (DCCPC, u, 14.8.50, page 2, emphasis added)

As these examples make clear, Durham County Council clearly accepted the overriding national importance of meeting coal production targets as a constraint on its own activities as a planning authority. This was partly because the NCB suggested that the 'short-term' policy of expanding production and 'protecting' its labor force in Durham would stabilize employment in the mines. The policy of the Board was consequently to maximize new recruitment, partly because of the high turnover associated with out-migration from areas such as West Durham.

As well as maintaining its labor force, the NCB was also concerned to preserve the reserves identified in the Ministry of Fuel and Power's 1944–5 surveys and in its own 1947–9 surveys (NCB 1947–9). Because of this, it became involved in most decisions concerning new industrial and housing developments on the coalfield considered by the county councils as planning authorities. In Durham, for example, it had already been agreed that the County Council Planning Department's searches for industrial sites would be conducted in cooperation with the Ministry of Fuel and Power (DCCPC, 29.10.46, item 7). As a result, the NCB, allied to the Ministry, could reject proposals—say for new industrial estates—because they entailed an unacceptable sterilization of coal. The Board also refused to guarantee the stability of proposed sites since the future pattern of coal extraction had yet to be decided.

The Board's power to control the introduction of new industries was frequently used. In North West Durham, for example, from 1946 onwards, lengthy delays in establishing new sites for industrial development occurred because the Board continually rejected proposed sites. The Planning Department's report on North West Durham in 1948 (Report of the Durham County Planning Officer 1948) claimed that there was serious difficulty in finding 'sufficiently large and flat sites which would be free from subsidence dangers or which would not involve the immediate sterilization of valuable coking coal reserves'. Perhaps the best-known case where a clash emerged between the

NCB's goal of not sterilizing coal reserves and other development proposals is that of Peterlee New Town in East Durham. This was resolved at considerable expense to the town's development corporation by constructing much of the housing in the town on concrete rafts to counter subsidence from mining (see, e.g. Steele 1962; Leishman 1971; Robinson 1978, 1983). In general, however, such solutions were not available to local authorities, and the interests of the dominant NCB prevailed.

Clearly Durham County Council was simultaneously dependent upon and subservient to NCB and central Government goals and interests—a position it shared with other planning authorities in coalfield areas. The NCB could block specific industrial development proposals that were central to County Council settlement policies. It also refused to release vital information on the future of individual collieries that the Council needed to devise appropriate planning policies of its own. Thus, the NCB had demonstrably and visibly become the key institution shaping economic development, housing, and planning in County Durham—and was acknowledged and accepted as such by the institutions of local government and other central government departments. The dominance of the NCB only began to weaken as coal production began to decline from the late 1950s in the face of growing competition from imported oil, and later natural gas and nuclear power. As output and employment fell, the economic and labor market bases of the institutional dominance of the NCB began to wane. Even so, it remained an influential institution in the region until the 1980s and the Thatcherite assault on the nationalized industries.

The Demise of the Nationalized Industries and the Resurgence of Markets as the Dominant Institution Shaping the Region ... Again

I have argued above that the state was centrally involved both in creating and reinforcing lock-in to ensure path-dependent development between the late 1920s and mid-1970s and that, within the north east, the dominant state institution was the National Coal Board for almost forty years from the late 1940s. Subsequently, the emphasis in state policies switched to seeking to erode such lock-in to facilitate new developmental trajectories, breaking the power of formerly dominant institutions and putting others into positions of dominance. This has involved seeking to address the problems posed to such a transition, especially in terms of the attitudes and behavior of people in the region as part of neoliberal supply-side approaches.

By the mid-1970s it was clear that the social democratic 'One Nations' politics that had been nationally dominant for the previous thirty years was an increasingly problematic project as economic growth rates fell, unemployment rose, and fears of a fiscal crisis of the state arose. Put another way, the previously dominant mode of regulation and dominant institutional arrangements became increasingly fragile, stretched to breaking point. This in turn led to a search for a new approach, which was encapsulated in the neoliberal 'Two Nations' Thatcherite project, centered on redefining relationships between state, economy, and civil society, reining back the scope of state involvement in economy and society and restoring the market to a preeminent place as the institution steering the trajectory of economic development. The UK state was at the forefront of making this transition, and while this was given particular impetus by the Thatcher governments of the 1980s, it was continued in the subsequent era of 'New Labour' to create a UK-specific variant among the 'many national capitalisms' (Schmidt 2002) of neoliberal late modernity.

As a central part of this, the nationalized industries were dismantled. First, they were subject to rationalization as their formerly sheltered markets were opened to the disciplining effects of international markets. Having been drastically slimmed down, they were then privatized, one after another. The combined effects of rationalization, privatization, and further postprivatization rationalization under the continuing impress of global market forces were to produce substantial cuts in capacity and employment. This had strongly regionally differentiated effects (Beynon et al. 1991).

In the north east of England, employment in coal mining, iron and steel production, and shipbuilding, fell to around 10,000 by the end of the twentieth century—fifty years earlier it had stood at around 350,000. Put another way, the nationalized industries had ceased—in dramatic fashion—to be the dominant institutions shaping economy and society in the region while the emphasis switched from even weak attempts at planning to strategies predicated on the assumption that there was no alternative to adapting to the forces of globalization and global markets as the dominant institution. High levels of unemployment created labor market conditions attractive to certain sorts of branch plant investment, as companies could be very selective as to who they recruited and retained—for example, Nissan had over 33,000 applications for 600 jobs advertised in its auto assembly plant in the early 1990s (Hudson 1995). Although Nissan remains in the region after some twenty years, many others remained for much less time (in extreme cases not even opening the factory).

The national *political* shift from predominantly social-democratic to a neoliberal politics was also reflected in the north east in the evolution in emphasis from plans (e.g. Teesside County Borough Council 1972) via strategic plans (Northern Regional Strategy Team 1997) to strategies (OneNorthEast 2000). This has entailed a shift from a belief in the possibility, legitimacy, and validity of socially—progressive redistributive planning via the institution of the state and central state action to one that embraces the institution of the market as the main economic steering mechanism. This had definite implications for people in the north east as the state sought to cut back the extent of its direct engagement with economy and society there and, not entirely successfully, to encourage greater mobility in the labor market and encourage entrepreneurial behavior.

The shift to neoliberalism has also involved redefining the geometry of state power, with a decentralization of responsibility for regional development issues to the regional level within the state. Thus, the region became socially constituted as an active subject in seeking to resolve the regional problem. Rather than regional policies designed and administered by the central state, there is now a more complex multilevel system of governance that conjoins EU, national, regional, and subregional in a more complex geometry. However, these new arrangements devolve greater responsibilities to regional and subregional levels for dealing with issues of regional economic development and regeneration. This has been emphasized within the region by the creation of the OneNorthEast Regional Development Agency, the four subregional partnerships to which it devolves most of its budget, and the local strategic partnerships now being established across the region under the leadership of local authorities (Liddle and Townsend 2002). However, many of these new institutions—not least OneNorthEast—were, or are, central government appointed QUANGOS. These unelected organizations have generated new forms of 'democratic deficit' as they are politically unaccountable within the region, with evident dangers in undermining the credibility of the case for devolving power as part of a new governmentality through which to address regional development problems (Beynon, Hudson, and Sadler 1994). Moreover, they often sit uneasily with neoliberal rhetoric as to the preeminent role of the market as the key institution steering the region's economic development trajectory.

The emergence of Task Forces is a further characteristic policy response of the new neoliberal governmentality and, more particularly, of the particular politics of New Labour to create new temporary institutions to tackle place, and/or industry-specific problems of economic decline. There are marked similarities between such Task Forces and the 'project teams' that have come to characterize much of the contemporary economy (Grabher 2002). Such Task Forces have exploded in number and have become endemic in north east England—though not only there. They have been established as ad hoc bodies intended to deal flexibly and rapidly with specific policy problems, typically associated with the (un)expected decline of a particular industry or sector (including coal mining, clothing, electronics, steel, textiles) and its consequences on the places in which it was formerly concentrated (Pike 2002). Others seek to arrest or reverse decline—for example the Teesside Chemical Initiative (Chapman 2003)—for reasons that are explicable in terms of subregional politics and the difficulties of imagining Teesside without chemical production, rather than a more realistic assessment of the global political-economy of chemicals production.

The membership of these bodies consists of a mix of private and public sector representatives, typically drawn from a cast of 'usual suspects'. Self-defined key players in the region find new niches in these partnerships from which to exercise power and preserve their own influence (Robinson et al. 2000), often drawn together around notions of partnership and the perception of a shared regional interest (as they first were in the 1930s). They can be characterized as nonstatutory (i.e. non-QUANGO) and multiagency organizations, with selected and defined membership, with initially an indeterminate but always temporary lifespan. Typically, however, like the earlier QUANGOS, they are opaque, unaccountable, closed off to wider political and public scrutiny, with the hand of central government often prominent and with limited links to, and coordination with, the actions of other public policy bodies. Fundamentally, they are designed to mop up and paper over the consequences of economic decline, a combination of sticking plaster and sponge. They symbolize the transition from a concern with planning to one with strategy, understood as developing ad hoc ways of coping with the consequences of unplanned, unexpected, and emergent changes in economic circumstances in a region marked by long-term structural economic decline.

As illustrated by many of the Task Forces, decentralization to the regional level has also often involved greater reliance on institutions within civil society acting together (in partnership) with regional, subregional and/or local state organizations. The notion of 'partnership' and collaborative working at, and between, these levels is important, although not all partners have equal power and influence in the partnership. In particular, many partnerships remain dominated, or led, by parts of the state as the preeminent institution. Even so, partnership signals a blurring of the boundaries between market, state and civil society as processes of governance partially replace those of government. Allied to this, there has been a discernible tendency toward 'the community' as both subject and object of intraregional policies to tackle uneven development. This in turn has often been linked to an emphasis upon the 'third sector', or social economy, as the route to tackling regional problems and problems of intraregional regeneration, encouraging the creation of new institutional forms beyond the formal economy (Amin, Cameron, and Hudson 2002).

The turn to the third sector signals recognition that state policy attempts to break unwanted forms of lock-in, for example, by encouraging greater labor mobility and entrepreneurial activity via establishing SMEs, have largely been ineffectual. People wish to remain in their places but not to become entrepreneurs in the formal mainstream economy. The growing focus upon the social economy is a recognition both of this and the fact that increasingly large swathes of the territory of regions such as north east England now fall outside the decisive circuits of capital. They have been eviscerated by capital flight and effectively abandoned by the state beyond a residual commitment to maintain a minimum level of welfare provision there. However, it is precisely the impoverished condition of such places that militates against the development of a vibrant 'alternative' social economy, amplified by a more general state suspicion of potentially 'subversive' social economies such as Local Exchange Trading Systems (LETS). Thus the turn to the social economy represents an attempt to reconcile tensions between immanent accumulation and rationality crises on the one hand and legitimation crises on the other as both capital and the national state lose interest in the region as a space for the production of surplus value. In its turn, however, it creates political tensions at local and regional levels as the developmental limits of the social economy become clear. For example, over much of north east England, the social economy is most notable by its absence, particularly in those areas in which it is needed most (Amin, Cameron, and Hudson 2002), and where it does develop tends to reproduce the socioeconomic inequalities of the mainstream within it (Bowring 1999).

Clearly, there has been an explosion of new and more-or-less compatible institutional forms in north east England, within and beyond the boundaries of the state, as part of the transition to neoliberalism and its associated form of governmentality. Many of these have originated in innovations by central government. It is important to emphasize, however, that the creation of such new institutions did not simply involve changes imposed externally upon the region. There were social forces within the region arguing in favor of such changes, with local politicians wanting greater decentralization of power and resources to their authorities and an emergent small but vociferous lobby seeking a regional assembly and much greater regional autonomy. In principle, these three levels are intended to produce a seamless web of 'joined up' socioeconomic development and regeneration policies in the region, with a heavy emphasis upon 'cluster' policies in economic development, seeking to develop complementary place-based clusters of firms and state institutions. Practice deviates somewhat from this principle, however—and there is scant recognition that successful cluster policies could engender precisely the forms of lock-in that were previously seen as a diagnostic feature of the regional problem.

Conclusions

In his account, Boyer emphasizes that the strict definition of the concept of 'supermodality' imposes strong limits as to its range of valid applicability and it is certainly the case that there has been and is a definite absence of evidence of supermodality among institutions in north east England. Equally, it cannot be claimed that institutions in the north east are complementry or coherent, easily coexisting, or interacting due to identical or common principles. Although there is some evidence of isomorphism—for example, as a result of public sector institutions mimicking private sector firms and markets—more generally institutions apparently operate according to differing and often incompatible principles, and this applies as much to institutions within the public sector as it does to differences between private and public sector institutions.

On the other hand, it is more defensible to claim that institutions in the north east are clustered and, to a degree at least, compatible—not least, they have managed to coexist and coevolve over many years, although not necessarily as intended by those responsible for creating and managing them, providing a degree of institutional 'glue' and helping generate a degree of stability in the social and economic life of the region. Institutional innovation has been a trial-and-error process of learning-by-doing in an emergent environment. As Coriat and Dosi (2002: 96–7) suggest, 'aggregate phenomena (e.g. regularities in the growth process or in industrial structures and so forth) are "explained" as emergent properties. They are the collective outcome of far-from-equilibrium interactions and heterogeneous learning'. These properties of emergence mean that there have often been unintended (and to some, unwanted) consequences. Often the result has been seemingly chaotic and competitive relations between institutions rather than smooth coordination. In part this is because there are strong power asymmetries in the relationships between these institutions, with important effects in shaping the region's development trajectory, its place in wider spatial divisions of labor, and the anatomy of sociospatial inequality within it. At different times, the dominant institutions have been private sector firms, nationalized industries, and the market as a space of decentralized economic decision-making in which actors pursue their rational interests (as shaped by the state).

Thus, while there is some evidence of coevolution among institutions—or perhaps more accurately, coincidence in temporal development trajectories—the forms of interinstitutional relationships in the north east are at the weaker end of the spectrum specified by Boyer, essentially relations of association and coexistence in the same time/space rather than relations of strong causality or necessary dependence. This conclusion has some powerful contemporary relevance in the context of debates about relationships between political devolution, and devolved regional government and regional economic success. It strongly suggests that claims as to direct causal links from former to the latter are likely to be misconceived and that regional economic revival will require more than some redefinition of the regional institutional landscape. This in turn raises important questions as to the likely adequacy and stability of the version of neoliberal regulation that has been emerging in north east England in recent years and the economic development models for the region that it embraces. There is little convincing evidence of this leading to economic revival. While there is some evidence of localized economic regeneration (e.g. around some business services and consumption on parts of the banks of the river Tyne in Gateshead and Newcastle), much of the region remains blighted by high levels of multiple deprivation, as the Office of the Deputy Prime Minister's (2004) *Index of Multiple Deprivation* only too graphically reveals. There is little evidence of the new institutional arrangements facilitating the emergence of an 'enterprise culture' and 'enterprise economy' in the region while it has ceased to be attractive as a location for inward investment in routine 'branch plant' operations by multinational capital in the face of competition from central and eastern Europe and south east Asia, especially China. Indeed, the plethora of new regional and subregional institutions, typically under close central Government supervision and monitoring, sits uneasily with the neoliberal rhetoric of the market as the preeminent institution for regulation of economic life in the region and steering the region's development strategy.

In conclusion, then, what judgment can be reached as to the adequacy of the new emergent neoliberal mode of regulation? Does it possess the coherence required to stimulate regional economic revival, grounded in a robust analysis of the relationships between regional institutions and regional economic performance, or is it based on a flawed and partial analysis of the relationships between regional institutions and regional economic performance and so doomed to failure in the medium-to-long term? Reflecting on the available evidence, the most reasonable interpretation may well be that the varied regional institutional innovations of the last decade or so constitute part of an incoherent and unfolding trial-and-error 'coping' or crisis-management strategy that seeks to contain the worst aspects of processes of economic restructuring within 'politically tolerable' limits in the short-term. Put another way, they constitute a series of relatively improvised actions located around a 'broad orientation'[3]—but an orientation that nonetheless sets quite precise limits as to what is permissible. One consequence of all this is a growing disillusionment with the political process in general and with yet more proposals for regional institutional innovation in particular, as central Government continues to use the region as a laboratory for its experiments in regional governance and regulation. This was sharply emphasized in the November 2004 referendum on proposals for an elected Regional Assembly. Only around half those eligible to vote did so; those who did rejected the proposals by an overwhelming 4:1 majority. This suggests that many residents of the north east were far from enamored with yet more proposals for regional institutional innovation—at least in the form of the proposed elected Regional Assembly—as the route to regional economic revival and that the basis of popular support for the tentatively emergent neoliberal mode of regulation of which it was a central element is at best weak. What will now emerge remains to be seen.

Acknowledgments

My thanks to Phil James and Geoff Wood for helpful comments on earlier drafts of this chapter. As always, responsibility for its remaining shortcomings rest with me.

References

Amin, A., Cameron, A., and Hudson, R. (2002). *Placing the Social Economy.* London: Routledge.

Beynon, H., Hudson, R., and Sadler, D. (1994). *A Place Called Teesside: A Locality in a Global Economy.* Edinburgh: Edinburgh University Press.

Bowring, F. (1999). 'LETS: An Eco-socialist Alternative', *New Left Review*, 232: 91–111.

Boyer, R. (2005). 'Institutional Complementarity', *This volume.*

Carney, J. and Hudson, R. (1978). 'Capital, Politics and Ideology: The North East of England, 1870–', *Antipode*, 10: 64–78.

—— Hudson, R., and Lewis, J. (1977). 'Coal Combines and Interregional Uneven Development in the UK', in P. Batey and D. Massey (eds.), *London Papers in Regional Sciences.* London: Pion.

Chapman, K. (2003). 'From "Growth Centre" to "Cluster": Restructuring, Regional Development and the Teesside Chemical Industry', *Paper presented to the International Workshop, The Restructuring of Old Industrial Areas in Europe and Asia'*, University of Bonn, 11–12 July.

Coriat, B. and Dosi, G. (2002). 'The Institutional Embeddedness of Economic Change: An Appraisal of the "Evolutionary" and "Regulationist" Research Programmemes', in G. Hodgson (ed.), *A Modern Reader in Institutional and Evolutionary Economics.* Cheltenham, UK: Elgar, pp. 95–123.

Durham County Council (1951). *County Development Plan.* Durham.

Durham County Council Planning Committee (1946). *Minutes*, 29 October, Item 7.

—— 1950. *Houghton le Spring Draft town* Map, 14 August.

Gilbert, M. (1976). *Winston S Churchill, volume 5*, 1922–39, Heinemann, London.

Grabher, G. (2002). 'The Project Ecology of Advertising: Tasks, Talents and Teams', *Regional Studies*, 36: 245–62.

Hadjimichalis, C. and Hudson, R. (2003). 'Networks, Regional Development and Democratic Control', Paper presented to the Aegean Seminar, 'Rethinking Radical Spatial Approaches', Naxos, 8–14 September.

Harvey, G. (1917). *Capitalism in the Northern Coalfield.* Newcastle on Tyne, UK: City Library.

Hudson, R. (1986). 'Nationalised Industry Policies and Regional Policies: The Role of the State in the Deindustrialisation and Reindustrialisation of Regions', *Society and Space*, 4: 7–28.

—— (1989). *Wrecking A Region.* London: Pion.

—— (1995). 'The Role of Foreign Investment', in L. Evans, P. Johnson, and B. Thomas (eds.), *Northern Region Economy: Progress and Prospects.* London: Cassell, 79–95.

—— (2006). 'Firms as Political Actors in Processes of Capital Accumulation and Regional Development', in M. Taylor and P. Oinas (eds.), *Conceptualising the Firm: Capabilities, Cultures and Coalitions.* Oxford: Oxford University Press, (forthcoming).

Leishman, A. D. H. (1971). *New Town Politics.* Unpublished MA dissertation, University of Durham.

Liddle, J. and Townsend, A. (2002). 'Reflections on the Development of Local Strategic Partnerships: Key Emerging Issues', *Paper presented to the Annual conference of the British Academy of Management,* September 9–11, London.

Moore, R. (1974). *Pitmen, Preachers and Politics.* Cambridge: Cambridge University Press.

National Coal Board (1947–9). *Annual Reports and Accounts.* London: Hobart House.

Northern Industrial Group (1943). *Considerations Affecting Post War Employment in the North East.* Newcastle on Tyne, UK: Literary and Philosophical Society.

—— (1944). *Memorandum on the Government White Paper on Employment Policy.* Newcastle on Tyne, UK: Literary and Philosophical Society.

Northern Regional Strategy Team (1997). *Strategic Plan for the Northern Region, Volumes 1–5.* London: HMSO.

Northumberland County Council (1951). *County Development Plan,* Newcastle on Tyne.

Office of the Deputy Prime Minister's 2004. *Index of Multiple Deprivation.* London: Bressendon House.

OneNorthEast (2000). *Regional Economic Strategy: Fulfilling Our Potential.* Newcastle on Tyne, UK: ONE North East.

Pepler, G. and MacFarlane, P. W. (1949). *North East Development Area Plan.* Interim report presented to the Minister for Town and Country Planning.

Pike, A. (2002). 'Task Forces and the Organisation of Economic Development: The Case of the North East Region of England', *Environment and Planning C,* 20: 717–39.

Report of the Durham County Planning Officer, 1948. *Preliminary Survey of the Employment Prospects of North West Durham.* Durham: County Hall.

Robinson, F. (1978). *Peterlee: A Study in New Town Development,* Unpublished PhD thesis, University of Durham.

—— (1983) 'State planning of spatial change: compromise and contradiction in Peterlee New Town,' in J. Anderson, S. Duncan and R. Hudson (eds.), Redundant Spaces in Cities and Regions. London: Academic press, 263–84.

—— Shaw, K., Dutton, J., Grainger, P., Hopwood, B., and Williams, S. (2000). *Who Runs the North East ... Now?* Newcastle on Tyne, UK: Millfield House Foundation.

Schmidt, V. A. (2002). *The Future of European Capitalisms.* Oxford: Oxford University Press.

Steele, D. B. (1962). *The Origins of Peterlee New Town,* Unpublished MA thesis, University of Durham.

Teesside County Borough Council (1972). *Teesside Structure Plan: Report of Survey.* Middlesbrough: Teesside County Borough Council.

6

Financial Change and European Employment Relations

John Grahl

Introduction

This chapter explores the changing consequences of financialization in liberal market economies, the effects of its gradual penetration into cooperative market economies, and the possibilities for new forms of institutional hybridity. In doing so, it suggests, first, that the financial changes taking place in many countries have been widely misunderstood and, second, that the consequences of these changes for employment relations, although often adverse, are not necessarily so.

Aspects of Financial Change

What is sometimes referred to as the 'financialization' (for one analysis see Froud, Johal, and Williams 2002) of socioeconomic systems involves a number of phenomena. Three economic aspects of financial change are frequently referred to; it is important to distinguish between them. (There are also important cultural and linguistic aspects—such as the widespread perception that financial institutions and financial markets are central locations in society today.)

The Growth of Finance

First, there is simply the growth of finance and of the financial sector. There is more finance about in that economic agents today hold more financial claims on each other than in the past, relative to GDP as a measure of economic development. Expenditures, both for investment and consumption, are more likely to be supported by credit or other forms of finance than in the past. The balance sheets of households and businesses carry a higher level of both financial assets and liabilities relative to real assets such as buildings or equipment.

This expansion of finance involves an expansion of the financial sector, of the corporations and other institutions which collect monetary resources from the public and channel them either to the agents who will use them or onto the financial markets. This is now a larger sector by all measures—the percentage of the workforce it employs, the share of national income for which it accounts, and the size of the financial flows and financial assets and liabilities involved. This expansion goes along with the expansion of closely related activities such as real estate: some commentators speak of a spreading FIRE (finance, insurance, real estate).

Disintermediation and Securitization

The second aspect of change is in the nature of finance. Financial markets, for company shares, bonds and other debt instruments, foreign exchange (FX), and derivatives, such as options and futures based on these assets, play an increasingly important role in the financial system; at the same time classical bank finance—the advance of credit from a bank, based on the deposits it receives from the public, is becoming relatively less important in quantitative terms. This shift, sometimes referred to as *disintermediation*, is linked to a liberalization of finance which allows investors in securities and issuers of securities to operate in many countries. The move away from classical bank intermediation should not be regarded as implying a decline in the importance of banks as institutions. In fact, the big banks are the key players in the whole transformation. Although deposit-taking and bank credit today make up a smaller proportion of the banks' activities, they are involved in every aspect of the security market-based finance which has emerged in recent decades. The banks issue securities on their own behalf and on behalf of corporate customers; they make markets in many securities; and provide many of the services linked to security trading, such as investment analysis, fund management, and the settlement of transactions.

This change in the nature of finance, however, also involves the rise of other financial corporations to rival the banks—these are the institutional investors: pension funds, insurance companies, and investment companies such as unit trusts in Britain or mutual investment companies in the United States. In classical bank intermediation the provider of funds, the depositor, has a claim on the bank, not on the borrower who actually uses the funds. He or she relies on the solidity of the bank to make the claim safe and liquid. In the security-trading financial system which has to some extent displaced classical bank intermediation, the provider of funds relies on the existence of a deep and wide market in securities to secure the same objectives.

In the 'secondary' markets, which account for the vast bulk of security trading, investors are able to liquidate their positions by selling to other investors. The 'primary' markets, where new securities are issued, are very much smaller—but it is usually price movements on secondary markets which set the terms on which corporations or governments can raise new money on the primary markets.

It has been known theoretically for a long time that portfolio diversification can reduce some of the risks of investment for a given expected rate of return. In practice, effective diversification is costly and only the richest investors could achieve it on an individual basis. The institutional investors (Davis and Steil 2001) offer the same advantage to the middle classes by aggregating thousands of small positions into an overall portfolio. But a savings plan with an institutional investor differs from a bank deposit in that it is the customer not the intermediary institution, who, in the first instance, bears the risk of the investment.

This process of *disintermediation* or *securitization* is not easy to explain. Why did one form of finance expand at the cost of the other? A full answer will not be attempted here, but it is interesting to see that this process might be *cumulative*: the ease with which securities can be traded, and hence the liquidity of an investment in securities, depends crucially on the scale of the security market. Thus, if security-based finance secures an advantage over bank intermediation, that advantage will tend to increase over time.

High Interest Rates

The third aspect of 'financialization' which will be discussed is financial tension—the pressure of financial constraints on economic agents. The same era—roughly the last quarter of the twentieth century—which saw the growth of finance and the changes in financial structure which have been referred to—was also marked by exceptionally high interest rates and thus by extraordinary pressure on debtors and on agents seeking finance. The most catastrophic result of these tensions has been the third world debt crisis, still unresolved some twenty years after it struck. But there have been other victims—for example, the EU member states failed to find a clear common response to rising interest rates in the world economy, and this put their socioeconomic systems under enormous pressure: both Keynesian economic intervention and high welfare standards became very difficult to finance. Likewise, the pressure for downsizing and closures in their manufacturing sectors were, although not caused, greatly exacerbated by the cost of credit.

Because the era of financial transformation coincided in this way with that of very high interest rates many commentators have closely associated, or even identified, the two developments (e.g. Duménil and Lévy 2004). This is one source of the misunderstandings that will now be explored.

Financial Demonology

A stylized account will be attempted here of the interpretation of the financialization process within critical political economy. Most of the difficulties are caused not by errors, but by emphasizing rather contingent or medium-term aspects of processes which have a wider significance. Financial sectors today are seen as overblown and parasitical; their growth is explained by political decisions taken in error or under the pressure of interested parties; the increasing role of security markets is seen as sacrificing enterprise to speculation and strategic concepts of investment to the short-term; where security trading is not put down to speculation it is attributed to the equally dysfunctional behavior of security dealers themselves, swelling transactions to gain commission.

Such positions obviously affect the positions adopted in wider debates on globalization, since the understanding one forms of the global economy is conditioned by the way one views financial change.

None of these positions is false—in fact all of them can be easily documented and illustrated by gruesome episodes of malpractice and inefficiency. The parasitism, the speculation, the abuse of political power—all are facts. Nevertheless, if one interprets the entire range of financial phenomena in these terms, significant developments in the nature and functioning of capitalist economies may be underestimated.

From Tight to Easy Money

Not all these issues will be addressed here, but as a start, it can be pointed out that the era of high interest rates seems to have come to an end, and thus that the changes in financial structures cannot be seen as essentially dependent on exceptional tributes extracted from borrowers. The eighties and to a lesser extent the nineties were characterized by exceptionally intense financial pressures, which in themselves tended to swell the profits of the banks. These developments suggested that financial transformations could be seen as a 'revolt of the lenders'. Indeed, the reactions of wealthholders to the inflation of the seventies was a key moment of the transformation, but, it is becoming clear, not an essential feature of it.

It is more difficult than is sometimes assumed to identify the interests which are advanced by the financialization process. We could distinguish debtors (and other issuers) from creditors (and other investors) and both from intermediaries. The general tendency to identify financial change with financial tensions would make the creditors the big winners; but this view is not easily reconciled with the position of the United States as the world's major debtor. A focus on the most powerful institutions and intermediaries is perhaps more realistic, but globalization has meant that even the largest of these are subject to new competitive pressures—and it is easy to find casualties among them, such as Deutsche Bank, Crédit Lyonnais, or the Midland Bank, all of which came to grief in their international strategies. It is clear, again, that stock markets are subject to much more competitive pressure in the new financial regime.

In retrospect, there may have been two forces behind the era of very high interest rates. First, a flight of investors toward liquid assets, prompted by the decline in profitability in Western economies to the late seventies and the uncertainties which this induced. Second, and partly in consequence, the turn of macroeconomic policy toward monetary disinflation, which drove up nominal interest rates while bringing down inflation rates, and thus led to a sharp rise in real rates of interest.

This era may now be at an end,[4] so that the surplus of capital which has been latent in the world economy for several decades has now broken into the open. This clearly has implications for employment relations in that the massive rates of return which investors have sought in recent decades are becoming quite clearly impossible. (In fact, it is not only the fall in interest rates which is bringing down rates of return; it seems that the risk premium between bond and equity yields may also be coming under pressure.[5] This would be a consequence of the risk-reducing portfolio diversification made possible by globalization and brought about by the institutional investors.)

A Casino Economy?

A second widely held view of finance today is that it is dominated by 'speculation'. Of course, if speculation is defined in a very wide and loose sense this becomes true almost by definition; capitalism as such involves buying in order to sell but one does not usually interpret all capitalist enterprise as speculative. If one adopts a tighter definition of speculation as the adoption of an open position (long or short) in some asset in the expectation of a favorable movement (up or down) in that asset's price, then it is by no means clear that current financial activities are dominated by speculation. Speculation is always present in financial markets and may even be necessary to their effective functioning but it has not been shown to be the dominant feature of their recent expansion.[6]

Consider first the special case of FX, where the Tobinistas of the social movements deduce from the sheer scale of transactions that only speculation can be taking place. This is a simple error, although one which is at least partly to be explained by the absence of any coherent account of FX markets in the orthodox literature. A glance at the currencies which are traded should be enough to call the speculation hypothesis into question. A handful of currencies—the most stable—account for virtually all the trading in FX

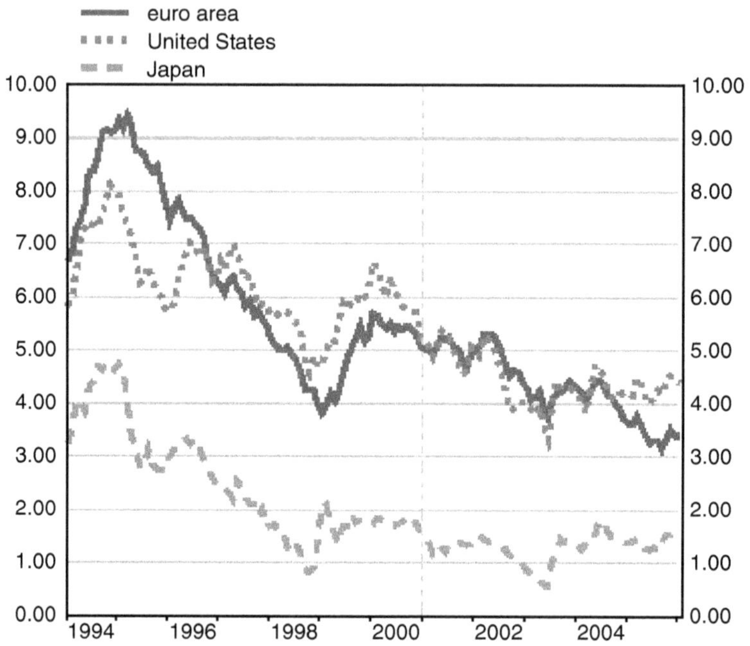

Figure 6.1. Yield on ten-year government bonds.

Source: ECB (European Central Bank) (2006). 'Hedge Funds and Policy Implications; ECB Monthly, January: 63–76

markets, with the exchanges among the three largest, dollar, yen, and euro, making up 48 percent of the total. The currencies of the developing world have, of course, been subjected to massively destabilizing speculation on many occasions. But it is a confusion of two completely different phenomena to believe that the $1.8 trillion FX trades taking place every day have anything to do with third world currencies.[7]

As well as the currencies traded, the character of the traders points in the same direction. A handful of giant banks do most of the dealing among themselves—and they are known not to take open positions in FX. But the most striking evidence comes from the *instruments* used. Transactions are dominated by the FX swap, which, because it combines a spot trade with a forward trade in the opposite direction, is a closed position as far as currency fluctuations are concerned. Today, these swaps account for half the transactions in the FX market.

In fact, most of these transactions are standard banking and money market operations, recycling liquidity from surplus to deficit agents in the normal way. The swap dealers do not even sit on the FX trading floors—because they

Foreign exchange market turnover at constant April 2004 exchange rates by market segment[1]

As a percentage of total reported turnover

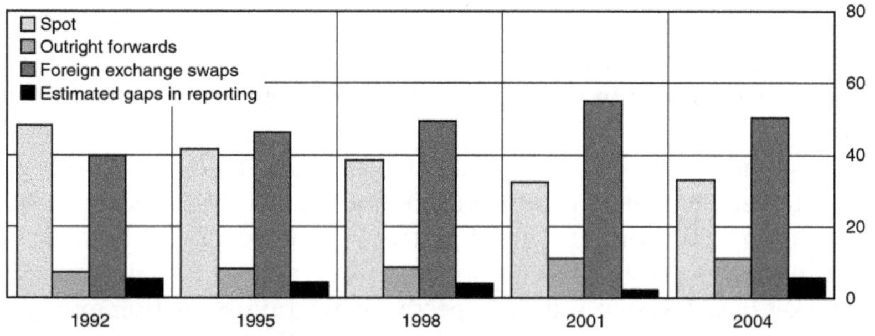

1 Non-US dollar legs of foreign currency transactions were converted into original currency amounts at the average exchange rate for April of each survey year and then reconverted into US dollar amounts at average April 2004 exchange rates.

Figure 6.2.

Source: BIS (2005) Triennial Central Bank Survey of Foreign Exchange and Derivatives Market Activity. www.bis.org.

are not taking open positions the price of currency is of no consequence to them. They sit where they belong—on the money market desk.

The size of the FX market testifies not to speculation but to integration—the very close money market integration of the major economies despite the persistence of separate currencies (for this argument in full, see Grahl and Lysandrou 2003).

Speculation in Securities

The same dubious notion of speculation as dominant prevails in many discussions of the securities markets. Clearly, such a view makes the broad move away from bank-intermediated toward security market-based finance an essentially negative phenomenon. It will be suggested here first, that this notion has little factual basis, second, that it obscures certain systematic features of financial development which are of considerable importance.

As with the FX markets, a simple examination of the structure of security market trading militates against an interpretation in terms of speculation. Markets—trading is concentrated on the oldest and most liquid markets with almost negligible fractions of turnover being found on the newer securities markets of emerging economies. Instruments—trading in bonds, especially those issued by the governments of rich and stable economies, dwarfs trading in equities. Within equity trading, it is the shares of blue-chip companies, least susceptible to price volatility, which are most traded.[8]

Likewise, with agents. The institutional investors which today predominate over individuals prefer the largest and most liquid security issues.[9] For example, the NASDAQ, massively affected by the dot.com bubble, is dominated by individual traders; the NYSE, much more stable, and much more quick to recover from the collapse of 2000–1, is dominated by institutional investors.

Of course, many bubbles and speculative episodes have been observed on security markets. But these exceptions are not the rule and it is certainly the case that more traditional financial systems, centered on bank credit have been far more exposed to speculation and upheaval than have the emerging, more market-based, systems. If a perspective based on speculation exaggerates some phenomena, it may obscure others. One substantial strength of the security-based financial structure is its capacity for expansion—because these markets are open to investors and issuers from different countries they are well placed to establish financial linkages across national boundaries, whereas classical bank-based systems, relying to a much greater extent on 'inside' investors, may have more difficulty in functioning outside the social environment in which they developed (Grahl 2001). In other words, there are good reasons why global finance should tend to take the form of security trading rather than bank credit.

Critics of the global system often trace crises and instability to liberalization as such. But it is equally plausible to trace them to premature or rushed liberalization and to the confrontation between primitive domestic and highly developed external systems.[10] Once again, as with the notion that financialization is linked to financial tensions, specific or temporary phenomena are being seen as essential to the emerging global system.

Hypertrophy of Finance?

The notion that there is, in some sense, 'too much' finance has a simple basis in everyday experience, in the observation that financial enterprises, financial products and advertising, employment in the financial sector and so on have grown explosively in recent decades. From there, however, it is a large leap to the conclusion that the increased prominence of finance is, in some way, dysfunctional. If more specific charges are laid, then differentiated judgments are required. On the one hand, the landscape of retail finance, in countries such as Britain or the United States, where market-based finance predominates, suggests very strongly that there are very often too many products and too many enterprises. Although the needs of the population for savings products, credit facilities, and payments services are relatively homogeneous; on the supply side there is massive differentiation. This is particularly the case in Britain where a series of authoritative reports, prepared by insiders, have issued comprehensive condemnation of retail finance for its high charges, opaque products, excessive marketing costs, and general failure to provide value for money.[11] Much of the sector is rather clearly characterized by Chamberlinian competition, centered on marketing rather than price and with the usual consequences—failure to obtain scale economies, excessive advertising and marketing expenditures, spurious product differentiation and so on. In the United States, very similar phenomena are seen but with rather more progress toward the control of these malfunctions by a standardization of products and procedures.

The other frequent claim that the sector is overdeveloped relates to trading on security markets. Here, as indicated above, it is much more difficult to reach a clear conclusion because the forces behind trading are not well understood. There are, however, good reasons to believe that the bulk of routine trading relates to portfolio management by the institutional investors, that it is not speculative in nature but rather heavily concentrated on the most stable and cognizable securities, and that it is not encouraged by 'excess liquidity' in and around the markets because, for the purposes of the big institutions, these markets are far from liquid.

More generally, the notion of hypertrophy has to be measured against the evidence that the expansion of financial activities is a reliable indicator of economic development in general, although the evidence concerning forms of finance and the structure of the financial sector is much more questionable.

Politics and Financial Liberalization

A very correct position, in the general debates on globalization, is that any simple opposition between the role of markets and states is likely to distort understanding of the processes involved. Many studies have analyzed the active policy measures leading to capital market liberalization as well as the reform strategies which inspired them (Helleiner 1994; Loriaux et al. 1997). Equally, the emergence of large integrated financial systems at an international level is dependent on a process of regime construction which has been going on for several decades and which has necessitated very high levels of intergovernmental cooperation and the construction of supranational authorities. The convergence of both institutions and practices in the field of financial supervision is an impressive example of this activism (Lütz 2002).

From this perspective, it is easy to interpret financialization as the latest wave of a neoliberal political strategy, designed to reshape the framework in which markets operate. The danger in such an assessment is that the economic forces behind these processes will be underestimated. Yet, many of the key developments were economic in their origin—for example, the first emergence of offshore finance, centered in London, arose out of the activities of US multinationals; it was accepted by governments but in no way their design. Similarly, the rise of the institutional investors, which worked to restore the central role of security markets in the financial system was an essentially economic phenomenon.[12] More broadly, the rise of global finance is logically linked to the growth of international trade, international investment and migration, and international technology transfer. Once scale issues are dealt with realistically, by applying the criteria of a security-based financial system rather than those of a bank-based one, the dimensions of the global financial system correspond well to those of the global economy. Of course, in both instances, relations among wealthy economies are much more developed than those with the South, but this is a general characteristic of contemporary economic life, not a consequence of financial relations in particular.

The Crash

One obvious objection to the argument made above is that the dysfunctionality of security-based financial systems is clearly demonstrated by the recent bubble and then collapse in share prices. Often, however, these dramatic episodes draw too much attention away from the more regular working of financial markets in less interesting times.

What lessons are to be drawn from the recent stock market crash and associated scandals?[13] No doubt, a great deal of *Schadenfreude* is well justified but it is not clear that the move toward a security-based financial system will be or should be reversed. Reactions by the authorities, on both sides of the Atlantic, seem inadequate to the problems revealed, both in corporate behavior and in the financial system. There have been strident calls for more 'transparency' but these are not obviously pertinent. The very status of the modern corporation can surely be called into question by malfunctions on the scale revealed. Similarly, the very ability of market agents to make rational assessments of investment proposals can be doubted after the excesses of the Internet boom.

As regards the first of these, the 'Corporate Social Responsibility' so much in fashion today seems to be essentially a cosmetic device designed to stave off the necessary recasting and tightening of regulatory structures to protect customers, employees, small businesses, local communities, the environment and, by no means least, investors from these overmighty subjects.

As regards the formation of expectations within the financial system, what is confirmed is the existence of a public good—the stabilization and crystallization of individual perspectives which public investment permits. Yet, there are at least two reasons to doubt that the transition from an 'inside-investor' and bank-based financial system to one centered on security-markets will be affected by the crash and its aftermath. First, although the gyrations of the stock market (encouraged by the Federal Reserve Bank) gave rise to the bubble, when it burst the economic damage was limited just by the highly developed system of security markets which moved risks away from the banking system. In less advanced financial systems it is the concentration of risks in the banking system which turns asset market collapses into major economic crises. Second, there is the simple fact that the whole EU economy was dragged into the bubble, and the supposedly more stable and conservative nature of the European business classes offered no immunity. In fact, huge outflows from the EU were attracted by the US bubble which they also helped to sustain. Much of this investment (quite legitimately characterized as speculation) took the form of FDI as EU corporations went on a spending spree in the United States. But the basic aim was the same as for stock market placements—that is to get exposure to United States and high-tech assets. (This outflow was the main reason for euro weakness in the early years of the new currency.)

It is also useful to distinguish the NASDAQ boom and bust, from the much milder developments on the NYSE. The former is much more influenced by individual investors, the latter by the big institutions. This is by no means

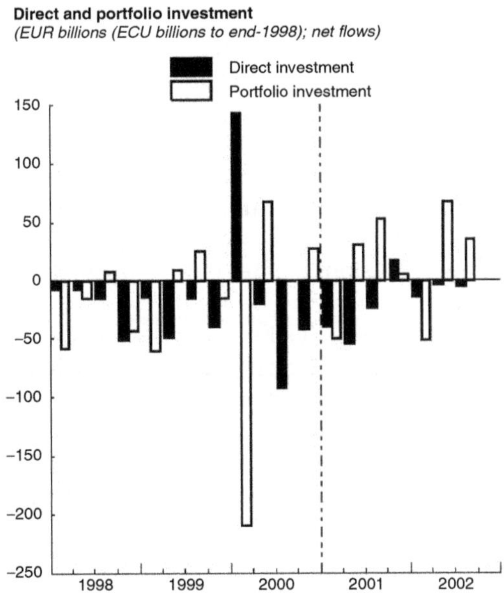

Figure 6.3. Eurozone financial outflows.

Source: ECB (European Central Bank) (2006). 'Hedge Funds and Policy Implications; ECB Monthly, January: 63–76

to exonerate the latter but merely to point out that the bubble in high-tech stocks was in the first instance the consequence of speculation by individual investors.

Consideration of the bubble, however, leads us to a key question. To what extent do the 'Anglo-Saxon' economies, that of the United States in particular, correspond to the necessary features of the security-based financial system? To what extent, in other words, does the financial transformation now taking place in European countries necessarily involve an Americanization of economic life? Clearly, this is a question of some significance from the point of view of employment relations.[14]

The question has tended to receive the same answer from political elites in Europe, whose frenzied imitation of all things American is well represented by the Lisbon agenda as from critical commentators who have often made the same identification of financial change with (undesirable) features of the US system.

The Shareholder Drive

An important issue where market-based finance has tended to be identified with the US practice concerns the role of shareholders. In the United States in the eighties, a drive for shareholder value was launched as means of resolving the conflicts of interest resulting from the separation of ownership and control in the corporate sector.[15] The new salience of the problem was to some extent contingent, in that very tight money and the pursuit of quantitative targets for monetary aggregates favored a further disintermediation of finance; however, the rise of the institutional investors, representing middle class wealth-holders, was working in the same direction. As the problem was formulated at that time, investor interests were mainly impaired by corporations undertaking excessive expansion, at rates of return less than the shareholders could expect to obtain elsewhere.[16]

The shareholder response involved several elements. One was a very positive assessment of the 'market for corporate control' and takeovers, especially hostile ones, which were seen as an important means of disciplining managements. A second feature was the use of new metrics to assess corporate performance. These attached a heavy weight to cash flows as a means of reducing managerial discretion in the presentation of results to shareholders. A third important element was the use of incentive systems intended to align managerial and investor interests—the massive use of stock options for this purpose began at this time. Various other devices attempted to strengthen the hand of dispersed shareholders against that of incumbent managements, including restructurings and disposals intended to refocus the enterprise on core activities and render it more transparent to investors. It was also often seen as useful to increase a company's indebtedness since this would both leverage shareholder interests and limit managerial discretion.

Now this entire agenda has to be seen as a comprehensive failure in that, although it certainly encouraged brutal corporate restructuring exercises, it failed to prevent managerial predation on a colossal scale so that in the course of a decade, 1992–2002, US CEOs raised their personal stake in corporate America from 2 to 12 percent (Brenner 2003). Michael Jensen, perhaps the most influential advocate of the shareholder agenda, recognized the need for major changes in his position. One key consideration was that the 'discipline' imposed by the stock market fails completely if a company is overvalued—indeed, when this happens, managements are able to find cheap finance for any project at all, no matter how contrary it might be to investor interests. Jensen has also changed his views on managerial incentives; whereas he used to argue that higher rewards were needed he cannot repeat that position today (see Jensen and Murphy 2004).

How then can the continuing tensions between principals (shareholders) and agents (managements) be addressed? The future performance of the US economy may depend on effective social and economic reforms to stabilize savings and restore general confidence in financial mechanisms. The issue will not be pursued here—rather the question of European financial development will be raised.

European Finance

The centrality of the United States to the global financial system arises in the first instance from effects of *scale*. The existence of a continentwide economy with very high incomes led to the initial advantages of market-based finance, because in such a context the ability to raise capital from dispersed investors and allocate it to any part of the economy is of particular value. Subsequently, the process became cumulative as the size and liquidity of dollar markets attracted investors and issuers from around the world.

This genesis of the global financial system clearly gave the United States enormous influence over the standards which governed financial practice. For example, regulatory structures have often followed American patterns, although there is certainly nothing optimal about them. Similarly, US interests have been promoted in international systems, such as the Basle accords on banking stability (see again Lütz 2002).

However, it is important to distinguish those characteristics of the US financial system which are indispensable to its functioning and its contingent features. Among the former are scale, liquidity, and a supportive macroeconomic policy; the latter, on the other hand, include many of the practices, in both finance and corporate governance, which have been called into question by the bursting of the high-tech bubble and the subsequent scandals.

Now, for very different reasons, both political leaderships and some of their strongest critics have neglected this vital distinction between intrinsic features of the global financial system and contingent practices and structures in the so-called 'Anglo-Saxon' economies. There has often been an empiricist tendency to conflate the two.

The European elites who formulated the Lisbon agenda seem to have been dazzled by the stock market boom which was then in full swing.[17] Their assessment of the productivity performance of the United States, which raises very thorny statistical issues, was close to a moral panic. The response was an attempt to ape the most superficial aspects of the dot.com bubble. In the realm of finance, the main components of Lisbon were the Financial Services Action Plan and the Venture Capital Action Plan (for an assessment, Frangakis 2005). The main objective of these initiatives—to build big, liquid capital markets in Europe on the basis of the euro—was very rational. The expectation, however, that such measures could transform the EU economies within a matter of years was utopian, while the endorsement of every aspect of the US financial model displayed much the same kind of 'irrational exuberance' that gripped stock market investors at that time.[18] As the weaknesses of US finance were dramatically revealed in the following years, the European Commission echoed the American authorities in demanding more transparency but rejected any deeper criticism of US practice.

Some influential critics of official Europe, on the other hand, also seemed to identify market-based finance as such with its US form. The notion of 'varieties of capitalism' emphasizes the mutually supporting nature of institutions and structures within a given model. These institutional complementarities together with path dependence are supposed to immunize given socioeconomic systems against piecemeal change or the introduction of foreign elements incompatible with their overall logic. Such a view may in practice coincide with that of the elites who drew up the Lisbon strategy: financial transformation amounts to the wholesale adoption of the US system in all its concrete details. As a corollary of the same view, preservation of the main characteristics of the 'coordinated market economy' might be seen to depend on the maintenance of its established, bank-based, inside-investor-dominated, financial mechanisms.

As against these excessively holistic approaches, more and more discussion seems to invoke the notion of *hybridity* in economic relations. Of course, the term itself only poses a question—what combinations of 'Anglo-Saxon' and European practice are viable or desirable? To indicate the scope of the question, reference will be made to two questions: corporate governance as it affects takeovers and executive rewards; and the changing strategies of German corporations.

Corporate Governance Issues

The Takeover Directive

Hostile takeovers, 'the market in corporate control', have often been presented as an essential feature of the market-based financial system. The capital markets will tend to mark down both the equity and the debt issued by an unsuccessful company but it was often suggested that the sanction of a higher cost of capital was not in itself sufficient to discipline underperforming or delinquent managements. Takeovers, encouraged by a low-share price, and resulting in the wholesale replacement of corporate leaderships, can be seen as a much more effective mechanism.

The European Commission clearly accepted this somewhat romantic view of shareholder capitalism. It took the view, first, that a uniform takeover code was necessary for the integration of EU security markets—if the conditions under which a company could be taken over were not the same in all member states, then the securities issued by these companies would not be fully comparable. Second, the Commission argued that the uniform code must be completely liberal—no barriers to hostile takeovers, determined by the acquisition of a controlling fraction of the target company's equity, were to be permitted. The Commission asserted that the decision to sell securities concerned only their owners—both an illogical and a cynical judgment in the context of a change in the control of an enterprise which obviously concerns many people. The draft directive on takeovers, however, was rejected by the European Parliament (EP) in a dramatic tied vote. The document subsequently accepted by the EP was a clear dilution of the original proposal and permitted, according to the country, a variety of defences to be used by incumbent managements. The appointed Commission did not hesitate to express its dissatisfaction with the elected Parliament: the compromise Directive was contrary to market principles and therefore unacceptable.

However, the hostile takeover may no longer be a key feature of the security-based financial system. On the one hand, the days when the key shareholder interest was to squeeze cash out of bloated corporations may have gone; the condition for the greenmail attacks of Carl Icahn or T. Boone Pickens was a level of interest rates so high that investors had no problem in placing their funds. Today, the hunger is not for cash but for assets, even if the yield is low. In the United States itself the excesses of the 1980s led to legislation in many states to obstruct hostile takeovers.

On the other hand, relations between corporations and the capital markets have evolved and are becoming more normalized: the liquidity of their equity (the more liquid the lower the required yield) is now a key consideration for the major corporations who are therefore constrained to pay continuous attention to the price of their shares. Under these new circumstances noncontested takeovers, often influenced by shareholder power, are increasingly frequent and can act to displace failing corporate leaderships. In Germany, for example, the takeover of Mannesmann by Vodaphone in 2000 did not introduce a wave of hostile takeovers in the way some commentators anticipated, but the continuously high level of agreed mergers suggest that a functional equivalent has been found, less at variance with German industrial traditions.[19]

The social costs of the associated restructuring were a key factor in the EP's refusal to endorse the Commission's proposals on takeovers.[20] In France the existence of strong regulations governing mass dismissals has not prevented vigorous growth in the equity market. No doubt, the present legal situation on mergers and takeovers is not ideal: rules are different from country to country and, although incumbent managements are permitted to build obstacles to hostile takeovers, there is no clear indication of when or in whose interests they should exercise this power. But a codification of the existing rules, with a strengthening of the safeguards for employees in cases of restructuring, would be quite compatible with the growth of European security markets and there is no convincing rationale for the extreme position adopted by the Commission.

Managerial Rewards

Similar considerations seem to apply to the incentive structures for senior managers which have developed in the United States. The usual justification for managerial excess has been that it is necessary to align the interests of top management with those of the shareholders, although the predation of CEOs has been on such a scale that this rationale has lost any plausibility it may once have had. Quite apart from this direct cost to investors there are the broader socioeconomic problems which an explosion of high incomes generates throughout the income distribution. The case of Britain, where there are few signs of the dynamism and international competitive success which these rewards are supposed to induce, is particularly egregious.[21]

But once again there is no good reason to take this malfunction as an essential component of a market-based financial system. The same contingency governed the development of the key practices—that is, interest rates so high that the extraction of cash reserves from corporations raised no difficulties in terms of alternative placements. Huge payouts to the top managements concerned might make some sense in that context but through the nineties and into the new century seem increasingly anachronistic.

The lack of countervailing power to the big corporations has meant that the momentum of executive pay inflation is still unchecked but there are some signs that institutional investors, in a changing political climate, are increasingly hostile to this predation.

The forms of control exercised by institutional investors will never replicate those available to 'inside' investors in the socially embedded financial systems of Germany or Japan in the past but increasingly they do not need to do so. Both parties are increasingly focused on the securities markets. The investors, especially the institutions which now dominate among them, want strong enterprise performance primarily to underpin the quality and the tradability of the securities they hold. Managements want good investor relations to support their share price and to maximize the liquidity premium above the price justified by profits alone. This does not mean that top managements are now in harmonious relations with investors but it does indicate that, as the securities markets become more important to both parties, their conflicts are more constrained by market forces. Of course big gyrations in security prices and unstable expectations among investors will negate this proposition, but one should not take exceptional episodes as typical of the functioning of the markets.

What is being suggested is not that market forces will rein in the explosion of corporate incomes, merely that it is not clear that market forces would prevent social and political forces from doing so. Thus, in this case, as with the codes governing takeovers, the EU may have much more scope than it realizes to challenge the norms and practices of the 'Anglo-Saxon' financial system (for an extended argument around this point see Aglietta and Rébérioux 2005).

Corporate Strategies in Germany

The impact of financial change on the strategies of European business is a vast question, and debates are in an early stage. By far the most developed discussion concerns the impact on large German corporations and this is the only case which will be considered here. However, it is obviously a case of central importance, given the strength of these enterprises and their weight in the eurozone economy.

Until the last ten years, Germany was a paradigmatic example of 'inside-investor' and bank-based finance. German companies were closely held and not for sale. There were many cross-holdings among financial and industrial companies; these were stable and worked to cement collaboration among the enterprises concerned. The equity market was much smaller than its counterparts in the United States or Britain. Big enterprises were seen, in 'stakeholder' terms, as coalitions of interest in which codetermination laws supported a strong voice for labor.

How extensive are the changes induced in Germany's 'coordinated' market economy by the emergence of an international financial system centered on the security markets? One tends to get conflicting answers, depending on whether what is examined is corporate strategy or employment relations. In the first case, the story is one of almost revolutionary reorientation; in the second, more of continuity and stability.

The adoption of shareholder economics by big firms in Germany has been rapid and comprehensive (Streeck and Höpner 2003). A closed system of corporate finance has been opened up to FDI and many companies have actively sought external investors. Legal changes have been introduced to permit the dissolution of cross-holdings among industrial and financial companies. The banks, although they still hold a lot of industrial equity, now tend to see these holdings as portfolios rather than as the support for specific relationships. Profitability metrics, oriented to the equity market, are increasingly deployed within the big firms, both to assess investment projects and to set targets for divisions. A host of other changes, for example, in accounting practices, have been stimulated by the same general shift.[22]

Within the financial sector itself the major banks are pursuing active globalization strategies, and an increasing share of their activities is connected to securities trading. As pointed out above, although the hostile takeover has not been institutionalized in Germany, merger and acquisition activity has grown very rapidly in close correspondence to stock market activity. Longstanding relations between big companies and their suppliers are, if not being dissolved, being placed under considerable pressure. From this point of view the stakeholder enterprises of the past seem to be dead.

A consideration of employment relations, on the other hand, calls this judgment into question. There are certainly unprecedented pressures on the German employment system. Not only have legislative changes reduced the level of social protection, but employers are also seeking to reverse some of the gains, especially on working time, made by the unions in the 1980s and 1990s. The Western employment relations system was never fully established in the Easter *Länder* and smaller companies especially in the East are pulling out of industrywide collective agreements. However, within the large enterprises, employee voice systems and structures of representation are stable (see, e.g. Vitols 2003). They may even be gaining a new importance because the shareholder economy emphasizes the enterprise as against the industry as a locus of decision-making. It certainly does not seem to be the case that *Mitbestimmung* and the high level of employee participation which it promotes are perceived as disqualifying the companies concerned in the securities markets. Indeed, the functional flexibility which depends on these systems is today, as in the past, a source of competitive strength.

Of course, large German enterprises are not the same thing as the German economy. Indeed, the dissociation between the two is certainly widening as the big companies pursue global strategies which many small and medium enterprises cannot imitate. A clear national economic interest then becomes harder to define, for instance because companies with an export orientation have a very different view of developments than companies dependent on the stagnant home market. It may also be the case that it is the smaller enterprises which are adversely affected by the financial changes under way, as they find it harder or more costly to obtain bank credit. It is probably within the *Mittelstand* that one finds the greatest pressures on employment relations. The larger enterprises on the other hand continue to derive enormous competitive advantages from the excellence of their industrial systems although this no longer has the same meaning for the national economy.

The suggestion here is that it may be an error to regard market-based finance as simply working to dissolve all established and socially embedded economic relations. The capital market's demand for transparency implies that the outcome of negotiations within the enterprise should be disclosed to outside investors and the profitability calculations which are intrinsic to the security-based financial system certainly apply a general test to established relations. However, the continuity and density of localized economic relations, including especially employment relations, are a real factor in the productivity and profitability of enterprises and cannot therefore simply be cast aside by the new financial system.

Conclusion

The general interpretation of 'financialization' in general and 'shareholder value' in particular is probably that they represent the latest wave of a neoliberal strategy which has now dominated European economic policies for more than two decades. This interpretation emphasizes above all the political determinants of economic change. Neoliberalism promotes, in a very selective way, the intensification of market forces in order to achieve specific objectives, such as reversing many of the socioeconomic gains of organized labor. Although an understanding of economic processes is obviously necessary to this view, the key issues are political—how such a strategy is arrived at, how it wins acceptance, how it is implemented.

This interpretation is not wrong. In the present context, for example, the Lisbon agenda of the European Union demonstrates that the rapid transformation of the EU's financial system was a clear choice of Europe's political elite. Their objectives were various but certainly not incompatible with those of neoliberalism and the adulation of the US economy they exhibited was hardly consistent with their professed attachment to the European Social Model.

However, this interpretation, although not wrong, may be incomplete and this is what the present chapter has tried to suggest. Particularly at the international level, we observe a massive growth in the scale and intensity of economic interactions which seems to go well beyond the scope of any of the political strategies referred to (Grahl 2005). Indeed, although the opening up of markets to external forces is very frequently part of neoliberal strategies, not all aspects of the global economy are welcome to neoliberals since overwhelming pressures are released in a way which tends to undermine the stable and conservative social order which most of them wish to combine with the market economy.

Many developments in the global economy are the result of basically economic forces and this is true of global finance as well. Indeed, when unrealistic notions about the appropriate scale of the financial sector are discarded, then global finance—in today's world inevitably *market* finance, can be seen to be intrinsic to emerging structures of international trade, international production, and international resource flows.

But, just because there are powerful economic forces working to transform financial systems, it is important to distinguish which features of the transformation are necessary and which are more or less contingent. This involves an assessment of finance in the United States where most of the ongoing changes began. The United States holds this pioneering position because the scale of its continental economy worked to promote deep and liquid financial markets. But this does not mean that financial markets in Europe have to replicate every feature of the US system. On the contrary, if the emerging European system builds in effective measures for the social control of corporate behavior and for the stabilization of investor expectations, then it may be able in some ways to outperform its US rival.

This argument applies to European employment relations. It cannot be denied that financial integration and the dissolution of existing financial structures are often a threat to employee interests. But it is suggested that this threat is not inscribed in financial market relations as such. More ambitious European strategies are possible which would combine the construction of an integrated financial system with effective measures for its social control.

References

Aglietta, M. and Rébérioux, A. (2005). *Corporate Governance Adrift: A Critique of Shareholder Value*. Cheltenham, UK: Edward Elgar.

BIS. (2005). *Triennial Central Bank Survey of Foreign Exchange and Derivatives Market Activity*, www.bis.org

Boyer, R., Dehove, M., and Plihon, D. (2004). *Crises Financières*, rapport du Conseil d'analyse économique, novembre. Paris: La Documentation française.

Brenner, R. (2002). *The Boom and the Bubble: The US in the World Economy*. London: Verso.

—— (2003). 'Towards the Precipice', *London Review of Books*, 25(3), February.

Davis, P. and Steil, B. (2001). *Institutional Investors*. Cambridge, MA: MIT Press.

Duménil, G. and Lévy, D. (2004). *Capital Resurgent: Roots of the Neoliberal Revolution*. London: Harvard University Press.

ECB (European Central Bank) (2006). 'Hedge Funds: Developments and Policy Implications', *ECB Monthly Bulletin*, January: 63–76.

Frangakis, M. (2005). 'The Drive for Financial Integration: Stability and Inclusion at Risk', in J. Huffschmid (ed.), *Economic Policy for a Social Europe: A Critique of Neo-liberalism and Proposals for Alternatives*. Basingstoke, UK: Palgrave Macmillan.

Froud, J., Johal, S., and Williams, K. (2002). 'Financialization and the Coupon Pool', *Capital and Class*, 78: 119–51.

Grahl, J. (2001). 'Globalised Finance and the Challenge to the Euro', *New Left Review*, March/April.

—— (2005). 'Scale and the Political Economy of Financial Change', in J. Hölscher and H. Tomann (eds.), *Globalisation of Capital Markets and Monetary Policy*. Basingstoke, UK: Palgrave Macmillan.

—— and Lysandrou, P. (2003). 'Sand in the Wheels or Spanner in the Works? The Tobin Tax and Global Finance', *Cambridge Journal of Economics*, 27(4): 597–621.

Helleiner, E. (1994). *States and the Reemergence of Global Finance: from Bretton Woods to the 1990s*. Ithaca, NY: Cornell University Press.

Jensen, M. and Murphy, K. (2004). 'Remuneration: Where We've been, How We Got to Here, What are the Problems, and How to Fix Them', ECGI working paper 44/2004, July.

King, M. (2006). 'Speech by Mervyn King in Kent', Bank of England website: www.bankofengland.co.uk 16 January.

Kok, W. (2004). *Report from the High Level Group: Facing the Challenge—the Lisbon Strategy for Growth and Employment*. Brussels: European Communities.

Loriaux, M. et al. (1997). *Capital Ungoverned: Liberalising Finance in Interventionist States*. London: Cornell University Press.

Lütz, S. (2002). *Der Staat und die Globalisierung von Finanzmärkten: Regulative Politik in Deutschland, Grossbritannien und den USA*. Cologne: Campus.

Myners, P. (2001). *Institutional Investment in the United Kingdom: A Review*. London: HM Treasury.

Sandler, R. (2002). *Medium and Long-Term Retail Savings in the UK*. London: HM Treasury.

Stiglitz, J. (2004). *The Roaring Nineties*. London: Penguin.

Streeck, W. and Höpner, M. (2003). *Alle Maccht dem Markt? Fallstudien zum Abwicklung der Deutschland AG*. Cologne: Campus.

Treasury Select Committee (2004). *Restoring Confidence in Long-term Savings*. London: House of Commons.

Vitols, S. (2003). 'Negotiated Shareholder Value: The German version of an Anglo-American practice', WZB working paper SP II 2003-25, December.

Williams, K. (2000). *Shareholder Value and the Political Economy of Late Capitalism*, special issue of *Economy and Society*, 29(1): 1–12.

Part II

Continuity and Change in Working Life

7

The Blurring of Organizational Boundaries and the Fragmentation of Work

Damian Grimshaw, Mick Marchington, and Jill Rubery

Introduction

The employment relationship is normally regarded as contracted between a single employer and an employee and shaped and formed within a single organization with a clear organizational boundary. This approach, taken as the bedrock for enquiry in areas such as industrial relations, human resource management (HRM), employment law, and labor economics, fails to consider the way in which differences in organizational forms (such as outsourcing, joint ventures, multiemployer sites, partnerships, agency working, and pseudo self-employment) impact on employment relations. Conversely, analyses of changing organizational forms tend to ignore the impact of changes to employment relationships on the likely performance and sustainability of a particular organizational form.

Appreciation of the variety of organizational forms raises a host of new issues and questions for employment research. Many workers now spend their working days not at the workplace of a single, easily identifiable, employer, but at the workplace of a client organization. Client organizations agree a contract with another organization to provide a product or a service but this interorganizational contracting, far from displacing the internal employment relationship as the means of delivering the product or service, serves to complicate the relationships that need to be managed to produce the outcome; now there is a relationship between the contractor and subcontractor and an employment relationship between the subcontractor and his/her employees. These employment relations underpin the subcontractor's capacity to meet the targets specified in the contract. The employment relationship within the subcontracting organization is now, however, shaped not only by the internal relationship between the employer and the workforce, but also by the contractual and power relations between the contractor and subcontractor, as well as informal understandings between the contractors with respect to the quality, timing, quantity, and reliability of products/services delivered. The subcontractor in managing their own internal employment relations consequently has to respond to diverse client needs regarding service quality, job design, employment contracts, and working conditions, which may present difficulties in constructing and maintaining consistent and fair human resource policies. Moreover, the client organizations, in their concern for the quality, reliability, or timeliness of the outsourced activities are liable to seek to intervene directly in the management of the subcontractor's employees, both indirectly, by specifying job tasks, and performance targets in interorganizational contracts, and directly, by assuming some of the control, authority, and training functions of the employer.

These complexities introduced by interorganizational contracting mean that processes of fragmentation of work associated with deverticalization and new organizational forms are likely to incur costs as well as benefits for employers. There is therefore no inevitable tendency toward fragmentation and the emergence of network forms of organizing work and employment; instead these developments will depend upon the institutional, regulatory, and competitive environment that shapes the incentives and the opportunities for deverticalization and fragmentation. Nevertheless, most societies are moving toward an institutional and regulatory environment in which organizations are both being permitted, and even urged, to consider the appropriateness of networked production systems. As such it is surprising how little attention has been paid both to the consequences of these trends for employment relations and to the importance of employment factors in shaping the performance outcomes of particular organizational forms.

To explore these issues the chapter is organized as follows. Section 2 provides a critique of mainstream management accounts of deverticalization and outsourcing that both fail to appreciate the complexity of the employment relationship and downplay the role of the institutional context. Section 3 argues that notions of trust, risk, and power are central to explanations of interorganizational contracting, and that these concepts have consequences for the linkages between interorganizational contracting and the reshaping of employment relations. Section 4 provides examples of how employment conditions are directly shaped by these organizational forms, leading to a fragmentation of work. Section 5 explores the implications of our research findings for policy, both for the governance of interorganizational contracting and for employment, and Section 6 concludes the chapter. Throughout, we draw on the theoretical arguments, and on the associated detailed empirical research, of a project on 'changing organizational forms and the reshaping of work', conducted by a team of researchers, which included the present authors, at the University of Manchester (then UMIST) as part of the Economic and Social Research Council's (ESRC) widely acclaimed 'Future of Work' research program (see Marchington et al. 2005 for full details).[23]

Socioeconomic and Institutionalist Explanations

Trends toward deverticalization and outsourcing tend to be explained in the organizational literature by managers responding to a matrix of pressures to improve efficiency. Within contributions to the 'competence' and resource-based views of the firm, managers are said to be adapting the organizational form to 'fit' with changing competitive conditions (Rumelt 1984; Wernerfelt 1984; Barney 1991). These rational efficiency-led explanations do not, however, fit well with the empirical evidence arising from both our own case studies and from other research on network forms.

A main reason for this is that the success of outsourcing and subcontracting depends upon numerous intangible variables and outcomes that are difficult to objectify or measure (Malecki 1997), including, for example, employee skill and knowledge, the extent of information exchange between organizations and client–supplier partnership relations. As a result, the assumption made by proponents of deverticalization that employers are easily able to distinguish between those forms of work that are central to added value, and thus need to be retained inhouse, and other forms of work that need to be outsourced is problematic (e.g. Lepak and Snell 1999). This is particularly so given that the types of issues identified above are not under the complete control of the contractor but depend, for example, on the external availability of labor of the required quality and on the costs at which other organizations are able to provide similar services.

Where there is a large cost advantage, organizations may be willing to risk outsourcing even 'core' functions. However, Purcell and Purcell (1999) point out that similar organizations have very different notions of what constitutes core and noncore activities, thereby suggesting that these decisions are contingent on a number of both internal and external variables. Furthermore, as we discuss further below, processes of outsourcing are shaped by both interorganizational and by employer–employee power relations; as such we would caution against universal predictions of mutual gains through efficiency savings for both client and supplier organizations, or for employers and employees. Indeed, the processes of interorganizational contracting can be seen as adding to rather than simplifying the dynamics of cooperation and conflict between employer and employee within the employment relationship (Hyman 1987). The fragmentation of processes across organizational boundaries both requires more input from employees to coordinate activities and provides a framework in which employers can seek to use outsourcing as a means for control and cost reduction.[24]

Further to these problems, in managerialist and strategy accounts of organizational change little attention is paid to the institutional context that may shape the extent and form of deverticalization. For example, in the United States and the UK outsider systems of corporate governance that emphasize the financial benefits of short-term organizational restructuring may promote a higher incidence of outsourcing compared to other countries. The deepening 'financialization' of the public and private sectors (Froud et al. 2000) has reinforced such principles, most notably with the application of the 'Economic Value Added' formula, which encourages managers to minimize and narrow capital invested (Ackroyd and Procter 1998; Thompson 2004). Such thinking also informs the controversial Private Finance Initiative in the UK where the government uses private capital to build prisons, schools, roads and hospitals, and leases outsourced services from the private sector.

Institutions that promote coordination and cooperation among employers and among employees may have opposite effects. Countries characterized by strong 'deliberative' institutions (such as works councils) and high participation among employers in trade associations governing technical standards and contracting rules are likely to experience a different dynamic between outsourcing and employment relations (Grimshaw and Miozzo 2006). In these types of countries, outsourcing and subcontracting are more likely to be accompanied by, for example, close checks on hiring and promotion practices in subcontractor firms and the dissemination of information about contracting practices among workers within different organizations in the network. Thus, while internationalization undoubtedly acts as an increasingly important pressure in all countries, institutional effects are likely to shape the performance and sustainability of interorganizational forms and influence the extent and form of changes in the employment relationship.

Trust, Risk, and Power in Interorganizational Relations

Interorganizational relations are shaped by both the distribution of risk between contractors and the extent and form of trust relations. However, the forms of trust and the distributions of risk are institutionally constructed with variation between sectors and countries (e.g. Hall and Soskice 2001; Lane and Bachmann 2002). Strong societal institutions (involving trade associations, employers' organizations, trade unions, and government legislation) shape the extent to which the potential risks of trusting relations may be minimized, or prevented, altogether. Hence, those who assert that network forms are characterized by high trust and mutual gains need to establish the particular conditions that make this feasible. On the basis of our research, these include, for example, a shared desire among organizations for long-term stability, or evidence of long-standing relations among organizations contracting for high quality/low risk products and services. Under different contracting conditions, trusting relations may be more difficult to establish, for example, where markets are highly competitive or where cost reduction is a principal organizational goal, particularly in countries where the pursuit of short-term shareholder value is dominant.

Interorganizational relations are also shaped by power relations, both internal to the contracting organization (e.g. between headquarters and subsidiary) and external between client and supplier organizations. Decisions within large, hierarchical organizations may be taken by the headquarters of multinational firms without any involvement of, or consultation with, individual parts of the business. What may apparently benefit the organization as a whole may not make economic sense for the individual subunit. Moreover, many examples of interorganizational contracting from the public to the private sector are driven primarily by political decisions about subcontracting which leave individual public sector units with little room for maneuver. The economic benefits of such deals are often hard to determine with any clarity. Power relations between client and supplier organizations will further influence the outcomes of outsourcing, in particular, how the distribution of any economic rent from contracting arrangements is distributed among client organizations, suppliers, and workforces (Grimshaw and Rubery 2005). For example, studies of the business services markets of contract cleaning and computer services find that the base of supplier firms has become very concentrated with a handful of powerful multinationals controlling a massive portfolio of deals, underpinned by knowledge of how to put successful tenders together rather than any obvious superiority in their performance (Ovum 2002; Crouch 2003). Attention to power relations and the dynamics of market structure thus contrasts markedly with the standard focus on individual, atomized, decisions to enter into network arrangements.

The empirical evidence from our own study suggests that interorganizational relations are typically characterized by an imbalance of power, shifting of risk, and weak and strong trusting relations. However, the qualitative data reveal the complexity of these dynamics and warn against establishing a neat typology of contracting arrangements—into those based on strong trust and mutual gains on the one hand and unequal, arm's-length arrangements on the other—or assuming consistent differences between organizations in terms of how and why they enter into contracting. We found, for example, that a client organization may establish different interorganizational relations with different suppliers—in some cases relations reflected a client's greater bargaining power, but in others relations were restricted by its dependency on a supplier because of a lack of suitable alternatives (Marchington and Vincent 2004). Similarly, a supplier may have reasons to establish strong trusting relations with some clients, but weak ones with others. For example, the supply teacher agency in our study sought to build a strong reputation through high trust relations and a commitment to supply high quality staff with schools in prosperous local areas, but weak trusting relations with some schools in underprivileged ones (Grimshaw, Earnshaw, and Hebson 2003).

Where trust underpinned interorganizational relations, it was also heavily circumscribed and typically accompanied by unequal power relations where the smaller firms usually—though not always—were dependent on their larger and more powerful collaborators in the network. At a chemical firm, the road haulage firms were required to meet the standards set by their client in order to remain on the preferred list. This involved rearranging delivery schedules to fit with the 'needs' of the client and negotiating with other agencies to increase the supply of drivers at short notice. Even though the language of trust might have been central to discussions about interorganizational relations, both parties were fully aware where the greater power in the relationship lay. The power balance in the four public–private partnerships studied was more complex, depending on the distribution of expertise in the relationship, the degree to which either party was sheltered from reputation effects, and the extent to which they were able to rely on external support (Grimshaw and Hebson 2004). Evidence of opportunistic behavior was especially associated with a strongly uneven balance of expertise in negotiating and working to contract. In three of the four cases investigated, this favored the private sector provider because they were able to draw on greater external resources and had an accumulated pool of expertise. In one case, the private sector firm possessed less expertise than the public sector team, but this reflected the highly idiosyncratic skills required to administer housing benefits and a business strategy of bidding for the contract as a short-term loss leader designed to win greater benefits in the long-term (Marchington, Cooke, and Hebson 2003). Of course, either party might also make a mistake in the bidding, for example, with a private sector provider making too low a bid to be able to service the contract effectively, or a public sector contractor allowing too much slack in the system so that it was easy for the subcontractor to make profits. Across all the cases, therefore, the evidence demonstrated imbalances in power relations, which led to shifting of risk rather than to shared goals and the search for mutual benefits. In the next section, we argue risk is transferred not only between organizational partners, but also between and down organizational hierarchies to different groups of workers.

Passing Risk Along the Chain and Down the Hierarchy

In this section we examine how workers' employment conditions are directly shaped by the shifting of risk that occurs within interorganizational relations, drawing primarily on the empirical evidence from our own research project. We illustrate these influences in six areas: employment security, pay and reward, fair treatment, skills, voice, and gender. These comprise areas of work that are central and important to workers, according to key studies in the field (Gallie et al. 1998; Noon and Blyton 2002; White et al. 2004). Our argument is that the blurring of organizational boundaries is leading to a fragmentation of work. First, outsourcing and greater use of agency workers lead to a disintegration of norms regulating behavior and social relationships. This is evident in, for example, the more limited opportunities for workers to exercise their collective voice and in the tensions created by differential approaches to the fair treatment of workers. Second, interorganizational contracting establishes a disconnection with respect to an employee's attachment to a single employer. Practices of staff transfers, working on client premises, and switching employers in multiemployer sites radically alter conventional perceptions of job security and establish instead a pattern whereby employers trade workers between organizations. Third, the nature of work is rendered less complete, with deficiencies especially notable in the extent to which employees are able to exercise skill and discretion in their day-to-day work. And fourth, the experience of work is fragmented in the sense of becoming disordered and more unequally distributed. In particular, standard rates of pay among colleagues become multitiered because of variation in who is the employer, and men and women experience unequal treatment because of an increased emphasis on result-based work and new feminized stereotyping of job positions.

Reduced Levels of Employment Security

To assess whether or not contract workers have low levels of employment security, we need to consider where the work they are doing was undertaken prior to contracting. Where work that has been done internally is subcontracted to a third party, the work may continue to be done by the same staff transferred to the new employer, may be transferred to existing employees of the new employer, or be performed by new employees hired for the purpose. In many cases all three options apply. Workers transferred to another employer enjoy some limited protection of their employment conditions under the Transfer of Undertakings (Protection of Employment) (TUPE) legislation but this protection is only partial and may be undermined by comparisons with other employees of the contractor, who may be cheaper and have lower expectations of employment security than the transferred workers. Agency workers may also be brought in by the subcontractor so that staff employed on the work may be transferred staff, direct hires by the subcontractor and agency staff employed by an external agency. While the threat of direct redundancy and replacement by new staff is reduced by

TUPE, downsizing of the staff employed can still occur for economic reasons. Moreover, there are dangers that once work is transferred or contracted out, this process may be repeated with new subcontractors such that transferred staff face employment by a chain of new employers.

Security does not just relate solely to the increased likelihood of redundancy, it also impinges on changed feelings of security and levels of work intensification, as well as to uncertainty about their future location and careers (Heery and Salmon 2000; Burchell, Ladipo, and Wilkinson 2003). If workers are transferred to another employer who has a quite different approach to managing people, they may also find they are required to move to other locations with that firm in order to maintain their employment. In a similar vein, if potential career paths are closed off, workers are likely to be made even more aware of how limited guarantees are of future employment and the need to maximize benefits over the short-term instead. This shows how issues to do with employment cannot just be considered subsequent to the decision to subcontract as workers on different contracts may have had wide variations in terms and conditions prior to the implementation of outsourcing. It also helps us to understand why some employers specifically seek to subcontract certain forms of work in order to reduce their reliance on (relatively) well-protected workers.

Differentials in Pay and Benefits

When workers from different organizations are employed alongside each other at the same site, it is highly likely that pay systems and levels will be disordered, and inconsistencies increase between workers. Of course, even in workplaces where workers are employed on time rates, differential rates of pay are common if people are on scales that reward length of service, or there are additional bonuses for acquiring skills. However, these are generally transparent and other workers know that if they remain with the same organization for long enough, or they learn new skills, they will become eligible for higher rewards. When workers with different employers work alongside each other, there is a chance that they will discover what each other earns and this can trigger demands for a pay increase, or lead to grievances about the fairness of the effort-reward bargain. Although this may not become explicit, underlying disgruntlement is hardly conducive to good employment relations.

Of course, differentials between workers are not just something that comes to light after the decision has been made to subcontract or bring agency workers into the organization. In many cases, employers are fully aware that they can pay new workers, or those working for different organizations, less than they have paid, and will have to continue paying, established workers, and indeed this is a major reason for decisions to subcontract in the first place. Rather than seeing such (often temporary) peripheral workers as an outer ring to protect and insulate the inner core, as some analysts believe, the introduction of new workers on worse terms and conditions might serve to undermine previous arrangements (Rubery et al. 2003). Evidence of the two-tier workforce associated with outsourcing of ancillary services in public–private partnerships (Unison 2003) suggests that as staff quit, they are replaced by cheaper labor. Yet, such inconsistencies are not always to the benefit of employers; resentment can arise between workers on different contracts; organizations employing workers on lower rates of pay may experience higher rates of labor turnover—and thus greater costs of replacement—and some workers who were loyal to their employer may decide postoutsourcing that there is little point offering more than an instrumental attachment to the organization.

Perceptions of (un)fair Treatment

One of the central tenets of employment relations is that there should be consistent disciplinary procedures and rules, at least at the same place of work. Whilst this is not always simple to achieve in workplaces which are governed by the rules of a single employer, it is much harder in multiemployer workplaces due to differing and sometimes competing influences on the employment relationship. Clients who are paying a subcontractor to provide services for them, perhaps in relation to professional work such as teaching or IT or to manual/clerical labor through office cleaning or a call center, might well feel they should have some control and influence over the type of staff employed. Some clients insist that specific individuals are deployed on their contract and, more importantly, refuse to have other staff on their premises. It is hardly surprising, therefore, if tensions emerge between employers and with workers given this scenario, even more so if there are a number of clients who want the same person to be employed on their contract in a multiemployer workplace. One client may want an individual to be disciplined for what they regard as poor performance or inappropriate behavior, but the employer may be rather more sanguine about how the same offence should be treated; this situation was most evident in the schools that hired supply teachers from a large private sector agency (Grimshaw, Earnshaw, and Hebson 2003). Moreover, if employers and workers are unsure of the identity of their immediate line manager, the likelihood of confused and confusing sources of authority relations becomes obvious, again to the potential detriment not only of the workers involved but also to customers.

Yet again we need to recall that changed expectations concerning fair treatment are not just a consequence of the contracting decision, but are often part of the rationale for outsourcing in the first place. Some employers may be keen to reduce the cost base or feel that workers are provided with too much protection or are too prepared to challenge management under existing regimes, and therefore decide to subcontract partly in order to remove what they regard as inflexible working practices. Similarly, decisions to seek a reduction in costs, even if not explicit, are also bound to impinge on impressions of fair treatment, particularly if workers have become accustomed to a positive psychological contract with their employer. Moreover, as with pay and employment security, some employers may decide to put pressure on existing staff, and cause them to question the sanctity of their current conditions, by exposing them directly to workers who are rather worse off than themselves.

Reducing Levels of Discretion and Skill

One of the consequences of contracting appears to be that work requires lower levels of skill and discretion than under previous in-house arrangements (Grugulis, Vincent, and Hebson 2003). Contract work lends itself to greater levels of specification and codification precisely because it is difficult to price contracts without clear definitions of needs. In a whole range of cases, such as hospital porters, housing benefit officers, and security personnel, jobs have been analyzed more systematically and described in more detail. Contrary to the idealized vision of the 'empowered' worker, or the assumption under the high commitment paradigm that workers are encouraged to use their discretion, the contract worker is under a much tighter set of instructions (Godard 2004). Moreover, since jobs are timed in order to ensure that the supplier extracts maximum profit from the contract, there is rarely time to do additional work of the kind that would have been typical prior to outsourcing. For example, maintenance personnel in hospitals are no longer able to attend to minor jobs whilst they are on the wards because it is not on the job docket, and they are rarely able to contribute to the wider goals of improved patient care through social interaction on the ward. Similarly, customer-facing staff, in post offices, for example, may find they are hard-pressed to justify a conversation with a lonely pensioner because it cannot be assessed directly in terms of added value.

Skills have also changed in many of the jobs that have been contracted out, and substantive, professional skills (such as a detailed experience of how the law relates to housing benefits cases), have been superseded by the need for a good telephone manner and an ability to follow detailed scripts when dealing with clients. We found that many professional staff had become alienated by this changing focus, feeling that the job now required greater attention to the speed of the interaction and the use of prespecified phrases designed to calm down customers rather than solving problems no matter how long it took. For experienced staff this represents a major—and in their view—negative change to working conditions. For people new to this work, however, or to those from agencies who are trained for relatively short periods of time in basic procedures, the emphasis on customer service skills might seem perfectly reasonable, and they can always ask a more experienced colleague if they are confronted with a problem. In the long term, as those with experience leave the workplace, skills deficiencies are likely to become more serious.

Fragmented Voice

Although trade union and collective voice has declined throughout most developed economies during the last twenty years (Ferner and Hyman 1998; Traxler, Blaschke, and Kittel 2001), it is particularly fragmented at workplaces that are subject to interorganizational contracting. To some extent this is inevitable as workers are confronted with increased difficulties collaborating with their colleagues in other organizations, partly due to logistical problems but also due to the fact they are often seen as competitors (Heery et al. 2004). Logistically, it is hard for agency workers to develop strong ties with colleagues on 'permanent' contracts because they may only be working with them for the odd day at a time. Even when agency workers are on longer-term placements, say, as a teacher at one school for a term, they are often resented by permanent staff, seen either as a threat to continued employment or as inadequately trained and insufficiently committed to student needs. At the same time, agency workers are likely to have different concerns from other staff at the school, thus making it more difficult to identify shared grievances or provide opportunities to unify their voice under a common cause. Agency workers, or those working at the workplace of another employer, face a further problem in that their own employer is not immediately available if they do wish to raise a grievance. On some occasions, as we discussed above, host employers may take action which potentially creates additional problems with consistency. But agency workers may also be reticent to raise concerns, either with their own employer or with the host employer for fear it will reduce their opportunities for work in the future if they are identified as someone prepared to argue for their rights (Marchington, Rubery, and Cooke 2004).

Yet again, we need to remind ourselves that contracting decisions alter existing work patterns if workers are transferred to another employer or work is subcontracted. In the case of public–private contracting, workers may find that they are still employed at the same workplace but by a different employer, and even though they continue to work alongside existing colleagues, opportunities to express voice or use procedures to raise grievances have changed. They may even be members of the same union, and even in the same branch as before, but issues that are relevant to their colleagues working in the public sector no longer have as much meaning for them; similarly, their own problems may find little support from other members of the union. Rights to union facilities may be withdrawn or at least severely curtailed by the new employer and pay discussions may become increasingly based on individual performance rather than collective bargaining. Some workers may be disenfranchised altogether compared to other workers at the same site or compared to the rights enjoyed by people who used to do their jobs prior to outsourcing. In short, voice is particularly susceptible to fracture and fragmentation.

Gender Equality

Changing organizational forms, especially where these lead to a dismantling of vertically integrated, bureaucratic, and patriarchal organizational hierarchies, have the potential to improve gender relations. New organizational forms can establish 'feminine' managerial qualities, such as relational work needed to manage contracts between organization partners, and erode long-standing norms of sex segregation by reorganizing work across workplaces (see Hebson and Grugulis 2005, for a review of the literature). However, interorganizational contracting also involves new patterns of risk transfer and trust relations, which complicate efforts to rationalize and modernize work organization with the goal of improving gender equality. These arrangements may also reduce transparency and consistency of human resource practices, thereby increasing the difficulties in identifying and eliminating sex discrimination.

Among low-skill workers and managers, our empirical evidence suggests both limited change of gender roles and a regendering of traditional stereotypes. At the National Health Service (NHS) trust, which had signed a Private Finance Initiative with a consortium of private sector firms, both male and female ancillary workers lost jobs as part of an agreement to transfer work to a cleaning firm. But while female cleaners in part-time jobs were forced to accept cuts in hours, the male porters maintained their full-time hours. Also, female cleaners were unable to resist, or to influence, radical plans by the private sector firm to create a new integrated 'patient service assistant' through combining the work of cleaners, caterers, and porters. By contrast, the strongly unionized male porters did resist and ultimately the new jobs excluded portering tasks. At the same time, several of our case studies included growing shares of women in middle manager positions, representing positive opportunities for relatively quick promotion into higher-skill jobs for women. However, further research is required to establish whether the 'soft skills' associated with these positions (communication, customer relations, teamwork, organizational culture) contribute to further progression in the organization, or whether the higher value given to what may be viewed as feminine attributes does not apply to more senior levels where values of competition, risk, performance, and finance still prevail.

The centrality of the interorganizational contract in shaping the pace and quality of work also meant that workers had to be sensitive to, and supportive of, the goals and demands of workers and managers in the client organization. Our evidence revealed a gendering of these new forms of relational work. Managers at the call center associated the work of processing benefit claims with women's work and identified a danger that male workers would respond too aggressively to angry clients. But the importance of such skills did not imply autonomy and discretion as such jobs were extensively monitored by managers. At the airport, the (mainly female) check-in agents had to follow a tight checklist concerning eye contact, script, and facial expression (with variations for each airline) and mistakes were logged daily and reported to the manager. Also, contractual cost pressures reinforced practices that deskilled work and favored the recruitment of women for whom external wage rates were lower. Thus, while relational work is central to the business of organizations operating within interorganizational contracts (not least because it establishes trust between partner workers and managers), our evidence suggests new employment opportunities for women have not ended gendered inequalities. Instead, lesser transparency, results-based work, and a stereotyped feminization of job tasks contribute to new gender inequalities at work.

Rethinking Policy

The previous sections have argued that the growth of contracting relations has led to a fragmentation of work and organization and reduced the effectiveness of existing forms of countervailing power, or voice, that have tended, in the UK at least, to focus on relations at the level of the single employer instead of the supply chain or interorganizational contract. If effective countervailing power is to be exercised, policies are needed to reduce opportunities for risk shifting and fragmentation; or, if this is not considered a feasible political option, the customary and legal boundaries of policy formation require redrawing. Typically, the least powerful are seen as most at risk from the fragmentation of work, at least in the short term, but there is evidence that the current system could also damage the interests of capital and, in the long term, the wider society in a context where workers are denied the opportunity to make more significant contributions to organizational and societal goals. Here we propose two main areas—the governance of interorganizational contracting relations and employment policy—where changes in policy orientation could offer a valuable way forward.

Governance of Contracting Relations

Existing modes of corporate governance are narrowly defined so as to privilege the needs of shareholders against those of other stakeholders. A broader conception of multi-stakeholders would allow for differing interests to be recognized, and thereby to be perceived as legitimate and supported by the wider community. We see this as offering a more conducive way to establish and maintain the condition of stability necessary to foster long-term economic prosperity. One way to extend involvement in corporate governance is to make information available in a form that has direct relevance to the plurality of stakeholders. However, despite some discussion of the need for change in corporate governance to take into account human resource policies, there has been little progress in this direction. For example, the Operating and Financial Reviews were introduced without the anticipated requirement for detailed information to be presented on human capital management, including equal opportunity policies (Kingsmill 2001; Accounting for People 2003).

A second way to improve corporate governance concerns better regulation by the government of contracting relations between private sector firms and public sector organizations. Our research unveiled a considerable imbalance of power in three of the four cases that favored the private sector partner and suggests an urgent need for public sector bodies to improve contacting expertise. Private sector firms are able to use their considerable market power and expertise to draw up tenders and to provide evidence of their ability to meet the requirements of initial performance expectations, such that they are bound to be accepted by the clients. However, meeting these short-term objectives does not guarantee that they will be able to deliver improved service provision in the medium, let alone, the long term. What is needed is for government to: (a) establish a coordinated approach to contracting that builds in the requirement for public sector bodies to make a more realistic assessment of the costs and benefits of contracting, (b) abolish the *de jure* (or de facto) obligation on public sector organizations to outsource activities to the private sector as part of its agenda to establish a mixed economy approach to services provision (as found in its Best Value program, or the capital investment (PFI) policy), and (c) invest resources in training personnel in how to design and manage contracts and to set up forums for public bodies to share information on their experiences with private sector firms. The approach of government should also embrace trade unions, such as UNISON, which have a wealth of detailed information about the past performance of leading contractors.

Third, the way in which interorganizational synergies are assessed needs to be rethought, with rather less attention to key performance indicators that may serve only to disrupt long-term organizational and societal goals. For example, an emphasis on the time taken to answer calls pays no attention to the quality of the advice offered once the call is answered or to the service required by the customer. Similarly, there is more to improved patient care than merely cutting waiting times or improving bed management. Our research suggests that managers acting as boundary-spanning agents are painfully aware that they need to develop stronger trusting relations with their counterparts in other organizations in order to make the contracts work in any real sense. Often, however, they are thwarted by a lack of shared understanding of agreed codes of conduct or by inappropriate standards for service provision defined in the original contract.

Employment Policy

In the realm of employment law and policy, much of the current framework remains predicated on notions of a single employer, with the attendant implications for responsibility and accountability. As the contracting culture becomes more widespread, questions of responsibility for employment policy are increasingly ambiguous. Here we focus attention on three aspects of this.

Training is a key part of state policy largely because of the acknowledged problems of market failure in this area. Interorganizational contracting intensifies these problems because whilst suppliers may be able to recruit sufficiently well-qualified and experienced staff in the short term (often through staff transfer), they lack a strong incentive to train staff beyond the most basic generic skills, in part because contracts are often of limited duration. Reduced career opportunities and redefinitions of skill around customer service as opposed to technical expertise further amplify the problem. The increased risk that, under interorganizational contracting, responsibility for training will be shifted between the parties means that the state has to take action. The reintroduction of universal levies on all companies to promote investment in training is one that the government has chosen not to support, instead believing that employer-led approaches and the NVQ system fill the gap (Keep 2000). If nothing else, the current emphasis on sector skills ignores the very real problem that much interorganizational contracting takes place across conventionally defined sectoral boundaries.

Employment rights are increasingly being undermined by a system of employment law that is constrained by the focus on single employers, and ambiguities in this area allow employers the opportunity to evade responsibilities and shift the risk to other parties. Earnshaw, Rubery and Cooke (2002) argue that clearer lines are needed in the UK to establish the identity of the employer in these circumstances, applying the principle that responsibility lies with the organization that has greater control over the working environment. In other areas, greater attention should be focused on the obligations of the legal employer so as to prevent the possibility that workers could be disciplined on the basis of claims by third parties without full investigation by their own employer. A case can also be made for extending the field for comparison in equal pay cases so that perceived inequities by colocated workers can be dealt with even though they might have different legal employers. Action should also be taken to provide a floor of minimum employment rights for all workers. Research into supply chains in the clothing manufacture industry in Australia, for example, shows how rights at work for many homeworkers are negligible: deficiencies in the law cause an 'entitlement gap' compared to other workers covered by the protective elements of the trade regulatory framework; even where the law can in principle be applied there is inadequate enforcement; and in the absence of legal obligations, powerful retailers encourage cost cutting among competing subcontractors (Nossar, Johnstone, and Quinlan 2003). Employment rights should also be extended in such a way as to provide protection for transferred workers beyond the initial contract as negotiated at the point of transfer and to encompass other workers at the same firm, thus eliminating the problem of the two-tier workforce. The UK government has strengthened protection in this area, including the announcement in October 2005 that all cleaning, catering, and portering staff employed by a private sector firm providing services to the NHS will have terms and conditions that are 'no less favourable overall than the Agenda for Change pay deal', described by the General Secretary of Unison as 'a great step forward towards ending the two-tier workforce in the NHS'. But while the government may have modernized its approach to employment, it has not benefited from a more intelligent approach to governance since it agreed to fund fully the annual costs of upgrading transferred workers' terms and conditions, resulting in a transfer of an estimated £75 million of government funds (*RxPG News* 08.10.05).

Finally, trade unions need to think beyond conventional responses that rely on the concept of the single employer. Workers with different employers working on the same site with the same trade union have divergent experiences and concerns, and these need to be properly represented by the union. Moreover, because the terms and conditions of the contract agreed between client and supplier organizations have a great influence on employment, unions need to become expert in shaping the content of interorganizational contracts in ways that improve working conditions. Unions may also need to consider novel ways of working, as some US unions have done, with community groups to strengthen the position of poorly paid workers at the bottom of the hierarchy. Social movement unionism has identified two ways in which unions might counteract fragmented capital—new methods of recruiting, and targeting multiemployers or those that have influence over them. There is some evidence that this is happening in the UK (e.g. in Living Wage campaigns in East London), but it needs to be extended to cover more groups of workers in diverse surroundings.

Conclusion

The empirical findings from our ESRC 'Future of Work' project undertaken at the University of Manchester provide an important illustration of the way different organizational forms, characterized by different patterns of trust, risk, and power and embedded in a UK socioeconomic context, impact upon the organization of employment and workers' conditions. In this chapter we have argued that interorganizational contracting leads to a blurring of organizational boundaries and a fragmenting of work across many areas of employment practice.

Our account rejects conventional managerial and strategic explanations of deverticalization, because they overstate the rational basis for decision-making, ignore the institutional context and, crucially, do not fully appreciate the interlinkages between interorganizational relations and the employment relationship. In our alternative framework, we highlight relations of trust, risk, and power, among managers of contracting organizations and workforce groups. The dynamics of these relations are complex and preclude stylized categorization of networks—as high trust, or high risk, for example—because organizations enter into multiple forms of contracting arrangements and because relations change over time. Our evidence shows clearly, however, that very often high trust relations do not equate with mutual gains since trust between contracting partners is often upheld despite an imbalance of power that skews the distribution of costs and benefits.

The main contribution of our research has been to show how these dynamics of interorganizational relations fragment work. We have adopted the word 'fragment' because it reflects a composite of terms that encompass the changes we have identified. It reflects the *disintegration* of informal norms shared by workers that have traditionally governed the collective representation of grievances and expectations of fair treatment within a single organization. It reflects the *disconnection* workers now experience with their employer as they adapt to practices whereby employers trade workers through staff transfer agreements and use agency workers, generating new forms of employment insecurities. It reflects the *incompleteness* of the working experience, especially notable with regard to use of skill and discretion under a regime of more intensive use of monitoring and evaluation of performance to meet contract requirements. And it reflects a *disordering* of employment conditions, observable, for example, in fragmented and unequal pay structures and the stereotyping of feminized qualities of relational work which creates new boundaries around what is perceived to be men's and women's work. We hope this brief review of our empirical findings will motivate further research on this topic, both to strengthen the related theoretical arguments and to shed greater light on the role of institutions and market structures at the sector and country levels.

References

Accounting for People (2003). *Report of the Task Force on Human Capital Management.* Available at www.accountingforpeople.gov.uk

Ackroyd, S. and Procter, S. (1998). 'British Manufacturing Organization and Workplace Industrial Relations: Some Attributes of the New Flexible Firm', *British Journal of Industrial Relations*, 36(2): 163–83.

Barney, J. B. (1991). 'Firm Resources and Sustained Comparative Advantage', *Journal of Management*, 17(1): 99–120.

Burchell, B., Ladipo, D., and Wilkinson, F. (eds.) (2003). *Job Insecurity and Work Intensification.* London: Routledge.

Cooke, F., Earnshaw, J., Marchington, M., and Rubery, J. (2004). 'For Better and For Worse: Transfer of Undertakings and the Reshaping of Employment Relations', *International Journal of Human Resource Management*, 15(2): 276–94.

Crouch, C. (2003). 'Commercialisation or Citizenship? Education Policy and the Future of Public Services', *Fabian Ideas*. London: Fabian Society.

Earnshaw, J., Rubery, J., and Cooke, F. (2002). *Who is the Employer?* London: Institute for Employment Rights.

Ferner, A. and Hyman, R. (eds.) (1998). *Changing Industrial Relations in Europe*. Oxford: Blackwell.

Froud, J., Haslam, C., Johal, S., and Williams, K. (2000). 'Shareholder Value and Financialization: Consultancy Promises, Management Moves', *Economy and Society*, 29(1): 80–111.

Gallie, D., White, M., Cheng Y., and Tomlinson, M. (1998). *Restructuring the Employment Relationship*. Oxford: Oxford University Press.

Godard, J. (2004). 'A Critical Assessment of the High Performance Paradigm', *British Journal of Industrial Relations*, 42(2): 349–78.

Grimshaw, D. and Hebson, G. (2004). 'Public Private Partnerships in the UK: The Limits to Contracting and the Prospects for Employment', *Economia & Lavoro*, 38(1): 39–163.

——and Miozzo, M. (2006). 'Institutional Effects on the Market for IT Outsourcing: Analyzing Clients, Suppliers and Staff Transfer in Germany and the UK', *Organization Studies* (forthcoming).

——and Rubery, J. (2005). 'Inter-capital Relations and the Network Organization: Redefining the Issues Concerning Work and Employment', *Cambridge Journal of Economics* (forthcoming).

——Earnshaw, J., and Hebson, G. (2003). 'Private Sector Provision of Supply Teachers: A Case of Legal Swings and Professional Roundabouts', *Journal of Education Policy*, 18(3): 267–88.

——Rubery, J., Willmott, H., and Marchington, M. (2005). 'Bringing Employment Back in: A Critique of Current Theorizing of Inter-organizational Relations', Paper presented at the SASE conference, Budapest (June).

Grugulis, I., Vincent, S., and Hebson, G. (2003). 'The Rise of the "Network" Organization and the Decline of Discretion', *Human Resource Management Journal*, 13(2): 45–59.

Hall, P. and Soskice, D. (eds.) (2001). *Varieties of Capitalism: The Institutional Foundations of Comparative Advantage*. Oxford: Oxford University Press.

Hebson, G. and Grugulis, I. (2005). 'Gender and New Organizational Forms', in M. Marchington, D. Grimshaw, J. Rubery, and H. Willmott (eds.) (2005), *Fragmenting*

Work: Blurring Organizational Boundaries and Disordering Hierarchies. Oxford: Oxford University Press.

Heery, E. and Salmon, J. (eds.) (2000). *The Insecure Workforce*. London: Routledge.

——Conley, H., Delbridge, R., Simms, M., and Stewart, P. (2004). 'Trade Union Responses to Non-Standard Work', in G. Healy, E. Heery, P. Taylor, and W. Brown (eds.), *The Future of Worker Representation*. London: Palgrave.

Hyman, R. (1987). 'Strategy or Structure? Capital, Labour and Control', *Work, Employment and Society*, 1(1): 25–55.

Keep, E. (2000). Learning Organisations, Lifelong Learning and the Mystery of the Vanishing Employers, SKOPE Research Paper No. 8, Country: University of Warwick.

Kingsmill, D. (2001). *Review of Women's Pay and Employment*. Women and Equality Unit.

Lane, C. and Bachmann, R. (2002). *Trust Within and Between Organizations: Conceptual Issues and Empirical Applications*. Oxford: Oxford University Press.

Lepak, D. and Snell, S. (1999). 'The Human Resource Architecture: Towards a Theory of Human Capital Allocation and Development', *The Academy of Management Review*, 24(1): 31–48.

Malecki, E. J. (1997). *Technology and Economic Development*. Harlow, UK: Longman.

Marchington, M. and Vincent, S. (2004). 'Analyzing the Influence of Institutional, Organizational and Interpersonal Forces in Shaping Inter-organizational Relations', *Journal of Management Studies*, 41(6): 1029–56.

——Cooke, F., and Hebson, G. (2003). 'Performing for the "Customer": Managing Housing Benefit Operations Across Organizational Boundaries', *Local Government Studies*, 29(1): 51–74.

——Rubery, J., and Cooke, F. (2004). 'Worker Representation Within and Across Organisational Boundaries: A Case Study of Worker Voice in a Multi-Agency Environment', in G. Healy, E. Heery, P. Taylor, and W. Brown (eds.), *The Future of Worker Representation*. London: Palgrave.

——Grimshaw, D., Rubery, J., and Willmott, H. (eds.) (2005). *Fragmenting Work: Blurring Organizational Boundaries and Disordering Hierarchies*. Oxford: Oxford University Press.

Noon, M. and Blyton, P. (2002). *The Realities of Work*. London: Palgrave.

Nossar, I., Johnstone, R., and Quinlan, M. (2003). 'Regulating Supply Chains to Address the Occupational Health and Safety Problems associated with Precarious Employment: the Case of Home-based Clothing Workers in Australia', Working paper 21, National Research Centre for OHS Regulation, Australian National University.

Ovum (2002). *Holway@Ovum: Market trends 2002*. London: Ovum.

Purcell, K. and Purcell, J. (1999). 'Insourcing, Outsourcing and the Growth of Contingent Labour as Evidence of Flexible Employment Strategies', *Bulletin of Comparative Labour Relations*, 35: 163–81.

Rubery, J. and Earnshaw, J. (2005). 'Employment Policy and Practice; Crossing Borders and Disordering Hierarchies', in M. Marchington, D. Grimshaw, D. J. Rubery, and H. Willmott (eds.) (2005). *Fragmenting Work: Blurring Organizational Boundaries and Disordering Hierarchies*. Oxford: Oxford University Press.

——Cooke, F., Earnshaw, J., and Marchington, M. (2003). 'Contracts, Cooperation and Employment Relationships: Working in a Multi-Employer Environment', *British Journal of Industrial Relations*, 41(2): 265–89.

Rubery, J., Earnshaw, J., Marchington, M., Cooke, F. L., and Vincent, S. (2002). 'Changing Organisational Forms and the Employment Relationship', *Journal of Management Studies*, 39(5): 645–72.

Rumelt, R. (1984). 'Towards a Strategic Theory of the Firm', in R. Lamb (ed.), *Competitive Strategic Management*. Englewood Cliffs, NJ: Prentice-Hall.

Thompson, P. (2004). 'Disconnected Capitalism: Or Why Employers Can't Keep Their Side of Their Bargain', *Work, Employment and Society*, 17(2): 359–78.

Traxler, F., Blaschke, S., and Kittel, B. (2001). *National Labour Relations in Internationalised Markets*. Oxford: Oxford University Press.

Unison (2003). *Pay and Conditions Claim for Private Contract Staff: Barts and the Royal London Hospital Trust*, Unison, supported by TELCO (March). London: Unison.

Wernerfelt, B. (1984). 'A Resource-based View of the Firm', *Strategic Management Journal*, 5: 171–80.

White, M., Hill, S., Mills, C., and Smeaton, D. (2004). *Managing to Change? British Workplaces and the Future of Work*. London: Palgrave.

8

The Limits of Numerical Flexibility: Continuity and Change

Geoffrey Wood, Mark Harcourt, and Ian Roper

Introduction

In recent years, the European social employment model has come under increasing scrutiny for its relative inability, compared to its Anglo-Saxon counterpart, to generate sustained employment growth. The problem, for critics, has been that the European model provides too much employment security leading to too little numerical flexibility for employers to make adjustments to the size of their workforces. This criticism has not only come from outside Europe, but increasingly from within. In Germany, the challenge to rigid labor markets has come from the business lobby—now wishing to be freed, post-reunification, from the constraints that had previously provided a useful institutional constraint on labor. This has found its way into the political arena. The 2005 general election was fought not on whether the government needed to dismantle established labor market rigidities; but at what speed. It seems likely that in France too, populist sentiment among elements within the Gaulist right, backed by business interests, may be preparing to challenge the fabled French social model, so long a focus of party consensus.

Yet, in 1991, Anna Pollert bid a rhetorical farewell to the fetishized concept of flexibility. The concept was ambiguous; was overly descriptive, yet based on little evidence; and was based on flawed determinist prescriptive theory. It had gained hegemonic status due to the predominance of neoclassical economic theory in policymaking circles. Tellingly, however, she notes that

> ... in the process of its dissemination, the concept has become a material force in the policy language of governments and employers; and in practice, in legislation, in the booming management consultancy business and in industrial relations bargaining.
>
> (Pollert 1991: xvii)

This description is as true now as it was in 1991. As noted above, the clamor for more flexibility dominates discussion about reforming employment in Europe. This indicates that 'flexibility'—especially the numerical variety, that provides advantages only for employers—continues to command honorific status among policymakers. Paradoxically, however, it would seem that the continued clamor for 'more flexibility' from policymakers indicates that inadequate headway has been made in dismantling the institutional barriers holding back flexibility since the 1980s. Yet does numerical flexibility really yield the promised dividends? And, are alternatives to the orthodoxy of numerical flexibility sustainable?

Against this background, the present chapter challenges the growing orthodoxy that actions to reduce regulatory constraints in order to enhance numerical flexibility provide an effective means of enhancing economic performance. It does so by, initially, examining national variations in such constraints and the arguments advanced in support and opposition to them, and, then, considering the available evidence concerning their relationship to variations in levels of national productivity. Thereafter, the broader theoretical implications are appraised.

Employment Security and Numerical Flexibility: Some Cross-National Comparisons

Employment security concerns the degree of protection afforded to incumbents of jobs, and the restraints imposed on employers against the arbitrary termination of employees' services. The latter can include severance payments, the provision of advanced notice, procedural requirements (consultation with unions or works councils), just cause provisions (e.g. being contingent on disciplinary matters or pressing economic reasons), and/or obligations to provide retraining and/or placement assistance for employees who have been made redundant. Within most West European countries employees have strong job rights, and, in many instances, firms are encouraged to make use of alternatives—such as adjusting working hours—to layoffs (Abraham and Houseman 1994). In contrast, in strongly market-orientated economies such as the United States, job protection is very much weaker.

In Germany, workers have the right to advanced notice, ranging from two weeks to six months (Abraham and Houseman 1994). The 1951 Protection against Dismissal Act and its subsequent amendments cover individuals who have six months uninterrupted service at firms employing more than five workers (Eger 2002). Dismissals have to be in terms of a predetermined just cause—'socially justified'. The latter encompasses personal characteristics (lack of capability), misconduct, and redundancy; pregnant women, disabled workers and Works Council members are accorded further protection (Eger 2002). There must be a high probability that past problems (such as individual incapacity or the viability of the firm) will continue to exist in the future, that there are no less serious alternatives (such as retraining or redeployment) available, and in the case of individual dismissals, that the situation has been fairly evaluated (Eger 2002). In the event of a collective dismissal, the relevant Works Council must be consulted, and a social plan that provides some form of compensation to affected employees should be agreed on (Kraft 1997); in the event of no agreement, the matter is referred to binding arbitration (Abraham and Houseman 1994). Employees are entitled to a payout determined by the years of service and the pay rate at dismissal (Kraft 1997). Because of these requirements, short-term layoffs are rare, with employers being encouraged to resort to alternatives such as ending overtime. Whilst critics have charged that severance pay arrangements are not really necessary given a generous social welfare system, proponents have argued that this induces employers to make more considered—and hence, ultimately more efficient—choices between dismissal and retention (Eger 2002).

In France, workers are entitled to a notice period and severance payments ranging from one to three months, in the case of redundancies. Employers are required to consult with the Works Council and, again, are encouraged to make use of alternatives such as adjustments to working time (Eger 2002). However, collective dismissals no longer require authorization from the Labour Inspectorate, as they did prior to 1984. In Belgium, employees subject to collective dismissals are entitled to a predetermined amount of compensation from their employer, even in the case of entire plant closures (Eger 2002). In addition, as is the case with Germany and France, Belgian employees are entitled to receive benefits if they are placed on short time. In Spain, redundancies have to be on technical, organizational, or production grounds, or a general dysfunction not posing a risk to the entire viability of the enterprise (Morin and Vincens 2001).

In contrast, in the United States, there is no national obligation on employers to make severance payments to laid off workers, although collective dismissals may lead to an increase in unemployment insurance liabilities (Abraham and Houseman 1994). In the United States, most employment contracts are covered by 'employment at will', and can be terminated at any time for any or no reason (Lowther and Naletilic 2004). Only public sector and unionized workers have 'just-cause' employment protection and collective bargaining only covers some 18 percent of wage agreements in the United States (compared to, say, 92 percent in Germany). Hence, in most cases the countervailing power of US employees is relatively weak (Lowther and Naletilic 2004). However, workers are afforded some protection under equal opportunities legislation, and through state-level protection for whistleblowers.

In Britain, the situation has been more nuanced: if the 1980s were characterized by the Thatcherite project to '... go on reducing the barriers which discourage employers from recruiting more staff, [and] help to make the job market more flexible and efficient' (Conservative Party 1983), then the New Labour project from 1997 has been to put a human face on this, through its 'fairness at work' agenda. In the 1980s, then, legislative protection accorded to individual employees was drastically reduced in parallel with the legislative neutering of union powers. Thus, the qualifying length of service for coverage under unfair dismissal legislation was extended from 6 months in 1979 to two years by 1985, while the previously existing statutory union recognition procedure was abolished in 1980 and a whole raft of legislation restricting strike action and the closed shop and regulating the union-member relationship was introduced (MacInness 1987; Wedderburn 1989). The 'reforming' Labour administration that came to power in 1997 was keen to display its new 'flexibility with fairness' agenda by reducing the unfair dismissal qualifying period to 12 months. On union power, a statutory union recognition procedure was restored in 2000 but the legislation restricting unions' ability to mobilize—against redundancy among other things—was left intact (Smith and Morton 2001). Without collective bargaining as a support mechanism, unorganized workers in Britain face significant obstacles accessing the individual employment rights granted by the government (Pollert 2005).

As a result, Britain's Labour administration continues to boast, much like their Conservative predecessors, that the country has one of the 'most lightly regulated labour markets in the world' (DTI 1997). However, evidence suggesting that such flexibility is the choice of British workers—rather than the restricted choice made available by employers—is more mixed. For example, the workplace employment relations survey (WERS) series indicates that part-time work is sector-specific, and found in low-paid, service-based work. Thus, in 1998 only 1 percent of manufacturing organizations employed a largely part-time workforce compared to 55 percent of hotels, 43 percent of retail organizations, 40 percent of education establishments, and 50 percent of health care organizations (Cully et al. 1998: 33).

Despite sharing certain common features, 'collaborative' continental European countries vary in key areas. The 1992 EU Directive 92/56/EEC, amending a 1975 Directive, sought to harmonize the degree of job protection in the EU, but has only been partially successful (Morin and Vicens 2001). As Bertola, Boeri, and Cazes (2000) note, there are considerable national variations in the number of disputes surrounding dismissal being brought to court and success rates, ranging from a 74 percent success rate in France in 1995, to only 16 percent in Ireland (Bertola, Boeri, and Cazes 2000). In most cases, a high incidence of litigation is mirrored in a high success rate for employees (Bertola, Boeri, and Cazes 2000). Tough sanctions may discourage employers from going to court, but limitations in unemployment insurance may encourage the courts to make rulings favorable to workers.

The French government has a history of directly intervening in large-scale redundancies; indeed, from 1975 to 1984, French employers needed formal authorization from the Labour Inspectorate for any dismissals (Abraham and Houseman 1994). This was then abandoned in the face of intense employer pressure, although most requests were approved (Kraft 1997: 346). Again, whilst the Directive simply obliges companies to inform their employees of impending redundancies, in Germany, worker representatives have a say in the selection process (Morin and Vincens 2001). There are also considerable variations in employer accountability when helping dismissed workers find alternative employment. In France, the employer has the primary responsibility in helping separated workers. In Germany, Italy, and Spain, support for dismissed workers is primarily an obligation of the authorities (Morin and Vincens 2001). However, whilst French managers can play the primary role in framing redundancy plans, in Germany this has to be a negotiated agreement between the employer and the Works Council. Finally, in all these countries, there has been considerable use made of early retirement schemes, and, despite legislative interventions, it seems that highly vulnerable categories of worker—the elderly and the unskilled—are most likely to face dismissal (Morin and Vincens 2001). Again, since the 1990s, a growing proportion of new jobs in the EU have been temporary or fixed-term positions; whilst, in most instances, such workers still enjoy a greater degree of protection than their US counterparts, such employment is nonetheless generally less secure than traditional permanent posts (Lowther and Naletilic 2004). Whilst there have been pressures to reduce the degree of job protection accorded to workers, in some cases, such as Spain in 1997, the statutory definition of unfair dismissals has been both expanded and clarified. In others, such as Germany, the 1985 Employment Promotion Act which liberalized fixed-term contracts (*inter alia*, extending their permitted duration), reducing the termination costs associated with redundancies, seems to have had limited effects (Kraft 1997: 346). Similarly, in a more detailed study of the effects of this reform, Hunt (1998: 179) found that it had little effect in speeding the time taken to adjust hours worked to changes in production.

Varieties of Capitalism and the Importance of Employment Security

The employment security debate is not just about job creation. There is little doubt that variations in job security provision constitute one of the defining features of national business systems, and have far-reaching effects on other areas of the firm's activities: differing degrees of job security may encourage greater or lesser investments in human capital, affect the degree of upward mobility afforded to employees, and productivity and national skills profiles.

The divergent and uneven performance of different national economies has highlighted the extent to which distinct trajectories of national development are possible, pressures toward globalization notwithstanding (Leborgne and Lipietz 2001: 384). Advanced forms of social compromise performed particularly well in the 1980s and early 1990s when compared to national economies that had chosen the path of deregulation. This led some writers to conclude that the former represented a more effective mode of national economic management than deregulation. However, by the late 1990s, it was evident that compromise-based systems were not immune from systemic crises, characterized by falling rates of profit, leading to renewed rounds of cost cutting and manufacturing shakeouts (Brenner 2002: 127).

From a rational choice perspective, firms pursue economic gain through rationally based decisions and actions; practices that promote optimal outcomes will rapidly spread, with uneven outcomes representing the product of either imperfect information or nonrational structural impediments (Gooderham, Nordhaug, and Ringdal 1999: 507). In other words, countries that subject firms to the greatest degree of regulation will inevitably hamper the diffusion of best practices, inevitably leading to suboptimal outcomes.

In contrast, critical institutionalist perspectives argue that a specific set of economic, political, and cultural-ideological institutional structures foster economic production and development (Kotz 2003: 265). However, whether seen as an impediment or a facilitator, both critical institutionalists and neoliberals have ascribed the differing fortunes of nations to the effects of various attempts to regulate economic activity through legislation or convention, or the lack thereof. In understanding the causes, nature, and effects of uneven performance a distinction is most commonly drawn between compromise-based national systems, and the deregulated alternatives. Hence, Kotz (2003: 265) argues that states with a liberal institutional structure are characterized by the state playing a limited role in economic activity, by aggressive and unilateralist strategies by management toward labor, and cutthroat competition, reinforced by neoliberal ideologies. In more regulated alternatives, relations between employers and employees are marked by a degree of cooperation and compromise, the rivalry between firms is corespective and muted, and both of these features are underpinned by an ideology of social democracy highlighting the dangers of untrammeled markets, and the role of the state as a guarantor of prosperity (Kotz 2003).

Dore (2000) draws a clear distinction between, on the one hand, varieties of capitalism emphasizing that the rights of shareholders be counterbalanced by the entrenched rights of other stakeholders—including employees and communities, with that of the shareholder-only driven Anglo-Saxon model.

Again, Hall and Soskice (2001) make a similar distinction between coordinated market economies and liberal market (Anglo-American style) ones, with the former characterized by a greater range of systemic checks and balances, and cooperation between stakeholders (cf. Lincoln and Kalleberg 1990). Other accounts, such as Whitley (1999) have pointed to a greater number of possible varieties of capitalism. However, whilst there is little doubt that each national business system has specific characteristics, the key differences are between the coordinated European/Rhineland model on the one side (and, to an extent, also the coordinated Japanese system) and the liberal market model. Other national business systems such as Italy incorporate important regional variations in regulation and practice, and represent more of a mixed model.

What all these accounts have in common is that they draw a close linkage between the wider regulatory environment, and firm-level governance and workplace practices. In coordinated market economies, firms are more comprehensively obliged to take at least some account of employee interests by formal legislation, bargained agreements, or simply embedded convention (Dore 2000). This means that, whilst some numerical flexibility may be possible through negotiated changes to working time, firms are restrained from responding to external challenges through excessive use of redundancies. This has forced firms operating in such contexts to seek competitive gains through high technology and highly skilled production, in other words, functional flexibility (Dore 2000; cf. Leborgne and Lipietz 2001: 347). In contrast, in liberal market economies, firms have fewer incentives to systematically invest in, actively secure the buy-in, and maximize the potential of their employees, as they may secure short-term competitive advantages through recourse to external flexibility. Firms are relatively free to rapidly adjust the sizes of their workforces, thereby gaining a high degree of numerical flexibility.

The 'optimal model of existing capitalism', an influential strand of regulationist theory echoes some of the assumptions of the Varieties of Capitalism school, in that it similarly suggests that specific national institutional frameworks are more conducive to economic growth than others (Amable 2003: 76). However, more recently, leading theorists such as Robert Boyer have reemphasized the complex and interconnected nature of complementary institutional features; again, the forces that shape institutional features are not the same as those that mould the governance of business organizations (see Chapter 2).

The post-World War II (WWII) social compromises in Western Europe forced a dilution of managerial power that many managers would have an interest in reversing should the external environment prove conducive (Kotz 2003); this represents only one of quotidian systemic instabilities, in addition to the broader volatility associated with the operation of technologies, capital, and markets under contemporary capitalism. Hence, Kotz (2003) argues that cooperative and liberal market institutional structures are likely to alternate over time within specific national contexts, and both may be superseded by new or hybrid forms of mediation. However, the existing nature of institutional complementarities within Western Europe would make it difficult to bring about regulatory changes that would optimize conditions for renewed growth.

In other words, the dominant social system of production in the cooperative economies of Western Europe represents not so much an embedded and stable set of institutions and practices, but rather a series of unstable and temporary compromises and rules that have provided both the foundations for a period of unprecedented growth and stability, yet one that is not indefinitely sustainable. Although cooperative economies may have reaped the benefits that have flowed from greater job security in the past, the sets of compromises that made this possible may not be as functional in the future. At the same time, while the US liberal market economy may have performed particularly robustly in the late 1990s and early 2000s, growth has been uneven (manufacturing has performed particularly poorly), volatile, and associated with rising income inequality. Hence, it is evident that the particular set of institutions associated with liberal market economies seems more conducive to certain types of economic activity than others, and remains more of an unstable interregnum than a coherent growth regime (Amable 2003; Kotz 2003: 76–7).

Neoliberal, critical institutionalist and regulationist accounts, nevertheless, all suggest that the employment contract and the manner in which it is governed is central to understanding the divergent fortunes of nations. If highly insecure employment contracts do encourage individuals to make more suitable lifestyle choices, and allow firms to most effectively respond to changing environments, then, it would seem that over time, the Anglo-American model will prove the more resilient. On the other hand, if insecure employment contracts yield suboptimal outcomes, the benefits of more closely governed forms of employment relations, and hence, alternative trajectories of national development are underscored.

Whilst proponents of employment security have often highlighted the incentive effects of employment protection—that it encourages mutual commitment, resulting in firms investing in organization-specific skills—critics have charged that employment protection has negative 'lethargy' effects (Suedekum and Ruehmann 2003: 48). However, as Suedekum and Ruehmann (2003: 49) note, it is likely that there will be a trade-off between these two mechanisms; the positive effects are likely to greatly outweigh the negative ones if there are strong incentives to build up human capital in the first place. In other words, within a particular national business system, there are a range of features that are essentially complementary; these are likely to facilitate certain outcomes, and preclude others (Hollingsworth 2004).

Behavioral Responses to Job Protection

To a large extent, preferences for one system of protection over another presuppose certain behavioral responses of actors within these systems. In relation to flexibility, relevant behavior relates to the effect of job security on worker motivation. Looking at the case of Germany, Riphahn (2004) explores the behavioral responses associated with a high degree of job security, more specifically in terms of propensity toward excessive absenteeism. She found that whilst there was little difference in behaviour between private sector and public sector workers with a low degree of job security, there was a significant degree of variation between public and private sector workers as a whole; this reflected the extended employment protection afforded certain categories of public sector worker, who were particularly prone to be absent from work: an average of 16.1 days per year, compared to 10.1 without this protection (Riphahn: 354). The job protection afforded this category of public sector workers is extremely high, in comparison to other categories of worker in Germany, especially to workers over 40; it should be noted that the differences between different categories of worker in the private sector were far less pronounced (Riphahn: 354). In addition, it needs to be borne in mind that, in most cases, in coordinated economies, it is possible for firms to dismiss workers for poor performance.

Again, research conducted in peripheral economies with little legal job protection has indicated that workers in particularly tenuous occupations are likely to be more prone to absenteeism, or simply deserting their jobs (Cohen 1994); it should be noted that these behavioral patterns are echoed among workers in peripheral occupations such as fast food in liberal market economies. Shirking may still occur in situations where job security is low, as employees may be able to count on a good reference for legal reasons and to encourage them to leave. Again, good behavior may often go unrewarded and bad behavior penalized (Schwab 1993). However, as noted elsewhere, at certain stages of a career life cycle individual employees may be particularly vulnerable and in other stages at a stronger bargaining position vis-à-vis the employer. It is precisely at the most vulnerable stages—early and late in the career—that employees are least likely to shirk for fear of job loss, but where statutory job protection will be the most valuable to them (cf. Schwab 1993).

Studies by opponents of job protection have asserted that employment falls when job security laws are introduced; this is based on the assumption that the only workers likely to be dismissed by rational profit maximizing firms are shirkers, and firms are more likely to take on workers if they can readily rid themselves of poor performers (Carter and Lancey 1997: 620). However, if even some workers are dismissed for unfair reasons—hence, making little or no efficiency gain in firing them—the firm will incur costs that would have been avoided had the workers enjoyed greater job protection (Carter and Lancey 1992). These include greater recruitment, induction, and training costs, and a reciprocal lower organizational commitment by employees, with even the most productive employees hedging by actively exploring alternative employment options. Indeed, in a real-world situation, both the employer and a job incumbent are likely to possess imperfect information as to her/his relative performance in a range of areas, leading to both periodic unjustified dismissals by the firm, and active hedging of employment options by the worker. Whilst shirkers may gain from job protection, so do nonshirkers through being relieved of the stress posed by the possibility of arbitrary termination (Carter and Lancey 1992). The firm gains costs advantages accruing from a lower staff turnover, even if these are somewhat offset by the retention of a greater number of shirkers than would otherwise have been the case (Carter and Lancey 1992).

Critics of employment security particularly argue that it makes employers more cautious in their recruitment choices, opting for workers who are already in jobs and 'proven', rather than the riskier option of choosing the already unemployed (Kugler and Saint Paul 2004: 553). Some also argue that employment protection laws can lead to the stigmatization of those who are dismissed, since only workers with very poor performance or guilty of major misconduct can be fired under such regimes (Canziani and Petrongolo 2001). However, in the absence of such laws, employees can be stigmatized instead through employment in the secondary labor market (see Chapter 15). Hence, those entering the highly insecure jobs that are a feature of deregulated labor markets may also be stigmatized—this time as 'losers'—and remain locked in poverty, albeit in low-end employment. Also, the lack of a predetermined period of notice will give dismissed employees less time to transfer to alternative jobs, and, hence, be more likely to be burdened with the stigma of unemployment. Finally, firing individuals who are less productive does not rid the economy of such workers; they may end up being disciplined by workfare or shunted between a succession of low-end jobs and, in doing so, become more widely distributed across the economy, but with nothing done to resolve the underlying causes of their poor performance. In contrast, firms that are 'stuck' with unproductive workers are forced to investigate the causes of underperformance, and through better voice and skill development mechanisms, actively seek to remedy underperformance, reincluding such individuals back into normal organizational life.

Moreover, there is a long-term 'bonding' effect in employment contracts; the possibility for employer opportunism where protection is weak encourages the employee to hedge her/his bets by actively monitoring alternatives. However, when the possibility for opportunism is reduced (through statutory job protection), employees may be encouraged to increase effort, in anticipation of a long-lasting relationship with the company, and more personally identify with company goals (Eger 2004: 387). When employers expect a lasting relationship with employees, they will have incentives to improve working conditions in order to provide a more stimulating and pleasant work climate to ensure continued employee buy-in (Eger 2004). The pros and cons of a high degree of job protection in these areas are summarized in Table 8.1:

Table 8.1 Behavioral responses to job protection

Potential problems	Countervailing issues
Lethargy effects (high job security likely to induce absenteeism and poor performance)	Little evidence except in cases where job protection is extremely high. Recent entrants into the job market and older workers are likely to be particularly vulnerable to arbitrary job loss in the absence of protection, but there is no evidence that such individuals are more prone to shirking.
Adverse selection ('shirkers' will not be deterred from applying for work if they can count on a high degree of security of tenure)	Signalling problem. If legal job protection is weak, there is likely to be a considerable unevenness in firm practices. Diligent workers who seek out job security—for example, owing to personal circumstances—may send out the wrong signals to potential employers.
Risk aversion (firms only hire 'proven' workers, shutting new entrants to the labor market out of many jobs)	Even if job protection is high, firms may still make use of temporary workers.
Natural selection (over time, firms will be able to weed out poor performers, and retain good workers)	Imperfect information. Even 'good' workers may be unsure as to whether their performance has been duly noted, and will be tempted to hedge their bets through actively exploring the external labor market. High cost of recruiting and inducting new staff if turnover is high. In terms of the 'bonding effect', longer serving workers are likely to be more committed to the firm.
Stigmatization problem (workers still losing their jobs in a situation where job security is high may be stigmatized as 'failures')	Upward mobility in highly deregulated economies is uneven. Unskilled workers can remain trapped in peripheral occupations, facing stigmatization as 'losers'.

Productivity Responses to Job Protection

Despite increases in US productivity growth rates, many countries that have substantially more restrictions on the termination of employment contracts still enjoy superior productivity levels and have, up until recently, surpassed US productivity growth rates. Proponents of greater regulation have suggested this reflected a greater sense of well-being amongst employees that comes from security, and that firms are forced to secure competitive advantage from investing in their people, rather than through the crudest forms of numerical flexibility (Wood 2004: 453). However, by the early 2000s, this trend was reversed, with the United States surpassing most Western European economies in productivity gains. Whilst proponents of highly flexible labor markets are quick to claim that their position has been exonerated, critics argue that much of this productivity gain was through the 'iron whip of hunger' (see Chapter 15). Low job security and the scaling back of benefits forced employees to work ever harder (see Wood 2004); however, these gains had a hidden cost in terms of increased workplace stress and poorer health, making such increases difficult to sustain. As Schwab (1993: 25) notes, the threat of the loss of employment and developed relationships within the workplace can have a devastating effect, leading to a range of physiological and psychological ailments. Although firms are quick to reap the resultant productivity gains, the cost in terms of reductions in overall health and well-being is borne by society as a whole.

One could argue that using contingent labor provides gains through numerical flexibility and its associated cost savings. However, it is harder to simultaneously make performance gains through predictability and continuity (Lautsch 2002: 26); numerical flexibility comes at the cost of less *functional* flexibility. In other words, allocative efficiency may be enhanced (resources are allocated to the uses likely to prove most immediately productive), but with less dynamic efficiency (more difficulty leveraging innovation off existing resource endowments). If it is not easy to adjust wages or overall employment figures, firms are forced to (and, Western European evidence would suggest they do) concentrate on achieving high productivity gains through the development of employee skills, and the more effective deployment of labor throughout the firm (Boyer 2000: 125).

Functional flexibility concerns the propensity of workers to change a job within a given type of organization, even if it is undergoing rapid change, as well as the adaptability of productive organization; the latter depends on both choice of technology and the type of organization (Boyer 2000: 117). The dissemination of functionally flexible methods across an economy is associated with high value-added forms of production, and is likely to mitigate the *Brazilianization* of society, high levels of social segmentation between a labor market elite, and those locked in a career trajectory of insecure and poorly paying jobs (Roobeek 2000: 161). The former may be facilitated through state interventions aimed at providing the framework in which entrepreneurs may more readily switch to new technological concepts through an effective national training and skills development infrastructure, and, increasing pressures on employers to invest in their people, through making labor less of a readily dispensable commodity (cf. Boyer 2000; Glyn 2000; Roobeek 2000).

As noted earlier, firms in coordinated economies may offset the costs posed by a high degree of job protection by adjusting the hours worked. A greater degree of regulation of working time arrangements is therefore likely to impede the speed with which firms can cope with changes. On the other hand, looser working time arrangements are likely to discourage employment growth during expansions (Nunziata 2003: 40). As regulation is likely to be lighter in both regards, in Anglo-American model economies, this means that the effect of one could diminish the other. Conversely, however, strict working time arrangements during slumps may encourage job shedding, even if it is deterred by stricter regulation (Nunziata 2003: 46). This would seem to indicate that a careful fine-tuning of working time governance regulations is in order, so as to optimize the effects of external shocks. Again, as the experience of Germany would indicate, regulations governing working time, do not necessarily seem to deter regular adjustments to the working day and week; rather, they seem to confirm specific practices and deter others, which may be particularly beneficial, or, in some cases result in sub-optimal outcomes.

The greater tendency to make use of reduced working hours rather than redundancies in coordinated economies has a number of benefits. First, workers who have been laid off may be uncertain as to whether they will be likely to be recalled, and, hence, may defer looking for new work (Abraham and Houseman 1994: 25). The underutilization of experienced workers represents a loss of resources to society. In contrast, if firms are deterred from taking on additional labor by the possible difficulties of shedding it again, then the principal costs are amongst those who are most able to bear it—young labor market entrants with few dependants—and who have the least on job skills and experience to offer. Second, job shedding places the cost of adjustment disproportionately on a few individuals, who suffer a large loss of income and benefits, in contrast to the rather lower costs experienced by the firm (Abraham and Houseman: 25). Table 8.2 shows, in ascending order, how average annual hours worked during 2003 for a number of coordinated and liberal market business systems compare. Neoliberal economies consistently have the highest figures, yet do not have productivity figures to match, suggesting a lack of efficiency in such an approach.

Across most of continental Europe, bargaining coverage is high and stable, and in many cases coordinated. Coordinated bargaining is where the

Table 8.2 Average annual hours worked, 2003 (in ascending order)

Country	Production regime	Annual hours (avg)
Germany	Coordinated	1,446
Denmark	Coordinated	1,475
Austria	Coordinated	1,550
Sweden	Coordinated	1,564
UK	Liberal market	1,673
Canada	Liberal market	1,718
USA	Liberal market	1,792

Source: OECD 2004.

aggregate employment implications of wage rates are taken into account in bargaining, examples being seen as Austria (where highly centralized bargaining takes place) and Germany (where effective employer federations assist bargainers to act in concert). Where bargaining is coordinated the adverse effects of other factors on employment are offset, and wages are able to more rapidly factor in the effects of output shocks (Nickell 2002).

General Issues

Two caveats should be added to this general picture. First, it should not be read into the analysis presented that there are not problems of function or legitimacy associated with coordinated market approaches. As was noted at the outset, the restrictions placed upon employers are increasingly being challenged by employers and reform-minded populist politicians. In addition, the operation of safe employment territory has also been associated with growing pockets of excluded workers: from those living in the former communist east in Germany, to second generation North African communities living on the peripheral estates in France. But it is not clear how the exclusion of these groups will be ameliorated by the levelling down of those currently occupying 'insider' status.

The second caveat is that liberal market economies incorporate a great deal of internal diversity (cf. Amable 2003; Chapter 11). Sectors and regions associated with innovation and relatively high pay—an often-cited example being the Silicon Valley region—coexist with widely distributed firms and sectors associated with high levels of labor repression, most notably in low value-added areas of the service sector. At the same time, liberal market systems remain considerably less favorable for large areas of manufacturing when compared to cooperative systems.

Furthermore, it is important to draw a distinction between the coexistence of particular sets of formal and informal rules, and firm-level practices and situations where they are genuinely complementary (see Chapter 2). The fact that a light regulatory environment may be favorable for sweatshop production paradigms does not mean that the former will gradually infuse greater sustainability or higher returns in the latter; the two are simply often found together. In contrast, more cooperative institutional frameworks seem to be conducive to more closely integrated supply chain relations (critical in key areas of manufacturing such as the motor industry) (Wood and Brewster 2005), encouraging more patient investor behavior, and cooperative production paradigms, centering on knowledge-sharing and development, and high levels of mutual commitment; a key dimension of the latter being high security of tenure. The situation is summarized in Table 8.3:

Table 8.3 Complementarity and coexistence between regulation and sectoral performance

		Sectoral performance:		
Institutional environment	Degree of employment protection	'High-tech'	Manufacturing	'Low value added' areas of the service sector
Liberal market	Limited	Complementarity in particular local environments	Destructive	Coexistence
Cooperative	High	Coexistence	Complementary	Uneasy coexistence

Conclusion

This chapter serves to highlight the limits of numerical flexibility when attained through low levels of job security. In contrast, the higher degree of job security associated with cooperative economies remains conducive to building organizational citizenship, human capital development, and sustainable productivity gains. However, it should be reemphasized that the complementarities associated with cooperative economies were attained through far-reaching class compromises that formed part and parcel of the post-World War II settlement. Constraints on the ability to hire and fire workers necessarily limit managerial power, and hence remain unattractive to the short-term interests of managers charged with dealing with day-to-day challenges and issues on the shopfloor, even if long-term organizational (and social) interests would be better served by high levels of employer–employee interdependence within a functionally flexible production paradigm (cf. Hassel 1999). As Anglo-American style ownership patterns gradually penetrate continental Western Europe, pressures mount to maximize short-term shareholder value, facilitated by the relentless ideological assault of neoliberalism, threaten to undermine the basis of what was always a contested compromise; the institutional foundations of cooperation and mutual interdependence at the workplace are both unstable and represent the product of a particular time and place. However, the volatility of the neoliberal alternative—and its ruinous track record in key areas of economic activity such as manufacturing, and in promoting greater social equity, inclusion, and well-being at work—would suggest that the most viable way forward is a reconfiguration and revitalization (not simply a watering down) of the cooperative model, or the development of a new alternative, retaining, and strengthening the best aspects of the latter, including mutual commitment between employers and employees centering on legally enforceable job security.

References

Abraham, K. and Housman, S. (1994). 'Does Employment Protection Inhibit Labor Market Flexibility?', in R. Blank (ed.), *Social Protection vs. Economic Flexibility: Is there a Trade-Off?* Chicago, IL: University of Chicago Press.

Bertola, G., Boeri, T., and Cazes, S. (2000). 'Employment Protection and Labour Market Adjustment in OECD Countries', *Employment and Training Papers*, 48: 1–15.

Boyer, R. (2000). 'Labour Flexibilities: Many Forms, Uncertain Effects', in B. Jessop (ed.), *Regulationist Perspectives on Fordism and Post-Fordism—Regulation Theory and the Crisis of Capitalism Volume 3*. London: Edward Elgar.

Brenner, R. (2002). *The Boom and the Bubble: The US in the World Economy.* London: Verso.

Canziani, P. and Petrongolo, B. (2001). 'Firing Costs and Stigma', *European Economic Review*, 45: 1877–906.

Carter, T. and De Lancey, P. (1997). 'Just, Unjust and Just Cause Dismissals', *Journal of Macroeconomics*, 19(3): 619–28.

Cohen, R. (1994). 'Resistance and Hidden Forms of Consciousness Amongst African Workers, in E. Webster et al. (eds.), *Work and Industrialisation in South Africa*. Johannesburg: Ravan.

Conservative Party (1983). *Conservative Party Manifesto*. London.

Cully, M., O'Reilly, A., Millward, N., Forth, J., Woodland, S., Dix, G., and Bryson, A. (1998). *Britain at Work*. London: Routledge.

Dore, R. (2000). *Stock Market Capitalism: Welfare Capitalism*. Cambridge: Cambridge University Press.

DTI (1997). *Fairness at Work. White Paper* Cm 3968. Department of Trade and Industry.

Eger, T. (2002). 'Opportunistic Termination of Employment Contracts, and Legal Protection of Dismissal in Germany and the USA', *German working papers in Law and Economics*, 2002-1-1049, pp. 1–24.

—— (2004). 'Opportunistic Termination of Employment Contracts, and Legal Protection of Dismissal in Germany and the USA', *International Review of Law and Economics*, 23: 381–403.

Glyn, A. (2000). 'Productivity and the Crisis of Fordism', in B. Jessop (ed.), *Regulationist Perspectives on Fordism and Post-Fordism—Regulation Theory and the Crisis of Capitalism Volume 3*. London: Edward Elgar.

Gooderham, P. N., Nordhaug, O., and Ringdal, K. (1999). 'Institutional Determinants of Organizational Practices: Human Resource Management in European Firms,' *Administrative Science Quarterly*, 44(3): 507–31.

Hall, P. and Soskice, D. (eds.) (2001). *Varieties of Capitalism: The Institutional Foundations of Competitive Advantage*. Oxford: Oxford University Press.

Hassel, A. (1999). 'The Erosion of the German System of Industrial Relations', *British Journal of Industrial Relations*, 37(4): 483–505.

Hollingsworth, J. R. (2004). 'The Impact of New Knowledge and World Affairs on Socio-Economics', Paper presented at the Annual Conference of the Society for the Advancement of Socio-Economics, Washington, July.

Hunt, J. (1998). 'Firing Costs, Employment Fluctuations and Average Employment', *Economica*, 67: 177–202.

Kotz, D. (2003). 'Neoliberalism and the Social Structure of Accumuilation Theory of Long-Term Capital Accummulation', *Review of Radical Political Economics,* 35(3): 263–70.

Kraft, K. (1997). 'Hiring and Dismissal Costs in Theory and Practice', *Kyklos*, 50(3): 341–68.

Kugler, A. and Saint-Paul, G. (2004). 'How Do Firing Costs Affect Worker Flows in a World of Adverse Selection', *Journal of Labor Economics*, 22(3): 553–84.

Lautsch, B. (2002). 'Uncovering and Explaining: Variance in the Features and Outcomes of Contingent Work', *Industrial and Labor Relations Review*, 56(1): 23–43.

Leborgne, D. and Lipietz, A. (2001). 'Conceptual Fallacies and Open Questions on Post-Fordism', in B. Jessop (ed.), *Regulation Theory and the Crisis of Capitalism 3—Regulationist Perspectives on Fordism and Post-Fordism.* London: Edward Elgar.

Lincoln, J. and Kalleberg, A. (1990). *Culture, Control and Commitment: A Study of Work Organization in the United States and Japan.* Cambridge: Cambridge University Press.

Lowther, J. and Naletilic, M. (2004). 'Labour Flexibility: A Survey of International Experiences and Their Application to Croatia'. Zagreb, Republic of Croatia.

MacInnes, J. (1987). *Thatcherism at Work. Industrial Relations and Industrial Change.* Milton Keynes, UK: Open University Press.

Morin, M. and Vincens, C. (2001). 'Redundancy, Business Flexibility and Workers Security', *International Labour Review*, 140(1): 45–67.

Nickell, S. (2002). 'A Picture of European Unemployment: Success and Failure', Unpublished working paper, London School of Economics, London.

Nunziata, L. (2003). 'Labour Market Institutions and the Cyclical Dynamics of Employment', *Labour Economics*, 10: 31–53.

OECD (1999).

—— (2004). *Employment Outlook 2004*. Paris.

Parker, S., Griffen, M., Sprigg, C., and Wall, T. (2002). 'Effects of Temporary Contracts on Perceived Work Characteristics and Job Strain: A Longitudinal Study', *Personnel Psychology*, 55: 689–54.

Pollert, A. (1991). 'The Orthodoxy or Flexibility', in A. Pollert (ed.), *Farewell to Flexibility?* London: Blackwell.

—— (2005). 'The Unorganised Worker: The Decline in Collectivism and New Hurdles to Individual Employment Rights', *Industrial Law Journal*, 34(3): 217–38.

Riphahn, R. (2004). 'Employment Protection and Effort Among German Employees', *Economics Letters*, 85: 353–7.

Roobeek, A. (2000). 'The Crisis of Fordism and the Rise of a New Technological Paradigm', in B. Jessop (ed.), *Regulationist Perspectives on Fordism and Post-Fordism—Regulation Theory and the Crisis of Capitalism Volume 3*. London: Edward Elgar.

Saint-Paul, G. (2000). 'Employment Protection, International Specialization and Innovation', *European Economic Review*, 46: 375–95.

Schwab, S. (1993). 'Life-Cycle Justice: Accommodating Just Cause and Employment at Will', *Michigan Law Review*, 92(8): 8–62.

Smith, P. and Morton, G. (2001). 'New Labour's Reform of Britain's Employment Law: The Devil is not only in the Detail but in the Values and Policy Too', *British Journal of Industrial Relations*, 39(1): 119–38.

Suedekum, J. and Ruehmann, P. (2003). 'Severance Payments and Firm Specific Human Capital', *Labour,* 17(1): 47–62.

TUC (nd). Things *Have Got Better. Labour Market Performance 1992–2002*. Trades Union Congress. http://www.tuc.org.uk/economy/tuc-6946-f0.pdf

Wedderburn, L. (1989). 'Freedom of Association and Philosophies of Labour Law', *Industrial Law Journal*, 18(1): 1–38.

Whitley, R. (1999). *Divergent Capitalisms: The Social Structuring and Change of Business Systems*. Oxford: Oxford University Press.

Wood, N. (2004). *Tyranny in America: Capitalism and National Decay*. London: Verso.

—— and Brewster, C. (2005). 'Trust, Interfirm and Supplier Relations', *Business and Society Review*, 110(4): 459–84.

9

The Remaking of Work: Empowerment or Degradation?

Jeff Hyman

Introduction

Though faced by accusations of vagueness, of 'paradoxes and inconsistencies' (Hales 2000: 511–12) and even of impoverishment (Boje and Rosile 2001), empowerment basically purports to provide a redistributive focus whereby a measure of control is transferred to employees over aspects of their work by managers, with the expectation that the resultant liberation from direct control will lead to heightened expressions of employee motivation and performance (Cunningham, Hyman, and Baldry 1996; Harley 1999).

This chapter aims to examine this ostensibly straightforward process and, in particular, to question the seemingly positive transformative properties of the empowerment process. The first section considers the nature of empowerment. It asks whether empowerment is a single unidimensional activity or comprises a range of potentially mutually reinforcing activities that either singly or in combination can influence employee and organizational performance.

The following substantive section reviews the experience of empowerment in 'traditional' work settings. Notwithstanding the unremittingly positive prognoses of empowerment evangelicals, the extent to which expressions of empowerment have actually been imported into manufacturing and 'old economy' organizations that proclaim its use is disputed. Bearing in mind the important qualification that organizational empowerment derives directly from management interests, initiatives, and policies, there is the question of whether any organizationally initiated shifts in task discretion confer qualitative or quantitative benefits to participants in terms of control over the broader dimensions of work or are introduced primarily to encourage 'responsible autonomy' and gain employee compliance in the service of their organization (Harley 2005: 42). In other words, empowerment may offer 'more responsibility, but not more power' (Marchington et al. 1992; Moynagh and Worsley 2005: 127).

Finally, the scope for empowerment in the so-called knowledge economy is considered. In particular, the question is posed whether acknowledged shifts to more flexible and knowledge-based work regimes can be associated with higher levels of work autonomy and discretion among workers, especially under conditions of the changing technology available to organizations.

The Nature of Empowerment

Notwithstanding lack of clarity, some limited and not especially satisfactory attempts at codification have been made, based on assumptions or perceptions of the depth and scope of the expanded influence (e.g. Bowen and Lawler 1992; Lee and Koh 2001). In probably the most widely recognized classification, Bowen and Lawler categorize empowerment practice in terms of a hierarchy, ranging from the low-impact informational approaches of suggestion schemes and attitude surveys, through more task-based initiatives such as teamworking, to those practices that ostensibly offer employee influence at organizational level. In practice, however, many studies that have investigated empowerment indicate a clustering at the lower levels, where any employee involvement is passive or heavily circumscribed with little observable impact on decision-making at any level (Cunningham, Hyman, and Baldry 1996). Even middle- and higher-order participation presents difficulties: as indicated below, the little additional discretion associated with activities such as teamworking may be offset by more intensified and longer work regimes.

Teamworking is cited by both proponents and critics as an integral component or defining characteristic of both empowerment exercises and so-called high-involvement work systems (see, e.g. Lawler 1986; Ichniowski et al. 1996; Beirne 2006: 20). Again, though, there are considerable doubts with respect to its contribution to worker autonomy or satisfaction, teamworking has, for example, been associated with work intensification and its deprivations in a process of 'social engineering' (Reinhart 1998) where peer pressure and interteam and interworker competition can displace supervisory 'authority and responsibility' (Sennett 1998: 114) through a 'new exploitative relation' (Martinez Lucio, Jenkins, and Noon 2000: 264) that 'generates new forms of control' (Harley 2001). These new forms of control in the team setting can include self-disciplining, peer surveillance, and self-enforced controls such as social ostracism for nonconformers (Hodson 2001: 175). Other observers, meanwhile, have questioned the compatibility of teamwork with a market orientation: for example, in the health service, neoliberal market reforms promoting interoccupational competition are seen to have 'undermined teamwork among professionals and organizations vital to patient-centred care' (Department of Health 2000: 56) and it has been noted, more generally, that a more direct efficiency-seeking ambition for teamwork is less likely to engage fulsome employee support (Findlay et al. 2000: 238–9).

The higher-order empowerment envisaged by Bowen and Lawler, such as employee share schemes, has not noticeably raised the profile of employee participation in executive decision-making and indeed these schemes are regarded by some authorities as principally serving to provide flexibility in remuneration and reinforce executive legitimacy rather than democratizing work, 'since employees have few control rights' under standard employee-owned regimes (Strauss 1998: 20). If this is the case, it is highly questionable whether financial participation should be regarded as a form of empowerment. These doubts are reinforced by more critical perspectives which propose that share-based participation is not actually directed toward empowering employees at all, but to the maintenance or reinforcement of employer control when macroeconomic conditions might be conducive to collective employee challenge (Ramsay 1977).

This critical labor process perspective toward financial participation is not, however, shared by all authorities. Hodson cites numerous studies that provide evidence for higher productivity, performance, and employee satisfaction because of 'the genuine overlap between the goals of the enterprise and those of employees' (2001: 180). He also suggests that share schemes can help to lubricate communication between the parties, give support to teamworking, and encourage employees to adopt favorable positions toward task participation. Nevertheless, caution is needed: Hodson refers to employee-*owned* enterprises, not to the vast majority of conventional companies where employees are simply offered a (small) financial stake in the enterprise as part of their overall remuneration. In these cases, there is less evidence of positive associations between share schemes and behavioral outcomes, with the opportunistic selling of shares by employees in conventional schemes and the rating of them primarily for their 'bonus' value both suggesting a less-than-binding relationship between employees and employers (Baddon et al. 1989).

Lee and Koh (2001) identify empowerment as consisting of two distinctive states: the reallocation of responsibilities to which most management empowerment programs subscribe and a 'psychological state of increased self-efficacy' (2001: 685), as perceived by the empowered. When unpicked, however, this elevated psychological state does not emerge from intrinsic affective states resulting from the independent action of the employee but rather the perceptions which result 'from his/her supervisors' empowering' (2001: 686). It is, then, the actions of the managers which are seen to provide the context for the psychological well-being of the employees, notwithstanding the point made by critics that '*feeling* empowered is not the same as *being* empowered' (Jacques 1996: 141).

Empowerment in the 'Old Economy'

Empowerment first rose to prominence as an idea and practice in the 1980s and 1990s on the back of concern at the competitive capacity of Western corporations to compete with their more highly productive Japanese counterparts. A recommended key action was to shift from control-centered to commitment-centered systems of management using employee empowerment as the catalyst (Walton 1985). Notwithstanding management celebration of successful ventures, most academic studies of empowerment practice in manufacturing and public services from this period point to either a negative or, at best, neutral impact of management-initiated empowerment on employees (Cunningham, Hyman, and Baldry 1996; Taylor 2003). These studies have shown that little extra discretion is distributed to employees; managerial controls are still very evident; material benefits, such as extra pay, are rarely provided, the reward, *pace* Hertzberg, being ostensibly intrinsic to performing the enhanced job itself; job security is not promoted; and there is little evidence for 'psychological ownership'. In short, it would appear that 'the aims of empowerment ... are not primarily democratic' (Wilkinson 2001: 337). In other cases, notwithstanding the powerful rhetoric emanating from employers and consultants about the success of their initiatives, scant evidence has been found for any significant move toward an emancipated workforce at all: using appropriate Glasgow phraseology, empowerment was all 'fur coat and nae knickers' (Hales 2000; Geary 2003).

Furthermore, all too frequently empowerment has become associated with two other less life-enhancing outcomes: the initiatives often accompanied or followed organizational restructuring and attendant job losses (Adler 1993), and/or they became associated with task enlargement or work intensification, heightened insecurity and with fewer numbers employed, restricted opportunities for organizational survivors to exert control over working hours or methods (Cunnningham, Hyman, and Baldry 1996) compounded by obstructionist behavior by supervisors and low-level managers fearful of loss of their hierarchical privileges (Beirne 2006: 9). In these circumstances, it is not surprising, perhaps, that empowerment, with its promise of fulfillment but reality of disillusion, has made little discernible impact on organizational decision-making processes.

At the same time, empowerment cannot simply be dismissed as a non-event. Proponents argue that its association with two other linked processes suggests that, under favorable conditions, it may well enhance employee influence over workplace decision-making. One identified process is the rise in employee involvement. There is no question that over the past few years there has been a marked growth in employer-led initiatives that purport to involve employees in aspects of workplace decision-making (see Cully et al. 1999). The majority of these techniques, following the Bowen and Lawler typology above, would fall into the low-influence classification. Nevertheless, evidence from successive national industrial and employee relations surveys confirms the presence of diverse communicative and consultative exercises. However, evidence of the presence of techniques does not of course mean that they are being applied or, if they are being applied, that they can be associated with any meaningful advance in terms of employee discretion. According to Hodson, it is not just new skills that are in demand in the new technologically based and service-orientated sectors of the economy, but 'greater worker initiative grounded on new values, attitudes and motivations' throughout the economy (2001: 171). On the basis of a meta-analysis of a range of studies, Hodson proceeds to argue that on aggregate these demonstrate two overall effects: first, higher productivity is associated with involvement; and second, employees experience greater autonomy and pride in their work (2001: 172) as a result of the application of involvement techniques. On the basis of further analysis, however, Hodson concludes that: 'current versions of employee participation and involvement are unlikely on their own to bring about an end to alienation at work' (2001: 172) because of their association with work intensification and job insecurity. The extent to which productivity is directly and positively related to autonomy or satisfaction is of course a relevant question, especially as many involvement programs, including empowerment, are introduced, usually unilaterally by management, alongside, or following, staff reduction exercises (Parker and Slaughter 1994); others appear to be associated with attempts to secure greater effort, longer working hours, or campaigns to win hearts and minds (presented as 'commitment') and to capture employees' tacit knowledge (Thompson and McHugh 2002) at a time of collective union weakness. Moreover, a number of studies point to only a weak or marginal impact of individual involvement approaches (Geary 2003).

If empowerment or employee involvement as a singular and specific management initiative has failed to live up to its claim to enhance employee autonomy in traditional sectors of the economy, a stronger claim for the organizationally beneficial impact of empowerment is through the synergy exerted by appropriate combinations of HRM techniques. Proponents argue that these high-involvement (HIWS) or high-commitment (HCWS) bundles constitute a system based on empowerment (see, e.g. Huselid 1995; Appelbaum 2002; Appelbaum et al. 2000) which serves to enhance employee autonomy and through this leads to heightened commitment and consequential beneficial impacts on organizational performance (Harley 2005: 38).

Management scholars have focused on identifying substantive sequential links between empowerment-centered practices and elements of organizational performance. The linkage trail, initially, consists of the application of progressive HR techniques, such as teamworking, share schemes, and systematic employee development, which lead to job satisfaction and raised organizational commitment (Patterson et al. 1997). This heightened satisfaction and commitment is, in turn, seen to result in a positive impact on organizational performance (Huselid 1995; Pfeffer 1998).

Other observers have been more skeptical about the impact of the HIWS, whether treated as individual elements or acting in concert. First, there is little consensus over which HR practices should be included. Legge (2001) notes, for example, that the number and types of practices designated as being involving or commitment focused vary from study to study and that few common practices have been identified among the different studies. Problems of identifying directions of causality and discriminating between whether inputs offer a positive or negative contribution to employee behavior have also been noted. Some commentators, for example, regard performance appraisal and performance-related pay as positive inputs, motivating individual employee effort and consolidating their commitment to the organization, while others identify performance-related pay as a factor in maintaining employee control (White et al. 2004), increasing work intensification, promoting discriminatory practices, compromising teamwork, and mobilizing worker dissatisfaction (Lloyd and Newell 2000: 194; Procter and Mueller 2000: 15). More generally, analysis of inputs and outcomes suffers from unresolved epistemological and methodological shortcomings, leading Legge to conclude that 'much of the research on HR "high commitment/performance" practices and organizational performance is at best confused and, at worst, conceptually and methodologically deeply flawed' (2001: 31, see also Harley 2005). To these criticisms can be added a further qualification, namely that HIWSs may be more talked about than applied. Analysis of the 1998 UK WERS, for example, revealed that 'the diffusion of high-commitment management practices was not especially widespread' (Cully et al. 1999: 295). Similar limitations in operation, reported by Taylor (2002), have been consistently reported in other recent UK studies.

These shortcomings raise the possibility that HIWSs may be instrumental in raising organizational performance not through its catalytic effect upon employee autonomy or discretion, but through exerting tighter, if indirect, management control over labor processes (Ramsay, Scholarios, and Harley 2000). Further, extraneous factors such as job reductions or tighter targets accompanying, or preceding, the HIWS initiative may account for (potentially short-lived) productivity gains. Certainly, recent research by Green and Tsitsianis (2005) provides evidence that job satisfaction among employees in Britain generally is deteriorating, with work intensification and *declining* discretion over work tasks cited as the main influences. In exposing these trends, the research further casts doubt on the argument advanced by some critics of empowerment and HIWS that, while these processes demonstrate a minimal impact on organizational decision-making, they can serve to enhance immediate task autonomy.

Anticipating the following section, shifts in work intensity and diminishing control could further feed dissatisfaction if expectations associated with the rising skill and educational levels among the UK workforce are not subsequently met through paid work; a suggestion that takes on added weight given that Felstead, Gallie, and Green (2002) have previously noted that the decline in discretion has been especially pronounced among professional employees (see also Green 2002). Alternatively, if empowering approaches are being adopted and one consequence is greater work effort, presumably brought about by these individual or group (teamworking) empowerment processes, then direct causality between these and the resulting dissatisfaction (but improved competitive performance) cannot be discounted. On the other hand, there may be positive impacts associated with empowering initiatives but these may be swamped by the deleterious effects of work intensification. Nevertheless, the observed decline in worker discretion and job quality would be more difficult to explain if worker participation was having the anticipated positive effect on worker attitudes to their jobs, especially as Green and Tsitsianis found that proportions of employees reporting 'quite a lot/a great deal' of participation had risen from 32 percent in 1996 to 36 percent in 2001 (2005: 412).

The Scope for Empowerment in the Modern Economy

The turbulent changes experienced in both regional and global economies over recent years have been accompanied by vigorous debates concerning the contemporary nature and potential future directions of work, at least in the developed world (see Moynagh and Worsley 2005 for a summary). The main contours of economic change in the UK are well rehearsed: continuing dimunition of the manufacturing base and the ascendancy of public and private sector services; policy reliance on deregulation of service provision; quality combined with cost-based competition, with potentially contrasting implications for people resourcing, management, and deployment; and associated with these pressures, continuous organizational restructuring. These changes have, of course, in turn been paralleled by continuing declines in both union membership and collective activity.

The employment consequences that flow from these institutional and structural changes can be summarized in divergent terms: on one hand, it is claimed that quality and service-based competition coupled with demand for people capable and willing to deliver high-quality inputs means that employees have 'never had it so good'. On the other hand, competitive pressures, escalating cost imperatives, and enduring insecurity ensure that there has been little or no change from traditional models of management control and dominance, with maintenance and indeed consolidation of

Taylorist management principles, albeit transferred to different sectoral contexts, but complete with their acknowledged attendant deprivations in terms of job fragmentation, deskilling, and submission to management control for employees.

The never had it so good scenario derives from a number of potential linked sources. First, it is claimed that with employee knowledge and expertise providing the critical component of competitive advantage, favored employees can exercise significant control over their work, thereby, according to one prominent commentator close to the UK government, requiring 'styles of management quite different from organizations of the old economy' (Leadbeater 2000: 61). A vital underpinning element to this scenario is of course the extent to which a distinctive new economy exists to provide scope for the exercise of knowledge work. Second, according to this 'new economy' scenario, the growing ranks of knowledge workers possessing precious ICT skills are increasingly able to control where they work, when they work, even (with work-life balance hovering near the top of the government's policy agenda) how much they work, and confronted by this expert power, managers are forced into providing the environmental organization conditions under which knowledge work can flourish: 'these organizations *will* be less hierarchical, less domineering and less intolerant of different life styles . . . work will *probably* be more creative and self-governing' (Leadbeater 2000: 63, emphases added). Even at this early stage, however, it is worth noting the futuristic and tentative note that provides a cautionary edge to these otherwise forthright statements.

A rather more contentious and ambiguous source for the optimistic scenario derives from the vast instrumental management literature which directs managers to optimize human resource contributions to organizational endeavor through manipulating the cultural capital of the organization and by capturing the hearts and minds of employees (Peters and Waterman 1982; Flecker and Hofbauer 1998). This alluring approach requires 'changing the corporate ethos, the core values, attitudes and beliefs that influence behaviour, socializing people into the role of "team players" and overcoming any ingrained tendency towards low trust, adversarial relations' (Beirne 2006: 61). It is through this cultural change framework that expressions of empowerment are most clearly stated (Walton 1985). Deriving from this prescriptive approach emerged the recent shifts toward high-involvement work systems. A further potential impetus is offered in the global shift toward flexible production. One argument suggests that only flexible work regimes located in nimble-footed organizations can respond adequately to the rapidly evolving patterns of volatile consumer behavior (Sennett 1998). Flexible work demands flexible workers unfettered either by time constraints or by task boundaries.

On the other hand, the 'no change' arguments suggest that Taylorist principles are being maintained and indeed, under different guise, imported into both existing and new areas of work, including technical and professional occupations where technological developments can serve to restrict and control employee discretion, heighten intensification, and reduce security. Current HIWS emphasis on outputs, outcomes, targets, and performance measures at the expense of resource inputs is also an inherently Taylorist approach to work organization (McMaster 2002). Sennett's masterful study of the role of technology in diminishing the 'art of baking' to a series of scheduled on-screen maneuvers provides clear evidence of this potential (1998: 68–9). In these skilled-reduced areas the emergence and spread of 'McDonaldization' (Ritzer 1996) into highly competitive sectors, such as food preparation, displaces and confines these occupations into low-skilled, low-discretion, and insecure tributaries of the working economy. Under this pessimistic scenario empowerment initiatives are established by organizational management to reinforce, rather than relax, their control. A related area of interest concerns the growing influence of information and communications technology (ICT) on monitoring levels and boundaries of employee discretion (Moynagh and Worsley 2005: 128).

In order to more fully examine these alternative viewpoints the remainder of the present chapter therefore examines the shape of the so-called new economy and, with an especial focus on software workers, explores the nature, extent and directions of empowerment initiatives within it and how these differ from projects in more traditional settings, notably with regard to their genesis, control, and outcomes.

The Knowledge Economy: An Emerging Positive Picture for Empowerment?

Both predictors and analysts have indicated far-reaching changes to the economy in directions in which innovation, creativity, and flexibility among employees are both required and rewarded. Castells has no doubts about the emergence of a new economy, based on information technology, globalization, and networks (2000: 77), interacting with environmental uncertainty and competitive demands to encourage large-scale and continuing organizational restructuring (2000: 256), and in the process leading to the demise of the Taylorist project as a 'historic relic' and the enhancement of 'work that requires analysis, decision, and reprogrammeming capabilities' (2000: 258). Whilst recognizing that these processes do not become the property of all workplaces, nor of all employees, the trends, whether in manufacturing or services, are therefore seen to be toward the growth of expertise; trends that appear to have been reflected in a massive expansion of professionalized, technical, and 'knowledge-' based occupations in the past few years and a corresponding (if slower) decline in low-skill and manual occupations (see, e.g. Wolf 2002: 49).

Linked to these developments has been the expansion of tertiary education. The main point here is not just the unprecedented increase in university-level enrollments but the speed with which higher education has changed from elite to mass status. From a base of about 5 percent fifty years ago, participation rates in the UK now exceed 45 percent (Wolf 2002: 170–2). Virtually parallel to these developments has been the doubling of people classified in middle-class occupations, with about a third of the population now designated as middle class (Roberts 2001: 141). An increasing and growing number of entrants to the workforce are therefore university educated, technically trained and proficient in IT, and with middle-class aspirations. In their roles as both employees *and* consumer/users, these groups may have the aptitude and confidence to confront hierarchy and challenge for more substantive levels of participation in organizational affairs.

Software Development: A Case Study

A prominent contemporary example of new work is provided by software development, where the recent annual market growth in Europe has averaged 10 percent and even higher in the UK. Numbers employed in software and associated work have been growing with comparable rapidity. According to successive Labour Force surveys, between the years 1996 and 2000 numbers of economically active software-associated workers rose to nearly three-quarters of a million, an increase of 39 percent. During the same four-year period, the number of designated software engineers nearly doubled to almost 200,000.

As part of a study for the ESRC *Future of Work* program, five software companies based in the central belt of Scotland between Glasgow and Edinburgh were researched between 1999 and 2001. The case study research included observation, formal and informal interviews, and a lengthy written questionnaire distributed to all employees in the four small- to medium-sized enterprises and to a representative sample of software engineers in the large, ex-public utility company. A total of 541 questionnaires were distributed and 328 returned (response rate 69 percent), of which 288 represented technical software employees used in the present analysis. Nearly three-quarters of respondents were men, confirming the masculinized culture of the sector. Nearly three-quarters were aged under 40 years.

The four smaller companies, privately owned and managed, with between 20 and 250 employees, did not recognize unions. The ex-utility with upwards of 100,000 employees (but only a small proportion of these employed as software workers) recognized unions and membership density among software workers was about 50 percent. Contextual conditions for empowering employees in all the companies were highly favorable. There was a tight labor market for software workers, meaning that if working conditions and management style did not meet aspirations, other options were readily available. In the words of an applications support analyst at *Beta*:

> ... you ... go somewhere else where the conditions are better ... I know that if I walked out of the door today I could be in another job by the end of next week.

Whilst not a profession in the traditional sense (von Glinow 1998), software work shares many of the attributes associated with professional work, though whether practitioners have the independence and level of autonomous control associated with professional status is an important question. The employees themselves, as prototypical 'knowledge workers', tended to be university-educated and engage in continuous development, albeit often at their own expense and time. There are numerous electronic community networks that keep 'members' informed of occupational developments and job opportunities.

Teamworking was common practice in all five companies. In the smaller companies there were few signs of sophisticated human resource practices and informal styles of management, emanating from the charismatic owner-managers, were common. These espoused styles, encouraging enterprise and use of discretion, were typified by an absence of bureaucracy and emphasis on individualism, including secrecy over pay, where individually determined performance-related pay increments were common. The owner of one company, *Lambda*, wanted people 'to join the club', but only those who were 'motivated to go places'. A senior manager at another company, *Omega*, emphasized the entrepreneurial culture with its flat structure supporting individual and team discretion. At *Pi*, the chief executive emphasized the flat and informal structure and open communications approach. At the ex-utility, *Beta*, there was more of a formally codified structure with formal appraisal systems and performance-related pay. In all the companies there was an expectation, among both managers and employees, of individual and team-based task autonomy and discretion.

These characteristics found expression in employee interviews. Thus, an applications support analyst at the more formally structured company *Beta*, confirmed that:

> ... what's particularly important is the working environment and we are allowed to get on with our job without any real interference. We are allowed to take decisions.

Further evidence of the discretionary action available to developers was remarked on by several interviewees: if a problem arises, 'I sort it out', (*Gamma*, software engineer) or 'I'd do something about it, I'd do it myself' (*Gamma*, business development manager). This sense of self-determination was experienced also in other aspects of work control, and notably between the boundaries of life and work, over which many employees desired to assert a measure of control (see, e.g. Kochan 2005: 37). In software, flexible work patterns, involving either home working or manipulating working hours, were utilized and accepted by management in return for employee commitment to work flexibly when required.

A team leader at *Beta* pointed out that:

> I guess the phrase I would use is you are responsible for your own hours. . . . There is nobody looking over your shoulder . . . so you are trusted to work your own hours.

A *Beta* software engineer also demonstrated the choices available to him when asked how he uses the home terminal provided by the company:

> I log on now and again to check my email. I work from home now and again depending on the circumstances. I use it to suit me. I don't want to work from home full time, because it suits me coming in here.

At *Omega*, similar flexibility was offered:

> I am contracted 35 hours but actually their other permanent staff, or some of them work part-time, but their full week is $37\frac{1}{4}$ I think . . . When I started with them I said that I couldn't . . . I have a family, so 35 hours was all that I could manage to work so that's what I'm contracted to do.

The majority of software workers were men, whose elevated status was reflected in their pay and work autonomy, assisted by working in an expanding and developing sector. These workers were able to exercise a measure of control over their work boundaries, both through formal provision in terms of part-time contracts and informally through adjusting working times; freedoms that are not available in other contemporary new occupations such as call centers (see, e.g. Taylor and Bain 1999; Taylor et al. 2002). Whilst teamworking was common and project deadlines needed to be met, task-work was relatively unconstrained by internal controls and the work environment open to manipulation and boundary flexibility by favored employees. Working arrangements such as part-time employment were formally accommodated by employers and working times could often be informally adjusted by employees to comply with domestic demands. Nevertheless, the long and often intense working regimes were explained and justified as being integral to the job. Hence, this partial control available to software workers was exerted within broader boundaries which allowed them to decide when they work but provided rather less discretion over the quantity of work or the conditions under which it was undertaken. This suggests that employee control may be less substantial than is sometimes proposed for so-called knowledge workers.

Men in the software companies had few difficulties in organizing their work-home environment, both because of the informal and formal organizational mechanisms made available to them but also because of supportive domestic circumstances in many cases. Notwithstanding favorable work contexts, the situation for women in exercising control over their working lives could still be problematic. In career terms, prospects for part-time women in a male-dominated occupation were not always favorable. The following comment from a woman software engineer, working part-time at *Beta* following maternity leave is instructive:

> I don't feel disadvantaged in my team. I feel it is a disadvantage within the company. If you wanted promotion, I don't think it would be looked upon favorably. Not at all.
>
> (*Beta*, female, software engineer,WI-14)

It is clear that relatively high levels of job control and autonomy arise partly as a function of gender but that they also reflect a flexible labor process and strong labor market situation.

Discussion and Conclusions

Our evidence suggests that many of the empowerment projects of the 1980s and 1990s focused on management-inspired low-level communication and task-based initiatives. In these situations employee discretion was commonly heavily circumscribed and line managers were often inadequately trained or uncommitted to the projects for which they shared prime responsibility to deliver (Cunningham, Hyman, and Baldry 1996; Geary 2003). Many employees had realistic expectations about the purposes of these exercises, especially when combined with job reductions and other cost-saving measures. Concomitant with empowerment, monitoring of employees and their performance increased and job satisfaction and discretion declined (Moynagh and Worsley 2005: 129). In the past few years, there have been noticeable shifts, as we have seen, in the structure and operation of the economy. Along with the rise in price and quality competition, these changes a priori offer opportunities for expanded employee discretion and autonomy in the so-called knowledge economy of the new millennium.

Software development as a prototype for 'new work' clearly represents a favorable location for empowerment to operate and we have seen that software workers have enjoyed some discretion in the ways they work. In contradistinction to the earlier projects, in some cases, work-flow flexibility has been employee initiated and management tolerated. But closer examination suggests that any empowerment enjoyed tends to be at a rather superficial level and that, even under these ostensibly favorable circumstances, for employees the impact of empowerment is limited and subject to managerial encroachment. The previous observations by Beirne, Ramsay, and Panteli (1998) concerning how 'performance metrics' and monitoring approaches are used to shape and discipline worker behavior in hi-tech contexts were therefore echoed in the present case study companies. At *Pi,* for example, the company's written remuneration policy statement was unequivocal:

As a meritocracy, the Company aims to discriminate heavily in favour of employees whose performance is judged to be above average.

This 'judgment' was undertaken unilaterally by the owner-manager. At *Omega,* further evidence of central control was apparent. No questions referring to trade unions were permitted in the survey questionnaire and whilst there was a flat organizational structure and espousal of an empowered culture, senior managers were in no doubt as to the operational orientations of the company. In the words of one manager: 'the managerial style is control', echoed by another who pointed out that:

the owners have had a problem letting go . . . we pay lip service to giving over authority and responsibility.

The software center manager at *Beta* considered the:

set of behaviours the business has decided our people must exhibit. And that's what we use to measure performance. There are paragraphs to tell you how people should behave and get certain marks.

Additional threats to employee autonomy were presented by the increasing presence of outsourced freelance and overseas agency employees recruited temporarily to specific software projects. Both for these and established employees, future prospective allocation to projects and teams was related to how well and in what ways they were deemed by senior managers and owners to have contributed to existing projects. Also, as we saw above, there is a strong gender divide. Women in software currently enjoy greater freedom than do women in more traditional sectors to limit and protect their work hours but this is potentially at the cost of advancement to more prestigious projects or to promotion within the company.

It should be borne in mind that the freedoms enjoyed by software workers were shaped and bounded by the nature of the task itself with which they strongly identified and to which they were chiefly committed (and not necessarily to the employer, see Baldry, Scholarios, and Hyman 2005). Thus, many software workers in our companies paid a heavy price for their temporal and task empowerment by working long and unpredictable hours, working unpaid overtime, taking work (and worries) home, often accompanied by feelings of stress and exhaustion (Hyman et al. 2003).

These manifestations suggest that the surface empowerment offered to, or captured by, workers in these new high-prestige occupations is more than compensated for by the degree and depth of commitment offered in return to the job itself. This suggests that boundaries surrounding workplace control are not static, but the result of a continuous process of social negotiation in which the differential power and resources available to employer and employees are critical to the outcome. When the employee has workplace resources available, whether derived from a tight labor market or coupled with the presence of a union, as at *Beta*, where negotiated workplace adjustments were possible, then a measure of autonomy over work tasks is possible and it is clearly in the employer's interest not to directly contest this limited control. Under these favorable conditions, it is perhaps not surprising that software workers felt empowered, but following Jacques (1996), did this necessarily mean that they were empowered?

For at the same time, there was clear evidence of traditional hierarchical and ownership control now overlaid and reinforced by new client-driven controls afforded to employers in ICT service operations and through labor competition provided by flexible and globalized labor markets operating in these high-technology conditions. These observations lead us to conclude that whilst the profile and depth of employee responsibilities may vary from sector to sector, the extent to which the new economy offers genuine opportunities for employees to gain substantive or strategic control over work, even for high-prestige knowledge workers, is bounded by the mandates determined by the employers themselves. As employee knowledge (rather than effort alone) increasingly grows to represent a principal source of organizational innovation, competitive advantage, and accumulation, it can be predicted that employers will seek out further ways in which to appropriate and control the deployment of this knowledge.

References

Adler, P. (1993). 'Time-and-Motion Regained', *Harvard Business Review*, Jan.–Feb.: 97–107.

Appelbaum, E. (2002). 'The Impact of New Forms of Work Organisation on Workers', in G. Murray, J. Belanger, A. Giles, and P. Lapointe (eds.), *Work and Employment Relations in the High-Performance Workplace*. London: Continuum.

——Bailey, T., Berg, P., and Kalleberg, A. (2000). *Manufacturing Advantage: Why High-Performance Work Systems Pay Off*. Ithaca, NY: ILR Press.

Baddon, L., Hunter, L., Hyman, J., Leopold, J., and Ramsay, H. (1989). *People's Capitalism: A Critical Analysis of Profit-Sharing and Employee Share Ownership*. London: Routledge.

Baldry, C., Scholarios, D., and Hyman, J. (2005). 'Organizational Commitment Among Software Developers', in R. Barrett (ed.), *Management, Labour Process and Software Development: Reality Bytes*. London: Routledge.

Beirne, M. (2006). *Empowerment and Innovation*. Cheltenham, UK: Edward Elgar.

Beirne, M., Ramsay, H., and Panteli, N. (1998). 'Developments in Computing Work: Control and Contradiction in the Software Labour Process', in P. Thompson and C. Warhurst (eds.), *Workplaces of the Future*. London: Macmillan.

Boje, D. and Rosile, G. (2001). 'Where's the Power in Empowerment', *The Journal of Applied Behavioural Science*, 37(1): 90–117.

Bowen, D. E. and Lawler, E. E. (1992). 'The Empowerment of Service Workers: What, Why, How and When', *Sloan Management Review*, Spring: 31–9.

Castells, M. (2000). *The Rise of the Network Society*, 2nd edn. Oxford: Blackwell.

Cully, M., Woodland, S., O'Reilly, A., and Dix, G. (1999). *Britain at Work*. London: Routledge.

Cunningham, I., Hyman, J., and Baldry, C. (1996). 'Empowerment: The Power to Do What?', *Industrial Relations Journal*, 27(2): 143–54.

Department of Health (2000). *The NHS Plan: A Plan for Investment, A Plan for Reform*, Cm 4818-I. London: HMSO.

Felstead, A., Gallie, D., and Green, F. (2002). *Work Skills in Britain 1986–2001*. Nottingham, UK: DfES Publications.

Findlay, P., McKinlay, A., Marks, A., and Thompson, P. (2000). 'Flexible When it Suits Them: The Use and Abuse of Teamwork Skills', in S. Procter and F. Mueller (eds.), *Teamworking*. Basingstoke, UK: Macmillan, pp. 222–43.

Flecker, J. and Hofbauer, J. (1998), 'Capitalising on Subjectivity: the "New Model Worker" and the importance of being useful', in P. Thompson and C. Warhurst (eds), *Workplaces of the Future*. Basingstoke: Macmillan: 104–23.

Geary, J. (2003). 'New Forms of Work Organization: Still Limited, Still Controlled, but Still Welcome?', in P. Edwards (ed.), *Industrial Relations*, 2nd edn. Oxford: Blackwell, pp. 338–67.

Green, F. (2002). 'Work Intensification, Discretion and the Decline in Well-Being at Work', Paper presented at *Conference on Work Intensification*, Paris, 20–21 November.

—— and Tsitsianis, N. (2005). 'An Investigation of National Trends in Job Satisfaction in Britain and Germany', *British Journal of Industrial Relations*, 43(3): 401–30.

Hales, C. (2000). 'Management and Empowerment Programmemes', *Work, Employment & Society*, 14(3): 501–19.

Harley, B. (1999). 'The Myth of Empowerment: Work Organisation, Hierarchy and Employee Autonomy in Contemporary Australian Workplaces', *Work, Employment & Society*, 13: 41–66.

—— (2001). 'Team Membership and the Experience of Work in Britain: An Analysis of the WERS98 Data', *Work, Employment & Society*, 15(4): 721–42.

—— (2005). 'Hope or Hype? High Performance Work Systems', in B. Harley, J. Hyman and P. Thompson (eds.), *Participation and Democracy*, Basingstoke, UK: Palgrave Macmillan, pp. 38–54.

Hodson, R. (2001). *Dignity at Work*. Cambridge: Cambridge University Press.

Huselid, M. (1995). 'The Impact of Human Resource Management Practices on Turnover, Productivity and Corporate Financial Performance', *Academy of Management Journal*, 38: 635–72.

Hyman, J., Baldry, C., Scholarios, D., and Bunzel, D. (2003). 'Work-Life Imbalance in Call Centres and Software Development', *British Journal of Industrial Relations*, 41(2): 215–40.

Ichniowski, C., Kochan, T., Levine, D., Olson, C., and Strauss, G. (1996). 'What Works at Work: Overview and Assessment', *Industrial Relations*, 55: 299–333.

Jacques, R. (1996). *Manufacturing the Employee: Management Knowledge from the 9th to the 21st Centuries*. London: Sage.

Kochan, T. (2005). *Restoring the American Dream: A Working Families' Agenda for America*. Cambridge, MA: MIT Press.

Lawler, E. E. (1986). *High Involvement Management*. San Francsico, CA: Jossey-Bass.

Leadbeater, C. L. (2000). *Living on Thin Air*. London: Penguin.

Lee, M. and Koh, J. (2001). 'Is Empowerment Really a New Concept?', *International Journal of Human Resource Management*, 12(4): 684–95.

Legge, K. (2001). 'Silver Bullet or Spent Round? Assessing the Meaning of the "High Commitment Management"/Performance Relationship', in J. Storey (ed.), *Human Resource Management: A Critical Text*. London: Thomson, pp. 21–36.

Lloyd, C. and Newell, H. (2000). 'Selling Teams to the Salesforce: Teamworking in the UK Pharmaceutical Industry', in S. Procter and F. Mueller (eds.), *Teamworking*. Basingstoke, UK: Macmillan, pp. 183–202.

Marchington, M., Goodman, J., Wilkinson, A., and Ackers, P. (1992). *New Developments in Employee Involvement*, Employment Department Research Paper No. 2.

Martinez Lucio, M., Jenkins, S., and Noon, M. (2000). 'Management Strategy, Union Identity and Oppositionalism: Teamwork in the Royal Mail', in S. Procter and F. Mueller (eds.), *Teamworking*. Basingstoke, UK: Macmillan.

McMaster, R. (2002). 'A Socio-Institutionalist Critique of the 1990s Reforms of the United Kingdom's National Health Service', *Review of Social Economy*, LX(3): 403–33.

Moynagh, M. and Worsley, R. (2005). *Working in the Twenty-First Century*. Leeds, UK: ESRC.

Parker, M. and Slaughter, J. (1994). *Working Smart: A Union Guide to Participation Programmes and Reengineering*. Detroit, MI: Labor Notes.

Patterson, M., West, M., Hawthorn, R., and Nickell, S. (1997). *The Impact of People Management Practices on Business Performance*. London: Institute of Personnel and Development.

Peters, T. and Waterman, R. (1982). In Search of Excellance, New York: Harper and Row.

Pfeffer, J. (1998). *The Human Equation*. Cambridge, MA: Harvard Business School Press.

Procter, S. and Mueller, F. (2000). 'Teamworking: Strategy, Systems and Structure', in S. Procter and F. Mueller (eds.), *Teamworking*. Basingstoke, UK: Macmillan, pp. 3–24.

Ramsay, H. (1977). 'Cycles of Control: Worker Participation in Sociological and Historical Perspective', *Sociology*, 11: 481–506.

——Scholarios, D., and Harley, B. (2000). 'Employees and High-Performance Work Systems: Testing Inside the Black Box', *British Journal of Industrial Relations*, 38(4): 501–32.

Reinhart, J. (1998). 'Transcending Taylorism and Fordism? Two Decades of Work Restructuring', Paper presented to *Work Difference and Social Change* conference, Binghamton, USA.

Ritzer, G. (1996). *The McDonaldization of Society*. Thousand Oaks, CA: Pine Forge Press.

Roberts, K. (2001). *Class in Modern Britain*. Basingstoke, UK: Palgrave.

Sennett, R. (1998). *The Corrosion of Character*. New York: Norton.

Strauss, G. (1998). 'An Overview', in F. Heller, E. Pusic, G. Strauss, and B. Wilpert (eds.), *Organizational Participation: Myth and Reality*. Oxford: Oxford University Press, pp. 8–39.

Taylor, P. and Bain, P. (1999). '"An Assembly Line in the Head": Work and Employee Relations in the Call Centre', *Industrial Relations Journal*, 30(2): 101–17.

——Mulvey, G., Hyman, J., and Bain, P. (2002). 'Work Organization, Control and the Experience of Work in Call Centres', *Work, Employment & Society*, 16(1): 133–50.

Taylor, R. (2002). *Managing Workplace Change*. Swindon: ESRC Future of Work Programmeme Series, Swindon, ESRC.

——(2003). *Skills and Innovation in Modern Workplaces*. ESRC Future of Work Programmeme Series, Swindon, ESRC.

Thompson, P. and McHugh, D. (2002). *Work Organisations*, 3rd edn. Basingstoke, UK: Palgrave.

von Glinow, M. (1998). *The New Professionals*. Cambridge, MA: Ballinger.

Walton, R. (1985). 'From Control to Commitment in the Workplace', *Harvard Business Review*, March–April: 77–84.

Wilkinson, A. (2001). 'Empowerment', in T. Redman and A. Wilkinson (eds.), *Contemporary Human Resource Management*. Harlow, UK: Pearson, pp. 336–76.

White, M., Hill, S., Mills, C. and Sweator, D. (2004). British Workplaces and Future of Work, Basingstoke: Palgrave Macmillan.

Wolf, A. (2002). *Does Education Matter?* London: Penguin.

10

Organizational Life: The Good, the Bad, and the Instrumental

Andrew Sayer

Introduction

Organizations as workplaces are inherently instrumental institutions, structured and oriented to meeting their goals, be they making profit, as in the case of capitalist organizations, or pursuing what might be termed use-value ends, such as education or sport, in the case of nonprofit making organizations. In either case, no one expects employers to hire employees out of charity or respect; they are hired for their usefulness to the organization.

Particularly in the face of competitive pressures and a changing environment, workplaces are commonly sites of insecurity, domination, overweening ambition and competitiveness, status seeking, callousness, strategizing, and dissembling (Jackall 1988). They may also be sites of prejudice, discrimination, bullying, and harassment. Yet at the same time one may find sociability, moral concern, the pursuit and granting of esteem and respect, concern for justice, gift exchanges, commitments to causes, projects and people, and intrinsic satisfaction in work and its effects. In other words, some actions are motivated by concern for others and for practices in their own right, for their own sake, rather than out of self-interest or that of the organization. Employment can thus involve a wide range of experiences and motivations from the moral to the amoral and immoral. These mediate the operation of firms.

Workplaces are therefore sites in which ethical and economic values are likely to be in tension. In any society it is possible for what is deemed to be ethical and what is economically feasible or expedient not to correspond, but this is particularly likely under capitalism because unlike any other economic system, it is not directed toward human welfare but toward making profit, this being the condition of survival of capitalist firms. Insofar as capitalism does benefit human welfare, this is a by-product of its profit-seeking orientation. At one level, therefore, capitalist organizations seem unlikely contexts for moral behavior. However, those within them have other concerns besides those of their organization, and these various interests and norms may in some cases converge and in others diverge.

Particularly if they have competitors or tight budgets, firms and other organizations are obliged to attempt to specialize and 'purify' activities under their control so that labor power is used efficiently in the pursuit of their goals and 'idle' time or time spent on other activities is minimized. But of course, employees are not like machines or materials but have multiple needs, interests, and concerns, which cannot be kept at bay for long. The attempted purification of activities within the space-time frame of the organization is never total, for the activities always take on other dimensions, meanings, and functions. Thus, workers may socialize, seek fulfillment, respect and esteem, get distracted or inspired, become ill, get pregnant, and generally allow life to intrude on work. Hence, the multidimensional nature of social action tends repeatedly to frustrate attempts to confine it to particular purposes, spilling out over the frames set by the organization. Consequently, despite their narrow instrumental focus, a great deal is going on within organizations. Some of these other motivations and interests may themselves be instrumentalized by the employer for organization's own ends, but there is always the danger that doing so may corrupt such values and become counterproductive. Paradoxically, they may be more successful in meeting their limited goals if they work with rather than try to suppress every aspect of this 'surplus'.

The diversity of motivations and interests present in any organization is familiar enough, but economic theory has tended to misunderstand it, because of its dogmatic and reductionist presumption of self-interest as the prime motive of action, and its treatment of actors as effectively autistic. In contrast, my aim in this chapter is to explore the relationship between the narrowly focused instrumentalism of organizations and some of the complex, mixed motivations of their members. I argue that to ignore the latter or force them into simplistic categories of egoism and altruism is not only to misunderstand what goes on in organizations, but to provide a misleading basis also for normative ideas about how organizations should change.

My analysis draws on moral philosophy, particularly Adam Smith's empirical analysis of lay morality,[25] Alasdair MacIntyre's analysis of internal and external goods, and Geoffrey Brennan and Philip Pettit's analysis of 'the economy of esteem'. The subject could easily warrant a book so I limit myself to discussions of commitments to work itself and the satisfactions that may derive from this, and the relation of these to esteem and recognition. I begin by discussing instrumentalism and the need to look beyond self-interest, and acknowledge the diverse interests, relationships, commitments, and sources of satisfaction that workers may seek in their jobs, including their need for recognition. The next section explores first how motivations are related to the internal goods afforded by work, such as the satisfactions from completing useful, demanding tasks, and to the external goods of esteem and disesteem, and second how organizations encourage or discourage workers through the way they provide, or fail to provide, recognition of their employees' contributions. I then discuss how the granting of esteem and disesteem is rendered problematic in the context of inequalities in pay and working conditions and conclude by arguing for a highly differentiated view of motivations, both instrumental and noninstrumental, in organizations.

Instrumentalism, Self-interest and Motivation

Although instrumentalism is often valued negatively, instrumental action may be oriented toward good or bad ends, and the means chosen are not necessarily bad. Instrumental rationality is a condition of survival, though it is not the only form of rationality. We also need practical rationality, involving the evaluation and balancing of diverse, often incommensurable ends.[26] While the members of organizations, whether workers or managers, may find some satisfaction in their work, from a normative point of view, this is secondary to the job of providing goods or services. Work, particularly within a division of labor, is just instrumental. Thus, the point of education is not the job satisfaction of the teacher but the education of the pupil; the health of the patient is more important than the job satisfaction of the nurse; the point of cleaning is cleanliness. In for-profit organizations, these use-values, whether goods or services, are themselves instrumental as means to the end of making profit. No matter how desirable job satisfaction may be, it is not the reason for the existence of, or the end, of economic work, whether capitalist or noncapitalist.[27] Moreover, the greater the competitive pressures, the more are organizations likely to try to purify activities and instrumentalize their members' faculties. The problems that result stem not only from the instrumental nature of organizations' activities but also from the narrowness of the ends to which they are directed. By contrast, as individuals we have many ends; insofar as we assess their value in themselves we use practical judgment; insofar as we seek ways of pursuing them, our actions are instrumental.

While instrumental rationality is therefore famously dominant in organizations, often taking a calculative, formal character, as theorized by Weber, this does not necessarily mean that it is entirely unethical. As Paul du Gay has argued with reference to bureaucracy, far from being amoral or immoral, bureaucratic rationality has its own ethic of procedural fairness and refusal of favoritism (du Gay 1999). Use of a criterion of 'fitness for purpose' and operating 'without regard for persons' can, for example, provide barriers to discrimination on grounds such as gender, 'race', age, or sexuality. Phenomena such as sexism, racism, ageism, and homophobia do not, after all, involve instrumental rationality, but rather an irrational, unjust, and immoral form of valuation of others in themselves. Although these forms of discrimination may be instrumentalized by organizations if it suits their interests—for example, by depressing the pay of stigmatized groups—they may be opposed for instrumental reasons where they obstruct efficient and effective operations. However, when a narrowly focused instrumentalism dominates a whole sphere of life, such as that of employment, it then becomes ethically problematic, because it fails to acknowledge, and where appropriate support, the diverse needs of the members of organizations—needs which are important for their well-being. It also becomes counterproductive even from an instrumental point of view, because it produces resistance and suboptimal performance.

Although the point of employment is the instrumental one of earning an income, employees are not mere instruments but ends in themselves who will treat themselves—and often others—as such, and they may vary considerably in how far they conform to the organization's priorities. Employees may effectively instrumentalize their work for other ends, such as pursuing ambitions, or making friends. It is common to theorize this kind of situation in terms of different self-interested actors, contracting with one another to further their own interests, and trying to find ways of preventing malfeasance, as in the case of Principal-Agent theory. However, this turns the empirical question of what kinds of motivation are present into a matter of assumption, and an implausible one at that. I wish to argue that we need to go not only beyond the assumption of self-interest if we are to understand organizations, but also beyond a simple distinction between egoism and altruism. Instead, we need a much richer, thicker analysis of motivation, such as that provided by Adam Smith's *The Theory of Moral Sentiments* (Smith 1759, 1984).

Approaches which assume that all action is, or should be, self-interested, often mistakenly invoking Adam Smith as mentor, or which reduce motivation to self-interest and altruism, are too crude to understand such matters. As Smith saw, individuals are not only self-interested but have a capacity for fellow-feeling and a concern for the welfare of others. They are profoundly social beings, psychologically in need of the company and approval of others and far removed from the autistic economic actors of mainstream economics.[28] Hence, people have a range of needs and capacities for flourishing and susceptibilities to suffering. They also have the capacity to develop *commitments* to others and to practices and causes, and often to work itself (Archer 2000). Their valuations of things and motivations are related to all of these.

People are evaluative beings and there are many forms of normativity and evaluation in everyday life, corresponding to different kinds of need and good

(Anderson 1993); for example, they may be aesthetic, performative (evaluating performances or actions or products), and moral or ethical, or some combination of these. The realm of morality is especially complex, relating as it does to these diverse human needs, capabilities, susceptibilities, and commitments. Through our relations to others we experience moral and immoral sentiments such as benevolence, selfishness, compassion, pride and shame, gratitude and remorse, envy and resentment, and a sense of justice, and we regulate our behavior in response to the actual and imagined responses of others (Smith 1759). We also make comparisons between different experiences and situations and between different people and how they are treated, from which resentments and a sense of injustice may arise.

Work satisfaction involves many dimensions and many kinds of goods—not only money and economic security, but intrinsic satisfaction in executing demanding and worthwhile tasks, in serving others, and in working with others who provide a source of company, friendship, solidarity, recognition, and esteem. At the same time, we would have doubts about any organization in which these goods were given a higher priority than meeting the needs of users. But of course most kinds of paid work—and much unpaid work—fail to provide many of these goods.

Although the pursuit of self-interest looms large in organizations, interpreting all motivation as self-interested is therefore a recipe for misunderstanding organizational life. Instrumental action is not necessarily self-interested, and even self-interest, as Smith recognized, is not necessarily selfish or greedy but can involve self-command and prudence and recognition of others as ends in themselves. (Someone who cannot value others as ends in themselves is not acting in their self-interest, for they will fail to enjoy friendship.) Much of what we do is neither simply self-interested nor altruistic in the sense of self-sacrificing (O'Neill 1998). Social virtues such as good humor benefit both self and others simultaneously and interdependently. Many young people 'want to work with people', not exclusively out of self-interest, but because they find others interesting and as worthy of concern in themselves.

The tenacity with which some theorists try to interpret everything in terms of pursuit of self-interest is curious and, in the face of counterevidence all round them in their daily lives, unscientifically dogmatic. Why should it be so important to make such a simplistic assumption, come what may? Possibly there is a kind of adolescent iconoclasm which assumes the most cynical explanations must always be the best. It is one thing to be skeptical, but skepticism is not the same thing as cynicism and we can be skeptical about cynicism itself. People can value others as persons in their own right including where they do not benefit from their actions; one might respect a competitor, for example, even when their success comes at one's own expense. To be excessively cynical is as naive as to be completely uncynical. Typically, those who claim that actors only ever act in their own self-interest would be shocked and embarrassed if they were accused of doing so in their own relationships to others.

Shame and pride are crucial influences on behavior, including that within organizations, and relate not only to achievements in carrying out tasks but to character, treatment of others, and appearance or social background. Shame may also be engendered by invidious comparison with others who have done better than ourselves in competition for goods which we value, such as work achievements or moral behavior (Tomkins in Sedgwick and Frank 1995: p. 161). Rom Harré suggests that actors continually seek out situations where they risk contempt and hence shame, in order to win respect, implying that unless they take such risks, they shall achieve little respect or self-respect (Harré 1979). In this way, shame and self-respect are linked.[29] Those who never risk contempt because they never put their beliefs 'on the line', whatever the situation, are likely to be seen as lacking the courage of their convictions, or having no convictions or commitments and hence lacking character. This strategy fails because it too invites contempt. One might also feel shame about not having any convictions. Maintaining integrity in the face of pressures to bend is a prime source of respect and self-respect but it is buttressed by the fear of the contempt and shame which failure would bring, and fear of misplaced, unjust contempt.

People generally need and expect recognition both as persons (unconditional recognition) and for their behavior and character (conditional recognition) (Taylor 1994). It is common to thank people for just doing their job, even if the job is unskilled, for example, thanking the cleaner for emptying the office bin, the shop assistant for serving us, more as a way of showing respect for them as persons than as a valuation of the way they have done their job. Jobs and work situations which fail to acknowledge workers' dignity, for example, by refusing them any autonomy or recognition as unique individuals, do not even provide this basic recognition (Sayer 2006). But even where this unconditional recognition is given, there may be a lack of possibilities for gaining conditional recognition, either because workers have no freedom to do anything which warrants it, or because even where they do, it will not be recognized.

Esteem and Internal and External Goods

Although we are social beings in need of others and their approval, we do not always merely do whatever will bring us approval, but often what we regard as right in itself. Smith makes a fundamental distinction between the love of praise and that of praiseworthiness (1759: III, 2.1), arguing that we generally want not merely to be the objects of praise—which is symptomatic of vanity—

but to deserve praise on account of having acted virtuously: 'To desire, or even to accept praise, where no praise is due, can be the effect only of the most contemptible vanity' (III, 2.8). He further argued that all but 'the weakest and most superficial of mankind' do what they believe to be praiseworthy even in the absence of praise (III, 2.7). Smith believed that commercial society encouraged vanity, and notwithstanding its effects in stimulating demand and economic growth, clearly saw this as a problem. (Note again that doing things because we believe them to be the right thing to do, even if it brings us no approval or reward, fits neither the categories of egoism nor altruism comfortably.)

MacIntyre provides a related useful distinction between internal and external goods (MacIntyre 1981). Certain kinds of complex activity or 'practice' which involve skill and have their own internal standards can provide satisfactions and achievements, or 'internal goods'. Examples would be those of architectural design or medicine, though less complex practices like web design may provide more modest internal goods. A key qualitative difference among jobs is the extent to which they provide opportunities for engaging in such practices and enjoying their internal goods. Some practices and internal goods may be purely self-indulgent, while others may benefit others too. Even less complex and interesting work may provide some limited satisfaction if done well.[30]

While actors may pursue their work for its own sake and the good that it contingently brings others, they may also expect and indeed may be motivated by 'external goods' of recognition, esteem, praise, status, or money. Although people may sometimes be primarily motivated by these, the external goods are normally awarded for, and hence are dependent on, the achievement of internal goods or good work. Normally actors want to *deserve* such external goods, and they are likely to find the internal goods rewarding in themselves. To get the external goods of recognition without the corresponding achievements would not only be to invite contempt, and perhaps shame, for not deserving them, but would lead the recipient to miss out on the satisfactions provided by the internal goods themselves, or at least the satisfaction of having done their job well.

Of course, even where jobs involving practices and internal goods are available, these goods are not enough on their own to motivate people to work, for they also need money to live. Wages and salaries are a precondition of wage-labor, though to the extent that they may be varied in response to performance, they may also function as external goods. However, while people work for money, they also work for other things, such as satisfaction and fulfillment, sociability and respect. Those who are lucky enough to do work that is both deeply satisfying in itself, and brings them external goods of recognition, might regard their pay as enabling them to do that work, rather than the reverse, although of course they are unlikely to admit this publicly. (Low pay is likely to be taken as a sign of lack of recognition.) Jobs that involve practices in this specialized sense necessarily tend to allow workers significant discretion and autonomy in the conduct of their work; this is also a source of power which they may use to assert their interests vis-à-vis managers or clients or customers. Workers in this position are doubly fortunate in having both fulfillment and power.

Within organizations, activities are instrumental for the goals of the organization, and this means that practices are governed or at least shaped by external standards. To some extent this may be quite proper, for as we noted earlier, the product is more important. But particularly where practices are instrumental for profit, as in the case of a private hospital, the internal standards and goods (in this case, of medicine) are likely to be compromised. For this reason, one of the problems of division of labor within organizations, whether primarily pursued so as to reduce costs or to increase managerial control, is that it tends also to diminish practices which are a source of internal goods, and/or instrumentalize them, and hence reduce the quality of working life, although where new kinds of job are introduced, new skills and practices may arise. This does not mean instrumental action cannot be satisfying or worthwhile; even those who are involved in maintaining and developing the instrumental, formal rationality of organizations—accountants, for example—may find satisfaction in the work itself and care about its results.

As Geoffrey Brennan and Philip Pettit argue, the need of actors for esteem and their aversion toward disesteem 'provides a gravitational field that silently shapes their dispositions and their doings, exerting a long, insistent influence that can only be resisted at the cost of considerable effort and self-sacrifice'. (Brennan and Pettit 2004: 23). The granting and withholding of esteem can, as a result, provide an 'intangible hand' that supplements the visible hand of management and the invisible hand of market pressures; depending on whether and how esteem and disesteem are signaled, workers can be motivated or demotivated to work well. Unlike respect for and goodwill toward persons as such (unconditional recognition), esteem is conditional on good performance, so that one cannot rationally choose in advance, without evidence of performance, to evaluate someone positively or negatively, though of course prejudice is possible. Esteem cannot be demanded irrespective of behavior. Thus, although gift-giving and gift-exchange among workers in terms of providing help and advice are common and important features of organizational life, esteem cannot be given as a gift. People can, however, exchange 'esteem services', for example, by putting themselves in a position where they can give them esteem or disesteem, and publicizing their evaluations (Brennan and Pettit 2004: 52).[31]

As Brennan and Pettit note, esteem has an *epistemic* as well as a social-psychological motivational function, insofar as it gives the actor feedback on their performance and what was good or bad about it. Thus, people's need for the approval of others can encourage not merely conformity but good practice and improvement. Of course, whether it does so, depends on the quality of the evaluation—whether, for example, it comes from someone with concrete knowledge and experience of the work in question or an external auditor lacking such qualifications and armed only with abstract criteria that are largely inappropriate to the job.

Esteem is an important external good, but as we noted, external goods are generally taken to be properly conditional on achievement of internal goods, or more generally, at least on some kind of merit. Undeserved esteem or disesteem are likely to induce cynicism and resentment. Furthermore, failure to give any recognition at all may cause low morale or, in the case of absence of conditional disesteem, complacency and indifference. People need recognition, but not just on any terms; although on the whole they may conform to what others expect of them and value, as Smith noted in his discussion of praiseworthiness, there may be circumstances under which they reject those valuations, and do what they think is best regardless. Teachers sometimes diverge from the curriculum they are supposed to teach if they think it is inadequate. Call center workers may diverge from their scripts if they think this is warranted. Workers may want to do a good job for their own sake and self-respect, and not merely for the recognition that good work may bring, though they may also expect some recognition as warranted, and become discouraged by its absence. To treat people either as incapable of being motivated in this way, and as only working well when it brings them some advantage, is an obvious empirical error. If they do a bad job, they may feel a sense of shame even if no one else notices. The intangible hand also works within our heads, as a form of self-regulation.[32] While these possibilities are not necessarily inconsistent with the pursuit of self-interest, they may also involve sacrificing self-interest.

Further, if management cynically *and naively* assumes that employees' sole motivation is self-interest and the pursuit of external goods of pay and recognition, and organizes payment systems and expressions of recognition accordingly, it may prove to be counterproductive (Frey 1997; Le Grand 2003; Brennan and Pettit 2004). To treat an employee's actions as purely motivated by the expectation of reward, is to reduce virtue to instrumental action for the purposes of exchange. Consequently, they may feel somewhat demeaned by such treatment and become more cynical and instrumental as a result. In other words, treatment of this kind may 'crowd out' virtuous behavior, done for its own sake. Of course, the point of employment for employees *is* to get an income, and some will be happy to be treated as if this were their only motivation. Piecework, and working on commission are common in some kinds of employment—usually ones where either there are no significant internal goods or satisfactions, or else ones that are not consistent with the goals of the organization and hence need to be controlled externally; some workers may be motivated by these. However, the immediate rewards in terms of pay and recognition are not necessarily the only motivation for many workers, and for some, they may play a secondary role.

Thus even from an instrumental point of view, it may be unwise for employers to use forms of payment and recognition which make workers feel that the only reason they work well is to get such payment or recognition. If rewards and recognition are too closely related to very specific actions they are likely to be seen as a form of control rather than appreciation, and as disrespecting workers' own discretion, self-command, and judgment. On the other hand, not to reward or recognize good performance may be de-motivating. To reconcile these two conflicting tendencies requires the maintenance of a certain distance between the actions and their recognition and reward, so that, for example, rewards are not given for each task, but over a period of time, in recognition of *general* good performance and citizenship. Then the employee is likely to feel valued *as a person*—or, in an older (Aristotelian) moral language, as a person of virtuous character—or at least as valued for the way they exercise their discretion and autonomy, and not merely as being rewarded for individual acts that happen to be useful to the employer.

The pursuit of esteem is not always individualistic and competitive; workers may want to be part of a good team and take pride in belonging to one.[33] The morale and motivation of individual workers is also powerfully affected by how they stand in relation to peers. As the study of *The American Soldier* showed, groups in which there are few prospects of promotion may be more harmonious than ones in which opportunities for inequalities to develop through promotion are strong (Stouffer, 1949). The practice now developing in some British universities of giving individuals rankings in terms of their research standing—in effect, naming and shaming them—can, for this reason have acutely demoralizing effects, and endanger collegiality. Furthermore, one of the reasons many may be troubled by such clumsy policies is that their ability to win this recognition depends partly on external influences such as family circumstances which employers and auditors do not take into account because they lie outside the narrow ends to which the organization is dedicated. In such a context, the strivings of individuals to balance their various ends or commitments, which are already difficult in a modern employment context, become still further distorted by the organization's priorities.

Esteem need not be shown in payments of money, indeed there are some expressions of esteem which would be debased by being expressed in monetary awards. Money is alienable: it shows no trace of where it has been, and is indifferent to what it is spent on or to whom it is given. In a sense, it is cheap. A pound earned as part of a work incentives scheme is no different from any other pound. It may appear merely as the price the firm is prepared to pay for performance. By contrast, that which cannot be exchanged, such as an award for some notable achievement, is beyond price; as Kant argued, it therefore has dignity.[34] On the other hand, in some circumstances a purely symbolic form of recognition could be seen as demotivating—as a worthless, perhaps even insulting, exercise in tokenism that fails to pay any bills. It might also be argued that since the best performers contribute more than others to the organization, they should be paid more. Just how symbolic and pecuniary rewards are valued is therefore a complex matter, depending very much on the wider culture, on how highly commodified it is and on how much material inequality there is, and on how far pay is seen as a measure of individual worth.

While people generally need esteem—we might have worries about someone who did not and was completely oblivious to what others thought about them—we are likely to be wary of those whose sole motivation seems to be the approval of others; in Smith's terms, they put the pursuit of praise above the pursuit of praiseworthy acts. The pursuit of esteem fails if it is seen as being too instrumental and for its own sake rather than as an expected—but not demanded—recognition of the good practice itself, in other words, if the external, rather than the internal, goods are treated as the goal. In contrast, if workers see their work as worthwhile in itself, they are likely to try to work well both for their own satisfaction and self-respect, and for any esteem it brings them, which will also enhance their self-respect. Further, working well may become a habit, or a virtue in the Aristotelian sense, and a source of self-respect.

Those attached to the dogma that motivations can only be egotistical will no doubt want to argue that the economy of esteem will result in actors' pursuing their self-interest by disguising it. This may happen. However, it is risky because if the motives of those who adopt this strategy are suspected by others, they may subsequently suffer a loss of face and a long-lasting refusal of recognition. Even where effort and good performance are initially motivated by the pursuit of esteem, it may become habitual over time, and hence no longer consciously instrumental. Some may also pursue the external good of esteem without achieving any internal good, for example, by trying to appropriate credit for the achievements of others, and offloading blame for their own failures onto others. Managers may conceal individual failures and deficiencies within their own departments so as not to lower their departments' standing. The 'aura effects' of success and failure, discussed by Smith (II, iii, 2.6), and noted by Jackall in his study of corporate managers, encourage competitive individuals to avoid association with the weak and unsuccessful and to associate with the strong and successful (Jackall 1988). Nevertheless, while such behaviors are common, it is a mistake to assume they are universal: actors may have commitments to others or principles which are capable of overriding their self-interest.

Esteem and Recognition in the Context of Inequalities

The extent to which the intangible hand works depends on whether there is a 'public' present, willing and able to give esteem and disesteem, and on what kinds of reference group are involved. Although hierarchies are sometimes defended as reflecting differential contributions and esteem, they also distort the intangible hand, principally because it is difficult for those in a subordinate position to express judgments on the performance of those above them (expressing disesteem signals 'insubordination' while expressing esteem arouses the suspicion of insincerity and strategies of ingratiation),[35] and superiors may feel threatened if the performance of subordinates is superior to their own. In addition, status differences and prejudices such as snobbery, sexism, racism, homophobia may also distort their judgments.

One of the paradoxes of the economy of esteem is that if, as many assume is appropriate, differential esteem is reflected in differentials in pay and power, the resulting inequalities are then likely to distort the functioning of the intangible hand, for the subordinate are likely to feel disesteemed relative to their superiors simply by virtue of their position and regardless of their performance. Esteem is not merely a matter of words but of deeds. It is easy for organizations to make pronouncements about valuing all their members equally as persons, but if they allocate resources to them unequally, and provide very unequal working conditions, such statements are bound to ring hollow.[36] Of course, pay differentials are not simply a function of the esteem in which different groups of workers are held, but affected by differential scarcity and power, as well as by social conventions—often ones that lack warrant in normative terms. However, although pay and conditions are not simply a reflection of how groups of workers are esteemed, they may be taken as such by workers themselves. Some may believe that the imagined payment according to merit is just: what Lerner termed 'the belief in a just world' is common in popular thought, encouraging the assumption that people get paid what they deserve and deserve what they are paid (Lerner 1980).

The problem here is not only that the expression of esteem and recognition is often deficient in organizations, in part because of the existence of major inequalities. There is a more fundamental problem: the inequalities themselves give only limited and unequal access to satisfying work, involving internal goods, and whose effective performance warrants the external good of recognition.

Conclusions

I have been arguing that it is important to acknowledge both the overarching instrumental nature of organizations, and the possibility for ends other than those of the organization to be pursued within them. The latter are important from the point of view of the members of organizations, and they may either help or impede the realization of the organization's goals. Organizations are more likely to succeed if they take account of these other goals, including things which are valued in themselves rather than instrumentally, for other purposes.

I have not argued that instrumental action is necessarily bad, and non-instrumental action necessarily good, but that both can be good or bad. In emphasizing the importance of noninstrumental and ethical motivation and action in organizations I certainly do not want to overlook selfish and manipulative behavior, though these tend to be encouraged or discouraged by the nature of the organization, the way it selects its members and the demands it puts on them, its incentive systems and its ways of evaluating workers and managers. We need an unromantic view of employment that acknowledges excessive ambition, selfishness, insecurity, harassment, bullying, sexism, racism, homophobia, 'ableism' and the like, inequality and domination as well as ethical behavior and commitment to principles, and others. Thus in arguing that economic organizations have a moral dimension, it has certainly not been my intention to legitimize the status quo. They still operate in a context in which the priorities and quality of life are subordinate to the economy rather than vice versa, and in which, for capitalist enterprises, the pursuit of money becomes an end in itself, a condition of survival, rather than a means to an end (Booth 1993).

In this chapter I have only had space to deal with a few of the diverse goods that people seek within organizations and things which they value. In addition to pay, fulfillment from work and recognition, workers and managers are also likely to seek respect and dignity (Sayer 2006), sociability and enjoyment, though for many, access to these may be minimal. Although the possibility of esteem is, and arguably should be important in any social situation, an organizational culture in which the *only* recognition was esteem for achievement and given only to individuals would be a bleak, unforgiving, meritocratic, and moralistic environment, encouraging extreme competitiveness, individualism, anxiety, and low morale. Other qualities besides achievement, such as collegiality, civility, sensitivity, concern for others, friendliness, ability to listen, and willingness to offer opinions and to disagree make a significant difference to the quality of organizational life, often in ways that promote the organization's interests. Although therefore 'useful', many of these qualities imply a noninstrumental or partially noninstrumental attitude toward others, and they are likely to be eroded if they are treated too instrumentally by individuals or by the organization.

Acknowledgment

I would like to acknowledge the assistance of an ESRC fellowship in writing this chapter.

References

Anderson, E. S. (1993). *Value in Ethics and Economics*. Cambridge, MA: Harvard University Press.

Archer, M. (2000). *Being Human: The Problem of Agency*. Cambridge: Cambridge University Press.

Booth, W. J. (1993). *Households: On the Moral Architecture of the Economy*. Ithaca, NY: Cornell University Press.

Brennan, G. and Pettit, P. (2004). *The Economy of Esteem*. Oxford: Oxford University Press.

du Gay, P. (1999). *In Praise of Bureaucracy*. London: Sage.

Frey, B. (1997). *Not Just for the Money: An Economic Theory of Personal Motivation*. Cheltenham, UK: Edward Elgar.

Harré, R. (1979). *Social Being*. Oxford: Blackwell.

Jackall, R. (1988). *Moral Mazes*. Oxford: Oxford University Press.

Le Grand, J. (2003). *Motivation, Agency and Public Policy: Of Knights, Knaves, Pawns and Queens*. Oxford: Oxford University Press.

Lerner, M. J. (1980). *The Belief in a Just World: A Fundamental Delusion*. New York: Plenum Press.

MacIntyre, A. (1981). *After Virtue*. London: Duckworth.

O'Neill, J. (1998). *The Market: Ethics, Knowledge and Politics*. London: Routledge.

Sayer, A. (2005). *The Moral Significance of Class*. Cambridge: Cambridge University Press.

——(2006). 'Dignity at Work: Broadening the Agenda', Paper produced for ESRC workshop on Dignity at Work, Lancaster University Management School, 24.6.05.

Sedgewick, E. K. and Frank, A. (eds.) (1995). *Shame and its Sisters: A Silvan Tomkins Reader*. Durham, NC: Duke University Press.

Smith, A. (1759:1984). *The Theory of Moral Sentiments*. Indianapolis: Liberty Fund.

——(1776:1976). *An Inquiry into the Nature and Causes of the Wealth of Nations*, ed. by E. Cannan. Chicago, IL: University of Chicago Press.

Stouffer, S. A. (1949). *The American Soldier* (4 volumes). MA/AH Publishing.

Taylor, C. (1994). 'The Politics of Recognition', in A. Gutmann (ed.), *Multi-culturalism: Examining the Politics of Recognition*. Princeton, NJ: Princeton University Press.

11

Varieties of Capitalism and Varieties of Firm

Chris Brewster, Geoffrey Wood, and Mick Brookes

Introduction

The varieties of capitalism literature suggests that specific national economies are likely to be associated with specific sets of firm-level practices, ensuring the continuation of distinct national varieties of capitalism. Regulationist critics point to the temporary and inherently unstable nature of any specific mode of regulation; the effects of institutions are likely to be uneven and shifting, potentially making for a greater diversity in firm practices at specific times, even if a limited number of systemic archetypes are likely to predominate. Based on large-scale survey evidence, this chapter explores the extent to which several distinct and viable varieties of firm may coexist within specific varieties of capitalism, whether specific varieties of capitalism are associated with a greater or lesser degree of diversity in firm-level practices, and, whether, over time, there is a global pressure toward a greater diversity in practice.

Context

Firm Practices and Socio-regulatory Setting

A key strand of theories on the relationship between the firm and wider society has been in terms of conceptualizations on the nature and role of compound groups. In his classical theoretical writings on the subject, Emile Durkheim (1947) argued that, within a specific national economy, there is an underlying coherence—a subtle solidarity—based on an interdependence of social collectives. Durkheim (1947) held that this was underpinned by shared, orientating, rules and norms. These rules not only represented formal legislation, but informal conventions, accumulated over time. Later writings attempted to infuse more complex notions regarding the interdependence of component parts, and the underlying rules governing the operation of the systemic whole (Parsons 1951). Drawing on this specific theoretical tradition, Dunlop (1958) held that national employment relations systems represented a shared set of rules, encompassing both regulations and conventions, and day-to-day decisions, the latter molded by the wider systemic context.

Informed by this rich sociological tradition, a range of writers in the 1990s and early 2000s directed their attention to the persistence of national variations in firm practice within different national contexts, and attempted to anchor this relationship to wider societal rules (Lincoln and Kalleberg 1990; Whitely 1999; Applebaum et al. 2000; cf. Dore 2000). In part, this developed as a critique of neoliberal assumptions that national variations represented the product of market imperfections, which provided temporary blockages to the operationalization of 'best practice' at firm level (Hall and Soskice 2001: 1). It also reflected interest in specific European and Far Eastern varieties of capitalism that performed relatively well in the 1970s and 1980s, and in identifying optimal regulatory characteristics that could be emulated elsewhere, which would, it was held, encourage individual firms to adopt specific practices that would enhance their competitiveness (cf. Olson 1982; Lincoln and Kalleberg 1990; Applebaum et al. 2000; Dore 2000; Hall and Soskice 2001: 4).

More recent writing has tended to be rather more critical as to what individual national governments can accomplish (Whitely 1999; Hall and Soskice 2001: 4). Not only are accumulated practices likely to make for a certain path dependence that may be difficult to escape, but specific sets of practices—such as neocorporatism—may restrict the patina of economic choices (Hall and Soskice 2001). Nonetheless, a large component of the varieties of capitalism literature tends to draw a sharp distinction between liberal market, Anglo-American style, 'compartmentalized' economies on the one hand, and more cooperative social market economies on the other (Applebaum et al. 2000; Dore 2000; Hall and Soskice 2001). The latter would encompass both Far Eastern economies such as Japan and Korea, and the 'Rhineland' economies of western continental Europe.

In contrast to the two-archetype models, writers such as Whitley (1999) and Amable (2003) have identified a wider range of systemic archetypes—six and five respectively—to take account of the variations between Mediterranean capitalism and North European varieties, and provide more nuanced insights into the nature and operation of the advanced societies in the Far East. More recent work has pointed to yet another systemic archetype, encompassing partially and unevenly developed economies in tropical Africa (Wood and Frynas 2005).

A limitation of such approaches is that, whilst escaping the generalizations of the two archetype model, it inevitably leads to questions surrounding internal national coherence on regional lines—such as between northern and southern Italy, or between the Flemish and Walloon speaking parts of Belgium, or the ethnically, linguistically, and legally different regions of Spain. There is also, potentially, a proliferation of models, and/or the need for further analysis on the relationship between regional, national, and transnational regulatory configurations, while changes in the relative functionality of specific models reopen the question of convergence, albeit that empirical evidence points to the persistence of specific distinct features (Hall and Gingerich 2004; Brewster et al. 2006).

In contrast to the varieties of capitalism literature, regulationist perspectives point to the inherent instability of any specific regulatory environment (Jessop 2001; cf. Hopner 2005). Whilst the varieties of capitalism literature focuses on the systemic characteristics and performance outcomes of specific contexts, regulationist thinking commences with an analysis of the long-term transformation of capitalism, and the specific regulatory interventions that have provided, at best, a temporary context for relatively optimal capital accumulation (Boyer 2005*a*). Given this concern about wider regulatory configurations, regulationist methodologies place particular emphasis on the specific nature of systemic and macroeconomic coherence; in contrast, the varieties of capitalism literature stresses the importance of firm-level governance (Boyer 2005*a*).

From a regulationist perspective, certain regulatory environments will be more effective than others in imposing a specific coherence on firm-level practices; others will be more open ended and experimental (Williams 2000; cf. Boyer 2005*b*). The viability of a specific institutional environment may depend on the ability of one institutional feature to compensate for weaknesses in others, underscoring the fragile nature of accumulation (Boyer 2005*b*). In other words, specific social systems of production may be characterized by a greater diversity in firm-level practices than others; a distinction needs to be drawn between diversities in regulatory environments and the internal organization of firms (Boyer 2005*b*). In some cases, the characteristics of firms may be more homogeneous than others, despite the fact that the emergence and viability of corporations of a particular size is contingent on the relative integration and size of product markets (Boyer 2005*a*). This is of critical importance given the current popularity of benchmarking approaches—regulationists would caution that the same possible interventions do not shape institutions or firms in the same way, leading to mixed outcomes (Boyer 2005*a*).

However, both the varieties of capitalism and regulationist approaches stress the fact that a relatively limited number of types of capitalism coexist. What is in contention is the relative stability of regulatory environments, whether the diversity between firms is likely to be greater within specific types of capitalism than others, and whether there is not one but many combinations of managerial practices that may prove optimal within a particular regulatory setting.

Diversity in Internal Practices

As Edwards and Kuruvilla (2005: 10) note:

> ...emphasizing the *national* aspect of business systems to capture *international* variations does not mean that this line of analysis needs to be blind to *intra-national* variations. Certainly, one of the weaknesses in the way national systems are conceptualized is that such variations within countries tend to be downplayed.

This argument is reflected in earlier work by Bloom and Milkovich (1999) and Ortiz (2002). Focusing on the automobile industry in Australia, Germany, Italy, Japan, Sweden, the UK, and the United States, Katz and Darbyshire (2000) found increasing variation in all areas and many commonalities, producing variation within employment relations in all countries and convergence across countries. Much of this work is case study based, and open to further empirical observation.

Hopner (2005) argues that, within national contexts, hierarchical arrangements are inevitably subject to ongoing change. At specific times competition intensifies, and shifts in the nature of ownership patterns will result in more or less direct pressures being placed on managers, resulting in a greater or lesser uniformity in practices. On the one hand, it could be argued that liberal market economies have certain characteristics particularly likely to make for diversity, including a low degree of regulation, decentralized financial systems, weak unions, and fragmented collective bargaining (Boyer 2000; Amable 2003). Rosenberg (2005) suggests that highly decentralized environments allow for a greater room for experimentation at firm level, again allowing for a greater innovation. Hence, lightly regulated and decentralized contexts are likely to result in a greater range of managerial strategies, even if some prove ultimately unsuccessful. A high degree of room for entrepreneurial activity is likely to make for a high degree of internal turbulence (Audretsch and Thurick 2001). On the other hand, even in liberal market economies, there are strong centripetal pressures, given, most notably, the relative role and importance of institutional investors. Since, in liberal market economies, investors are less 'patient', this is likely to make for greater short-termism (Williams 2000; Amable 2003).

Centrifugal and centripetal pressures may make for internal regional and sectoral clusters of firms within particular national contexts. In other words, it is possible that a specific institutional context may prove optimal for more than one set of workplace practices. For example, within the United States, particular industries—the 'California type' (focused on high-technology) and wealthy financial sectors, characterized by individually negotiated involvement—coexist alongside large areas of the retail and fast food sectors, characterized by high levels of labor repression (Leborgne and Lipietz 2001). Hence, Jacoby (2004: 12) suggests that the internal differences within national business systems have the potential to exceed the differences between them (cf. Sako 2005); an argument which accords with Katz's suggestion (2005) that there is a tendency toward greater internal diversity in national economies.

Indeed, Wright and Dwyer (Chapter 14) have found that the decline of the manufacturing sector in the United States and the growth of different areas of the service sector has resulted in the bifurcation of the US labor market: low-end jobs concentrated in the retail trade and service sector, and better rewarded jobs in the high-technology sector, with a decline in the number of middle-level jobs. Low-end jobs are those of low quality, poorly paid, and commonly associated with low security of tenure or autonomy. In contrast, high-end jobs are better rewarded, and likely to be associated with better working conditions, although not necessarily greater security of tenure (Harcourt and Wood 2005). This would seemingly indicate the coexistence of several alternative models of workplace practices—and, given the correlation between quality of job and sector—the presence of several viable varieties of firm within a specific national context. The national context could represent an inherent feature of individual national business systems—in this case, liberal market—or reflect a greater tendency toward diversity given global pressures toward ever-greater deregulation. In other words, pressures on countries to adopt lighter regulation on the lines of the Anglo-Saxon model may result in firms drifting toward different models rather than toward a single model (cf. Guest 2001: 111). Indeed, Boyer (2005*b*) cautions that we lack a proverbial Mendelief table of all possible mixes of institutional arrangements and outcomes (Boyer 2005*b*).

Much of the international convergence literature addresses these issues, but is focused on convergence or divergence of national systems (see, e.g. Hickson et al. 1974; DiMaggio and Powell 1983). These discussions have been replicated in the field of HRM (see, e.g. Lammers and Hickson 1979; Brewster 1999; Gooderham and Brewster 2003, Brewster, Mayrhofer, and Morley 2004). A new strand of the convergence literature has identified the notion of 'majority convergence': the extent to which a population of organizations in a country become more homogeneous in the use of a certain management concept or tool. For example, if 50 percent of the organizations in a country use a specific management tool and 50 percent do not, one can assume maximum divergence within a country since there is a clear 'split' in the concrete use of this tool. In more general terms: the closer a value in a country has moved to the 50 percent level, the greater the majority divergence has become. Vice versa, the more the value approaches the 100 percent or 0 percent level, the greater the majority convergence has become (Mayrhofer et al. 2002; Mayrhofer and Brewster 2005). In overall terms, the question here is whether national sets of practices can be determined at all: is there greater variety within national systems than there is between them?

Defining Features of Firm Practice

So, what are the defining features of internal firm-level practice? Whitley (1999: 42) clusters firm employment relations practices into two broad categories: the degree of employer–employee interdependence, and the amount of delegation to employees (cf. Hollingsworth 1997; Amable 2003). The former would encompass relative security of tenure and the willingness of employers to invest in training and development: in short, the factors immediately impacting on the conduciveness to human capital development (Harcourt and Wood 2005). The latter would encompass the presence of different voice mechanisms encompassing collective or individual voice, and taking the form of limited, tightly constrained forms of involvement, or more open ended participation, as depicted in Figure 11.1.

Within the HRM literature, a common distinction is drawn between high and low road HRM practices (see Kochan and Ostermann 1994; Storey 2001). The former are characterized by high levels of employer–employee interdependence and delegation to employees (Kochan and Ostermann 1994; Pfeffer 1994; Ulrich 1997; cf. Whitley 1999). This would encompass high levels of

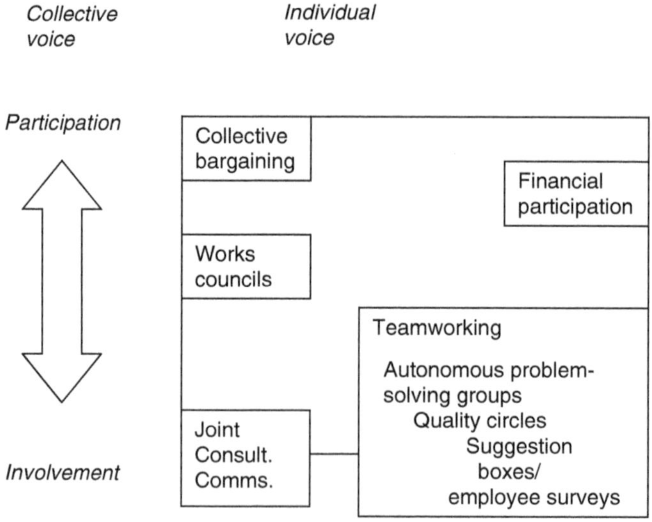

Figure 11.1. Different voice mechanism.
Source: Brewster et al. 2006.

security of tenure, formal channels, and procedures for employees to voice their concerns on a collective basis, and a strong emphasis on training and development (cf. Kochan and Ostermann 1994). In contrast, 'low road' practices would center on a low security of tenure, a lack of recognition of the collective concerns and rights of employees, and a strong emphasis on cost-cutting (Greider 1997).

However, within different settings, other combinations of practices are possible (Webster and Wood 2005). Even if vested with a high degree of autonomy, managers may adopt strategies that represent a sophisticated mix of policy options: hence, in liberal market economies, firms that make predominant use of classic Taylorist methods may coexist with those deploying managerial strategies that provide room for constrained but complex forms of participation, most notably of the financial variety (Pendleton et al. 2002), even if employees within both categories of firm may have relatively weak security of tenure and few collective rights. Four of the principle alternative managerial strategies are highlighted in Table 11.1.

Regulatory environments that pose fewer constraints on management may indeed make employee collectives more vulnerable to managerial action (Brewster et al. 2006); however, managers still have at their disposal a range of strategies (Webster and Wood 2005). Whilst it is argued that employers may, if relatively free of institutional restraints, naturally opt to do certain things—such as weakening the countervailing power of organized labor as much as possible—they still have a wide range of policy options, molded by past experience and subjective reinterpretation of present realities (see Wood 2001). Although this may make for a strong emphasis on individual voice and relatively low security of tenure, reward systems may follow tried and tested Taylorist methods, or encompass sophisticated forms of financial participation (Pendleton et al. 2003), and training and development may be informal and focused on a limited range of tasks, or be orientated toward specific categories of labor (cf. Webster and Wood 2005). Meanwhile, more pluralist/'high road' HR strategies may center on traditional collective bargaining, or encompass a range of different forums for exercising collective voice (cf. Guest 2001). Hence, it could be argued that a number of distinct varieties of practices are possible, with more than one being widespread within any particular national economy.

There is, as noted above, considerable merit to those theories of varieties of capitalism that identify not one, but several systemic archetypes. However, for the sake of analytical convenience, it has been decided to follow the common convention of distinguishing between liberal market economies, and more cooperative alternatives; this also allows more attention to be directed on the nature and extent of diversity within those economies where institutional mediation is relatively weak, in other words, liberal markets.

Table 11.1 Key firm-level employment relations practices

Type of HRM strategy	Autocratic Fordist	Sophisticated hard HRM	Traditional collectivism	Advanced cooperation
Associated form of work organization	'Bloody Fordism'	Numerically and financially orientated flexibility paradigms	'High Fordism'	Functional flexibility
Employee–employer interdependence				
Degree of investment by firm in training and development	Slight	Yes, to selected categories of employee	Mixed	High
Job security	Low	Low, particularly within certain job categories	Traditionally high	High
Delegation to employees				
Individual participation	Low	Financial participation	Limited	High—financial participation, etc.
Individual involvement	Confined to top-down briefings	Quality circles, team briefings, etc.	Limited	High—quality circles, etc.
Collective participation	Low	Low	High—centring on traditional collective bargaining	High—collective bargaining supplemented by works councils and autonomous teamwork
Collective involvement	Low	Limited forms of teamwork	Low	Some

Sources: Hollingsworth 1997: (274–5); Whitley 1999: 34; cf. Guest 2001; Webster and Wood 2005.

STATEMENT OF HYPOTHESIS

There are not one but several viable sets of firm-level practices within specific national business systems or types of capitalism.

Hence, for example, a specific variety of capitalism may be conducive to both autocratic fordism and sophisticated HRM, with most firms falling into one or other camp.

Method

This chapter is based on the findings of the 2004 Cranet Survey, which examines HR policies and practices within both private and public sector organizations in twenty-two European countries, and a dozen other nations with significant industrial and commercial sectors (Brewster, Mayrhofer, and Morley 2004). Respondents were the most senior HR official within the organizations encompassed; technical details on the survey are discussed in Brewster, Mayrhofer, and Morley (2004). The data used is selected from the overall database, and focuses on a number of cooperative and liberal market economies in order to shed further light on these two very distinct varieties of capitalism. The data for each country is representative of medium and larger organizations therein. Smaller firms were excluded given that there are very significant differences in practice between them and their larger counterparts; the practices in the smaller enterprise sector would constitute a fruitful area for future enquiry. Factor analysis was employed; this enables characteristics that go together to be identified, assessing the extent to which different questions are tapping the same underlying concept or shared set of practices (Morris, Wood, and Yaacob 2001: 69). In other words, it is a way of bringing order to the underlying issues, determining which items are related and which are not.

Findings

Table 11.2 presents the findings of factor analysis for all observations from a number of different liberal market and cooperative economies. It is evident that various forms of individually orientated downward communication, some of which incorporate an upward (individual voice) and direct dimension, are correlated (Component 1). This included team briefings, and workforce and direct face-to-face communication with management. The two principle forms of individual indirect voice—suggestion schemes and attitude surveys—are similarly correlated; firms using one were likely to use the other (Component 2). Meanwhile, firms making use of financial participation, such as share option schemes (again individual voice, this time of the participative variety), are found to be more likely to make use of redundancies, with this form of participation being in particular vogue amongst organizations placing a strong emphasis on maximizing shareholder value, and to also be more willing to consider them (Component 3).

Hardly surprisingly, there is also a correlation between the amount spent on training and the extent of training provided to employees (Component 4). In contrast, it is revealed that collective bargaining and works councils are not closely correlated with each other: this does not, however, indicate that they are inimical to each other, as the relationship between the two is weakly positive rather than inverse. Even more interestingly, the presence of collective bargaining and a works council is not correlated (either positively or negatively) with a range of other practices. In other words, there is not a strong correlation between those firms who have instituted a range of individual voice mechanisms and those who engage in collective bargaining or have a

Table 11.2 Factor analysis for all observations, 1,439 in total, from the UK (liberal market), Germany, Sweden, Netherlands, Norway, and Austria (cooperative)

Rotated component matrix	Factor 1	Factor 2	Factor 3	Factor 4	Factor 5
Decrease by compulsory redundancies	.047	−.108	**.644**	−.240	−.063
% employees on fixed-term or casual contracts	−.067	−.012	−.132	.019	**.903**
% of wage bill spent on training	.038	.135	−.063	**.663**	−.055
% employees receiving external training	.096	.025	−.049	**.684**	.111
Financial participation through profit sharing, share options, etc.	−.055	.302	**.642**	.084	−.099
Downward communication through team briefings	**.548**	.047	.379	.062	.151
Communication to management—direct to senior managers	**.716**	.008	−.132	.068	−.172
Communication to management through immediate superior	**.773**	.076	−.143	.001	−.126
Communication to management through TU reps	.254	.341	−.375	−.286	.019
Communicate to management through works council	.198	.448	−.204	−.439	.147
Communicate to management through regular workforce meetings	**.518**	.289	−.043	−.078	.009
Communicate to management through team briefings	**.635**	.136	.269	.096	.298
Communicate to management through suggestion schemes	.105	**.737**	.086	.077	−.138
Communicate to management through attitude surveys	.108	**.717**	.065	.135	.104

Note: Extraction method: Principal component analysis. Rotation method: Varimax with Kaiser normalization. A rotation converged in 6 iterations.

Variables that are relatively strongly correlated are highlighted in bold under the relevant factor they help constitute, using 0.5 as a cut-off point, a generally accepted standard.

works council. Indeed, it is also striking that there is not a strong correlation between the use of compulsory redundancies and the presence, or absence, of individual or collective voice mechanisms. As a result, what the factor analysis reveals is the presence of overlapping clusters of practices that may coexist, but are neither positively nor negatively associated with each other.

Table 11.3 provides the regression results obtained when each of the five factors identified above are treated as dependent variables and regressed against the independent ones of organization size, sector, and variety of capitalism (liberal market or collaborative).

First, it seems that there is not an association between the size of the firm and the use of individual and direct voice mechanisms (embodied in factor 1)—in other words, such voice mechanisms are relatively evenly distributed between differing sizes of firm. In addition, firms operating in a liberal market setting seem just as likely to make use of such mechanisms as their counterparts in more cooperative settings and while there are some sectoral variations, no clear divide emerges between the manufacturing and service sectors. Meanwhile, it would seem that individual and indirect voice mechanisms (factor 2, encompassing suggestion schemes and employee surveys) are more likely to be found in cooperative economies than their liberal market counterparts and are less likely to exist in the service sector; the relative importance

Table 11.3 Regression results with each of the 5 factors scores as the dependent variables and size, sector, and liberal market/collaborative economy as the explanatory variables

Variable	Factor 1		Factor 2		Factor 3		Factor 4		Factor 5	
	Coeff.	*t*-ratio	Coeff.	*t*-ratio	Coeff.	*t*-ratio	Coeff.	*t*-ratio	Coeff.	*t*-ratio
Constant	0.103	1.4	−0.194***	−2.6	0.631***	8.7	0.058	0.8	−0.439***	−5.6
Size	0.000	−0.5	0.000***	4.5	0.000***	2.6	0.000	−2.4	0.000	−1.1
Agric	0.230	1.1	−0.253	−1.2	−0.552***	−2.7	0.167**	0.8	0.487**	2.2
Ener	−0.268*	−1.7	0.121	0.8	−0.596***	−3.9	0.420***	2.7	0.053	0.3
Chem.	−0.429***	−2.6	0.175	1.0	0.048	0.3	0.234	1.4	−0.072	−0.4
Omanu	−0.050	−0.5	−0.126	−1.3	−0.244***	−2.6	−0.039	−0.4	0.063	0.6
Build	−0.153	−1.0	−0.448***	−2.9	−0.139	−0.9	0.253*	1.6	0.148	0.9
Retail	−0.229*	−1.9	−0.374***	−3.1	−0.279**	−2.4	0.587***	4.8	0.064	0.5
transport	−0.182	−1.2	0.132	0.9	−0.378***	−2.7	0.251*	1.7	0.112	0.7
Bank	−0.071	−0.6	−0.268***	−2.5	0.000	0.0	0.671***	6.1	0.174*	1.6
Pers	0.089	0.3	−0.382	−1.3	−0.600**	−2.1	0.636**	2.1	−0.146	−0.5
Health	−0.197	−1.6	−0.170	−1.4	−1.071***	−8.9	0.220*	1.8	0.548***	4.3
Oserv	−0.152	−1.1	−0.650***	−4.6	−0.636***	−4.7	0.510***	3.6	0.218	1.5
Educ	0.005	0.0	−0.314***	−2.7	−1.186***	−10.6	0.250**	2.1	0.735***	6.1
Sserv	−0.260*	−1.7	−0.233	−1.5	−1.260***	−8.6	0.027	0.2	0.428***	2.7
Padmin	−0.005	0.0	−0.261***	−2.5	−1.019***	−10.3	0.146	1.4	0.195*	1.8
Other	−0.093	−0.9	−0.162*	−1.6	−0.378***	−3.8	0.355***	3.4	0.448***	4.2
Collab	0.032	0.6	0.582***	10.8	−0.303***	−5.8	−0.469***	−8.7	0.372***	6.7
r-sq	0.014		0.135		0.213		0.113		0.083	

Note: *, **, and *** denote significance at the 10%, 5%, and 1% levels respectively.

of the latter within liberal market economies perhaps helping to explain this last association. On the other hand, firms in liberal market economies seem more likely to make use of large-scale redundancies and/or financial participation (factor 3), reflecting the stronger emphasis on maximizing shareholder value in such economies and those in cooperative economies less likely to spend resources on staff training (factor 4), a finding probably indicative of their more effective statutory training infrastructures. Finally, a tendency to a higher proportion of employees on fixed-term contracts in collaborative economies probably represents a response to stronger rights enjoyed by those in permanent (either de facto or *de jure*) posts in such regulatory environments; indeed, this higher usage of nominally insecure contracts is not correlated with a greater propensity to make use of compulsory redundancies.

In summary, it is evident that the regulatory context has only limited effects on whether firms make use of individual and direct voice mechanisms. However, the national setting does seem to impact on the use of indirect forms of individual voice, and relative propensity to make use of redundancies and financial participation. Second, whilst firms operating in private sector areas of the service sector seem more likely to make use of in-house training, they seem less likely to make use of indirect individual voice mechanisms, the latter often associated with specific manufacturing production paradigms.

Given these differences in practice on national lines, we now more closely examine which factors are most likely to be associated within collaborative economies (Table 11.4).

Again, it is evident that firms who made use of one form of direct individual voice mechanism are more likely to make use of others as well. It is also further evident that the two principle forms of indirect individual voice are likely to coexist, that financial participation is associated with compulsory redundancies and both the resources devoted to training and the extent to which it is provided by firms. At the same time, considerable internal diversity of practice is also highlighted, as is the fact that individual voice is not, either strongly or negatively, associated with collective voice.

Overall, then, given the various combinations of practices identified, it is apparent that *sophisticated varieties of hard HRM, traditional collectivism,* and *advanced cooperative paradigms* (see Table 11.1) may be encountered in cooperative economies. The fact that one or other of the latter two may predominate does not, as a result, seem to preclude alternative combinations of practices from emerging or persisting.

Roughly similar patterns are apparent when a liberal market economy—the United Kingdom—is considered (Table 11.5).

However, an important distinction here is that various forms of individual and direct voice are not at all as closely correlated; thus suggesting that there is an even greater variety of practice within liberal market economies, as suggested by some of the literature (cf. Sako 2005). This greater diversity in

Table 11.4 Factor analysis replicated for the collaborative economies only, that is, Germany, Sweden, Netherlands, Norway, and Austria, 881 observations

Rotated component matrix	Component 1	Component 2	Component 3	Component 4	Component 5
Decrease by compulsory redundancies	−.031	−.046	−.170	**.758**	.086
% employees on fixed-term or casual contracts	−.118	−.072	.143	−.032	**.796**
% of wage bill spent on training	.047	.128	**.578**	.104	.230
% employees receiving external training	.052	.028	**.757**	−.158	−.069
Financial participation through profit sharing, share options, etc.	−.047	.147	.290	**.568**	−.325
Downward communication through team briefings	.437	.151	−.042	.329	−.038
Communication to management—direct to senior managers	**.754**	−.073	.096	.014	.021
Communication to management through immediate superior	**.837**	.043	.026	−.074	−.039
Communication to management through TU reps	.307	.390	−.284	−.159	.381
Communicate to management through works council	.487	.295	−.250	−.249	−.019
Communicate to management through regular workforce meetings	**.554**	.283	.022	−.096	−.117
Communicate to management through team briefings	**.539**	.196	.139	.254	.327
Communicate to management through suggestion schemes	.116	**.770**	.020	.099	−.166
Communicate to management through attitude surveys	.107	**.744**	.197	.026	.118

Note: Extraction method: Principal component analysis. Rotation method: Varimax with Kaiser normalization.
A rotation converged in 7 iterations.

Table 11.5 Factor analysis replicated for the UK firms only, 558 observations

Rotated component matrix	Component 1	Component 2	Component 3	Component 4	Component 5
Decrease by compulsory redundancies	.180	−.020	−.138	−.359	**.554**
% employees on fixed-term or casual contracts	.202	−.125	.024	−.004	−.710
% of wage bill spent on training	−.114	.139	.158	**.668**	.096
% employees receiving external training	.160	.101	.056	**.581**	−.140
Financial participation through profit sharing, share options, etc.	.195	−.087	.287	.049	**.625**
Downward communication through team briefings	**.838**	.129	.077	.049	.017
Communication to management—direct to senior managers	.104	**.763**	.055	.071	.012
Communication to management through immediate superior	.160	**.786**	.012	.039	.009
Communication to management through TU reps	−.233	.332	.309	−.401	−.262
Communicate to management through works council	.029	.208	.218	−.493	.098
Communicate to management through regular workforce meetings	.348	.445	.104	−.076	.035
Communicate to management through team briefings	**.808**	.261	.093	.014	.042
Communicate to management through suggestion schemes	−.009	.151	**.737**	.091	.110
Communicate to management through attitude surveys	.207	−.029	**.761**	−.047	−.037

Note: Extraction method: Principal component analysis. Rotation method: Varimax with Kaiser normalization.
A rotation converged in 8 iterations.

practices may, therefore, be indicative of the existence of fewer complementarities flowing from practices that are stable and systemically embedded.

Conclusions

This chapter has highlighted the fact that whilst specific sets of practice are correlated, and often coincide with national setting, a wide range of different sets of practices may *coexist* within and amongst individual firms. The fact that the presence or absence of collective voice mechanisms is not closely correlated with individual voice mechanisms would indicate that the presence or absence of one is not necessarily *complementary* to the other; the two simply may or may not occur together (coexist). However, given that a range of individual direct voice mechanisms are often encountered together, this would indicate that a certain complementarity *may* exist; the same is true for individual indirect voice mechanisms. Again, there is no evidence that the relative propensity of firms to make greater use of compulsory redundancies is associated with a great reluctance to invest in training; any national or firm-specific skill shortfalls still have to be plugged regardless of whether or not it may be necessary to upsize or downsize. However, a specific combination of practices may prove *complementary* within a particular national, regional, and sectoral setting.

The lack of correlation between specific clusters of practices may be indicative not of a disorderly diversity, but rather of a range of combinations of practices—such as embodied in sophisticated hard HRM, traditional collective and advanced collaborative paradigms. Moreover, it seems that such paradigms do coexist in national regulatory settings, even if one or the other is likely to predominate within a particular regulatory environment. Indeed, this coexistence may be complementary—for example, a manufacturer of capital or consumer goods founding functionally flexible production on advanced forms of cooperation with staff may, at the same time, rely on suppliers being able to effectively cut costs, even if, in doing so, they make use of less 'people friendly' production paradigms. Of course, the latter may force suppliers to relocate production in more lightly regulated environments, making for greater diversity on global rather than simply national lines.

This chapter underscores the persistence of different national forms of regulation, making for variations in practice on national lines. Quite simply, firms in particular national settings are more likely to do certain things—such as engage in collective bargaining (Brewster, Brookes, and Wood 2005) or make use of suggestion schemes. However, this chapter also highlights the degree of internal diversity encountered in national business systems, with a wide range of practices coexisting, without sufficient complementarities necessarily emerging to ensure that a greater uniformity in practices diffuses across the economy in question. Hence, the central hypothesis is confirmed. This is not to preclude the possibility that specific combinations in practice may predominate in particular regions or industries. Yet, within a broader national setting, very different combinations of practices may be encountered—'bloody' fordism may coexist with traditional collective paradigms (or more complex clusters of practices)—and persist, despite wider regulatory and market pressures toward homogeneity. This would underscore the relative fragility of individual national social systems of production (SSPs) and the extent to which the latter represent more temporary combinations rather than durable frameworks for indefinite growth.

References

Amable, B. (2003). *The Diversity of Modern Capitalism.* Oxford: Oxford University Press.

Applebaum, E., Bailey, T., Berg, P., and Kalleberg, A. (2000). *Manufacturing Advantage: Why High Performance Work Systems Pay Off.* Ithaca, NY: Cornell University Press.

Audretsch, D. and Thurik, A. (2001). 'What's New About the New Economy?', *Industrial and Corporate Change,* 10(1): 267–315.

Bloom, M. and Milkovich, G. (1999). 'An SHRM perspective on International Compensation and Reward Systems', in P. M. Wright, L. D. Dyer, J. W. Boudreau, and G. T. Milkovich (eds.), *Strategic Human Resources Management in the Twenty-First Century. Research in Personnel and HRM.* Supplement 4: 283–303.

Boyer, R. (2000). 'Is a Finance-Led Growth Regime a Viable Alternative to Fordism', *Economy and Society,* 29(1): 111–45.

—— (2005*a*). 'How Do Institutions Cohere and Change', in P. James and G. Wood (eds.), *Institutions and Working Life.* Oxford: Oxford University Press (forthcoming).

—— (2005*b*). 'How and Why Capitalisms Differ', *Economy and Society,* 34(4): 509–57.

—— and Hollingsworth, J. R. (1997). 'From Embeddedness to Nestedness', in J. R. Hollingsworth and R. Boyer (eds.), *Contemporary Capitalism: The Embeddedness of Institutions.* Cambridge: Cambridge University Press.

Brewster, C. (1999). 'Different Paradigms in Strategic HRM: Questions Raised by Comparative Research', in P. Wright, L. Dyer, J. Boudreau, and G. Milkovich (eds.), *Strategic Human Resource management in the Twentyfirst Century. Research in Personnel and HRM.* Supplement 4: 213–38. Greenwich: JAI Press Inc.

—— Brookes, M., and Wood, G. (2005). 'Social Relations, Firms and Societies: A Study in Institutional Embeddedness', *International Sociology,* 20(4): 403–26.

—— —— Croucher, R., and Wood, G. (2006). 'Collective and Individual Voice: Convergence in Europe?', Working paper, Middlesex University, London.

—— Mayrhofer, W., and Morley, M. (eds.) (2004). *Human Resource Management in Europe: Evidence of Convergence?* London: Butterworth Heinemann.

DiMaggio, P. J. and Powell, W. W. (1983). 'The Iron Cage Revisited: Institutional Isomorphism and Collective Rationality in Organizational Fields', *American Sociological Review,* 48: 147–60.

Dore, R. (2000). *Stock Market Capitalism: Welfare Capitalism*. Cambridge: Cambridge University Press.

Dunlop, J. T. (1958). *Industrial Relations Systems*. New York: Holt.

Durkheim, E. (1947). *The Division of Labour in Society*. Glencoe, IL: Free Press.

Edwards, T. and Kuruvilla, S. (2005). 'International HRM: National Business Systems, Organizational Politics and the International Division of Labour in MNCs', *International Journal of Human Resource Management*, 16(1): 1–21.

Gooderham, P. and Brewster, C. (2003). 'Convergence, Stasis or Divergence? The Case of Personnel Management in Europe', *Beta*, 17(1): 6–18.

Greider, W. (1997). *One World, Ready or Not*. Harmondsworth, UK: Penguin.

Guest, D. (2001). 'Industrial Relations and Human Resource Management', in D. Storey (ed.), *Human Resource Management: A Critical Text*. London: Thomson.

Hall, P. and Gingerich, D. (2004). 'Varieties of Capitalism and Institutional Complementarities in the Macro-Economy', Max Planck Institute Discussion Paper O4/O5, Cologne.

—— and Soskice, D. (2001). 'An Introduction to Varieties of Capitalism', in P. Hall and D. Soskice (eds.), *Varieties of Capitalism: The Institutional Foundations of Competitive Advantage*. Oxford: Oxford University Press.

Harcourt, M. and Wood, G. (2005). 'Varieties of Capitalism: The Criticality of Employment Security in Western Europe', Working paper, University of Sheffield.

Hickson, D., Hinings, C. R., McMillan, C. J., and Schwitter, J. P. (1974). The Culture-free Context of Organisation Structure: A Tri-national Comparison, *Sociology*, 8: 59–80.

Hollingsworth, R. (1997). 'Continuities and Change in Social Systems of Production', in R. Hollingsworth and R. Boyer (eds.), *Contemporary Capitalism: The Embeddedness of Institutions*. Cambridge: Cambridge University Press.

Hopner, M. (2005). 'What Connects Industrial Relations and Corporate Governance?', *Socio-Economic Review*, 3(2): 331–58.

Jacoby, S. M. (2004). *The Embedded Corporation: Corporate Governance and Employment Relations in Japan and the United States*. Princeton, NJ: Princeton University Press.

Jessop, B. (2001). 'Series Preface', in B. Jessop (ed.), *The Parisian Regulation School—Regulation Theory and the Crisis of Capitalism Volume 1*. London: Edward Elgar.

Katz, H. C. (2005). 'The Causes and Consequences of Increased Within-Country Variance in Employment Practices', *British Journal of Industrial Relations*, 43(4): 577–84.

—— and Darbyshire, O. (2000). *Converging Divergences: Worldwide Changes in Employment Systems*. Ithaca, NY: Cornell University Press.

Kochan, T. and Osterman, P. (1994). *The Mutual Gains Enterprise*. Boston: Harvard Business School.

Lammers, C. J. and Hickson, D. J. (1979). 'Are Organizations Culture-Bound?', in C. J. Lammers and D. J. Hickson (eds.), *Organizations alike and unlike. International and interinstitutional studies in the sociology of organizations*. London: Routledge.

Leborgne, D. and Lipietz, A. (2001). 'Conceptual Fallacies and Open Questions on Post-Fordism', in B. Jessop (ed.), *Regulation Theory and the Crisis of Capitalism 3—Regulationist Perspectives on Fordism and Post-Fordism*. London: Edward Elgar.

Lincoln, J. and Kalleberg, A. (1990). *Culture, Control and Commitment: A Study of Work Organization in the United States and Japan*. Cambridge: Cambridge University Press.

Mayrhofer, W. and Brewster, C. (2005). 'European Human Resource Management: Researching Developments Over Time', *Management Review*, 16(1): 36–62.

——Müller-Camen, M., Ledolter, J., Strunk, G., and Erten, C. (2002). 'The Diffusion of Management Concepts in Europe—Conceptual Considerations and Longitudinal Analysis', *Journal of Cross-Cultural Competence & Management*, 3: 315–49.

Morris, D., Wood, G., and Yaacob, A. (2001). 'Securing Diversity in Human Resources?: Lessons From Malaysia', *Asia Pacific Business Review*, 8(1): 58–74.

Olson, M. (1982). *The Rise and Decline of Nations: Economic Growth, Stagflation and Social Rigidities*. New Haven, CT: Yale University Press.

Ortiz, L. (2002). 'Unions' Response to Teamwork: The Case of Opel Spain', *Industrial Relations Journal*, 29(1): 42–57.

Parsons (1951). *The Social System*. Glencoe, IL: Free Press.

Pendelton, A., Poutsma, E., van Ommeren, J., and Brewster, C. (2002). *Financial Participation in Europe: An Investigation of Profit Sharing and Employee Share Ownership*. Dublin: European Foundation for the Improvement of Living and Working Conditions.

Pfeffer, J. (1994). *Competitive Advantage Through People*. Cambridge, MA: Harvard University Press.

Rosenberg, N. (2005). 'Economic Experiments', in G. Dosi, D. Teece and J. Chytry, *Understanding Industrial and Corporate Change*. Oxford: Oxford University Press.

Sako, M. (2005). 'Does Embeddedness Imply Limits to Within Country Diversity', *British Journal of Industrial Relations*, 43(4): 585–92.

Ulrich, D. (1997). *Human Resource Champions*. Cambridge, MA: Harvard University Business School Press.

Webster, E. and Wood, G. (2005). 'Human Resource Management Practice and Institutional Constraints', *Employee Relations*, 27: 4.

Whitely, R. (1999). *Divergent Capitalisms: The Social Structuring and Change of Business Systems*. Oxford: Oxford University Press.

Williams, K. (2000). 'From Shareholder Value to Present-Day Capitalism', *Economy and Society*, 29(1): 1–12.

Wood, G. and Frynas, G. (2005). 'The Institutional Basis of Economic Failure: Anatomy of the Segmented Business System', *Socio-Economic Review* (in print).

Wood, S. (2001). Business and Labor Market Policy', in P. Hall and D. Soskice (eds.), *Varieties of Capitalism: The Institutional Foundations of Competitive Advantage*. Oxford: Oxford University Press.

12

'Bear With Me . . . .' —The Problems of Health and Well-being in Call Center Work

Chris Baldry, Phil Taylor, and Peter Bain

Introduction

The call or contact center is now the accepted organizational vehicle for the delivery of virtually all personal services from airline ticketing, through theater or holiday booking to insurance and banking and the public sector. The high level of integration of information and communications technologies has made the customer contact center a 'unique working environment' (HELA 1999) which in the UK by the end of 2003 had become the workplace of 790,000 employees, according to the DTI (Incomes Data Services 2005). Envisaging further growth, the call/contact sector is expected to grow to over 1 million employees by 2007.

Walk around a call center and at first glance it would seem to the casual observer to be the epitome of the modern workplace: no dangerous machinery, few overtly toxic materials, carpets on the floor, maybe potted plants. Yet absence and turnover figures for call centers in the UK remain at significantly high levels and by 1999 the Health and Safety Executive (HSE) had commissioned a research program specifically to look at 'the potential physical and psychological health risks associated with the working practices employed' in call centers, subsequently issuing a set of guidelines for employers in the public sector (HSE/HELA 2001). In 2001 the Trades Union Congress (TUC) ran the *'It's Your Call'* campaign which reflected the perception that the disturbing trends in their health and well-being reported by many union members were directly related to the structure and content of call center work. Despite the conclusion of a recent study from a work psychology perspective that 'call center work compares favorably with shop-floor manufacturing and clerical work with regard to well-being' (Holman 2002: 46), the occupational health and safety literature has therefore become increasingly filled with reports of a wide variety of complaints of ill health being reported by call center employees and for which the current health and safety regulatory framework seems to offer inadequate safeguards (see Taylor et al. 2003).

From the now extensive literature on call center work and organization, we know that working in call centers offers both potential job satisfactions deriving from directly helping the customer and significant dissatisfactions from repetitive and intensive work, stringent targets and tight supervisory control and monitoring (Taylor and Bain 1999, 2001; Bain and Taylor 2000; Callaghan and Thompson 2001; Bain et al. 2002; Taylor et al. 2002). However, while these dissatisfactions, and related stressors and employee 'burn-out', have been regularly discussed in such studies, the claim that call center work can be positively unhealthy has only recently been researched as a separate phenomenon (Deery, Iverson, and Walsh 2002; Holman 2002; Taylor et al. 2003).

This chapter builds on this latter strand of work. Initially, it puts forward an explanatory framework for examining the relationship between call center work and worker health aimed at enabling discussion of this relationship to move away from a monocausal model of individual conditions of unwellness by locating call center work within its surrounding political economy and demonstrating how occupational ill health within it is socially constructed. Following this, existing evidence on the implications that work of this type has for worker health is reviewed and case study evidence, then, used, to explore the extent and causes of the ill health that it generates.

An Integrated Model of the Office

In previous work (Baldry, Bain, and Taylor 1997; Taylor et al. 2003) we have argued that the ways in which occupational ill health can be generated by the social processes which both constitute and contextualize office work can be understood through examining the interaction and 'fit' between three interrelated components of any work system: the social environment (work organization, job design, managerial control systems, industrial relations context); the proximate environment (work technology, workstation design); and the ambient environment (work building, lighting, temperature, air quality, acoustics). These comprise the totality of any work system and none of these *on their own* can deliver healthy and satisfying work. Rather, the provision of such work depends on the establishment of a good fit between these three components: the design of the job, the technical system on which the job depends, and the environmental system in which these subelements are located. Thus, only if the surrounding built environment and technology *support* the work that has to be done and the job itself is designed on human-centered principles will work be healthy and satisfying.

If there is a disjunction between any two of these components of the work system, it is the employee who usually bears the consequences, as one attempts to make up the difference or bridge the system gap, usually through the expenditure of additional effort. The result is often physical discomfort or actual ill health. To take an example of a mismatch between social and proximate environments, information technologies typically perform mental calculations faster than the human brain, yet still rely on human data input at the start of the process. If data input jobs are poorly designed, so that the human is put under pressure to try to match the speed of the computer, the result may be some form of repetitive strain injury (RSI). Similarly, if repetitive jobs with short task cycles are performed in an office building with poor air quality, low humidity, and inadequate temperature control, the result for the building's occupants may be, as a result of a social/ambient mismatch, the cluster of symptoms known as sick building syndrome (Baldry, Bain, and Taylor 1997). In both these examples, the other components of the work system (technology and building), instead of supporting the organization of work, can be seen, then, to act as obstacles to its effective performance. Occupational ill health in contemporary workplaces like call centers, particularly for such a nonspecific complaint as occupational stress, may consequently be the result of the interaction between factors related to all three dimensions.

Up to this point this may look like a conventional (and static) systems model. We would stress, however, that it should be regarded only as an heuristic device because of the need for call center work systems to be understood as processes which reflect the dynamics of the economic context in which they are located. Hence, factors such as the structure of finance capital and the nature of market competition need to be seen as serving to shape organizational goals and managerially defined measures of performance and acting to create problematic tensions within the organization of work. For example, as the ensuing work organization struggles to deliver these goals (and the frequent goal revision which characterizes contemporary workplaces), with the existing technological system and built environment, the result may be more than one bad fit between its three associated subcomponents.

This approach serves to suggest limitations to some current ways of regarding or evaluating the state of workplace well-being and ill health. The conventional distinctions, made in organizational behavior, between intrinsic and extrinsic satisfactions (e.g. Holman 2002) do not really offer much analytical leverage as they limit themselves to the social environment and tend to take technology and the built environment as given. This would explain how it is quite possible to find a job intrinsically satisfying even though doing the job may make you ill. Thus, rather than just examining job design or the IT system on its own, we argue that a holistic or integrated examination of the workplace is necessary to identify the factors contributing to employee ill health. We will take the three components in turn to get a better picture of the characteristics of the call center work system and the consequences of their interaction. While there may be centers which are exempt from some of these characteristics, for this profile we can use the most recently available research to build up a composite picture of the typical center.

The Organizational Environment

The call center, typically, has a 'flat' organizational structure. Figures for Scotland (Taylor and Bain 1997) indicate an average composition to be: operators/agents, 71.3 percent, other clerical, 11.6 percent, professional/technical, 4 percent, supervisory grade, 8.8 percent, and managers, 4.3 percent. The workforce is around 61 percent female and predominantly young (two-thirds under the age of 35). Slightly less than a third of workers are part-time, and part-timers are more likely to be women than men, while temporary workers account for around 14 percent of the overall workforce (Taylor and Bain 2003).

The call center operator or agent's job can involve long periods sitting at a workstation, working simultaneously with screen-based equipment, keyboards, and telecoms. In the main, jobs are repetitive, tightly structured with little room for employee discretion or control, and usually governed by a combination of output and time targets. Teamworking is almost universal. Yet, in many instances these are pseudoteams, comprising merely administrative units, of say eight to twelve, rather than co-operative ones where work is shared and distributed according to the team's own decision-making.

Call centers, of course, are not homogenous and there are wide degrees of variation in cycle-times, degree of employee autonomy in call handling, and in the degree to which targets set are measured qualitatively or quantitatively. However, recent research (Batt and Moynihan, 2002; Kinnie et al. 2000) has suggested that most operations prioritize call volumes, throughput and strict measurements of operator performance, frequently combining this with monitoring to ensure qualitative standards are maintained (Taylor and Bain 2001; Rose 2002).

In a by now well-known phrase, one of Taylor and Bain's respondents referred to the work as 'an assembly-line in the head', aptly summing up the repetitive, system driven, and apparently inexorable nature of the work. However, the line in the head is not a Fordist one but rather emulates the model of lean production. Under Fordist flow-line assembly, with its consecutive sequence of specialized tasks, a holdup by one worker causes all others to wait (Askenazy 2001) whereas in call center working the automatic call distribution (ACD) system automatically distributes the calls to the next available agent and any holdup is covered by the work of other team members. Call centers are also 'lean' in that the goal is constantly to reduce 'unproductive' labor time, so that scripts, where used, are designed to get maximum information from the customer in the shortest time and targets are constantly revised upwards to remove every moment of down time. Further, staffing levels are also microscopically calibrated to match actual or anticipated customer demand. As Callaghan and Thompson (2001) point out, the work may resemble a mental assembly line in terms of its relentless machine pacing but not in terms of the production system. Most agents do not simply add a stage to the product and pass it on, they deal with the whole call process on a 'single-unit production' basis, completing one full production cycle after another.

The Technical Environment

Call centers represent of course a melding and integration of IT and telecommunications technology. Increasingly sophisticated ACD systems allow calls from customers to be diverted not only to any available operator in a given center but also, in a multicenter organization, to that center with the lowest waiting time. Similarly, predictive dialing systems allow the rapid generation of outbound calls from a database. During the call the operator interacts with the customer via the voice in the headset and the customer's details on the screen. One can neither see the customer (no body language to enrich communication), nor see how much work is likely to come in that day or that morning—one can only see how many are currently in the queue for the center as a whole from the ubiquitous digital readout on the office wall. There is, therefore, a high degree of machine-pacing of the rate at which workload is delivered to the agent, plus tight supervisory control of the pace and quality with which one processes the calls.

As is now well chronicled, the technology is both the means of service delivery and the means of performance monitoring, making a combination of audio and visual monitoring available to supervisors or team leaders in addition to the normal visual oversight. In addition, there is increasing use of call management software systems to secure a closer matching of staff availability to fluctuations in workflow, with the result that headcount, shift patterns, and break patterns are system generated and may vary daily.

The Ambient Environment

Call centers are of necessity open-plan, with each team's workstations grouped into cluster or row formation. Mostly located in offices built or refurbished within the last fifteen years, these will usually be sealed structures with mechanically (computer) controlled indoor climates; the amount of employees' local control over their working environment is usually minimal. Many of these offices were not designed to be used as call centers and most were not designed to be run on 24 hour occupancy. There are thus an increasing number of design unknowns here in terms of heat load and thermal adequacy, acoustics, air quality, and lighting levels. Most organizations do not really know how their building will behave until they fill it full of people and technology. This offers a good example of three-way interaction between the work system components. As pointed out by the HSE in their guidelines for local authorities:

> The large number of computers . . . can be generating heat 24 hours a day, seven days a week, and this can dry the air to unacceptable levels. Low relative humidity can lead to dehydration which, in turn, can contribute to sore eyes, voice loss and headaches. Skin rashes may also appear. (HSE 2001: 9)

The Economic Context

All this takes place within a highly competitive business environment which compels managers to strive to achieve maximum attainable call volumes (Bain and Taylor 2000; Taylor and Bain 2001*a*). This puts pressure on individual centers to meet and exceed set targets so that, within each center, similar pressures are put on teams and, within each team, the agent is the final recipient of these composite pressures. It is the constraints of competition which sustains the often-observed reluctance by management to take call-handlers off phones for any length of time or to increase the frequency and length of breaks.

The consequences of this are, first, that like so many aspects of contemporary office ill health, the complaints experienced by call center workers have become a contested terrain. As many of the conditions described below are invisible, particularly those labeled 'psychosocial', such as stress, this means that the affected worker is always faced with the problem of validity, of proving that one is 'really' ill, often in the context of increasingly severe sickness absence policies. Second, many of the best practices recommended by bodies such as the HSE to alleviate the onset of health problems run counter to the commercial logic by which center management is guided. 'Adequate rest breaks' and breaks 'away from intensive use of display screen equipment' (HSE/HELA 2001: 11) are always going to be problematic in an organization characterized by lean staffing and a productive time maximization strategy. Similarly, Holman's suggestion that 'job control should be maximized and practices such as insisting that calls are handled within an exact time and excessive call scripting should be resisted' (Holman 2002: 46) ignores the pressures of market competition that brought call centers into being in the first place. Finally, the sparse distribution of trade union representation means that in many centers there is no vehicle for workers to voice health grievances and challenge effectively this prevailing business logic; an absence that takes on added significance gives the evidence which indicates that a trade union presence is associated with a reduction in the incidence of injury and ill health (Reilly, Paci, and Holl 1995).

Ill Health in the Call Center

We can begin to see that, when these aspects of the call center work system come together, the results can be deleterious to employee health and well-being. Health complaints experienced by call center workers fall into roughly three categories: those particularly associated with call center work, such as voice loss, or hearing impairment; those already associated with working with display screen equipment, such as eyestrain, and musculoskeletal problems-higher work-related upper limb disorders, repetitive strain injury (WRULDs, RSI); and those associated with organizational or office work in general, such as stress, and sick building syndrome. These are of course not discrete categories and, as we shall see, what is significant is that call center employees can experience clusters of several of them contiguously.

Voice complaints. As early as 1996, the Banking, Insurance, and Finance Union examined the causes of 'voice loss' affecting their members in telephone banking (BIFU 1996) and other trade unions representing call center workers have increasingly reported their members complaining of voice-related symptoms such as sore throat or swelling, smarting, burning, irritation, croakiness, and whispering. If these symptoms persist over a period of time, this may indicate such forms of occupationally induced damage to the vocal apparatus (larynx and upper airways) as voice loss (dysphonia), throat pain and soreness (odynophonia), nodules and polyps on the larynx, excessive blood on the edges of the vocal chords (hyperaemia), thickening of the blood vessels, or ulcers on the larynx (Hazards 2004). The type of voice most likely to contract these malignant states is what is known as the 'projected voice', as used by salespersons, teachers, barristers/advocates, preachers, politicians, lecturers, radio and TV commentators, and actors, with the deliberate intention of exercising an influence on others. Like actors, call center employees have to 'project' their side of the dialog with the customer, but with the difference that the voice is used like this all day and every day and 'speaking the script' does not have the same vocal range as normal conversation.

In 2005, the UK white-collar union Unison voted for a program of six key demands to cut the risk of voice loss—regular voice breaks of at least five minutes of nonvocal time per hour, easy access to fresh drinking water, the facility to rerecord introductions, measures to minimize background noise, measures to ensure that calls are rotated and measures to ensure that workers with colds or sore throats are rested from telephone work (Trades Union Congress, 2005). It can be seen that this list usefully combines elements from all three of our work system components. If we apply the three-component model to the problem of potential voice damage, then the worst possible scenario would be:

- A work system which is high volume, repetitive and where breaks are discouraged and no training has been given on effective voice use.
- A technical system which uses poor quality or badly maintained audio equipment.
- An environmental system with poor acoustic integrity and thus high levels of ambient noise, with low levels of humidity and with a poor cleaning regime and consequent higher than average dust levels.

We could predict that whole one of these factors on its own might result in voice problems for some employees, two or three of them in combination will increase both the likelihood of problems and the number of those affected.

Hearing impairment. There has been an increasing concern with the phenomenon of acoustic shock, hearing damage caused by a random frequency surge resulting in an unexpected short loud burst or spike of noise delivered through the headset, the results of which may include pain, hearing loss, tinnitus, and noise sensitivity (CWU 2006). Modern headsets now contain software that filters out such spikes but the number of complaints dealt with by the unions, plus recent evidence from Denmark and Australia (HSE 2004), would seem to indicate that these are far from universal. Ear infections have also recently surfaced as an health issue which seem to be caused by sharing audio equipment, for example, on continuous shift systems, and where (unlike in aircraft for example) headsets are not sterilized. Examining hearing problems as a whole we find very similar factors to the above in that a combination of high levels of surrounding noise in the center and/or poor equipment can mute or distort the customer's voice and induce the operator to turn up the volume.

Eyestrain. Like all office work, call centers combine a mix of both desk and screen work and so require adequate levels of both natural and artificial light and the elimination of glare. Because centers are increasingly run on a 24-hour basis, night workers are often required to operate at the same levels of artificial light as are available during the day shift, which are usually insufficient as artificial light levels at night should be *increased* to compensate for the lack of natural light.

Musculoskeletal problems: After twenty-five years experience of IT in offices we now know a lot more than we did in the early 1980s about musculoskeletal disorders (MSDs) and their association with long periods of repetitive and sedentary work at PCs, with insufficient breaks (Caletano 1994). We know that the components of workstations, VDUs, and chairs should be adjustable to suit individual differences and the personal characteristics of *any* user.

However, where the same workstation is used on a continuous three-shift system or where hot-desking is practised, the evidence seems to indicate that such ergonomic adjustments are less likely to happen.

Bowel problems: The competitive pressures on employers to minimize off-phone time has been commented on above and there have been several accounts reported in the media of employers setting stringent conditions for workers taking toilet breaks or emphasizing system-generated break patterns. A good example is found in the memo sent by the AA to employees in its Cardiff center in October 2005:

> 'With effect from Tuesday 1st November 2005 everyone who works a shift of at least 3.5 hours duration will have breaks scheduled for them. These breaks will replace personal allowances. What you do in your break is of course entirely up to you, visit the toilet, get a coffee, go for a stroll, whatever. *However you must be back at your desk, logged in ready to take a call, by the time your scheduled break is over'.*
>
> (GMB 2005; emphasis in original)

Medical specialists on bowel control (Norton, cited in Hazards 2004) have detailed a number of medical consequences, including haemorrhoids and even renal damage, of not being able to take toilet breaks when necessary.

Stress. The most commonly accepted model of stress is where work loading is high but the individual's capacity to control the work is low (Karasek and Theorell 1990), exactly the combination of job design elements which, as we have seen, often characterize call center work.

Sick building syndrome. Despite the flurry of attention given to this syndrome in the early 1990s this still has not gone away. We still find huge numbers of call center workers (many in recently constructed buildings) complaining of stuffed noses, upper airway infections, sore eyes, headaches, lethargy, skin rashes, and the other major components of the syndrome cluster, and continuing to say that these symptoms were not experienced before they worked in this particular building and/or that they go away when the sufferer is absent from the building for any length of time. Without going into the debate on the causes of SBS here, we can simply remark that from our own research it seems to be another case of a bad fit between the way a building works and what people are asked to do inside that building. When sat in a given location for the best part of 7 or 8 hours a day the agent's personal biology becomes less tolerant of any levels of temperature, air quality, and humidity that do not suit their personal requirements.

The Work-System Model in Action

From our discussion of the typical call center we can see that there are several areas of potentially poor fit between its subsystems: where, instead of the environment and the technology supporting people in their work, they act as either an obstacle to effective performance or an externally experienced pressure which, in the worst cases, can push the human body to its physical limit, as exemplified in the various health conditions outlined above. We now draw on evidence from two case studies to illustrate how ill health is socially constructed in practice.

The first of these focused attention on a large call center operated by a national utility provider, *Energyco*, that was privatized in the late 1980s. At its Grampian House site, 1,100 were employed on inbound and outbound operations dealing largely with payment, billing, and debt services. At the time of the research (September 2000 to June 2001), 70 percent were directly employed, while the remainder were long-term agency temps. Women comprised a majority (55 percent) of the workforce and full-time workers accounted for three-quarters (for fuller details see Taylor et al. 2003). The second case comprised an investigation of working conditions amongst call-handlers and dispatchers working in police control and communication rooms (PCR), conducted between September 2004 and February 2005 (see Bain, Taylor, and Dutton 2005*a* and *b*).

Both studies utilized a combination of qualitative and quantitative research methods. At Grampian House, the former included thirty observations of task performance, lasting in most cases a complete shift, during which the research team listened into calls and conducted unstructured interviews with over seventy call-handlers, as well as formal semistructured interviews with management, who supplied essential company data, and with Unison officers and representatives. In the police control room research, six forces (encompassing eleven sites) and reflecting contrasting metropolitan, large county and small county geographies, and differing call-handling processes, were selected as being representative of the fifty-three UK forces. In most control rooms, work observation involved listening in to the interaction between call-handlers and the public and, similarly, included unstructured interviews with the staff. Formal, semistructured interviews with control room and HR managers and with Unison representatives and officers were recorded and transcribed. In addition, this latter study gathered and analyzed extensive documentation from the Government, the Home Office, and the Police Service.

Both studies also used a self-completing survey, composed of common and bespoke questions, the latter directed at the unique characteristics of each milieu. The fact that a considerable number of the questions were identical in both surveys enables us to make comparisons between the perceptions of call-handlers in the two environments. Many of the generic questions had been successfully employed in other studies undertaken by the authors of call centers in financial services (see Taylor and Bain 2001; Bain and Taylor 2002) or were drawn from earlier studies of the office environment (Wilson and Hedge 1987; Raw 1992; HSE 1995; Baldry et al. 1997). Additional questions were

Table 12.1 Comfort and discomfort at the workstation

	Comfortable or very comfortable Energyco %	Comfortable or very comfortable PCR %	Uncomfortable or very uncomfortable Energyco %	Uncomfortable or very uncomfortable PCR %
Height of desk (n=445; 573)	91	81	9.4	19
Height of chair (n=443; 564)	89	74	11	26
Position of screen (n=444; 574)	87	81	13	19
Position of keyboard (n=446; 568)	86	79	14	21
Support from chair (n=445; 572)	74	59	26	41
Headset (n=430; 558)	71	68	29	32
Earpiece (n=355; 404)	68	62	32	38
Amount of workspace (n=446; 575)	59	72	41	28

adapted from a survey instrument used in an ESRC 'Future of Work' project[(1)] and from the Health and Safety Executive's (HSE) call center research. At Grampian House, 634 usable completed questionnaires were received, yielding a response rate of 58 percent. To enable effective comparisons to be made between the two studies, we have filtered out those who were not customer-facing call-handlers. In the police control room research, from a national sample of union members, randomly selected by Unison's data management tool (RMS), and distributed by post, 583 (>20 percent) usable responses were received.

The Proximate Environment

Table 12.1 displays responses to questions relating to workstation comfort or discomfort. For all eight aspects in both surveys those reporting comfort outweighed those reporting discomfort. Large numbers considered the height of their desks and chairs, and the position of their screens and keyboards, to be either comfortable or very comfortable. However, the fact that minorities did report a degree of discomfort, particularly in the police control rooms, should not be overlooked; for example, more than a quarter experienced discomfort from the height of their chair.

Ergonomic aspects specifically related to call-handling activity were undoubtedly issues of concern to large minorities. Almost a third in both environments reported discomfort with their headsets. The reasons given by respondents for hearing problems were similar in both milieux: background noise, poor equipment, customers using mobile phones, customers not speaking clearly enough, bad connections. It would appear that space was more of a problem for workers in police control rooms than in Energyco, although

Table 12.2 Perceptions of the effects of heating and ventilation

	'Daily' or 'Several Times a Week' Energyco %	'Daily' or 'Several Times a Week' PCR %
Temperature—too hot (n = 414; 572)	52	60
Temperature—too cold (n = 417; 572)	51	62
Air circulation—too stuffy (n = 405; 570)	52	57
Air circulation—too draughty (n = 395; 569)	41	57
Humidity—too dry (n = 394; 573)	43	57

even in the latter case more than a quarter expressed problems. A final factor contributing to discomfort was hot-desking. Ninety percent of call-handlers in control rooms and 38 percent at Energyco reported that they did not always sit at the same workstation. Despite HSE advice that a self-assessment should be carried out each time a worker occupies a new workstation (HELA 2001), only 11 percent in control rooms reported that this happened.

In sum, sizable minorities reported ergonomic problems. However, given our holistic and integrated analysis, these should not be seen as operating in isolation from other sets of factors.

The Ambient Environment

As intimated above, the working environment is not a neutral factor in the construction of occupational ill health (Baldry, Bain, and Taylor 1997). Table 12.2 displays the responses of call-handlers in respect of the ambient environment. Given the reported extremes of temperature, large numbers of call-handlers in both case study organizations very regularly experienced thermal discomfort. Further, poor air circulation was causing many to feel that the building was either too draughty or too stuffy, complaints that are classically associated with malfunctioning heating, ventilation and air conditioning systems (HVACs). Finally, a large minority at Grampian House experienced their working environment as too dry on a daily basis, while almost six in ten in police control rooms reported this to be the case.

Patently, then, the built environment was failing to deliver satisfactory levels of thermal comfort and air quality to call-handlers in both Energyco and the PCRs. Interview data and questionnaire comments flesh out these descriptive statistics, with many articulating the conviction that the ambient environment was contributing significantly to high levels of illness and sickness absence.

> Our room is very uncomfortable to work in. There are very few windows, none of which open. The air conditioning is woefully inadequate and throughout the room there are pockets of hot and cold air. Operators can be freezing cold at one end of the room and too hot at the other. It is a breeding ground for infection.
>
> (Police Communications Operator, female, aged 40)

Table 12.3 Control over aspects of the job. 'To what extent do you . . .'

	'Not at all' + 'Just a little' Combined % Energyco	'Not at all' + 'Just a little' Combined % PCR	'Quite a lot' + 'A great deal' Combined % Energyco	'Quite a lot' + 'A great deal' Combined % PCR
. . . set your own pace of work? (*n*= 452; 579)	70	70	14	15
. . . plan how you carry out your work? (*n*= 451; 577)	62	63	18	21
. . . set your own targets (*n*= 451; 571)	84	77	6.4	13
. . . repeat the same tasks over and over (*n*= 453; 577)	10	10	79	81
. . . deal with difficult problem (*n*= 453; 576)	19	13	49	60
. . . use personal initiative and judgment (*n*= 452; 580)	24	6.6	45	80

The company will have to do something about the air conditioning—today there are draughts and we are frozen. It's also an incubator of germs. In an office of 800 people, one person with a little bug leads to germs rattling about the place.

(Customer Service Advisor, male, aged 32)

Social Environment: Work Organization and Job Design

The principal conclusion from both studies was that it was the way in which call-handlers' tasks were structured, organized, and performed that was perceived to contribute most to ill health. First, it is important to note that call-handlers were obliged to spend a considerable proportion of their working day on calls (75 percent of working time at Energyco and 88 percent in the PCRs) and, during this time, employees were subject to a labor process over which they exercised very little control (Table 12.3).

The majority of call-handlers, then, perceived an absence of, or very little control over, key aspects of task performance. The evidence confirms the conclusion of recent research (Taylor et al. 2002: 141–5) that most call-handlers do not, contra Frenkel et al. (1999: 71), enjoy 'expanded levels of discretion'. In having calls routed to them by Automatic Call Distribution (ACD) systems, the majority of call-handlers exercised very little control over the pace and planning of work, and task performance was commonly described as 'repetitive'. Demonstrably, also, call-handlers saw themselves as exercising little control over their targets. At the same time, almost a half of Energyco respondents, and clear majorities of PCR staff, reported that they both had to deal with difficult problems and had to use their personal initiative and judgment 'quite a lot' or 'a great deal'. To make sense of this apparent contradiction, we have to draw a distinction between content and

Table 12.4 Extent of feeling pressurized as a result of work on a normal day

Survey/location	Quite & very pressurized %	Not at all & not very pressurized %
Energyco (n= 447)	69	31
Police control rooms (n= 578)	84	16

Table 12.5 Extent to which aspects of job contribute to pressure

	Energyco %	PCR %
Inadequate staffing levels (n/a; n= 563)	n/a	88
Number of calls queuing/waiting (n/a; n= 547)	n/a	79
Dealing with calls of a serious nature (n/a; n= 552)	n/a	70
Having to meet targets (n= 441; 545)	71	64
Difficult members of the public/customers (n= 440; 555)	70	65
Not enough time between calls (n= 441; 538)	67	57
Fear of making mistakes (n/a; n= 567)	n/a	61
Repetitiveness of calls (n= 434; 548)	57	34
Call monitoring (n= 423; 511)	57	53
Having to keep to a script (n= 409; 345)	52	16
Monotony of the job (n= 435; 540)	49	21
Not enough breaks (n= 429; 540)	49	46
Always having to smile down the phone (n= 426; 538)	44	34
Breaks not long enough (n= 415; 528)	47	42
Not enough time to talk to colleagues (n= 423; 547)	36	34
Pressure from a supervisor (n= 427; 555)	32	42
Having to work on a computer screen (n= 424; 549)	24	34
Physical discomfort at the workstation (n= 417)	18	

process. Obviously, the content of calls can vary, particularly, in the control room where they are frequently unpredictable and may even deal with 'life or death' situations, yet the process by which staff deal with them is essentially imposed. For many control room staff, it was the exercise of judgment and responsibility in encounters with the public and the police within a highly structured framework where work routines were intense and repetitive that caused particular difficulties for staff.

As can be seen from Table 12.4, large numbers in both studies experienced their work as quite or very pressurized on a daily basis, although it appeared that police control rooms were a comparatively more pressurized environment. It is instructive to examine the aspects of the job that the call-handlers reported as causing pressure (Table 12.5).

The missing data for Energyco reflects differences between the studies in the questionnaire items used, so that respondents in police control rooms were presented with an expanded list of job aspects. Some of these were identified as the most important sources of pressure. Reprising the argument that the call center represents a 'lean production' model of service delivery, inadequate

Table 12.6 Increase/decrease in aspects of job over the last 12 months

	Increased a lot & a little Energyco %	Increased a lot & a little PCR %	Decreased a lot & a little Energyco %	Decreased a lot & a little PCR %
Speed of work (*n*=428; 537)	83	84	6.2	3.3
Volume of work (*n*=427; 539)	82	90	4.6	2.6
Intensity of work (*n*=427; 537)	80	89	4.8	1.9
Pressure of work (*n*=428; 534)	80	89	5.6	1.5

staffing emerged as the most significant source of pressure in control rooms, and is integrally related to many others. For example, the pressure that call-handlers experienced from waiting or queuing calls—identified as an important source of pressure—was a clear manifestation of understaffing; although for control room staff, the intrinsically demanding, perhaps even traumatic, nature of the incidents they were dealing with also clearly contributed to the pressures of their job.

Notwithstanding some variation in the findings between the two studies, it is possible to build a composite picture of what creates pressure for call-handlers. It is evident that having to meet targets is seen as a major problem. While much of the literature on call centers scarcely mentions targets, others have argued (Bain and Taylor 2000; Taylor and Bain 2001; Bain et al. 2002; Taylor et al. 2002) that the imposition of quantitative targets (measuring output, timings, etc.) and qualitative targets (evaluating interaction with customers) are central to managerial control strategies in the call center, and constitute the single most disliked aspect of its work. In addition, other distinctive, and closely related, aspects of the call center labor process—lack of time between calls, repetitiveness of calls, monitoring, brevity, and infrequency of breaks—are perceived to be important. The fact that difficult customers/members of the public are seen to contribute so greatly to the pressure of the job should compel us to treat with caution, if not skepticism, the arguments of those who regard the interaction of customers with call-handlers as essentially enriching for the latter (Frenkel et al. 1999; Korczynski 2002). In sum, the experience of targets, high call volumes, lack of breaks, and the pressure from supervisors and customers, etc., that is to say factors relating to job design, work organization and management policy, were the principal perceived cause of pressure in both studies.

It should be remembered that this is not a static picture, as indicated by the many call-handlers who reported a considerable increase in the volume, pressure, intensity, and speed of work (Table 12.6).

These figures provide striking confirmation that overwhelming majorities of call-handlers in both locations at the time of the survey believed that they had experienced a remarkable intensification of effort.

Table 12.7 Extent of complaints and symptoms

Symptom/complaint	'Very regularly' % Energyco	'Very regularly' % Control rooms	'At least regularly' % Energyco	'At least regularly' % Control rooms
Physical tiredness (n= 448; 575)	39	62	69	86
Mental fatigue (n= 446; 573)	35	57	61	84
Stress (n= 446; 569)	30	46	58	77
Stiff neck (n= 445; 572)	26	43	49	66
Stiff shoulders (n= 449; 575)	26	45	49	70
Sore eyes (n= 444; 565)	25	34	51	63
Backache (n= 445; 570)	19	40	40	66
Headaches (n= 446; 568)	18	22	52	60
Impaired vision (n= 434; 537)	9	16	18	31
Pain/numbness in hands/wrists (n= 443; 567)	9.9	19	23	38
Sore throat (n= 444; 569)	9.9	10	26	34
Blocked nose (n= 441; 561)	8.2	9.4	23	26
Sinus trouble (n= 444; 567)	7	8.7	15	20
Coughs (n= 444; 566)	6.5	5.2	13	16
Runny nose (n= 443; 568)	5.6	8.8	21	23
Earache (n= 439; 566)	4.6	4.6	9.2	14
Voice loss (n= 443; 562)	2.9	4.3	9	12

Sickness and Ill Health—Complaints and Symptoms

As suggested in our theoretical model, when these three aspects of the work system in our two call center cases are taken together, the results are frequently unhealthy. Both surveys asked call-handlers to report on the frequency with which they experienced the kinds of identifiable and often related symptoms and complaints that were outlined at the start of this chapter. Table 12.7 presents the extent to which these symptoms and complaints were reported; the frequency category 'very regularly' aggregates the 'daily' and 'several times a week' responses, and the 'at least regularly' column adds to this the numbers who report 'several times a month' responses.

The most notable difference between the cohorts is that the PCR staff were more likely than those at Energyco to report these symptoms and complaints, although this is merely a difference of degree. Given the constraints of word length it will be necessary to précis the discussion by considering evidence from both case studies together.

The two most frequently reported complaints were physical tiredness and mental fatigue. It would seem that some call-handlers in both milieux must be close to exhaustion and emotional withdrawal. Whilst acknowledging the distinction between the self-reporting of a condition and its medical diagnosis, the extent and frequency with which stress was reported is clearly indicative of a serious problem. It is remarkable that almost one-third of

Energyco respondents, and one-half of those in police control rooms, stated that they experienced stress either 'daily' or 'several times a week'.

Musculoskeletal complaints, including stiff shoulders and necks, backaches, and pains or numbness in hands wrists and arms, were also found to be prevalent. Clearly, these were problems of some importance for employees in these call center environments. Eye complaints, although clearly associated with extensive VDU usage, may be caused by the interaction of ambient factors (air quality and circulation, lighting), and proximate and social factors (scanning a screen for long periods). Headaches, which may have individual or multiple causes, were experienced 'at least regularly' by a majority in each of the cases. Complaints relating to nose and throat differed both in terms of their extent and between locations, but even in Grampian House relatively sizable minorities reported problems.

Earache and voice loss were the two conditions that might be seen as specifically related to call handling. Again, while clearly not as extensive as other complaints, it is clear that the number of workers affected is not negligible. For example, one in eleven at Energyco and one in eight in the PCRs reported that they suffered from voice loss at least several times a month.

Several additional points are pertinent. First, while many of these symptoms, when considered individually, are insufficiently serious as to cause absence from work, we found that large numbers experienced them in clusters. For example, 23 percent at Energyco and 47 percent in control rooms experienced at least five of these complaints 'daily' or 'several times a week'. While some symptoms can be attributed to one of the three environments (proximate, ambient, social), the experience of symptom clusters gives a good indication of how a poor fit *between* the dimensions of the overall work system aggravates workers' ill health. Second, the sickness absence policies in both settings were widely perceived to be unfair to the genuinely sick and draconian, with, for example, majorities reporting that they felt pressurized in returning to work. Consequently, many call-handlers (Energyco—63 percent, control rooms—54 percent) said that they 'often' or 'sometimes' came to work when unwell. Given what appears to be widespread and acute problems with heating, ventilation, and air conditioning (HVAC) systems, the presence of sick workers serves to exacerbate levels of illness by encouraging the circulation of germs and viruses (Baldry, Bain, and Taylor 1997). Thus, punitive sickness absence policies are, it would seem, often counterproductive.

Conclusion

Of the few studies of health and well-being in call centers, those by Holman and Deery appear to reach diametrically opposed conclusions (Deery, Iverson, and Walsh 2002; Holman 2002). While Deery, Iverson, and Walsh found that routinized work and use of scripts was associated with emotional exhaustion, Holman concluded that center work compared favorably with other forms of clerical work. The analysis presented in this chapter, including the case study findings reported, adds weight to the first of these interpretations by highlighting the scale of the work-related ill health experienced by call center workers. In doing so, however, it also draws attention to the need to locate the analysis of the relationship between such work and worker health in a much broader explanatory framework than those offered by these authors.

In their studies both Holman and Deery, Iverson, and Walsh only looked at job design and variables within job design such as the degree of job autonomy, or style of supervision. As a result, the approaches that they adopted ignored the fact that call center work is by its nature interactive—part of the stress of the job is not simply task repetition or the tight time allotted to the task cycle, but an outcome of the (unpredictable) nature of customer responses, including rudeness and verbal aggression (as at Energyco) or the traumatic incidents that form the focus for them (as in the PCRs).

The evidence from the two very sectorally dissimilar case study locations also, more fundamentally, indicates that it is wrong to seek the causes of occupational ill health in call centers in solely the technology, *or* the work organization, *or* the built environment. Instead, the findings obtained point to the fact that account also needs to be taken of the way in which these three elements of the work context interact to affect the health of workers. In particular, they clearly suggest that when a task which is itself stressful (difficult customers, demanding performance levels), requires protracted periods of human–technical interaction above the limits of recommended best practice and where the whole operation is performed in an unsupportive working environment, a reduction of employee health and well-being must inevitably occur.

This last observation, in turn, draws attention to a worrying aspect of the case study findings, namely the increase in the pace, intensity, and volume of work that appeared to be occurring in both locations as a result of the wider economic context of enhanced market competition and squeezed public sector finances. For, insofar as such tendencies are sustained, it suggests that call centers, as the favored and near universal means of delivery of personal services, may become even less (rather than more) healthy places to work in.

Acknowledgment

(1) ESRC award number L212 25 2006 'Employment and Working Life Beyond the Year 2000: Two Emerging Employment Sectors'.

References

Askenazy, P. (2001). 'Innovative Workplace Practices and Occupational Injuries and Illnesses in the United States', *Economic and Industrial Democracy,* 22: 485–516.

Bain, P. and Taylor, P. (2000). 'Entrapped by the Electric Panopticon?: Worker Resistance in the Call Centre', *New Technology, Work and Employment,* 15(1): 2–18.

—— —— (2002). 'Ringing the Changes?: Union Recognition and Organisation in Call Centres in the UK', *Industrial Relations Journal,* 33(3): 246–61.

—— ——, and Dutton, E. (2005*a*). 'The Thin Front Line': Call Handling in Police Control Rooms', Paper to *23rd International Labour Process Conference,* Glasgow: University of Strathclyde, 21–23 March 2005.

—— —— —— (2005*b*). *Working in Police Control Rooms: A Report for Unison.* Universities of Strathclyde and Stirling.

—— Watson, A., Mulvey, G., Taylor, P., and Gall, G. (2002). 'Taylorism, Targets, and the Pursuit of Quantity and Quality by Call Centre Management', *New Technology Work and Employment,* 17(3): 170–85.

Baldry, C., Bain, P., and Taylor, P. (1997). 'Sick and Tired? Working in the Modern Office', *Work Employment and Society,* 11(3): 519–39.

Batt, R. and Moynihan L. (2002). 'The viability of alternative call centre production models', *Human Resource Management Journal* 12(4); 14–34.

BIFU (1996). *Occupational Voice Loss*: a *Negotiations Guide,* London BIFU.

Caletano, D. (1994). 'Health Issues in Office Work', in G. Green and F. Barker (eds.), *Work Health and Productivity.* Oxford: Oxford University Press.

Callaghan, G. and Thompson, P. (2001). 'Edwards Revisited: Technical Control in Call Centres', *Economic and Industrial Democracy,* 22: 13–37.

Communication Workers' Union (2006). 'Accoustic Shocker: British Industry's Ticking Timebomb', *CWU Voice,* 13(1): 8–9.

Deery, S. J., Iverson, R. D., and Walsh, J. T. (2002). 'Work Relationships in Telephone Call Centres: Understanding Emotional Exhaustion and Employee Withdrawal', *Journal of Management Studies,* 39(1): 471–96.

Frenkel, S., Korczynski, M., Shire, K., and Tam, M. (1999). *On the Front Line: Organisation of Work in the Information Society.* Ithaca, NY: Cornell University Press.

GMB (2005). *GMB Calls the AA to Come Clean on the Work Standards and Toilet Breaks for its Call Centre Workers,* www.gmb.org.uk/Templates/PressItems.asp?NodeID=92734; accessed January 2006.

Hazards (2004). 'Toilet Breaks', *Hazards,* 81.

—— (2004). 'Work Hoarse', *Hazards,* 88, October–December 2004.

Health and Safety Executive (1995). *How to Deal with Sick Building Syndrome.* Sudbury, Canada: HSE Books.

—— (2004). *Noise—Acoustic shock,* www.hse.gove.uk/noise/acoustic.htm; accessed January 2006.

—— Local Authorities Enforcement Liaison Committee (2001). *Advice Regarding Call Centre Working Practices,* LAC 9a4/1 rev. Sudbury, Canada: HSE Books.

Holman, D. (2002). 'Employee Wellbeing in Call Centres', *Human Resource Management Journal,* 12(4): 35–50.

Income Data Services (2005). *Pay and Conditions in Call Centres, 2005/06.* London: IDS.

Karasek, R. and Theorell, T. (1990). *Healthy Work, Stress, Productivity and the Reconstruction of Working Life.* New York: Basic Books.

Kinnie, N., Hutchinson, S. and Purcell, S. (2000). ' "Fun and surveillance": the paradox of high commitment management in call centres', *International Journal of Human Resource Management* 11(5): 967–85.

Korczynski, M. (2002). *Human Resource Management and Service Work.* Basingstoke, UK: Palgrave.

Raw, G. (1992). *Sick Building Syndrome: A Review of the Evidence on Causes and Solution.* HSE Contract Research Report No. 42, Watford, Building Research Establishment/HMSO.

Reilly, B., Paci, P., and Holl, P. (1995). 'Unions, Safety Committees and Workplace Injuries', *British Journal of Industrial Relations,* 33(2): 275–87.

Rose, E. (2002). 'The labour process and union commitment within a banking services call centre' *The Journal of Industrial Relations,* 44(1): 40–61.

Taylor, P. and Bain, P. (1997). *Call Centres in Scotland: A Report for Scottish Enterprise.* Glasgow Scottish Enterprise.

——— (1999). 'An Assembly-line in the Head: Work and Employee Relations in the Call Centre', *Industrial Relations Journal,* 30(2): 101–17.

——— (2001). 'Trade Unions, Workers' Rights and the Frontier of Control in UK Call Centres', *Economic and Industrial Democracy,* 22(1): 39–66.

——— (2003). *Call Centres in Scotland and Outsourced Competition from India.* Stirling, UK: Scotecon.

—— Baldry, C., Bain, P., and Ellis, V. (2003). '"A Unique Working Environment": Health, Sickness and Absence Management in UK Call Centres', *Work Employment and Society,* 17(3): 435–58.

—— Hyman, J., Mulvey, G., and Bain, P. (2002). 'Work Organisation, Control and the Experience of Work in Call Centres', *Work, Employment and Society,* 16(1): 133–50.

Trades Union Congress (2005). 'Voice Loss Threat to Call Centre Workers', *Risks: Weekly Health and Safety Update,* 212, 25 June, TUC online.

Wilson, S. and Hedge, A. (1987). *The Office Environment Survey.* London: Building Use Studies.

13

The Reshaping of Workplace Risks

Phil James

Introduction

The risks of injury and ill health faced by workers during their course of employment are influenced by a range of factors both internal and external to the workplace. Internally, these factors include the type of work activities carried out, features of the equipment and substances involved in these activities, the nature of the preventive arrangements put in place by employers to protect workers, the form of employment relationship under which work is undertaken, and the ability that workers have, both individually and collectively, to challenge the presence of hazardous and risky working conditions. Externally, they encompass the nature of the surrounding labor and product markets, as well as the legal frameworks that exist to protect their health and safety and the degree to which these are enforced.

It follows that changes in these factors can have both negative and positive consequences for both the risks that workers face and their propensity to suffer injury and ill health. Given this, the present chapter explores, primarily in relation to Great Britain, but with reference being made to other developed economies, the implications in this regard of a number of the key economic and regulatory developments that have been taking place in recent decades.[37] The changes concerned are the shifts that have taken place in the occupational, contractual, and sectoral composition of employment, the way in which work processes and systems have been reformed, the rise of more fragmented, or networked, organizational structures, the decline of collective 'voice', and developments in the structure and operation of the regulatory framework for workplace health and safety.

The chapter proceeds as follows. First, attention is paid to the potential relationship that exists between the above changes and the extent of the risks to their health and safety faced by workers. Following this, attention turns to a consideration of what the currently available evidence tells us about the way in which the levels of the risks confronting workers have recently been changing and how far it lends weight to the previously offered analysis.

Shifts in the Composition of Employment

The composition of employment has changed dramatically in Britain, as well as in other advanced economies during recent decades. Employment in the primary industries, utilities and manufacturing, as Table 13.1 shows, has fallen sharply, the balance between manual and nonmanual work has shifted in favor of the latter and various forms of contingent or nonstandard employment, such as temporary and part-time work and self-employment, have become more common.

On the positive side, a beneficial impact would seem likely to flow from the reduction in employment in the primary industries, utilities and manufacturing given that these are areas of employment which have above average rates of injuries (see Figure 13.1) and where a number of 'traditional' occupational diseases have been relatively common (Health and Safety Executive 2005). The same would seem likely to be true of the fall that has taken place in manual work.

On the other hand, some of the other compositional changes previously mentioned can be viewed as more problematic. For example, the self-employed have been found to experience higher rates of fatal and major injuries, both generally and among particular occupational groups, such as construction workers and long-distance truck drivers, and significant proportions of homeworkers have been found to suffer from work-related injuries and ill health (Health and Safety Laboratory 2002; Mayhew and Quinlan

Table 13.1 Employment by broad industrial sector, 1982–2002

Industrial sector	Percentage employment share		
	*n*1982	1992	2002
Primary and utilities	5.2	3.5	2.2
Manufacturing	22.7	16.6	13.2
Construction	6.7	7.0	6.3
Distribution, transport, etc.	28.3	29.0	29.6
Business and misc. services	16.5	21.1	25.6
Nonmarketed services	20.6	22.7	23.1
All industries	25,186	26,639	29,336
	100	100	100

Source: Adapted from Davies and Jones (2005).

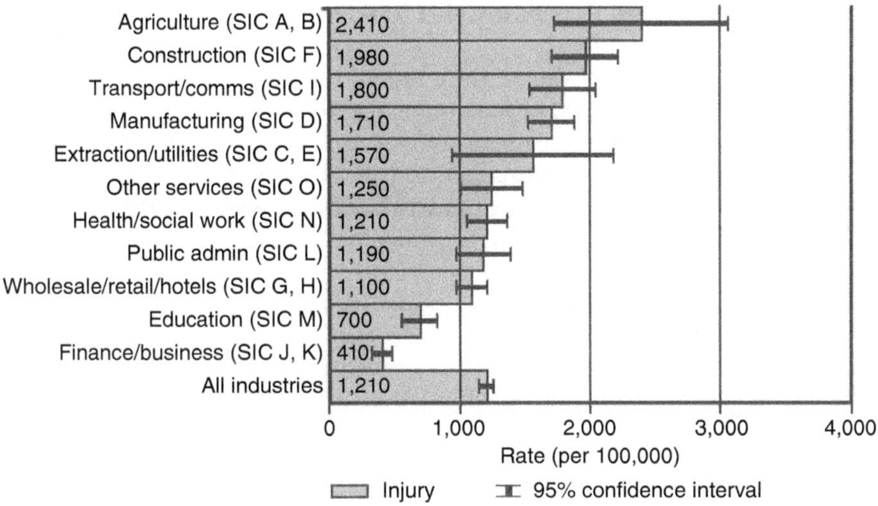

Figure 13.1. Estimated rates of reportable nonfatal injury to workers by SIC industry section, per 100,000 people, average 2002/03–2004/05.
Source: HSE (2005).

2006). Meanwhile, the available evidence, on balance, suggests that the working conditions of temporary and fixed-term workers are generally worse than those of 'permanent' ones, notably with regard to aspects of their physical work environments, such as working in painful or tiring positions, exposure to high noise levels and engagement on work involving repetitive tasks and movement (Goudswaad 2002). It, further, suggests that they more commonly suffer from musculoskeletal conditions, fatigue and, in the case of temporary agency staff, accidents, and that the financial insecurities faced by such workers, as a result of a combination of low pay and insecure employment, themselves generate a number of other adverse occupational outcomes including high work intensification, long working hours, a reluctance to take leave and an acceptance of poor working conditions (Mayhew and Quinlan 2006).

The observations made in the last paragraph do not, of course, mean that all of the growing proportion of workers engaged on nonstandard forms of employment is exposed to less favorable health and safety conditions and outcomes. They do, however, suggest that many of them are; a conclusion that is given added weight by the fact that over 80 percent of the studies examined in one major review of the relevant international research evidence were found to have obtained findings pointing in this direction (Quinlan, Mayhew, and Bohle 2001).

The Reform of Work Processes and Systems

As other chapters in this volume have noted, the organization of work has been undergoing a profound process of change in recent decades, prompted, in part, by the need of employers to cut costs and improve efficiency against the background of increasing competition, both domestically and globally, and, in part, by technological developments. Differing views, as has also been noted, however, exist as to the implications that these changes have had for workers.

These differing viewpoints can for present purposes be broadly, if somewhat crudely, divided into optimistic and pessimistic scenarios. The former, which is associated most clearly with proponents of 'high performance work systems', is premised on the viewpoint that in today's economic environment employing organizations need to secure the commitment, or 'hearts and minds', of those that they employ and as a result are moving to establish employment arrangements which enhance worker autonomy, skill, and discretion and, in doing so, acting to improve job satisfaction and worker commitment and motivation (Applebaum et al., 2000). In contrast, the latter is based on the view that the main trend is toward employers adopting 'lean and mean' systems of employment which simultaneously act to reduce task discretion and autonomy, increase managerial surveillance, sometimes with the aid of new information technology, and raise the intensity of work; developments that are seen to have rather less favorable outcomes for worker satisfaction, motivation, and commitment and to further increase the levels of stress they experience (Delbridge, Turnball, and Wilkinson 1992).

In reality, both of the above scenarios may contain elements of truth as a result of differences in the strategies adopted by individual employers, either generally, or in relation to different occupational groups. However, insofar as the 'lean and mean' interpretation of recent developments is correct, then it seems that they are likely to be leading to adverse occupational health outcomes given the well-established linkages which exist between such features of work organization as high levels of work intensity and low task discretion and control and both reported levels of stress and MSDs, as well as poorer general mental and physical health (Stansfield, Head, and Mamot 2000; Anderson-Connolly 2002; Taylor 2003; Brenner, Fairris, and Ruser 2004).

The analysis of the impact of call center work on workers' health by Baldry and his colleagues in Chapter 12 serves to add weight to this last point, demonstrating, as it does, how the work pressures and lack of control involved, as well as the nature of the surrounding proximate and ambient environments, can generate a range of adverse health effects. The same is true more generally of the available quantitative evidence in Britain which sheds light on recent aggregate developments in the organization of work. For this indicates that the intensity of work has been increasing, as has the degree of control and surveillance exercised by management, while task discretion has been falling; despite the fact that skill levels have been tending to rise and employers have been making increasing use of group forms of employee involvement (Green 2001; Gallie, Felstead, and Green 2004; Taylor 2004; Green 2006).

The Rise of Small Firm Employment

An important element of the changing face of employment in Britain, as well as other advanced economies, has been a growth in the proportion of employment based in small- and medium-sized enterprises (SMEs). An obvious consequence of this is that the actions of such enterprises now exert a more important influence over standards of workplace health and safety at the aggregate level.

Once again, this development cannot be viewed as wholly negative. For there is evidence to suggest that 'job-related well-being', a composite measure that comprises combined responses in respect of how far jobs generate feelings of calmness, tenseness, worry, uneasiness, contentment, and relaxedness, is higher in both small workplaces and organizations, that stress and MSDs are less of a problem in such organizations and that levels of work intensity in them are also lower (Kersley et al. 2005; Jones, Huxtable, and Hodgson 2005).

At the same time, this generally positive evidence exists alongside other data which indicates that injury rates vary negatively with both workplace and organization size. Eurostat data, for example, shows in respect of the then, fifteen European Union member states, that the average fatal injury rates per 100,000 workers for micro (1–9 employees) and small-sized enterprises (10–49 employees) were around double that which applied to larger undertakings in 1999 (Eurostat 2002). In a similar vein, a number of British studies have found the incidence of fatal and major injury accidents to be significantly higher in small workplaces (Nichols, Dennis, and Guy 1995; Cully et al. 1999; Stevens 1999).

A range of British studies have, moreover, highlighted the poor health and safety knowledge and expertise within small firms and their less sophisticated approach to the issues management. For example, one study investigated employers' awareness of, and responses to, six sets of regulations and found that knowledge of them varied considerably between small (less than fifty employees) and medium and large (more than fifty employees) employers, with just 41 percent of the former having heard of the Management of Health and Safety at Work Regulations, one of the most generally applicable and important sets of British regulatory requirements, compared with nearly 80 percent of the latter (Hanson et al. 1998). Meanwhile, another found that whereas 59 percent of companies employing more than 250 people had a health and safety practitioner, this was the case for 43 percent of small firms (11–49 employees) and 37 percent of microenterprises (ten or less employees) (Pilkington et al. 2002). In addition, this last study further found that the proportions of companies which engaged in the three activities of hazard identification, risk management and the provision of information to employees similarly varied, with the relevant percentages for large-, small-, and microfirms being found to range from 74 percent through 34 percent to 13 percent.

Organizational Fragmentation

The last two decades or so have also seen a marked trend toward the fragmentation of previously integrated systems of production and service delivery, a trend that has variously been associated with the advent of boundaryless, networked, and porous organizational forms (Marchington et al. 2005). Central to this trend has been the externalization or outsourcing of service and production activities to third party organizations in both the public and private sectors and a related move toward their control by market forces and contracts rather than internal managerial hierarchies (Williamson 1975).

Conceptually, it cannot be straightforwardly assumed that this greater use of control by market forces inevitably leads to adverse occupational health and safety outcomes. Insofar as, for example, externalization is associated with, say, the shift of manufacturing activities to more specialist producers, it could lead to the 'transferred work' being carried out in an environment where relevant work-related risks are better understood and better controlled. Similarly, insofar as internally utilized temporary and subcontract labor are to be employed in high risk production environments where the results of something going wrong are potentially catastrophic, the user employer may have substantial business incentives to ensure that their employment does not result in the undermining of existing standards of risk management.

There would, though, seem three reasons why the net aggregate effect of the de-integration of production and service delivery is likely to be adverse. The first, which links to the discussion above, is that much of the externalization of work activities would appear to have gone to smaller organizations and, in particular, small- and medium-sized enterprises, which possess less adequate and sophisticated systems of risk management. The other two relate to the problems that can arise with regard to the coordination of such management in situations where subcontractor and temporary staff work in physical proximity to in-house personnel, and the way in which the associated commercial contracts can potentially limit the ability of those organizations engaged in the supply of labor or the provision of manufacturing and other services to invest in preventive health and safety measures.

There is evidence to suggest that the coordination of risk management can become problematic in situations of subcontracting and labor outsourcing due to the fact that overall management control and responsibilities become more diffused. In the case of subcontracting, for example, Rebitzer (1995), in a study of contract and directly employed workers in the US petrochemical industry, found that the former category of worker received markedly lower levels of supervision and training than the directly employed staff with whom they often worked in close proximity and Kochan et al. (1994) found that poor communication between company management and contract workers created tensions that could have potentially serious implications for occupational health and safety. In a similar vein, Dawson et al. (1985) in a study of construction sites found that where subcontracting occurred, many people were unclear about the division of responsibilities for health and safety and that systems of authority did not run in a clear way through line management as they might in other forms of industrial organization, and a number of official inquiries into the causes of disasters in the offshore oil and rail industries have similarly drawn attention to the difficulties that can arise with regard to the adequate management and control of workers employed by subcontractors (Baldry 2006).

Existing research evidence relating to the management of the health and safety risks faced by temporary workers paints a similar picture. A British study, funded by the HSE and undertaken in 2000, for example, revealed that around half of the recruitment agencies did not have measures in place to ensure that they were fulfilling their legal obligations, that agencies were frequently unaware whether risk assessments have been carried out by host employers, and that the exchange of health and safety information between agencies and host employers was often poor (Wiseman and Gilbert 2000). Meanwhile, and more generally, a parliamentary inquiry in the Australian state of Victoria recently concluded that the use of 'labor hire arrangements' can complicate the coordination of work processes, including occupational health and safety (OHS) standards, and that weak lines of communication between labor hire workers and agencies, and host employers and employees, can lead to the obfuscation of occupational health and safety responsibilities (Economic Development Committee 2005).

There is also evidence that the market relationship between the different organizations involved in supply chains can lead to situations whereby the larger and financially stronger parties in them can secure financially beneficial contractual terms that can detrimentally affect the management of health and safety in those organizations with whom they contract. Thus, in a recent study of health and safety in small firms, a number of the owner/managers interviewed reported how their ability to invest in health and safety was limited by the narrow profit margins that they were operating under as a result of the contract prices demanded by larger clients (Vickers et al. 2003). Similarly, the Victorian Parliamentary report referred to above noted how the cost-sensitive nature of the labor hire industry could lead agencies to compromises or even noncompliance with OHS duties in relation to measures such as induction training or risk assessment.

More generally, and also in the context of Australia, on the basis of an investigation of the experiences of those working under subcontract/outsourcing arrangements in four sectors, child care, hospitality, transport, and building, the researchers involved reached the conclusion that they were associated with increased economic competition, as well as work disorganization, regulatory failure, and a divided workforce, and that in 'any organization where outsourcing has become common, OHS standards deteriorate...' (Mayhew, Quinlan, Bennett 1996).

The Decline of Collective Voice

Trade union membership and organization has declined substantially in Britain, as well as most of the rest of the industrialized world, over the past quarter of a century. Indeed, in the case of Britain, where these declines have been particularly marked, the position now is that, in the case of the private sector, union membership density stands at less than 10 percent, while unions are only recognized for bargaining purposes in around 11 percent of workplaces with ten or more employees (Kersely et al. 2005).

This decline in union membership and recognition has not been accompanied by the widespread putting in place of alternative, nonunion, channels of collective voice. As a result, in 2004, management in nearly 80 percent of workplaces possessing ten or more employees did not consult or negotiate with either union or nonunion representatives over the issue of health and safety (Kersely et al. 2005: 22).

There are good grounds for believing that this combination of declining union influence and the corresponding rise in the unilateral management of workplace health and safety issues by employers is problematic (James and Walters 2005). Thus, British evidence, as well as that stemming from studies in other countries, indicates that the presence of joint arrangements for worker consultation and representation is associated with better health and safety outcomes (Walters 2005). It further suggests that they are also linked to the existence of superior risk management arrangements, including the presence of written health and safety policies, the better provision of health and safety information and training, the use of health and safety practitioners, the carrying out of health and safety audits and inspections, and the undertaking of risk assessments.

Regulatory Policies

There is a substantial body of international evidence to indicate that legal requirements, as well as the likelihood that noncompliance with them will be discovered and penalized, both act to influence positively how employing organizations approach the management of health and safety (Wright 1998; Davis 2004). Trends in these two areas can consequently be expected to influence the degree to which employers are motivated to protect workers from work-related injury and ill health.

In terms of the legal duties imposed on employers in Britain, the advent of the Health and Safety at Work Act 1974 heralded a marked shift of approach in terms of their formulation or nature; a shift that has been subsequently replicated in other countries, including Canada, Australia, and the member states of the European Union (Gunningham and Johnstone 1999). This shift, initially, entailed a move away from the use of prescriptive requirements that effectively tell employers what they need to do to protect workers toward the utilization of goal-setting duties that lay down the standards of protection that must be achieved—a change exemplified by the core duty imposed under the 1974 Act to 'ensure, so far as reasonably practicable, the health and safety at work of employees'. More recently, it has also come to encompass the additional use of 'process' standards which detail the actions that employers should take with regard to such matters as the assessment of risks, the provision of relevant information and training, and the utilization of 'competent' health and safety advice.

These changes in regulatory approach have proved a challenge for many smaller organizations because of the less prescriptive and clear nature of the new legal duties and the resultant uncertainty this creates with regard to what they need to do to protect the health and safety of their workers (Health and Safety Commission 1994). During the period of Conservative rule from 1979–97 they also existed alongside a neoliberal inspired desire at the political level to reduce 'burdens on business', a desire that saw pressures emerge to both remove 'unnecessary' legal obligations and avoid imposing new ones. In reality, however, these pressures, ultimately, led to little direct 'deregulation' and existed alongside, much to the frustration of successive Conservative governments, the introduction of a host of new sets of regulatory duties stemming from European directives which themselves reflected the generally more favorably inclined approach of other member states toward 'social regulation' (James 1995). The period 1979–97 consequently saw, in practice, an increase in the legal duties of British employers.

Deregulation did occur during this period in another guise, namely via the reduction in the funding of the Health and Safety Executive (HSE), the body responsible for enforcing health and safety laws in the 'higher risk' parts of the economy, such as construction, manufacturing, mining, and agriculture. This funding reduction, in turn, led to a significant fall in the number of inspectors employed by the Executive, and substantial declines in the number of investigations and inspections they undertook and the number of enforcement notices issued and prosecutions brought by them.

Initially, the election of a Labour government in 1997 appeared to hold out the promise of a rather different regulatory agenda emerging (James and Walters 2005). Thus, shortly after it came to power the Labour government announced an increase in HSE funding and, in establishing a Better Regulation Unit, more generally, indicated that deregulation was no longer to form a fundamental philosophical touchstone of government policy. In addition, after the carrying out of an extensive consultation exercise, the government, in conjunction with the Health and Safety Commission (HSC), the tripartite body responsible for overall national policy regarding workplace health and safety, launched, in June 2000, a revitalizing health and safety strategy which raised the possibility of a number of legal reforms being introduced and, more generally, gave a clear public indication that the achievement of improved standards of workplace health and safety constituted an important policy objective (Department for the Environment, Transport and the Regions/Health and Safety Commission 2000).

More recently, the direction of regulatory policy has been effectively reversed. Funding to the HSE has been cut in real terms and, in 2004, the HSC (2004) published a new strategy document which placed more emphasis on 'partnership working' and educational and information initiatives; emphases which, in the context of falling resources, inevitably raised the prospect of fewer inspections and investigations and associated formal enforcement actions. Furthermore, following the publication of this strategy, the government accepted the recommendations of a review of the work of regulatory agencies which, among other things, called for an end to 'unnecessary' inspections and the commitment of more resources to the provision of advice to employers and, in doing so, committed itself to a 'risk based approach to regulation under which there would not just be a 'light touch' but a 'limited one' (Hampton 2005; Industrial Relations Services 2005). Unsurprisingly, against this background, the latest indications are that there has been a renewed fall in the numbers of inspections, investigations, enforcement notices, and prosecutions.

Britain, it should also be noted, has not been alone in pursuing this approach to regulation. In the United States, for example, one of the first acts of the Bush Administration was to rescind a new legal standard on workplace ergonomics that had only just come into force after years of discussion and the subsequent period has seen significant cuts in the resourcing of the Occupational Safety and Health Administration (OMB Watch 2004). Somewhat similarly, at the level of the European Union (EU), recent years have seen a marked reluctance to propose further legal measures and growing pressures to focus attention on the role of 'soft' regulation via the placing of greater emphasis on economic incentives, the publication of guidance and social dialogue (Woolfson 2005).

The Changing Context of Risk: Its Aggregate Effects

What impact the above changes are having, at the aggregate level, on the level of workplace risks being faced by workers, and their propensity to suffer harm as a result of them, is a matter of speculation, given the lack of studies that have sought to systematically explore their combined effects and the methodological problems that, more generally, confront the undertaking of such research. It is, however, possible to speculate in a reasonably informed way about these effects in relation to the period since the end of the 1980s.

A useful starting point is to note that the existing evidence points to the fact that the occupational distribution of jobs exerts an important influence over the level of work-related injuries suffered by workers. Indeed, one recent British study has suggested, on the basis of projected changes in the occupational composition of employment, that the rate of major injury is likely to decline by 7.6 percent over the period 2004–12 (Davies and Jones 2005). Given this, it seems reasonable to argue that the long-term reduction in manual work, along with the decline in employment in the primary industries, utilities, and manufacturing, has served, and is serving, to reduce, at the aggregate level, the probability of workers suffering an injury.

At the same time, other evidence which indicates that injury rates vary procyclically with the business cycle suggests that any such reduction will not be a straightforward and continuous one. It further suggests, given the role that variations in work intensity are postulated to play in this linkage, that any general rise in the intensification of work will act to counter it to some degree or other.

This likely countereffect of work intensity would, given the evidence reviewed earlier, further seem likely to be compounded by several of the other employment-related changes mentioned earlier; the growth in nonstandard forms of employment, the rise of employment in the small firm sector, the trend toward the use of more fragmented organizational structures and the decline in collective voice. It would further seem that the countereffects of these developments may well be compounded by those occurring in the sphere of regulatory policy. Thus, the hesitancy they embody with regard to the extension of legal regulation suggests that little legally is likely to be done to (a) reverse the decline in collective voice over workplace health and safety matters, (b) require employers to better design work tasks and processes in order to alleviate the potentially adverse consequences of growing work intensity, and (c) address the risks associated with organizational fragmentation, by, for instance, the imposition of more onerous duties on those at the head of supply chains with regard to the monitoring of health and safety standards lower down them. Meanwhile, the encouragement of regulatory agencies to place greater emphasis on business cases arguments and educational and advisory functions and devote, by extension, less resources to the carrying out of investigations and routine inspections seems to fit uneasily, to say the least, with the lack of evidence available as to the value of these alternative strategies and the strong evidence which indicates that small firms are most responsive to 'face-to-face' contacts, and that a meaningful threat of enforcement can do much to motivate employers to adequately manage workplace health and safety (Davis 2004).

In essence, then, although the inherent (occupational) 'riskiness' of jobs has been falling, it cannot be safely assumed that this decline will necessarily lead to a reduction in injury rates. Certainly, the only reliable recent trends in injury rates suggest that this caution is well warranted (Health and Safety Executive 2005). Thus, while the annual number of deaths per 100,000 employees fell substantially and consistently over the period from 1981 to 1999–2000, this rate subsequently rose in 2000–01 before falling back in 2004–05 to the level achieved in 1999–2000 (see Figure 13.2). In addition, although the rate of major injuries per 100,000 employees fell steadily between 1997–98 and 2000–01, the trend during the following four years encompassed both upward and downward movements, with the figure for 2004–05 being higher than that for 2000–01 (see Figure 13.3).

A somewhat similar picture is apparent from self-report data which sheds light on the extent and nature of occupational ill health over the period 1990 to 2003–04 (Jones, Huxtable, and Hodgson 2005).Thus, while these show the annual prevalence of work-related illness among people who had worked during the previous twelve months to have fallen during this period, they also reveal that this decline has been a relatively small and discontinuous

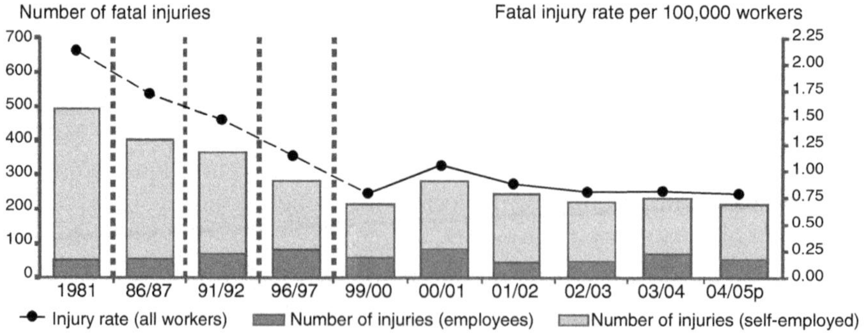

Figure 13.2. Number and rate of fatal injuries to workers.
Source: HSE (2005).

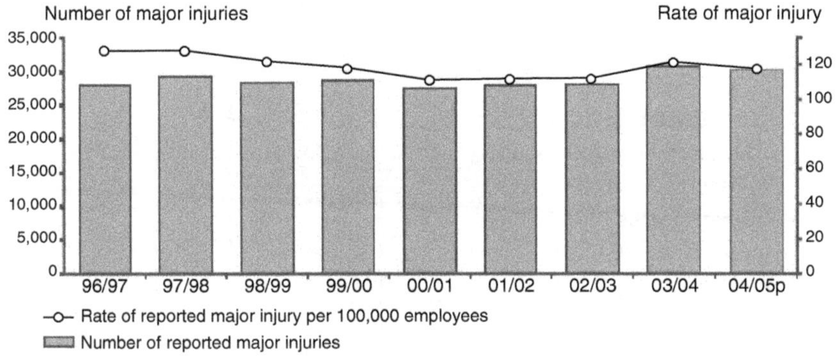

Figure 13.3. Number and rate of reported major injuries to employees.
Source: HSE (2005).

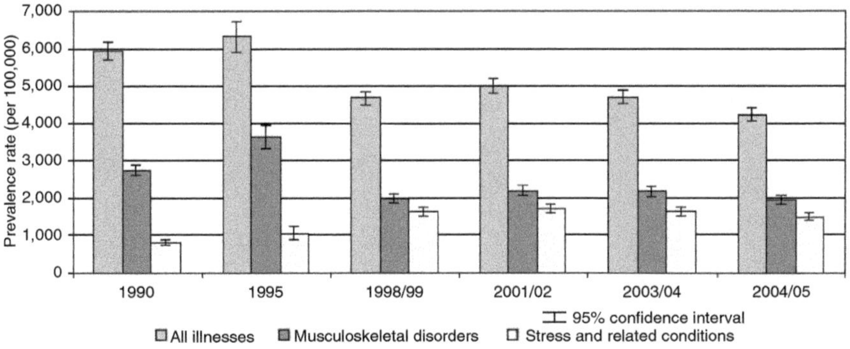

Figure 13.4. Comparison of estimated prevalence rates of self-reported work-related illness, for people working in the last 12 months in England and Wales, 1990 to 2004–05.
Source: HSE (2005).

one. Furthermore, if attention is focused on the two most commonly reported forms of such illness, while the trend for MSDs broadly mirrors this pattern, the 2003–04 prevalence rate for stress and related (mainly) heart conditions was around double of that for 1990 (see Figure 13.4).

Unlike with the case of workplace fatalities and injuries, it can also less easily be assumed that occupational changes have been, and are, acting to reduce the likelihood of workers, at the aggregate level, suffering work-related ill health. For, as Figure 13.5 shows, such ill health is most common in the health and social work, public administration, construction, and education sectors.

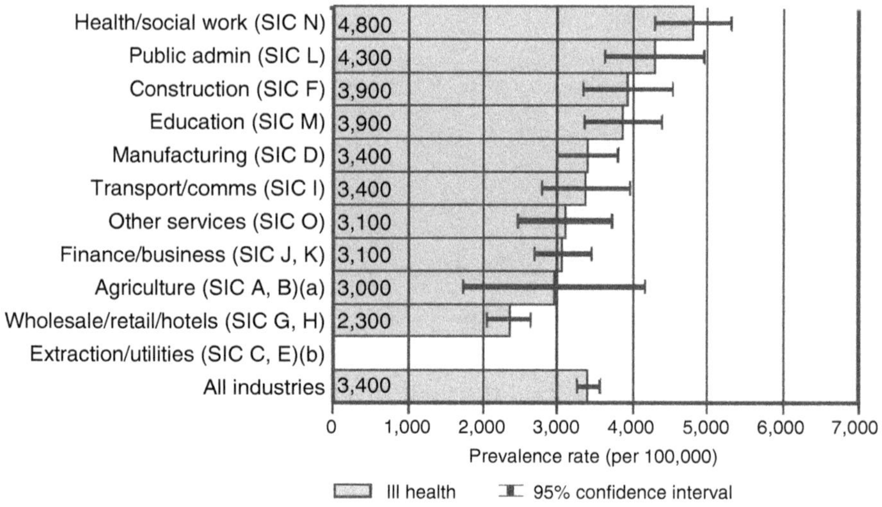

Figure 13.5. Estimated prevalence rates of self-reported work-related illness, by SIC industry section, per 100,000 people working in the last 12 months, 2004–05.

Source: HSE (2005).

Notes: (a) based on fewer than 30 sample cases; (b) sample size too small to give reliable estimates.

Conclusion

This chapter has explored, primarily in relation to Britain, but with some reference made to other developed economies, the implications of recent economic and political developments for both the workplace health and safety risks faced by workers and their related propensity to suffer work-related injury and ill health. The exploration provided has inevitably, given the research evidence available, been far from conclusive, but suggests that the implications concerned embody both positive and negative elements.

On the positive side, it would appear that the decline in manual work and the shift of employment away from manufacturing and other 'high risk' sectors of employment have acted to reduce 'inherent' risks of injury. At the same time, this reduction exists alongside a number of developments that appear to be working in the opposite direction, most notably by adversely affecting the way in which such risks are managed. These include increased work intensity, the growth of employment in smaller workplaces and enterprises that possess less sophisticated risk management arrangements, the establishment of more fragmented management systems as a result of the growth that has occurred in the use of networked organizational structures and various forms of non-standard employment, and the decline that has taken place in 'collective voice'.

In a similar vein, while there would seem good grounds for believing that the above changes in the occupational and sectoral composition are leading to a reduction in a number of 'traditional' types of occupational ill health, it would seem, on the basis of self-report data, that the last decade and a half has seen the prevalence rate of stress and related conditions increase significantly; an increase which has occurred against the background of increasing levels of work intensity and declining worker discretion. In addition, this same data, although suggesting that there has been a fall over the same time period in the overall prevalence of work-related ill health, further indicates that not only has this decline been a small one, but that it has been a product of both positive and negative fluctuations; fluctuations that therefore do not provide a firm basis for viewing the downward trend as a long-term one, particularly when it is borne in mind that trends in such harm would seem likely, in common with those relating to injuries, to be influenced by variations in levels of economic activity.

In conclusion, it cannot be argued that the aggregate risks of work-related harm faced by workers are therefore straightforwardly declining or increasing. Rather, it would seem that future trends in this regard will be the unpredictable result of a variety of contradictory forces which, in combination, are serving simultaneously to differentially increase and reduce levels of risk, as well as engender changes in the nature of the workplace risks which exist. Nevertheless, it seems reasonable to argue that these forces, on balance, may well lead, on average, to some, although not necessarily large, reduction in injury rates. In contrast, the position with regard to trends in work-related ill health appears to be far more open to question; with a real possibility existing that they could embody upward rather than downward movements in the cases, at least, of MSDs and stress and its related conditions.

It cannot, then, be complacently assumed that work is becoming less risky. Given this, current politically driven attempts to reduce the regulatory burden on employers would seem highly questionable. Indeed, if account is taken not only of trends in work-related harm, but also its total scale, there would seem good grounds for increasing this burden. Thus, not only does the evidence, as noted earlier, indicate that protective health and safety laws and their effective enforcement do act to motivate protective employer action, but it also indicates that the scale of this harm remains enormous, with current estimates suggesting that around three-quarters of a million workers suffer an injury each year and that over 600,000 new cases of work-related illness occurred during the year 2003–04 (Davies and Jones 2005; Health and Safety Executive 2005).

The fact that over half of these new cases of work-related ill health stem from two sources, MSDs and stress, depression and anxiety (Jones, Huxtable, and Hodgson 2005), also raises an important issue of policy, particularly when account is taken of the further fact that, against a background of increasing work intensity and declining worker discretion, the prevalence rate for stress and related conditions has recently considerably increased (see Figure 13.4). For this means that it is unlikely that the number of cases of such ill health can be reduced significantly without securing a major fall in the occurrence of these two types of condition. It also further suggests, given the way in which these conditions are intimately connected to workload levels and the nature of work tasks (Buckle and Devereaux 1999; Cox, Griffiths, and Rial-Gonzalez 2000), that the achievement of reductions of this type will require employers to be placed under much greater pressure to design work tasks and establish workloads that are not detrimental to worker health.

References

Anderson-Connolly, R., Grunberg, L., Greenberg, E., and Moore, S. (2002). 'Is Lean Mean? Workplace Transformation and Employee Well-Being', *Work, Employment and Society*, 16(3): 389–413.

Applebaum, E., Bailey, T., Berg, P., and Kalleberg, A. (2000). *Manufacturing Advantage: Why High Performance Systems Pay Off.* Ithaca, NY: ILR Press.

Baldry, C. (2006). 'Off the Rails: Factors Affecting Track Worker Safety in the Rail Industry', *Employee Relations*, forthcoming.

Brenner, M., Fairris, D., and Ruser, J. (2004). 'Flexible Work Practices and Occupational Safety and Health: Exploring the Relationship between Cumulative Trauma Disorders and Workplace Transformation', *Industrial Relations*, 43(1): 242–66.

Buckle, P. and Devereux, J. (1999). *Research on Work-related Neck and Upper Limb Musculoskeletal Disorders*. Luxembourg: Office for Official Publications of the European Union.

Cox, T., Griffiths, A., and Rial-Gonzalez, E. (2000). *Research on Work-Related Stress*. Luxembourg: Office for Official Publications of the European Union.

Cully, M., Woodland, S., O'Reilly, A., and Dix, G. (1999). *Britain at Work as Depicted in the 1998 Workplace Employee Relations Survey*. London: Routledge.

Davies, R. and Jones, P. (2005). *Trends and Context to Rates of Workplace Injury*, HSE Research Report 386. Sudbury, Canada: HSE Books.

Davis, C. (2004). *Making Companies Safe: What Works?* London: Centre for Corporate Accountability.

Dawson, S., Clinton, A., Bamford, M., and Willman, P. (1985). 'Safety in Construction: Self Regulation, Industrial Structure and Workforce Involvement', *Journal of General Management*, 10(4): 21–38.

Delbridge, R., Turnball, P., and Wilkinson, B. (1992). 'Pushing Back the Boundaries: Management Control and Work Intensification Under JIT/TQM Factory Regimes', *New Technology: Work and Employment*, 7(2): 97–106.

Department for the Environment, Transport and the Regions (2000). *Revitalising Health and Safety: Strategy Document*. London: DETR.

Economic Development Committee (2005). Inquiry into Labour Hire Employment in Victoria.

Eurostat (2002). *European Social Statistics: Accidents at Work and Health-Related Problems—Data 1994–2000*. Luxembourg: Statistical Office of the European Communities.

Gallie, D., Felstead, A., and Green, F. (2004). 'Changing Patterns of Task Discretion in Britain', *Work, Employment and Society*, 18(2): 243–66.

Goudswaad, A. (2002). *New Forms of Contractual Relationships and the Implications for Occupational Health and Safety*. Luxembourg: Office for the Official Publications of the European Communities.

Green, F. (2001). 'Its Been a Hard Day's Night: The Concentration and Intensification of Work in Late Twentieth Century Britain', *British Journal of Industrial Relations*, 39(1): 53–80.

——(2006). *Demanding Work: The Paradox of Job Quality in the Affluent Economy*. New Jersy: Princeton University Press.

Gunningham, N. and Johnstone, R. (1999). *Regulating Workplace Health and Safety*. Oxford: Oxford University Press.

Hampton, P. (2005). *Reducing Administrative Burdens: Effective Inspection and Enforcement*. London: Stationary Office.

Hanson, M., Tesh, K., Groat, S., Donnan, P., Ritchie, R., and Lancaster, R. (1998). *Evaluation of the Six Pack Regulations*. Sudbury, Canada: HSE Books.

Health and Safety Commission (1994). Review of Health and Safety Regulation. Sudbury, Canada: HSE Books.

——(2004). *A Strategy for Workplace Health and Safety in Great Britain to 2010 and Beyond*. Sudbury, Canada: HSE Books.

Health and Safety Executive (2005). *Health and Safety Statistics Highlights 2003/04*. Sudbury, Canada: HSE Books.

Health and Safety Laboratory (2002). *Scoping Exercise for Research into the Health and Safety of Homeworkers*. Sheffield, UK: HSL.

Industrial Relations Services (2005). 'Brown Takes Scalpel to Red-tape Herring', *Health and Safety Bulletin*, 341: 1.

James, P. (1995). 'Occupational Health and Safety: The Impact of the Single European Act', *Review of Employment Topics*, 3(1): 74–102.

James, P. and Walters, D. (2005). *Regulating Health and Safety at Work: An Agenda for Reform?* London: Institute of Employment Rights.

Jones, J., Huxtable, C., and Hodgson, J. (2005). *Self-reported Work-Related Illness in 2003–04*. Sudbury, Canada: HSE Books.

Kersley, B., Alpin, C., Forth, J., Bryson, A., Bewley, H., Dix, G., and Oxenbridge, S. (2005). *Inside the Workplace: First Findings from the 2004 Workplace Employment Relations Survey (WERS 2004)*. London: Department of Trade and Industry.

Kochan, T., Smith, M., Wells, J., and Rebitzer, J. (1994). 'Human Resource Strategies and Contingent Workers: The Case of Safety in the Petrochemical Industry', *Human Resource Management*, 33(1): 55–77.

Marchington, M., Grimshaw, D., Rubery, J., and Wilmott, H. (2005). *Fragmenting Work: Disordering Organizational Hierarchies and Blurring Boundaries*. Oxford: Oxford University Press.

Mayhew, C. and Quinlan, M. (2006). 'Economic/Reward Pressures, Multi-tiered Subcontracting and Occupational Health and Safety: Evidence from the Australian Long Haul Trucking Industry', *Employee Relations*, forthcoming.

——— and Bennett, L. (1996). *The Effects of Subcontracting/Outsourcing on Occupational Health and Safety*, UNSW Studies in Australian Industrial Relations No. 38. Sydney: University of New South Wales.

Nichols, T. (1997). *The Sociology of Industry Injury*. London: Mansell.

—— Dennis, A., and Guy, W. (1995). 'Size of Employment Unit and Industrial Injury Rates in British Manufacturing', *Industrial Relations Journal*, 26: 45–56.

OMB Watch (2004). *The Bush Regulatory Record: A Pattern of Failure*. Washington, DC: OMB Watch.

Pilkington, A., Graham, M., Cowie, H., Mulholland, R., Dempsey, S., Melrose, A., and Hutchinson, P. (2002). *Survey of Use of Occupational Health Support*. Sudbury, Canada: HSE Books.

Quinlan, M., Mayhew, C., and Bohle, P. (2001). 'The Global Expansion of Precarious Employment, Work Disorganization and Occupational Health: A Review of Recent Research', *International Journal of Health Services*, 31: 335–414.

Rebitzer, J. (1995). 'Job Safety and Contract Workers in the Petrochemical Industry', *Industrial Relations*, 34(1): 40–57.

Stansfield, S., Head, J., and Mamot, M. (2000). *Work Related Factors and Ill Health: The Whitehall II Study*, Contract Research Report 266. Sudbury, Canada: HSE Books.

Stevens, G. (1999). 'Workplace Injuries in Small and Large Manufacturing Workplaces 1994/5—1995/6', *Labour Market Trends*, 107: 19–26.

Taylor, P., Baldry, C., Bain, P., and Ellis, V. (2003). 'A Unique Working Environment: Health, Sickness and Absence Management in UK Call Centres', *Work, Employment and Society*, 17(3): 435–58.

Taylor, R. (2004). *Britain's World of Work—Myths and Realities*. Swindon, UK: Economic and Social Research Council.

Vickers, I., Baldock, R., Smallbone, D., James, P., Ekanem, I., and Bertotti, M. (2003). *Cultural Influences on Health and Safety Attitudes and Behaviour in Small Firms*, HSE Research Report 150. Sudbury, Canada: HSE Books.

Walters, D. (2005). 'Worker Representation and Health and Safety in the United Kingdom', *International Journal of Health Services*, 36(1): 87–111.

Williamson, O. (1975). *Markets and Hierarchies: Analysis and Antitrust Implications*. London: Free Press.

Wiseman, J. and Gilbert, F. (2000). *Survey of the Recruitment Agencies Industry*. Sudbury, Canada: HSE Books.

Woolfson, C. (2005). 'Health and Safety at Worker After Enlargement: A New European Strategy, or More of the Same?', *Policy and Practice in Health and Safety*, 3(2): 21–40.

Wright, M. S. (1998). *Factors Motivating Proactive Health and Safety Management*, HSE Contract Research Report 179. Sudbury, Canada: HSE Books.

Part III

Changing Labor Markets and the New Outsiders

14

The Patterns of Job Expansions in the United States: A Comparison of the 1960s and the 1990s

Erik Olin Wright and Rachel Dwyer

Introduction

This chapter examines the quality of jobs generated during periods of job expansion from the 1960s through to the 1990s in the leading liberal market economy, the United States. The central results of the study are as follows. First, the long 1990s economic boom produced a pattern of *asymetrically polarized job expansion*: very strong expansion of jobs in the top tier of the employment structure combined with very limited growth in the middle. Second, while job growth at the top was strong in the 1990s, the overall pattern of job expansion was much less favorable for the labor force as a whole than in earlier expansions. Third, there has been a dramatic change in the racial and gender patterns of job expansion since the 1960s: gender differences in job expansion were very sharp in the 1960s and quite muted in the 1990s, while the racially polarized character of job expansion has increased, especially at the bottom of the employment structure. Finally, immigration, especially of Hispanics, is deeply connected to the employment expansion in the bottom tiers of the employment structure. Underlying these descriptive patterns are dramatic changes in the sectoral patterns of job expansion in the 1990s compared to the 1960s: the much slower growth of middle-level jobs in the 1990s is rooted in the decline of manufacturing; the stronger growth of bottom-end jobs is rooted in accelerated growth of retail trade and personal services in the 1990s; and the very strong growth of high-end jobs is rooted in high-tech sectors.

The 1990s witnessed the most extended period of sustained economic growth, and with it employment expansion, in the United States in the twentieth century: the 120 months of expansion surpassed the previously longest boom of 106 months in the 1960s. While no one disputes the fact of this enormous employment expansion, there is considerable disagreement over its character and implications. Two images have dominated both scholarly analyses and the popular media. One image characterizes this expansion as dominated by the creation of *McJobs*—low paid, low security, dead-end service sector jobs. The 1990s is seen as a continuation, perhaps in some ways even an intensification, of trends already present in the 1980s of increasing inequality, transfers of well-paid industrial jobs to the Third World, wage stagnation for the large majority, and real economic improvements limited only to the highest tiers of the employment structure. As Robert Kuttner (1994: 16) wrote in the *Business Week* in the first Clinton administration:

> As labour day approaches the economy is generating jobs—4 million since President Clinton was elected—but too few good ones. If anything the trends of the 1980s have intensified: astronomical earnings gains for the economy's superstars. In the middle: relentless downsizing, with new pressures on once-secure professionals as well as depletion of solid blue-collar jobs. At the bottom: growing part-time and temporary hires, low wage jobs in services, especially retailing, and dismal starting wages.

The other image sees the expansion as a job creation miracle, reflecting the emergence of a dynamic 'new economy' of well-paid jobs, deepening prosperity and enhanced opportunities. As an ad placed by the Pfzier Corporation in *The Economist* in 1999 declared:

> But what about the quality of the new jobs created? The figures about the American labour market tell us a quite different story from the 'trash-job-and-working poor' litany that we so often hear. Since 1983 about 50 percent of the new net jobs created in the US economy—about 15 million—were in the managerial and professional sector, and adding the medium skilled occupation, the figure rises to over 80 percent. Furthermore, around 70% of the new net jobs were in occupations remunerated above the median income for all full-time employees.
>
> (Rojas 1999)

One might have thought that with such divergent descriptions of the employment expansion there would be a great deal of academic research carefully charting the patterns of job creation in the 1990s. This is in fact not the case. There is a large body of research examining individual income and earnings inequality and how this has changed in recent decades (e.g. Gottschalk 1997; Morris and Western 1999; Mishel Brenstein, and Schmitt 2001), and studies which chart the broad trends of expansion and contraction of employment by economic sectors (Plunkert 1990; Godbout 1993; Levy 1998; Meisenheimer 1998), as well as numerous technical reports from the Department of Labor about employment trends and prospects for different kinds of occupations (Rosenthal 1995; Ilg 1996; Bureau of Labour Statistics 2002), but there is almost no research that looks in detail at the overall distribution of the quality of jobs generated in the 1990s employment expansion as such (for exceptions see Council of Economic Advisors 1996; Farber 1997; Ilg and Haugen 2000), and none that we know of that compares the 1990s job expansion with earlier expansions, especially the long, robust employment expansion of the 1960s. The central objective of this chapter is to fill this gap in the existing literature.

The central punchline of the chapter is that the employment expansion in the 1990s can be described as a pattern of *asymmetrical polarization*: very strong growth in the top tier of the employment structure, moderately strong at the bottom, and extremely weak growth in the middle. This is a novel pattern. The employment expansion of the 1960s constituted a nonpolarized upgrading of the employment structure, and the expansions of the 1970s and 1980s involved relatively even job growth across the employment structure. In the 1990s, for the first time, there was sharply slower job growth in the middle. The task of this chapter is to carefully describe these patterns and provide some preliminary explanations for the changes.

We begin in Part I by elaborating a method for studying changes in the quality of employment that focuses on *jobs* rather than simply on *individual earnings*. Most research on inequality and changing patterns of inequality focuses on distributions of earnings across individuals and income across households. For reasons we will elaborate below we believe it is also important to study the distribution of jobs as such and how this changes. Part II uses this method to chart the changing patterns of job expansion and contraction in the United States since the early 1960s. Since these results are not available in the literature we will devote a considerable amount of space to fine-grained descriptions of these patterns. Part III then provides some preliminary explanations of the patterns we observe. In particular, we will examine the extent to which the dramatic changes in the pattern of job expansion in the 1990s compared to the 1960s are driven by changes in the sectoral distributions of employment.

Methodological Issues

A Methodology for Studying Job Expansions and Contractions

The methodology we will use is an extension of the empirical strategy of one of the few pieces of research that examined the overall pattern of job expansion in part of the 1990s economic boom, research done under the supervision of Joseph Stiglitz when he was the chairperson of the President's Council of Economic Advisors in the first Clinton administration. Stiglitz studied the job expansion over a fairly short span of time, 1994–6. His objective was to see what proportion of the job expansion in this period were 'good jobs' and what proportion 'bad jobs'.[38] His method was the following: Using Current Population Survey data, he constructed an occupation-by-sector matrix with 45 occupations and 22 sectors. This yielded a total of 990 potential kinds of 'jobs' (cells in the matrix). Many of these cells were, of course, empty or near-empty. After eliminating the small cells, there were some 250 or so jobs left in the analysis accounting for roughly 95 percent of total employment. The median weekly earnings of full-time employees in each cell were then calculated and job quality defined by the distribution of these cell medians. In the simplest model, good jobs were defined as all cells with median earnings above that of the median cell and bad jobs were defined as cells with median earnings below the median cell.[39] The change in the number of people in each cell was then calculated for the period 1993–5. The central finding was striking: roughly 70 percent of all job growth was among the 'good' jobs, and roughly 50 percent of all job growth was in jobs in the top three deciles of the median-earnings-ranked job distribution. The conclusion offered in the report was that the job expansion was strongly weighted toward the creation of good jobs.

While the Stiglitz paper received a great deal of press attention at the time, it did not provoke a body of subsequent research. We therefore do not know if the patterns he observed at the very beginning of the job expansion of the 1990s held for the entire decade, or whether the 1990s expansion was in any way unusual compared to earlier periods of job growth.

The research in this chapter extends and refines Stiglitz's analysis in several ways: First, we will adopt a much more fine-grained set of categories than Stiglitz used in his analysis, and use these categories to examine the quality of jobs generated throughout the entire 1990s employment expansion, rather than simply in the first two years of the expansion. Second, we will focus not simply on the question of what percentage of the job expansion consists of good jobs, but on the whole distribution of job quality. Of particular concern here will be the extent to which job growth has a polarized character. Third, we will carry the analysis backward to the 1960s to see the extent to which the 1990s constitute a distinctive pattern of employment growth. Fourth, we will explore the demographic aspects of the job expansion: the racial and gender composition of the job expansion in the 1960s and the 1990s, and the immigration composition in the 1990s (data on immigration status for job holders are not available in the earlier periods). This will further help us to identify the distinctive characteristics of the two periods of extended employment growth. Finally, as part of an explanation of the changes in patterns of job expansion between the 1960s and 1990s, we will examine the sectoral patterns of the two expansions.

Classifying Jobs and Measuring 'Job Quality'

The basic descriptive task of this project is to chart the quality of jobs created in the employment expansion of the 1990s compared to earlier job expansions. To do this we need to solve two methodological problems: first, how should we classify the millions of jobs in the US economy into various general categories, and second, how should we measure the quality of jobs so classified. What we want is a typology of *types of jobs* and then a criterion for ranking these types of jobs in terms of their 'quality'. Once this is done we can investigate where in this quality ranking of jobs, job expansion is concentrated.

Job Classification

There are, of course, many alternative ways one can classify jobs. In previous work, Wright and his collaborators classified jobs by their class character: working class, manager, employer, etc. (Wright and Martin 1987; Steinmetz and Wright 1989; Wright 1997). For some purposes it would be useful to classify jobs by the type of organization generating the job: government, nonprofit, large corporation, small business, etc. For the purposes of the present investigation, we will follow the basic strategy adopted in Stiglitz's analysis and classify jobs by economic sector and occupation. For the analysis of job expansion in the 1980s and 1990s we construct a labor force matrix of 104 occupational categories by 23 economic sectors. We will treat the 2,392 cells of this matrix as types of jobs. Examples of the cells in this matrix include: janitors in business repair services; bus and truck drivers in retail trade; secretaries, typists and stenographers in nondurable manufacturing; and financial managers in wholesale trade. Of course, even in a very large dataset, many of these cells have very few people in them, although surprisingly few are literally empty. While we will include all the job-cells in our analysis that have any people in them, about 479 of these job types account for over 90 percent of total employment.[40] The available data for the 1960s and 1970s did not allow for so fine-grained a set of occupational distinctions, so in the earlier period we use a job matrix of 30 occupations by 23 economic sectors which generate a total of 690 potential types of jobs.[41]

Job Quality

The second task is to rank-order the jobs in the occupation-by-sector matrices from the 'best' type of job to the 'worst'. This, of course, immediately raises the problem of what precisely one means by job quality. There is a wide range of heterogeneous attributes of jobs which matter to people and thus contribute to their desirability. Some of these attributes can be measured with readily available data—such as earnings, fringe benefits, educational levels of incumbents of jobs; others are in principle measurable, but data are not readily available—such as opportunities for advancement, job security, and levels of authority; and some involve job attributes that are difficult even in principle to measure—such as stress levels, degree of personal autonomy within the labor process, or opportunities for social connectedness on the job. Ideally in order to fully assess the extent to which economic growth in the United States is generating good or bad jobs one would want data on a full range of such attributes. Such data are simply not available for any extended periods of time for the entire employment structure. In practice, therefore, if we want to evaluate trends in the entire employment structure the only possibility is to measure job quality primarily on the basis of earnings generated by jobs. The cells in the occupation-by-sector matrix will thus be rank-ordered on the basis of median earnings of incumbents of the cells. The details of the procedure used are explained below. To the extent that the various other desirable features of jobs are correlated with earnings, then this can be considered a proxy for a more general gestalt of job quality attributes. But even if this is not the case, earnings are a sufficiently salient aspect of job quality that it is important to know the distribution of well-paying compared to badly paying types of jobs in the employment expansion.[42]

Why Study Growth of Earnings-Indexed Jobs Rather Than Simply Individual Earnings?

With this set of job categories rank-ordered by median earnings, we can determine what proportion of job growth occurs among the higher-ranking rather than lower-ranking categories of jobs in this list. But why go through the step of assigning median earnings to *types* of jobs and then examining the contributions of these *categories* to job growth rather than simply examining the changes in the number of individuals at different points in the earnings distribution? Is it not better to know, say, that 20 percent of the job expansion was among *individuals* earning more than $25 per hour than to know that 20 percent of the job expansion was in *job categories* whose median earnings were above $25 per hour? Since there is a distribution of earnings around the median within each of the job cells, these two statistics could mean very different things in the lives of the people holding these jobs. In the job category analysis, for example, it could conceivably be the case that while 20 percent of the expansion of jobs was in *cells* with medians above $25 per hour, most of the job expansion in these cells was in *individual jobs* that earned below $15 per hour. It would therefore seem that if the basic point of caring about the quality of jobs is its impact on the economic conditions of the lives of people in those jobs, then focusing directly on individual earnings would be more relevant than examining broader categories of jobs indexed by their median earnings.

There are two reasons why we feel it is important to study the growth of job categories indexed by median earnings rather than simply studying the changing distribution of the individual earnings themselves. First, we believe that the cells in the occupation-by-sector matrix tap real categories of jobs created in an economy. Jobs are not just employment contracts to 'work' at a given earnings level; they are contracts to perform sets of tasks to produce specific outputs. The occupation-by-sector categories, therefore, map this task dimension of jobs. Second, we believe the earnings *potential* embodied in an employment expansion is better measured by the growth of job categories than simply by individual earnings. A job type, defined by cells in a 100 occupation by 23 sector matrix, can be thought of as demarcating labor market opportunities for a particular kind of employment with a particular earnings potential. The growth of managerial occupations in the finance, insurance and real estate sector constitutes the growth of good jobs because the earnings potential of this specific job type is high, even if many of the jobs that may be created earn below the median of that category. The growth of jobs in specific locations within the earnings-ranked job distribution may therefore give a better picture of the longer-term real economic impact of job growth than simply the changing patterns of individual earnings.[43]

Although we will present data on both job expansions and contractions, we will focus our attention primarily on periods of job expansion, especially the 1990s and 1960s. Changes in the overall job distribution, of course, are the result of the specific patterns of job creation and destruction, and it could in principle be the case that periods in which the rate of job destruction is greater than the rate of job creation (i.e. periods of net employment contraction) generate bigger changes in job distributions than do periods of employment expansion. In the four decades under study here this is simply not the case: there is much less job decline in periods of contraction than there is job growth in periods of expansion, and the variation in net changes across the job distribution is much more dramatic in periods of expansion than contraction. It thus appears that periods of job expansion have a bigger impact on the distribution of quality of jobs, and it is for this reason we focus on the expansionary periods.

None of this implies, of course, that it is foolish to study the distribution of individual earnings or the growth of employment at specific locations in the individual-earnings distribution. All that we claim is that it is also important to understand the patterns of job expansion and contraction across categories of jobs in the job-type-earnings distribution, not simply the individual-earnings distribution.[44]

Data

The data come from the Current Population Survey (CPS) annual outgoing rotation group files for the period 1983–2000, and from the CPS March annual demographic supplement files for the period 1963–80. Because of problems in data quality, sampling and weights for the early 1960s, we had to begin the analysis of the 1960s job expansion in 1963 rather than in 1961 when the expansion began. Similarly, because of changes in the occupation coding in the early 1980s we had to begin the analysis for the 1980s expansion in 1983 rather than 1982.[45]

Throughout this analysis we will restrict our investigation to jobs held by employees, thus excluding the self-employed. In principle the problem of job expansion should include all jobs filled by active participants in the labor force, both employees and self-employed. However, the CPS does not contain comparable earnings data for both self-employed and employees, and thus it is difficult to create comparable earnings-based job category rankings for these segments of the labor force. For present purposes, therefore, we will restrict the analysis to employees.

We will also restrict our attention to full-time jobs. Part-time jobs pose a number of problems for the analysis of job growth. Should a 20 hour-a-week job be considered half a job? If so, should a 60 hour-a-week job be weighted 1.5 in a measure of job growth? If we did this, then in effect the analysis would shift from an investigation of job expansion to person-hours-in-jobs expansion. On the other hand, if we consider a half-time job the equivalent of a full-time job—a job is a job is a job—then the overall patterns of job expansion could potentially be distorted by the presence of jobs filled primarily by teenagers and others with relatively marginal attachments to the labor force in part-time work. Since the 1990s job expansion was in any case overwhelmingly dominated by the expansion of full-time employment, for the present analyses we will restrict the investigation to such jobs.[46]

Variables

Occupations

For the CPS data for 1983–2000 it is possible to construct a quite fine-grained occupational typology. We began with the standard 45-category two-digit occupational variable constructed by the CPS. We then went through each of these categories and examined the median earnings of the three-digit occupations within the broader category. Wherever there were substantial differences in the median earnings among these three-digit occupational categories we tried to group them into more homogeneous subcategories.[47] For example, the CPS two-digit occupational category 'Other Executives, Administrators, and Managers' accounts for just under 10 percent of all full-time employee jobs in the 1990s. This is a very heterogeneous collection of occupations, ranging from managers of food services with median earnings of $10.25 per hour to marketing managers with median earnings over $22 per hour. Accordingly, we broke this broad manager occupation category down into eight distinct manager occupations. The result is a 104-category occupational variable.

In the 1960s, the CPS data only contains a 30-category two-digit occupational variable. For the earlier period, therefore, we were not able to generate this refined set of occupational categories.[48]

Economic Sectors

The classifications for industry change less over time than the codes for occupation. We code industries into 23-categories, which can be created for each period. Because of minor changes to the 3-digit Census classifications we use to create the 23-categories, a few of the sectoral categories are not perfectly comparable across all expansions, though they are very close.

We also constructed, for certain specific purposes, two more aggregated categories. The first, 'personal services', consist of four sectors from our full typology: private household service, repair services, entertainment and recreation services, assorted personal services (which include hotels, laundry, barber and beauty, miscellaneous personal services). The second, which we will refer to as the 'high-technology domain', consists of all jobs in high-technology sectors plus all high-technology-using occupations in nonhigh-tech sectors.[49]

Earnings

We use hourly earnings to index job quality rather than weekly earnings, as in the earlier Stiglitz report. The results are not substantively affected by this shift, but we felt that hourly earnings was a better measure of job quality. In the data for the 1980s and 1990s, the CPS collected earnings per hour for hourly workers and per week for all others. To calculate hourly wages, we divide the 'usual weekly earnings' of nonhourly workers by their 'usual hours worked per week'. Within each expansion, earnings were converted into constant 2000 dollars. In the 1960s respondents were not directly asked about their hourly earnings for their *current* job. Instead, they were asked about their earnings for the longest job held the previous year. We therefore had to use this retrospective data to calculate the median earnings of the cells in the occupation-by-sector matrix based on data for people who had not changed jobs since the previous year. It is possible that the restriction of the sample to people who had not changed jobs will bias the estimates of median earnings, since on average one might expect that people in any given job category who change jobs have lower earnings than those who do not change jobs. In order to assess this bias, we used March CPS files to analyze the 1990s estimated wages using the same method we used in the 1960s, restricting the sample to people who had not changed jobs. Our results using this method for the

1990s were similar to our results produced with the ORG files, indicating that the method used in the 1960s does not distort the results.

Median Earnings of Job Types

Median earnings for cells in the jobs-matrix are calculated separately for each of the periods of job expansion we examine (1963–70, 1975–80, 1983–90, 1992–2000). In each period, we combine all of the relevant CPS samples across all the years within the period and then calculate median earnings in constant dollars for this multiyear sample for each period. This creates a very large sample for each period so that there are significant numbers of cases in nearly all cells of the matrix. This procedure also means that if earnings change in a cell over the period of a job expansion, the rank-order position of the job in the hierarchy of job quality will be based on a weighted average of the earnings over the period (weighted by the number of people in the job in each year of the CPS sample). It turns out that although median earnings of job types do change over time, the rank-order of cells changes hardly at all, and this is all that really matters for our analysis. For example, in the 1992–2000 job expansion, the correlation of quintile or decile position of a job cell in 1992 (calculated on the basis of only 1992 data) and those same cells in 2000 is 0.99 and the correlation of cell median earnings (for cells with at least fifty people in the 1992 CPS sample) was 0.95.[50]

Strategy of Analysis

Our empirical goal is to measure the relative contributions to job expansion of jobs of differential quality defined by the median hourly earnings of job categories. Our strategy of analysis is to rank-order these jobs from the highest median hourly earnings to the lowest and then group this ranked-ordered set of cells into five ordered-categories each containing as close as possible to 20 percent of the employment *at the beginning of a job expansion.*[51] We refer to these aggregated categories of jobs as 'Job Quality Quintiles'. The bottom quintile contains the roughly 20 percent of the employment at the beginning of a job expansion that are in the jobs with the lowest median earnings, the highest quintile contains the roughly 20 percent of the employment in jobs with the highest median weekly earnings, and so on. To convey a sense of what sorts of jobs fall within each of the quintiles, the three largest job categories within each quintile in the 1990s are given in Table 14.1.

The rank-ordering of job categories and their aggregation into quintiles is done separately for each period we are studying. Because of the differential growth and decline of specific job categories over time, a few jobs do change their location within this job-earnings distribution from one period to

Table 14.1 Characteristics of jobs in different job quality deciles

1992–9 job quality deciles	1999 median hourly earnings	Three largest jobs within decile		Number, 1992	Number, 1999	% of labor force in decile, 1992	% of labor force in decile, 1999	Number of jobs in the decile
		Occupation	Industry					
Lowest decile	$6.90	Retail sales workers	Retail trade	2,173,356	3,282,779	12.4	13.2	75
		Food services	Retail trade	1,604,542	2,638,460			
		Farm workers	Agriculture	878,056	1,036,160			
2nd decile	$8.00	Health services	Hospital service	476,787	382,093	7.9	7.9	94
		Cleaning, bldg.	Educational service	408,700	425,308			
		Clerical & other admin. support	Retail trade	366,953	630,632			
3rd decile	$9.40	Machine operators, tenders	Manuf. nondur. goods	2,456,242	22,448,674	9.7	9.0	67
		Clerical & other admin. support	FIRE	1,225,830	1,564,182			
		Secretaries, typists stenogrphrs.	Educational service	428,112	380,546			
4th decile	$10.25	Machine operators, tenders	Manuf. durable goods	1,767,374	1,814,287	10.1	9.1	61
		Sales supervisors, proprietors	Retail trade	1,166,147	2,075,191			
		Secretaries, typists stenogrphrs.	FIRE	5,832,233	282,264			
5th decile	$11.43	Fabricators, assemblers, inspectors, samplers	Manuf. durable goods	1,558,050	1,742,771	9.7	9.4	64
		Other exec., admin., mgrs.	Retail trade	626,453	1,069,286			
		Mechanics, repairers	Retail trade	515,716	521,165			

Continued

Table 14.1 (Contd.)

1992–9 job quality deciles	1999 median hourly earnings	Three largest jobs within decile		Number, 1992	Number, 1999	% of labor force in decile, 1992	% of labor force in decile, 1999	Number of jobs in the decile
		Occupation	Industry					
6th decile	$12.50	Other precision production	Manuf. durable goods	1,638,890	1,788,761	11.1	11.1	88
		Motor vehicle operators	Transportation	783,126	1,444,684			
		Other precision production	Manuf. nondur. goods	660,458	672,427			
7th decile	$14.40	Construction trades	Construction	2,073,887	2,920,937	10.1	10.2	84
		Protective services	Public administration	954,129	1,376,709			
		Sales reps, commodities	Wholesale trade	790,559	833,924			
8th decile	$15.80	Teachers except coll. & univ.	Educational service	2,512,687	3,402,299	9.3	8.8	30
		Sales reps, finance-business	FIRE	745,516	1,061,633			
		Mechanics, Repairers	Manuf. durable goods	651,778	549,874			
9th decile	$17.55	Other exec., admin., mgrs.	FIRE	708,130	1,188,612	10.0	10.9	77
		Mgt. rel.	FIRE	517,805	844,528			
		Mail, message dist.	Transportation	493,841	652,136			
Highest decile	$21.33	Health treating, assessment	Hospital service	917,691	1,239,898	9.6	10.3	98
		Engineers	Manuf. durable goods	709,870	792,805			
		Executives, admin., managers	Manuf. durable goods	698,520	1,075,867			

Distribution of net job expansion of job quintiles within race/gender categories

1960s	Job quality quintiles	White male	White female	Black male	Black female	Other male	Other female		
	Lowest	0.9%	19.1%	−17.2%	25.1%	−18.3%	20.9%		
	2nd	4.8%	39.0%	14.7%	35.9%	1.1%	19.4%		
	3rd	19.3%	19.9%	51.4%	19.1%	35.0%	19.9%		
	4th	30.9%	10.9%	34.9%	12.4%	1.4%	9.1%		
	Highest	44.2%	11.1%	16.2%	7.5%	80.8%	30.8%		
	Total	100.0%	100.0%	100.0%	100.0%	100.0%	100.0%		
1990s	Job quality quintiles	White male	White female	Black male	Black female	Hispanic male	Hispanic female	Other male	Other female
	Lowest	−0.3%	12.7%	15.3%	27.0%	32.8%	47.4%	14.0%	23.3%
	2nd	14.5%	8.0%	22.3%	20.9%	28.8%	24.0%	16.4%	15.5%
	3rd	9.8%	−22.5%	20.4%	8.6%	18.5%	7.9%	11.2%	9.7%
	4th	12.5%	41.2%	19.5%	23.9%	10.8%	12.8%	13.9%	20.7%
	Highest	63.6%	60.5%	22.4%	19.7%	9.0%	8.0%	44.5%	30.8%
	Total	100.0%	100.0%	100.0%	100.0%	100.0%	100.0%	100.0%	100.0%

Distribution of job expansion of race/gender categories within job quintiles

1960s	Job quality quintiles	White male	White female	Black male	Black female	Other male	Other female	Total		
	Lowest	5.6%	88.2%	−11.3%	17.2%	−1.2%	1.5%	100.0%		
	2nd	12.7%	72.9%	3.9%	9.9%	0.0%	0.6%	100.0%		
	3rd	46.7%	34.4%	12.6%	4.9%	0.9%	0.5%	100.0%		
	4th	70.8%	17.9%	8.1%	3.0%	0.0%	0.2%	100.0%		
	Highest	79.3%	14.3%	2.9%	1.4%	1.5%	0.6%	100.0%		
1990s	Job quality quintiles	White male	White female	Black male	Black female	Hispanic male	Hispanic female	Other male	Other female	Total
	Lowest	−0.3%	11.4%	28.9%	27.2%	6.0%	15.5%	4.6%	6.7%	100.0%
	2nd	16.1%	7.8%	27.7%	15.0%	9.6%	13.1%	5.8%	4.8%	100.0%
	3rd	33.2%	−66.7%	54.1%	15.0%	26.7%	16.3%	12.1%	9.2%	100.0%
	4th	13.0%	37.5%	9.7%	7.5%	7.8%	13.9%	4.6%	6.0%	100.0%
	Highest	37.1%	30.9%	4.5%	2.6%	5.0%	6.5%	8.3%	5.0%	100.0%

another. In no instance, however, has a job category moved either up or down more than one quintile in the distribution. In any case, the interpretation of the job quality quintiles remains the same even if there are such shifts in detailed jobs.

In order to facilitate comparisons across demographic categories, when we analyze the race and gender compositions of jobs we will use the same job-aggregations as we use in the total employment sample. That is, we will not recalculate median earnings of categories in the job matrix, nor recalibrate the job-quality quintile categories within given demographic groups.

We will use these job-quality quintiles to generate graphs showing the distribution of *net changes in the number of jobs within each quintile* during periods of job expansion and contraction. Figure 14.1 illustrates four different ideal-type patterns we might find in these results. The numbers in these graphs refer to *net* job expansion rather than job creation per se. That is, employment growth is always a simultaneous process of the creation of new jobs and the destruction of already existing jobs within any given job category. When we observe that a particular cell in the occupation-by-sector job matrix increased by 10,000 over a period of time, this could mean the creation of 25,000 new jobs and the destruction of 15,000 previously existing jobs. All that we observe is the net effect of these two processes.

In the hypothetical illustrations in Figure 14.1, there is an expansion of 5 million jobs in each of the graphs, but the pattern of job expansion varies sharply across the different cases. The *McJobs* image of job growth looks something like the second graph in this figure: job growth is concentrated in the lower deciles of the employment structure with only marginal growth among jobs in the upper tiers. The jobs miracle vision is closer to the third graph. The image of highly polarized job growth in some accounts of the 'New Economy' (e.g. Reich 1992) would look something like the fourth graph. Our primary task in this chapter, then, is to chart in this manner various aspects of the patterns of job expansion since the 1960s.

Descriptive Results: Patterns of Job Expansion

Overall Patterns of Job Expansion in the 1990s

Over 15 million full-time jobs were added to the American employment structure in the period 1992–2000. Figure 14.2 indicates that job growth was especially strong in the top quintile and especially low in the middle quintile of the employment structure.[52] These results are broadly consistent with those in the Stiglitz study: in his research, using cruder categories over a much shorter period, just under 70 percent of the job expansion occurred in jobs above the median (i.e. in the top five job quality *deciles*) whereas in our

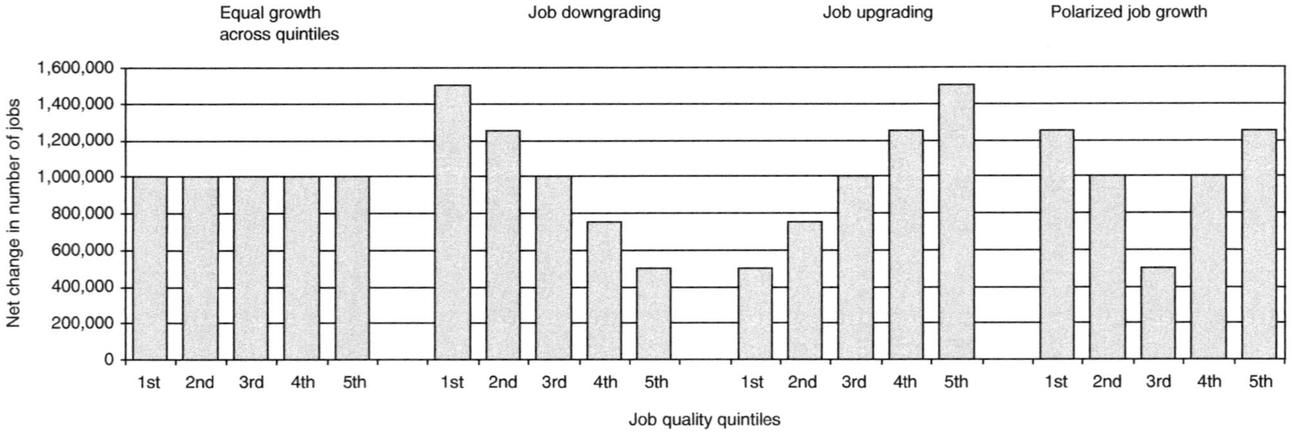

Figure 14.1. Hypothetical patterns of net job expansion.

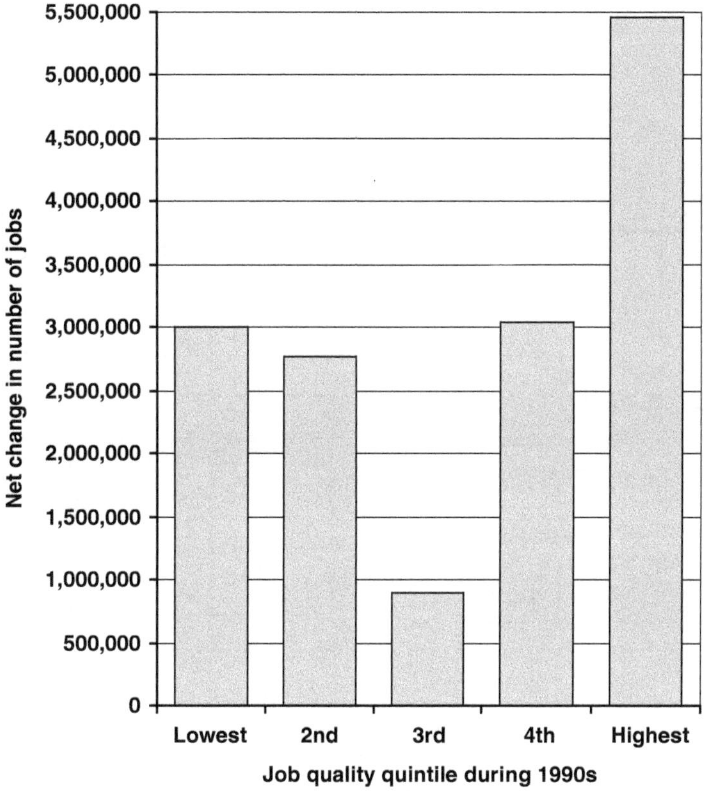

Figure 14.2. Patterns of job change, 1992–2000.

analysis for the entire expansion of the 1990s the comparable figure is just under 63 percent. But the results also indicate something not revealed in the Stiglitz analysis, namely that job growth was especially weak in the middle of the employment structure: only 6 percent of the job expansion occurred in the middle quintile. The result is therefore a polarized pattern, albeit one weighted toward the better jobs.[53]

The Trajectory of Job Expansions: 1960s–1990s

To fully assess the character of the 1990s job expansion it is important to compare it with earlier episodes of sustained job creation. Figure 14.3 presents the patterns of job expansion for each job expansion and contraction since the 1960s for which we have reliable data.[54] Four features of these patterns are important to note. First, the 1990s expansion is the first in which a clear polarized pattern of job growth occurs. Even in the 1980s, a period in which

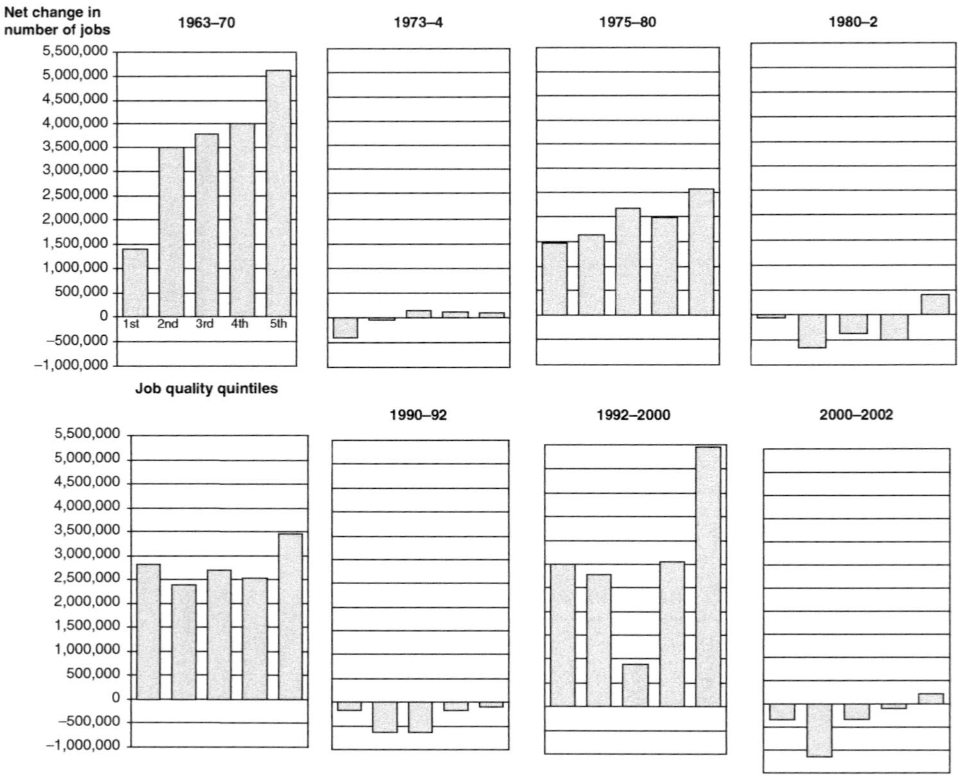

Figure 14.3. Patterns of job change during periods of expansion and contraction by job quality quintiles, 1960s–2000s.

there was a sharp rise in earnings inequality, it was not the case that job growth in the middle of the employment structure was lower than at the tails of the distribution.[55] This polarized pattern also appears in the recession of the early 1990s and the early 2000s. If these two periods are added to the job expansion of the 1990s, then there is absolutely no growth in the middle quintile of the employment structure from 1990 to 2002. Second, in every expansion, job growth is highest in the top quintile of the employment structure. Indeed, if we further break down the results into deciles, in every period of expansion job growth is strongest in the top decile. This is thus not a unique feature of the 1990s expansion. What is new in the 1990s expansion is the extent to which the top quintile grew disproportionately relative to other quintiles: in the 1990s the ratio of the growth of top quintile to the 4th quintile was 1.8:1, whereas in the three earlier periods of sustained job growth the ratios were between 1.3:1 and 1.4:1. Third, the contribution of the bottom quintile of jobs to total job growth increases dramatically over time: in the 1960s just under 10 percent of the total job growth occurred in the bottom quintile of jobs; in the 1970s the figure was 15 percent; and in both the 1980s and 1990s, this figure was 20 percent. Fourth, if we look at the trends across this entire period, the patterns of job expansion in the 1970s and 1980s appear to be intermediary between the patterns of the 1960s and 1990s: from a strong, unequivocal pattern of job expansion upgrading in the 1960s, to muted upgrading in the 1975–1980 expansion, to a relatively flat pattern of job growth in the 1980s and, finally, the polarized pattern of the 1990s. The 1970s and 1980s therefore appear as a kind of transition from the 'golden age' of upgrading job expansion of the 1960s to the polarized pattern of the 1990s.

Race and Gender Patterns of Job Expansion, 1960s versus 1990s

The quality of jobs created in employment expansions matters not simply because employment is the principle means by which individuals acquire their standards of living, but also because of the ways it reinforces or undermines other dimensions of social inequality. In particular, periods of robust job expansion in the upper tiers of the employment structure potentially offer relatively favorable conditions for disadvantaged social categories to make especially rapid gains, since in these conditions there is less of a zero-sum character to their movement into relatively privileged jobs. Figures 14.4 and 14.5 present the patterns of job expansion within race/gender categories in the 1960s and the 1990s. In the 1960s CPS data Hispanics are not distinguished from non-Hispanic whites, and thus only two racial categories are reported: whites and African-American. In the 1990s Hispanics and non-Hispanic whites are treated as separate categories.

The data in these figures indicate a fairly complex set of changes in the demographic patterns of job expansion between the 1960s and the 1990s. One

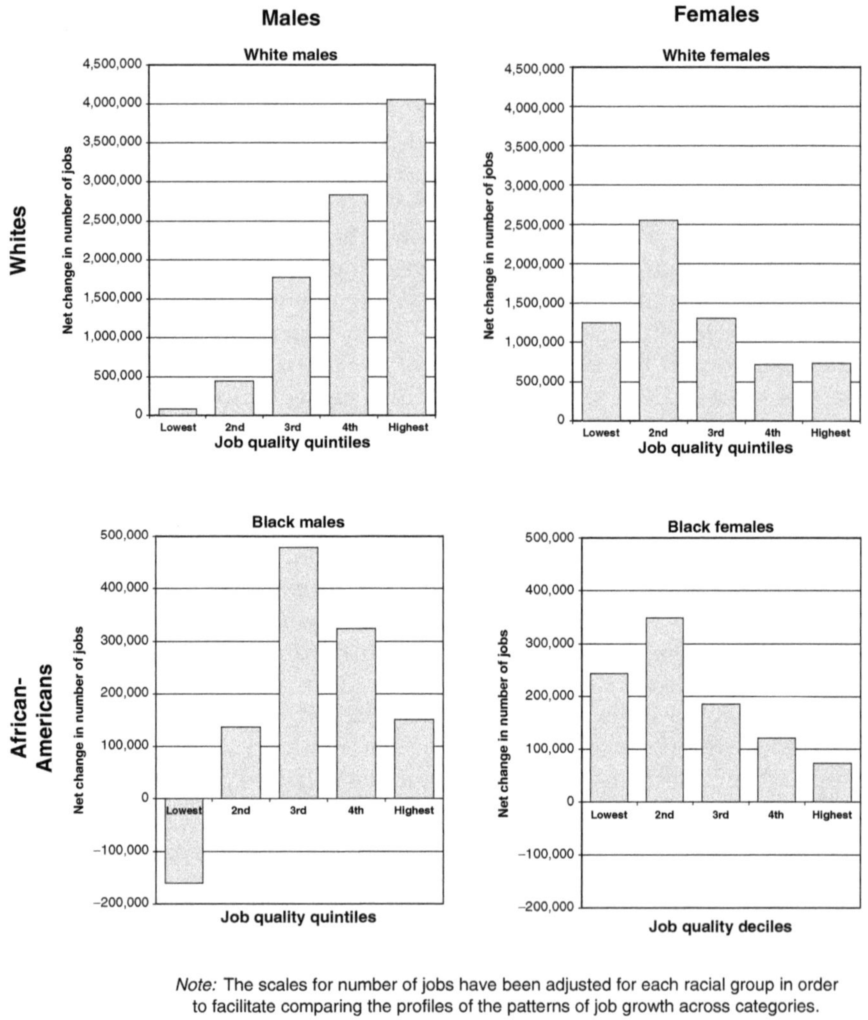

Figure 14.4. Patterns of job growth in race by gender categories in the 1960s.

way of characterizing the overall contrast in gender/race patterns between these two episodes of massive job expansion is that in the 1960s gender differences in patterns of job expansion are sharper than the racial differences, whereas in the 1990s the racial differences are generally more striking than the gender differences. In the 1960s the patterns for white and black women are almost identical: job expansion was highest in the second quintile and lowest in the top quintile. Among men, there is some racial difference—among white males job expansion is highest in the top quintile whereas for black men it

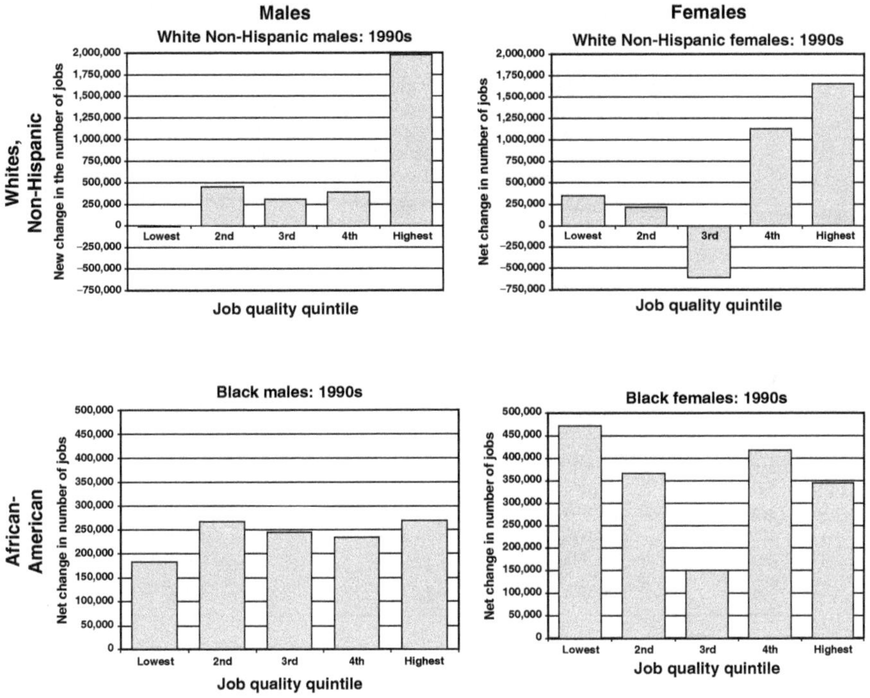

Figure 14.5. Patterns of job growth among race-gender categories, 1990s.

is highest in the middle quintile. Yet, for both white and black men, there is very little (or even negative) job expansion in the bottom two quintiles, whereas this is where job growth is concentrated for women, both black and white. Now, compare this to the 1990s: for both white men and white women, job growth is concentrated in the top of the employment structure; for both Hispanic men and Hispanic women, job growth is heavily concentrated at the bottom of the employment structure. The pattern of job growth among African-Americans is also sharply different from that of whites, although in this case there is some gender difference as well: job expansion is polarized among black women (the only demographic group within which there is a polarized pattern) whereas among black men job expansion is fairly evenly distributed throughout the employment structure. Overall, then, relative to the 1960s, the job expansion of the 1990s is less gendered, but more racialized.

The decline in the gender polarization of the job expansion occurs at both the top and bottom of the employment structure. As indicated in Table 14.2, in the 1960s 79 percent of the job expansion in the top quintile was filled by men and only 21 percent by women; in the 1990s the corresponding figures were 56 and 44 percent. In the bottom quintile, on the other hand, in the

Table 14.2 Race–gender distributions within job quality quintiles of job expansion

Job quality quintiles	Percentage durable manufacturing jobs that are in each quintile	Percentage of jobs in each quintile are in durable manufacturing	Percentage of total job expansion for each quintile that occurred in durable manufacturing
	1963	1963	1963–1970
1st	0.0%	0.0%	0.0%
2nd	4.7%	4.3%	−6.1%
3rd	54.9%	48.3%	65.5%
4th	15.6%	15.6%	21.2%
5th	24.8%	23.7%	26.2%
Total	100.0%	18.7%	27.3%
	1992	1992	1992–2000
1st	1.9%	1.2%	−0.2%
2nd	32.9%	20.7%	13.0%
3rd	21.8%	14.3%	−29.9%
4th	19.6%	11.8%	−1.3%
5th	23.8%	16.3%	10.6%
Total	100.0%	12.8%	4.1%

1960s for men as a whole there was a decline in employment, so women accounted for more than 100 percent of the job expansion in that category. In contrast, in the 1990s, men accounted for nearly 40 percent of the job expansion in the bottom quintile.

The increasingly racially differentiated pattern of job expansion in the 1990s is concentrated at the bottom and middle of the employment structure, not the top. In fact, if anything, the job expansion in the top quintile is somewhat less dominated by whites in the 1990s than in the 1960s: in the earlier job expansion over 93 percent of the job expansion in the top quintile was filled by whites, whereas in the 1990s this declined to 68 percent (or 79.5 percent if Hispanic whites are added).[56] In the bottom quintile, in contrast, the percent of the job expansion filled by whites declined from over 90 percent in the 1960s, to around 11 percent in the 1990s, and in the second quintile from just over 85 percent to around 24 percent.

Putting all of these observations together suggests that the aggregate pattern of job expansion polarization we observe in the 1990s in Figure 14.2 is a highly racialized, but not strongly gendered, pattern.

Immigration in the 1990s

The striking pattern of employment growth for Hispanics in the 1990s suggests that, perhaps, a significant part of the employment growth at the bottom

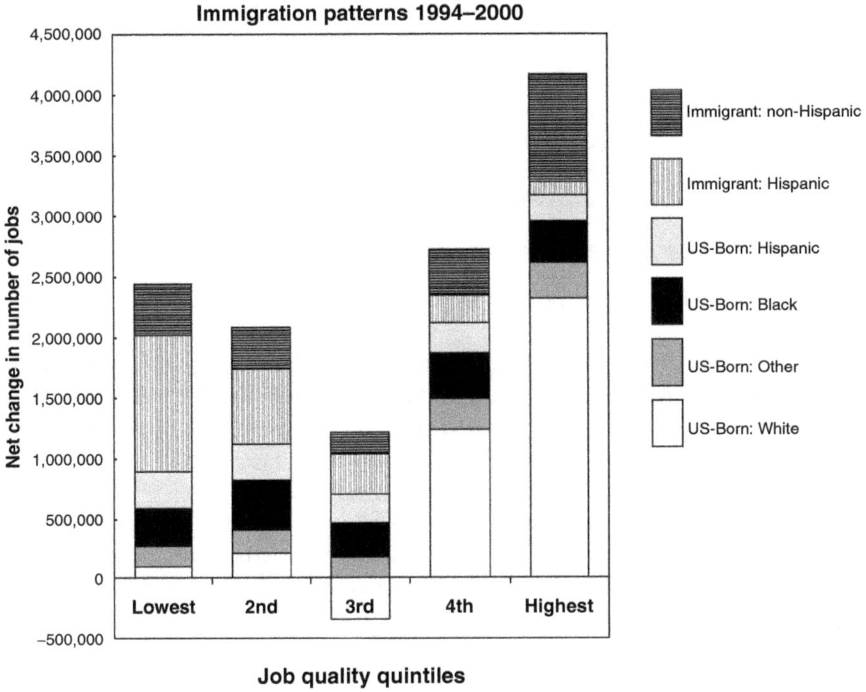

Job quality quintiles	US-born white	US-born other	US-born black	US-born Hispanic	Immigrant Hispanic	Immigrant non-Hispanic	Total
Lowest	4.2%	6.7%	12.8%	12.5%	46.9%	16.9%	100%
2nd	9.7%	9.4%	19.8%	14.7%	29.6%	16.7%	100%
3rd	–40.6%	19.5%	33.2%	28.2%	38.9%	20.7%	100%
4th	45.3%	8.9%	14.3%	9.3%	8.0%	14.1%	100%
Highest	55.3%	7.3%	8.3%	5.1%	2.6%	21.4%	100%

Figure 14.6. Immigration, race, and job expansion, 1994–2000.

of the job structure in the 1990s was due to immigration. Figure 14.6 shows that this is in fact the case. In the period 1994–2000, nearly 64 percent of the job expansion in the bottom quintile of the employment structure was filled by immigrants (of these, almost 75 percent were Hispanic), and 58 percent of the expansion below the median was filled by immigrants.[57] What is more, in the course of the 1990s, this concentration of immigrants in the expansion of jobs at the bottom increased: in the second half of the period, 1996–2000, 79 percent of the job expansion in the bottom quintile and 68 percent of the job expansion below the median was filled by immigrants. Although not as large as at the bottom of the employment structure, immigration also contributed significantly to employment expansion in the top two job quality quintiles in which over 20 percent of the job expansion was filled by immigrants. Unsurprisingly, non-Hispanic immigrants predominate here: almost 90 percent of the job expansion filled by immigrants in the top quintile in the 1990s consisted of non-Hispanic immigrants compared to under 30 percent of the bottom quintile.

A Preliminary Descriptive Summing Up

The descriptive results we have so far reviewed can be distilled into four basic observations:

First, the long 1990s economic boom produced a pattern of *asymetrically polarized job expansion*: very strong expansion of jobs in the top tier of the employment structure combined with very limited growth in the middle, and moderately strong at the bottom. This is the only job expansion among those studied here in which this polarized pattern occurred.

Second, while the claim that the 1990s job expansion is significantly weighted toward good jobs is correct, the overall pattern of job expansion is much less favorable for the labor force as a whole than the pattern in the previous longest episode of job expansion, the 1960s, and less favorable for people in the middle of the employment structure than the expansions of the 1970s and 1980s.

Third, there has been a dramatic change in the racial and gender patterns of job expansion since the 1960s: gender differences in job expansion were very sharp in the 1960s and quite muted in the 1990s, while the racially polarized character of job expansion has increased, especially at the bottom of the employment structure.

Finally, immigration, especially of Hispanics, is deeply connected to the employment expansion in the bottom tiers of the employment structure. To a significant extent the overall polarization of the employment expansion in the 1990s is linked to immigration.

Explaining the Patterns of Job Expansion: 1990s versus 1960s

There are three principle contrasts between the overall patterns of job expansion in the 1960s and the 1990s that we need to explain: first, the deep trough in job expansion in the middle quintile of the job quality distribution in the 1990s; second, the much higher contribution of the bottom quintile to job growth in the 1990s; and third, the especially strong growth in the 1990s in the top quintile relative to the fourth. Each of these contrasts is closely linked to the fate of specific sectors of the economy.

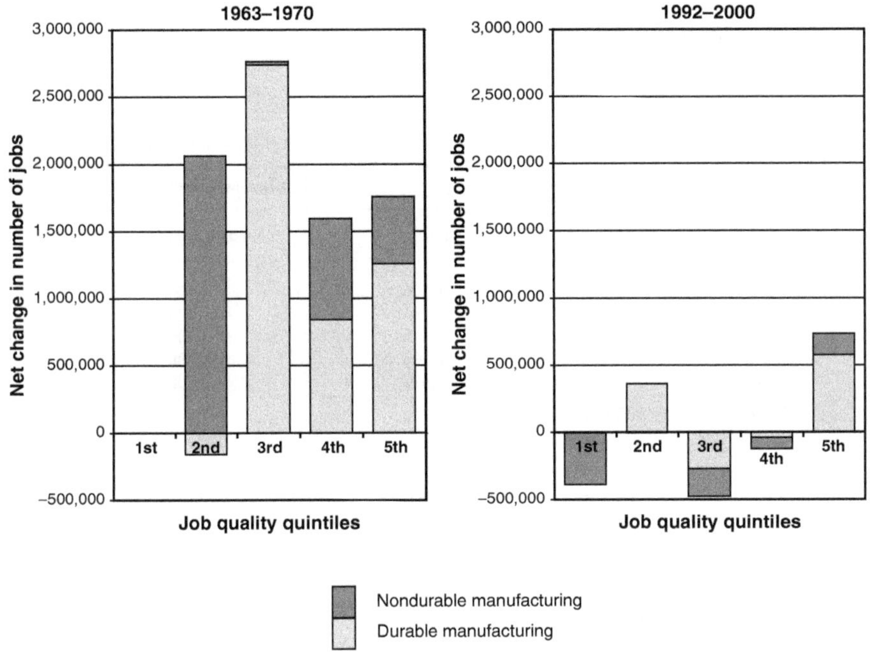

Figure 14.7. Net change in numbers of jobs in manufacturing by job quality deciles, 1960s and 1990s.

The Middle of the Employment Structure: the 1990s Trough

To understand the slow growth of middle quintile jobs in the 1990s we must examine closely two sectoral contrasts with earlier periods: first, a striking difference between then 1960s and the 1990s in the contribution of durable manufacturing to job expansion; and second, a difference between the 1980s and the 1990s in the contributions of service sectors to the growth of jobs in the middle of the employment structure.

DURABLE MANUFACTURING

Of the twenty-three economic sectors in terms of which we have analyzed the patterns of job expansion, there is one which is massively linked to the weak growth in the middle job quality quintile in the 1990s compared to the 1960s: durable manufacturing (see Figure 14.7). As indicated in Table 14.3, in 1963 18.7 percent of all full-time employee jobs in the American economy were in durable manufacturing, and nearly half—48 percent—of all middle quintile jobs were in that sector (no other sector contributed as much as 20 percent of the middle quintile jobs). Durable manufacturing was thus the pivotal sector within which jobs in the middle of the employment structure were located.

Table 14.3 Distribution of jobs and job expansion by quintiles for durable manufacturing, 1960s and 1990s

Retail trade			
Job quality quintiles	Percentage retail jobs that are in each quintile	Percentage of jobs in each quintile that are in retail	Percentage of total job expansion for each quintile that occurred in retail
	1963	1963	1963–1970
1st	54.4%	44.3%	31.9%
2nd	18.1%	14.5%	−13.1%
3rd	24.0%	18.3%	16.7%
4th	1.1%	1.0%	−1.2%
5th	2.3%	1.9%	−0.3%
Total	100.0%	16.3%	4.9%
	1992	1992	1992–2000
1st	48.3%	30.3%	46.9%
2nd	38.7%	24.0%	34.3%
3rd	10.0%	6.5%	4.9%
4th	1.4%	0.8%	2.2%
5th	1.5%	1.0%	1.9%
Total	100.0%	12.6%	17.0%

Personal services*			
Job quality quintiles	Percentage personal services jobs that are in each quintile	Percentage of jobs in each quintile that are in personal services	Percentage of total job expansion for each quintile that occurred in personal services
	1963	1963	1963–1970
1st	78.2%	31.3%	15.4%
2nd	4.8%	1.9%	1.1%
3rd	12.8%	4.8%	4.8%
4th	3.1%	1.3%	1.9%
5th	1.1%	0.5%	1.1%
Total	100.0%	8.1%	3.6%
	1992	1992	1992–2000
1st	59.7%	24.8%	37.0%
2nd	22.7%	9.4%	6.8%
3rd	13.0%	5.6%	29.1%
4th	4.0%	1.6%	3.9%
5th	0.7%	0.3%	0.2%
Total	100.0%	8.4%	11.1%

*personal services is an aggregated category that includes 5 of the 23 detailed sectors in our analysis: private household services; hotels, laundry, barber and beauty, misc. personal services; entertainment and recreation services; automotive and repair services; eating and drinking places.

In the course of the long 1960s employment expansion, jobs within durable manufacturing increased by nearly 4.7 million accounting for 27 percent of the total job expansion in the period. Durable manufacturing, therefore, accounted for a higher proportion of job growth in the period (27 percent) than of jobs at the beginning of the period (18.7 percent). Of this expansion of employment in durable manufacturing, over 2.5 million jobs were in the middle quintile. This constituted 58 percent of the expansion of jobs in durable manufacturing and just under two-thirds of the total expansion of jobs in the middle quintile in the 1960s.

The contrast with the 1990s could not be starker. In 1992, at the beginning of the employment expansion, durable manufacturing was still the largest single sector of full-time employment in our twenty-three-sector categories, but it had declined from 18.7 percent of all jobs to only 12.8 percent. What is even more striking, the concentration of durable manufacturing among middle quintile jobs declined from 48 to 14 percent. In the course of the 1990s boom, durable manufacturing jobs increased by only 600,000, or about 4 percent of total job growth, and within the middle quintile there was actually a loss of around 250,000 jobs. In the 1960s the strong expansion of durable manufacturing fueled strong job expansion in the middle of the employment structure. The absence of such growth in the 1990s is one of the crucial reasons for the trough in growth in the middle.

SERVICES

The decline of durable manufacturing is only part of the story. After all, as much research has argued, the decline of good jobs in manufacturing began in the 1970s and accelerated in the 1980s, and yet it is only in the 1990s expansion that aggregate slow growth of middle quintile jobs occurs. Figure 14.8 helps explain what happened in the 1980s that muted the effects of the decline in manufacturing.

This figure indicates the contributions of the middle job-quality quintiles within two broad sectors—manufacturing (durable and nondurable) and services—to total job expansion in each of the periods we have examined. The results confirm the standard view of the decline of manufacturing in the 1970s and 1980s. By the 1980s expansion, the middle quintile of jobs in manufacturing contributed nothing to total job expansion. And yet there was no trough. The reason is that in the 1980s there was a sufficiently strong growth of middle quintile jobs in a number of service sectors to compensate for the absence of such growth in manufacturing. In the 1990s this countervailing trend had largely disappeared: whereas in the 1980s, 16 percent of the overall expansion of employment was generated by job growth in the middle quintile within services, in the 1990s this had declined to under 6 percent.[58] The low-overall growth of middle quintile jobs in the 1990s, therefore, is the result of

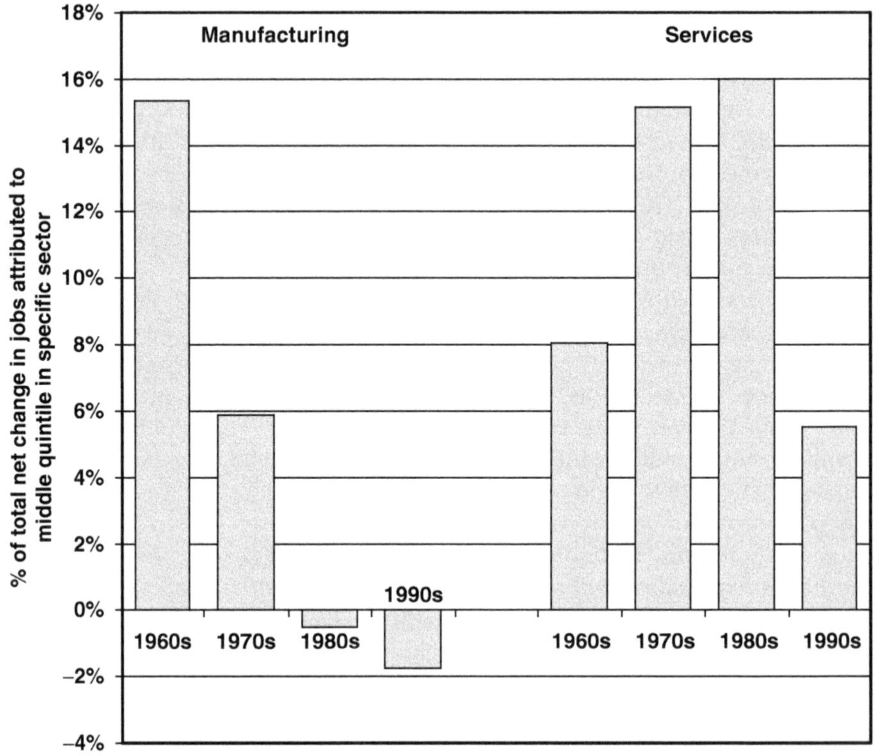

Figure 14.8. Contributions of middle job quality quintiles in manufacturing and in services to total net job growth, 1960s–1990s.

decline in manufacturing, especially durable manufacturing, since the 1960s, combined with the sharp decline in the growth of middle quintile jobs in service sectors compared to the 1980s.

The Bottom Quintile of Jobs: Strong Growth in the 1990s, Weak Growth in the 1960s

The strong growth of employment in the bottom quintile of the employment structure in the 1990s relative to the 1960s is especially concentrated in retail trade and the various sectors which comprise the aggregated personal service sector (see Figure 14.9 and Table 14.4). If anything, these results probably understate the growth of employment in the bottom quintile in the 1990s because of problems of undercounting low-wage minority and immigrant workers, especially in activities like personal services that are often in the informal economy.[59] Retail trade and personal services together accounted

Table 14.4 Distribution of jobs and job expansion in retail trade and personal services, 1960s and 1990s

	Business services		
Job quality quintile	Percentage business services jobs that are in each quintile	Percentage of jobs in each quintile that are in business services	Percentage of total job expansion for each quintile that occurred in business services
	1963	1963	1963–1970
1st	6.3%	0.4%	1.7%
2nd	40.2%	2.6%	7.1%
3rd	1.6%	0.1%	0.2%
4th	6.8%	0.5%	0.4%
5th	45.1%	3.0%	3.9%
Total	100.0%	1.3%	2.5%
	1992	1992	1992–2000
1st	31.7%	5.3%	13.2%
2nd	16.7%	2.8%	7.6%
3rd	8.2%	1.4%	4.6%
4th	15.6%	2.5%	19.2%
5th	27.7%	5.0%	22.2%
Total	100.0%	3.4%	16.1%

for 18 percent of the full-time employed labor force in 1992, yet during the 1990s period of job growth these sectors accounted for just over 23 percent of the total expansion of jobs in the economy (just over 3.5 million additional jobs). Within this large sectoral expansion of employment in retail trade and personal services, a growth of 1.9 million jobs occurred in the bottom quintile of the job structure. This accounted for almost two-thirds of the growth of jobs in the bottom quintile and 13 percent of the expansion of jobs overall.[60] As in the case of manufacturing, the contrast with the 1960s is striking. The expansion of 1.16 million jobs in retail trade and personal services in the 1960s accounted for only 6.5 percent of total job growth (in contrast to the 23 percent of total job expansion in the 1990s), and furthermore, the job expansion in these two sectors was less concentrated in jobs in the bottom quintile than in the 1990s. In the 1960s, in fact, more of the growth of employment in retail trade occurred in the middle quintile (almost 700,000 jobs) than in the bottom quintile (about 540,000 jobs).

This very large expansion of low-end services in the 1990s clearly indicates that there was a demand on the part of employers for such jobs. But demand alone is not sufficient to explain actual job creation; there must also be a pool of people willing to fill such jobs. Here the pivotal issue is immigration. As already noted, immigrants account for nearly two-thirds of the job

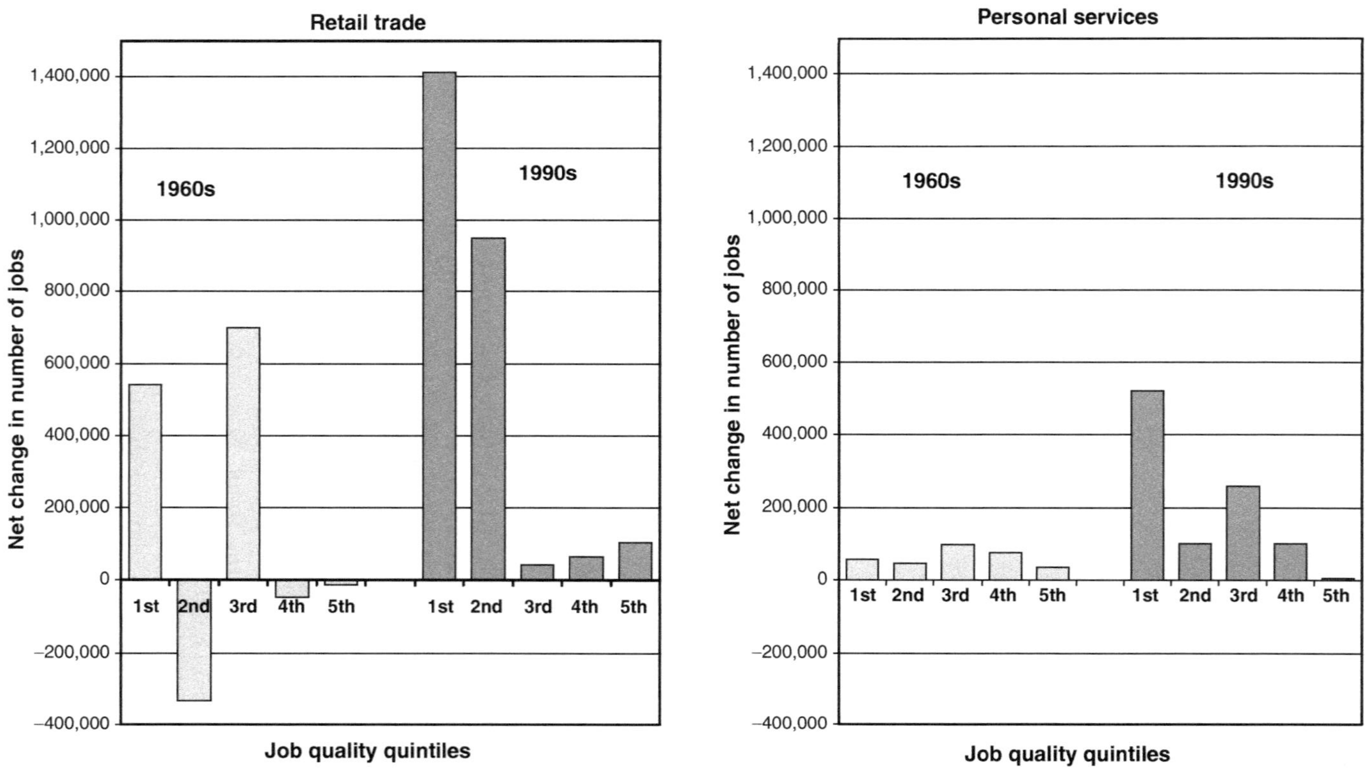

Figure 14.9. Patterns of job expansion in retail trade and personal services sectors, 1960s and 1990s.

growth in the bottom quintile of employment in the period 1994–2000. In personal services, the figure was even higher—91 percent. These figures, if anything, probably understate the impact of immigration at the bottom of the employment structure since the CPS survey almost certainly significantly undercounts illegal immigrants. While we do not have corresponding CPS data for the 1960s, we know from general census data that there was very little immigration to the United States in the 1960s: the percentage of the population that was foreign born actually declined between 1960 and 1970 from 5.4 to 4.8 percent (US Census Bureau 2001*a*: 44), while between 1990 and 2000 it increased from 7.9 to 10.4 percent (US Census Bureau 2001*a*: 45). Of course, one cannot tell from the sheer presence of immigrants in low-end job expansion whether immigration as such is primarily a cause of the expansion of jobs at the bottom of the employment structure or primarily an effect of the supply of such jobs. Nevertheless, it seems unlikely that in the absence of substantial immigration there would have been an alternative domestic labor supply to fill the several million jobs in the bottom quintiles of the employment structure generated in the 1990s. The result would have been either that the wages of those jobs would have had to rise significantly to attract a labor supply from other sectors within the US labor force, or—more likely—those jobs simply would not have been created.

While immigration may have made the growth of jobs in the bottom quintile of the employment structure possible by providing a labor supply willing to work in such jobs, one other factor probably contributed significantly to the actual creation of these jobs: the very low minimum wage in the 1990s compared to the 1960s. Using 1999 dollars, the minimum wage rose from $6.26 per hour in 1963 to a high of $7.07 in 1968 (Mishel, Bernstein, and Schmitt 2001: 187). In 1992, the minimum wage (in 1999 dollars) was $5.03, and it fluctuated slightly up and down from this level throughout the 1990s job expansion, ending at $5.00 per hour in 2000. Given how much the overall productivity of the economy had grown since the 1960s, the 1990s minimum wage in the $5 range was even lower in effective economic terms relative to the 1960s. Even though there is much debate among economists about the impact of the minimum wage on the demand for labor, it seems very likely that if the minimum wage in the 1990s was as high as it was in the 1960s this growth of jobs in the bottom quintile would have been considerably less robust.[61]

The Top of the Employment Structure

The exceptionally strong relative growth of employment in the top quintile in the 1990s is a story of the growth of business services (Figure 14.10 and Table 14.5) and, to an even greater extent, of the 'high-tech domain'

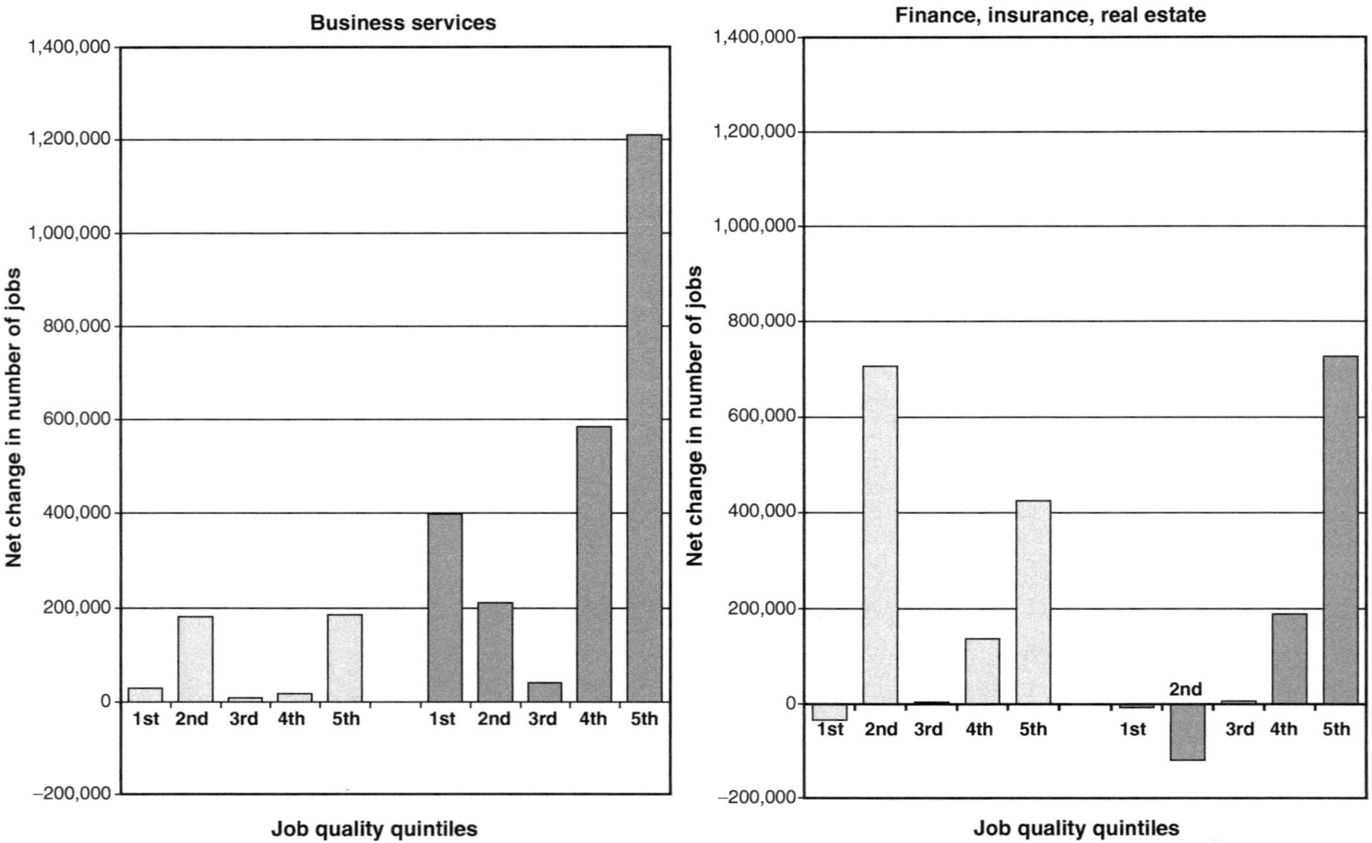

Figure 14.10. Patterns of job expansion of business services and FIRE, 1960s and 1990s.

Table 14.5 Distribution of jobs and job expansion in business services and FIRE, 1960s and 1990s

Finance, insurance, real estate			
Job quality quintiles	Percentage FIRE jobs that are in each quintile	Percentage of jobs in each quintile that are in FIRE	Percentage of total job expansion for each quintile that occurred in FIRE
	1963	1963	1963–1970
1st	5.9%	1.6%	−2.0%
2nd	52.4%	13.6%	27.8%
3rd	3.4%	0.8%	0.1%
4th	15.2%	4.3%	3.4%
5th	23.1%	6.2%	8.8%
Total	100.0%	5.3%	7.2%
	1992	1992	1992–2000
1st	11.2%	4.0%	−0.2%
2nd	22.6%	8.0%	−4.3%
3rd	19.1%	7.0%	0.7%
4th	24.9%	8.4%	6.2%
5th	22.2%	8.6%	13.3%
Total	100.0%	7.2%	5.2%

(Figure 14.11 and Table 14.6). As indicated in Table 14.5, in 1963 business services was a very small sector, accounting for only 1.3 percent of full-time jobs in the economy and 3 percent of the top quintile jobs. During the 1960s, there was an expansion of about 420,000 jobs in this sector (about 2.5 percent of the total expansion). Of these, 186,000 were in the top quintile, which accounted for about 4 percent of the overall job expansion in the top quintile. By 1992 the sector had nearly tripled as a percentage of the full-time employee labor force, but was still a relatively small sector (3.4 percent of full-time employment and 5 percent of the employment in jobs in the top quintile of the employment structure). In the 1990s job expansion, however, 16 percent of the expansion of employment occurred in this sector, and 22 percent of the top quintile job expansion. That is, business services, which at the beginning of the period accounted for only 5 percent of the jobs in the top quintile generated 22 percent of the job expansion in the top quintile.

One of the popular images of the growth of well-paying jobs in the 1990s is that they are closely connected to 'high tech'. The exact meaning of such claims is usually pretty vague: sometimes high tech refers to sectors which produce high technology (e.g. the software or computer industry), sometimes to sectors which use lots of high technology (e.g. medical care), and sometimes to occupations involving high tech regardless of the sector (e.g. computer

Table 14.6 Distribution of jobs and job expansion in the high-technology domain, 1990s

	High-Technology domain		
Job quality quintiles	Percentage HIGH TECH jobs that are in each quintile	Percentage of jobs in each quintile that are in HIGH TECH DOMAIN	Percentage of total job expansion for each quintile that occurred in HIGH TECH DOMAIN
	1992	1992	1992–2000
1st	1.6%	1.4%	3.4%
2nd	10.4%	8.8%	1.1%
3rd	17.5%	15.5%	−57.5%
4th	23.1%	18.7%	13.3%
5th	47.4%	43.9%	51.3%
Total	100.0%	17.3%	18.6%

scientists). For our analysis of this problem we have constructed a synthetic category consisting of all jobs within high-tech sectors and all high-tech jobs in all other sectors.[62] Unfortunately, it was impossible to construct even a rough version of this category for the 1960s since only 2-digit occupation and industry classification schemes were available in the CPS in that period, so our analysis here will be restricted to the 1990s.

Table 14.6 and Figure 14.11 clearly indicate how important the expansion of this high-tech domain was for the growth of jobs in the top quintile of the employment structure in the 1990s. In 1992, 17.3 percent of all full-time jobs were in the high-tech domain. During the 1990s, this sector increased by 2.8 million jobs—or 18.6 percent of the total expansion. The expansion of jobs in this domain, however, accounted for over 50 percent of the expansion of jobs in the top job quality quintile for the economy as a whole. The growth of high tech thus fueled the expansion of the highest quintile of jobs in the 1990s almost as much as the growth of durable manufacturing dominated the expansion of middle quintile jobs in the 1960s.

Conclusions

The extraordinarily robust pattern of job creation in the American economy of the 1990s was heralded by many in the United States and abroad as a triumph of deregulated, 'free market' capitalism. The rigidities of the much more regulated European labor markets were seen by many as central components of 'Eurosclerosis', leading to relatively weak job creation and stubbornly high rates of unemployment, especially among young workers. European

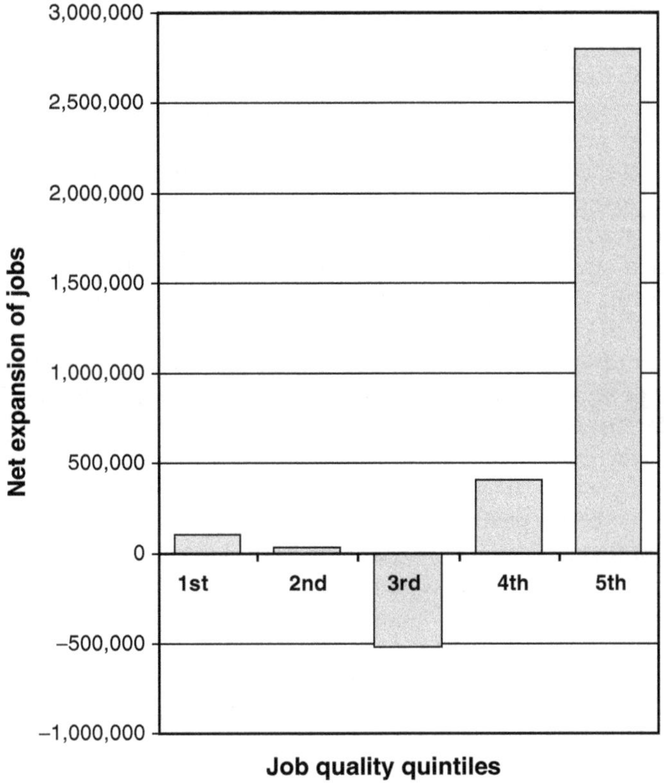

Figure 14.11. Job expansion in the high-technology domain, 1992–2000.

governments were thus urged by leading economists to emulate the American model if they wanted to generate their own 'jobs miracle'.

The results of this study suggest a complex set of lessons from the American experience. If all one cares about is the sheer number of new jobs being generated in an economy, then it is certainly the case that masses of new jobs have indeed been created in the United States in the 1990s. It is also the case that a disproportionate amount of this job expansion occurred in the top tier of the employment structure, particularly in those sectors and activities dominated by high tech. This was not a job expansion dominated by McJobs in low-paid services.

The overall robust job creation and the expansion of well-paying high-tech jobs of the 1990s, however, are only part of the story. When we compare the 1990s with the 1960s, a much less rosy picture emerges. In the 1960s, the sustained job expansion was unequivocally a process of *upgrading the employment structure*: slow growth at the bottom reflecting the relatively modest expansion of retail trade and personal services; strong growth in the middle anchored in durable manufacturing; and even stronger growth at the top. In the 1990s, the job expansion is characterized by an *asymmetrical polarization of employment opportunities* weighted toward the high-end of the job structure. Of particular salience is the deep trough in employment expansion in the middle of the employment structure, a trough generated by the collapse of durable manufacturing as a source of employment growth, the absence of a countervailing expansion of middle quintile jobs in high-end services, and a much stronger growth at the bottom than in the 1960s, generated by the expansion of retail trade and personal services. Moreover, this polarized pattern of job expansion is highly racialized. Employment for whites—both men and women—has expanded sharply among the better jobs in the employment structure, whereas expanding employment for blacks, Hispanics and immigrants is much more concentrated at the bottom of the employment structure. The sustained period of economic growth in the 1990s may indeed be creating masses of new jobs, and in the aggregate many of these jobs may be among the better paying kinds of jobs in the American economy, but the net effect of this employment expansion has been to increase polarization in the employment structure in a particularly racialized form.

The patterns we have been studying are distributions of *marginal changes* in the employment structure, not directly the patterns of job distributions as such. The deep trough in middle quintile jobs is thus a trough in the growth of those jobs, not a description of the relative size of jobs in the middle compared to the tails of the employment structure. The long-term ramifications of these changes depend, then, upon the extent to which they are reinforced or counteracted in subsequent periods of job expansion and contraction.

Assuming that these trends do continue, there are a number of implications of the change in the pattern of employment expansion from the 1960s to the 1990s for the character of social inequality in the United States. First, the polarization of employment growth may suggest that poverty in the United States increasingly involves the working poor rather than simply people largely marginalized from the system of employment altogether.[63] The minimum wage of $5.15 in 2001 means that a person working 50 weeks a year at 40 hours a week would earn just over $10,000 per year, or about 58 percent of the official poverty line for a family of four. In the late 1960s the minimum wage was sufficient to support a family at about 90 percent of the official poverty line. This is not to say that the link of poverty to unemployment and exclusion from the labor force has disappeared, but rather that an increasing proportion of poor people are working full-time in those kinds of jobs which pay below poverty-level wages. To seriously tackle poverty in America today requires more than just getting poor people into jobs; it requires changing the quality of jobs available to them or reducing the linkage between income and employment.[64]

Second, the very slow rate of growth of jobs in the middle range of job quality suggests that it may become increasingly difficult for people working in the worst jobs to move up in the employment structure. In the 1960s the very strong growth of middle quintile jobs in durable manufacturing meant that people from economic origins in the bottom tier of the employment structure or who currently occupied such jobs faced expanding employment opportunities in the middle of the employment structure in jobs that did not require high levels of education. The subsequent sharp decline in the 1990s in the growth rate of middle quintile jobs in general (the middle quintile grew at about a quarter of the rate of all jobs in the 1990s), and of durable manufacturing jobs in particular (middle quintile jobs in durable manufacturing declined in the 1990s), means that this mobility channel has been sharply curtailed. A similar point could be made about retail trade: in the 1960s a significant proportion of job growth in retail trade occurred in the middle quintile of the employment structure; in the 1990s there was virtually no growth in middle quintile retail jobs. This suggests that people employed in the rapidly expanding bottom quintiles of the employment structure will confront much more limited opportunities for significant improvements in employment in the future. This may pose a particular problem for immigrant communities who already face disadvantages because of cultural and linguistic issues.[65]

Third, there may be significant long-term political ramifications of the deep trough in the growth of middle quintile jobs when combined with such strong growth of jobs at the top. The question here is the social structural basis for what might be called a progressive-egalitarian political coalition in capitalist democracies. In the past, as a broad generalization, this coalition involved substantial numbers of people in jobs around the middle of the employment structure as well as in jobs at the bottom. This constituted a potential majoritarian coalition because of the strength of job growth in the middle. If the current pattern of economic development was a simple 'hour glass' pattern of job growth of symmetrical polarization or polarization weighted at the bottom as some have implied (Massey and Hirst 1998; Miller 1999; Rayman-Read 2001), then the prospects for a new majoritarian progressive-egalitarian coalition might seem promising since a coalition with people in the middle of the employment structure might be less important. However, the combination of very rapid expansion of jobs in the top tier of employment with stagnation in the middle may mean that in the future it will be increasingly difficult to rebuild such a majority coalition even in the face of deteriorating conditions at the bottom of employment.

Fourth, if the specific sectoral and occupational character of the patterns of employment growth were to continue into the future—high-tech jobs being created at the top of the employment structure, personal services and retail trade jobs being created at the bottom—then this could signal the emergence of a new cultural reality of social inequality in which an increasing proportion of the people at the bottom are engaged in providing personal services to the people at the top. While it would be a gross exaggeration to describe this as a transformation of the working class into a servant class, nevertheless aspects of the servant relation may become an increasing part of the cultural context of inequality.

Finally, the pattern of job expansion in the 1990s suggests significant transformations in the structure of racial stratification. Since the 1960s there has been a considerable expansion of employment of African-Americans and other racial minorities in what are loosely described as middle class jobs. The proportion of doctors, lawyers, professors, managers, and even executives who are African-American has increased significantly. Among higher-level jobs, therefore, there has been a partial deracialization. Among jobs at the bottom of the employment structure, on the other hand, the 1990s has generated a process of deepening racialization. Only 12 percent of the expansion of jobs among non-Hispanic whites occurred in the bottom three quintiles of employment compared to nearly 65.5 percent of job expansion among minorities.

This heightened racialized polarization at the bottom of the employment structure raises difficult moral and political issues. On the one hand, the expansion of jobs in the bottom quintile, even if badly paid, may constitute a real improvement in the lives of some people. This is especially the case for many immigrants, but also at least in some cases for people who otherwise might be marginalized from employment altogether. It is obviously too simple to unequivocally condemn the creation of such jobs if the real alternatives were materially much worse for the people who filled them. On the other hand, this racialized pattern of job growth, especially when combined with the slow rate of growth of accessible jobs in the middle of the employment structure, may contribute to new, deepened forms of racial division.

Acknowledgment

A modified version of this paper appeared in *Socio-Economic Review*, 1(3): 289–326. We would like to thank OUP for extending permission to use copyright material.

References

Anderson, M. J. and Fienberg, S. E. (1999). *Who Counts? The Politics of Census Taking in Contemporary America*. New York: Russell Sage Foundation.

Benner, C. (1998). 'Win the Lottery or Organize: Economic Restructuring and Union Organizing in Silicon Valley', *Berkeley Planning Journal*, 12: 50–71.

Bureau of Labor Statistics (2002). *Occupational Outlook Handbook, 2002–03 Edition.* Washington, DC: Bureau of Labor Statistics, U.S. Department of Labor.

Cherry, R. and Rodgers, W. M. III, (eds.) (2000). *Prosperity for All? The Economic Boom and African Americans.* New York: Russell Sage Foundation.

Council of Economic Advisors with the U.S. Department of Labor (1996). 'Job Creation and Employment Opportunities: The United States Labor Market, 1993–1996', Washington, DC: Office of the Chief Economist.

Farber, H. (1997). 'Job Creation in the United States: Good Jobs or Bad?', Working Paper No. 385, Industrial Relations Section, Princeton University.

Godbout, T. M. (1993). 'Employment Change and Sectoral Distribution in 10 Countries, 1970–90', *Monthly Labor Review*, 116: 3–20.

Gottschalk, P. (1997). 'Inequality, Income Growth and Mobility: The Basic Facts', *Journal of Economic Perspectives*, 11: 21–40.

Grubb, W. N. and Wilson, R. H. (1989). 'Sources of Increasing Inequality in Wages and Salaries, 1960–1990', *Monthly Labor Review*, 112: 3–13.

Ilg, R. E. (1996). 'The Nature of Employment Growth, 1989–95', *Monthly Labor Review*, 119: 29–36.

—— and Haugen, S. E. (2000). 'Earnings and Employment Trends in the 1990s', *Monthly Labor Review*, 123: 21–33.

Immigration and Naturalization Service (2001). *Estimates of the Undocumented Immigrant Population Residing in the United States.* Washington, DC: Immigration and Naturalization Service.

Juhn, C. and Potter, S. (1999). 'Explaining the Recent Divergence in Payroll and Household Employment Growth', *Current Issues in Economics and Finance*, 5: 1–6.

Levenson, A. R. (1996). 'Recent Trends in Part-Time Employment', *Contemporary Economic Policy*, XIV: 78–89.

Levy, F. (1998). *The New Dollars and Dreams: American Incomes and Economic Change.* New York: Russell Sage Foundation.

Massey, D. S. and Hirst, D. S. (1998). 'From Escalator to Hourglass: Changes in the U.S. Occupational Wage Structure 1949–1989', *Social Science Research*, 27: 51–71.

Meisenheimer, II, J. R. (1998). 'The Services Industry in the "Good" Versus "Bad" Job Debate', *Monthly Labor Review*, 22–47.

Miller, D. W. (1999). 'Scholars on Immigration Focus on the Children', *Chronicle of Higher Education*, A19–20.

Mishel, L., Bernstein, J., and Schmitt, J. (2001). *The State of Working America 2000/2001.* Ithaca, NY: Cornell University Press.

Morris, M. and Western, B. (1999). 'Inequality in Earnings at the Close of the Twentieth Century', *Annual Review of Sociology*, 25: 623–57.

—— Bernhardt, A., and Handcock, M. S. (1994). 'Economic Inequality: New Methods for New Trends', *American Sociological Review*, 59: 205–19.

Plunkert, L. M. (1990). 'The 1980's: A Decade of Job Growth and Industry Shifts', *Monthly Labor Review*, 113: 3–16.

Portes, A. and Zhou, M. (1993). 'The New Second Generation: Segmented Assimilation and its Variants', *Annals of the American Academy of Political and Social Science*, 530: 74–96.

Rayman-Read, A. R. (2001). 'Is the New Economy Family-Friendly?' *The American Prospectives*, 12(1).

Reich, R. B. (1992). *The Work of Nations: Preparing Ourselves for 21st Century Capitalism.* New York: Vintage Books.

Rosenthal, N. H. (1995). 'The Nature of Occupational Employment Growth: 1983–93', *Monthly Labor Review*, 118: 45–54.

Steinmetz, G. and Wright, E. O. (1989). 'The Fall and Rise of the Petty Bourgeoisie: Changing Patterns of Employment in the Postwar United States', *American Journal of Sociology*, 94: 973–1018.

Van P., Philippe et al. (2001). *What's Wrong with a Free Lunch?* Boston, MA: Beacon Press.

Wright, E. O. (1997). *Class Counts: Comparative Studies in Class Analysis.* Cambridge, UK: Cambridge University Press.

—— and Martin, B. (1987). 'The Transformation of the American Class Structure', *American Journal of Sociology*, 93: 1–29.

—— and Dwyer, R. (2003). 'Methodological Appendices to "The Patterns of Job Expansions in the United States: A Comparison of the 1960s and 1990s"', Posted at: http://www.ssc.wisc.edu/~wright/SERapnx.pdf

15

Neoliberalization at Work: The Long Transition from Welfare to Workfare

Jamie Peck

Introduction

The welfare state has been on of the key battlegrounds of the neoliberal offensive, the state-assisted 'market revolution' that has been unevenly ascendant for more than two decades now. In neoliberalizing countries, entitlement programs have been eroded, benefits and eligibilities have been cut back, welfare systems and welfare recipients have been subjected to sustained political attack, and recurrent waves of reform have sought to strengthen 'work incentives' (see Handler 2005). In the process, *welfarist* rationalities, like the decommodification of wage labor for designated social groups, the provision of limited shelters from labor market competition, and the standardization of services in the context of legally embedded entitlements, have progressively given way to an emergent set of *workfarist* logics, based on the selective recommodification of wage labor, the marketization of the labor market's boundary institutions, the activation and socialization of welfare recipients for contingent employment, and the replacement of entitlements with obligations.

Focusing mainly on the US case, this chapter places the shift toward workfare in the context of the wider ascendancy of neoliberal politics, government practices, and modes of regulation. This shift, for all its ideological and material significance, should not be understood as the preordained unfolding of a functionalist master plan. Rather, the winding path toward workfarism—and its tendential stabilization in the context of an increasingly flexibilized labor market—exposes the exploratory and contradictory nature of this ostensibly paradigmatic reform effort, just as it also highlights reasons for its doggedness.

Toward Neoliberal Workfare

If there is an epicenter for workfarist reform, it is surely the United States, where the 1996 'welfare repeal' was associated with, *inter alia*, the termination of federal entitlements, which had been enshrined in the New Deal for sixty years; the devolution of residual welfare responsibilities to the fifty states; the imposition of strict work requirements, welfare time limits, and spending caps; and the gutting of food programs and assistance to immigrants. In many respects, this really did mean, to borrow Bill Clinton's fateful campaign slogan, 'ending welfare as we know it'. But this was not a singular 'moment' of reform. Recall that Murray's *Losing Ground* (1984), which first made the case for systemic welfare reform by rejuvenating arguments about the dysfunctional consequences of 'welfare dependency', was denied a job in the Reagan White House on the grounds that he (and his ideas) were too right wing (Miller 2002). By the mid-1990s, even centrist Democrats had largely accepted Murray's thesis. The ground had shifted. But of course the reform of welfare was just one aspect of a wider ideological realignment.

The shift from welfare-as-federal entitlement to devolved forms of work-oriented, active programming, or workfare, represents a defining moment in the wider process of neoliberalization. As Pollin (2003: 174) points out, the passage under the Clinton presidency of both NAFTA and welfare reform 'serve[d] the crucial function of defining a left boundary for the neoliberal model against which George W. Bush could retreat rightward'. Both of these momentous events, however, were the culmination of long and often circuitous processes of escalating ideological and institutional struggle, processes that continue to play out. The momentum for systemic welfare reform had been building for more than a quarter century prior to the passage of the euphemistically named Personal Responsibility and Work Reconciliation Act (PRWORA) of 1996. Moreover, the dramatic reductions in the welfare rolls that followed, with more than two-thirds of the caseload exiting the system in many parts of the country, were secured not simply by administrative fiat, but more fundamentally through the interpenetration of work-enforcing welfare reform and a brutally accommodating labor market.

The structural expansion of contingent jobs—part-time, temporary, insecure, and invariably low-paid—that had been underway for some time in the United States, and driven by processes like deunionization, labor market 'deregulation', and the shift to services (see Peck 2002), effectively facilitated welfare reform by generating millions of 'destinations' for former recipients. While the process of welfare reform may have been animated by some of the lowest forms of opportunistic and reactionary politics, its much-touted 'success' can be largely attributed to the policy's *post hoc* complementarity with a polarizing labor market (Peck 2001; Prashad 2003). For individuals, poverty on benefits has been replaced by working poverty, as the porous boundaries of the job market have been adjusted to accommodate a new class of forced laborers, most of whom are single mothers with young children. Workfare in the United States has helped recalibrate the 'boundary institutions' of the labor market, lowering the floor of wages, regulatory standards, and expectations along the way. But this process was not accomplished without a great deal of institutional searching and skirmishing, many false dawns, and some outright policy failures. To the extent that workfare 'works', this is not a function of superior programming or some inevitable structural logic; it is the outcome of a concerted ideological offensive to dismantle welfarism, enabled by the simultaneous restructuring and 'deregulation' of the labor market.

These contradictory, complex, and prosaic, if not tawdry, processes of welfare 'reform' call attention to some of the realities of regulatory restructuring in the context of advanced neoliberalization. Far from a unilinear, cohesive, and monolithic transition, it is more appropriately understood as a tendential process of creative institutional destruction (see Brenner and Theodore 2002; Peck and Tickell 2002). Contrary to self-serving representations of neoliberalization as a simple transition to a market order, policed by a minimalist state, the reality is that transformed states are endlessly embroiled in contradictory processes of 'market-making', experimental reform, trial-and-error policy development, deregulation, and reregulation. Far from an historic process of once-and-forever state withdrawal, felicitously leaving in its wake liberated individuals and reanimated market forces, real-world neoliberal reforms are more appropriately characterized as historically distinctive *forms of intervention.*

Neoliberalization does not mean the replacement of states with markets, it implies a reorganization of state–economy relations in the context of a set of ideological parameters and priorities, generically favoring market-oriented, (finance) capital-centric, desocialized, decollectivized strategies. Moreover, this is not a one-way and functionally preordained march toward a market utopia, which remains both a stark and unattainable destination (after Polanyi 1944), but a process of concerted institutional searching, imbued by pragmatism, electoral calculation, and beset by failures of implementation, legitimacy, and logic. And in many cases these projects encounter real resistance, quite often defensive, but in some cases potentially transformative (see Prashad 2003).

This destructively creative process of political-economic transformation contains moments of both reaction and proaction. It is destructive of 'alien' social and state forms, such as the central institutions of the Keynesian welfare state, just as it gives rise to *new* social and state forms, such as the vast political and institutional apparatus constructed around projects like free trade or flex-labor markets. One side of the neoliberal project is therefore consumed with the *roll-back* of obstructive and antithetical institutional forms, where the

Table 15.1 From roll-back to roll-out neoliberalism

	Roll-back	Roll-out
Mode of intervention	State withdrawal	Governance
Market regulation	Deregulation	Experimental reregulation
Political style	Ideological conviction	Pragmatic learning
Change agents	Vanguardist politicians	Technopols
Ideological program	Explicitly programmatic	Institutionally embedded
Frontline	Economic policy	Social and penal policy
Taxation	Selective givebacks	Systemic regression
Monetary policy	'Cold bath' monetarism	Prudence
Public expenditure	Cuts	Fiscal responsibility
Labor market regime	Mass unemployment	Full employability
Employment relations	Deunionization	Flexibility
Social policy	Retrenchment	Workfare
Financial regulation	Liberalization	Standards and codes
Development ethos	Structural adjustment	Social capital

Source: Developed from Peck and Tickell 2002.

fundamental objective is to dismantle, disorganize, and deregulate, through measures like antiunion legislation and the downsizing of social service programs. Given the far-reaching scale of these tasks—and given the visceral, mobilizing role of such political antipathies within neoliberal ideology—these roll-back tendencies are enduring and in some respects defining characteristics of all forms of actually existing neoliberalism. This said, the time may have passed here since these were *dominant* tendencies within the project—as they were, for example, in the UK and the United States in the 1980s—because as the project has spread, deepened, and in some respects matured, so its creative and reregulatory moments have come to the fore, spawning new rounds of neoliberal institutional invention in spheres like the regulation of trade and finance, education and social security reform, and the management of poor and marginalized subjects. Needless to say, these efforts tend also to be flawed and contradictory, only further extending the process of reform.

As a result, neoliberal politicians and technocrats have been increasingly drawn into the tasks of *managing* deregulated and privatized 'markets', just as they have been impelled to contain the social fallout of earlier rounds of neoliberalization by recourse to extra-market strategies like faith-based interventions, authoritarian social and penal policies, social capital building, and localized governance (see Naim 2000; Peck 2003). There have, in other words, been significant transformations and discontinuities within the project of neoliberalization itself, summarized in Table 15.1 as a stylized distinction between roll-back and roll-out neoliberalism.

Even in strategically significant policy domains like welfare/workfare, the reality of the reform process has often been messy and inconclusive. The much-touted American reforms have left millions stranded in working poverty, and typically in jobs lacking adequate regulatory protection, workplace benefits, or promotion prospects (see Mishel, Bernstein, and Allegretto 2005). Meanwhile, the process of systemic welfare reform in Europe is at a comparatively early stage, even if the broad direction of the reform effort seems similarly inclined (Handler 2005). The European welfare state will not simply be 'Americanized', however. Here, the reform process is generating distinctive institutional outcomes and political responses (see Torfing 1999; Barbier and Fargion 2004). The welfare/workfare transition has not only been a long and incremental one, with each national and local experience exhibiting a measure of path-dependent distinctiveness; even the most far-reaching reform efforts, such as the shift to decentralized workfare in the United States, reflect complex combinations of roll-back and roll-out tendencies, together with powerful institutional residues from previous rounds of policy development. This said, amid the institutional clutter and political contingency, various forms of tendential patterning are clearly evident in the multiple paths from welfare to workfare. More precisely, multiple transitions are evident, from (various forms of) welfare statism to (even more variegated forms of) workfarism (see Lodomel and Trickey 2001; Peck 2001; Handler 2005), transitions that are increasingly interconnected and mutually referential. Moreover, these workfarist transformations are being consolidated, both in reorganized institutional-cum-political settlements and in restructured labor markets, such that they can be seen to be generically indicative of a normalizing *postwelfare* policy configuration. The remainder of the chapter reflects on this transformation, with particular reference to the US case, 'home' to what has become a transnationalizing project of workfarism.

Workfare at Home and Abroad

Workfare is a social policy neologism referring to mandatory work programs for welfare recipients or, more generically, to the process of work-oriented welfare reform. It has become a powerful signifier of the prevailing method and philosophy of welfare reform in the United States. Here, work-based or work-enforcing welfare policies have been favored by politicians of the right for some considerable time, bolstered by the perennial concern that 'no strings attached' welfare entitlements erode the employment habits, job skills, and work ethics of the poor. Support for workfare-style policies, however, widened during the 1980s, as centrist liberals became increasingly convinced of the argument for 'tough love' approaches to welfare reform.

The PRWORA would later crystallize this bipartisan realignment, replacing the federal entitlement to welfare with a post-New Deal system of time-limited cash benefits, restrictive eligibility rules, and strict work requirements. The PRWORA can be regarded as a 'workfare settlement' in that it embodies a defining objective of helping-and-hassling welfare recipients into the job market, establishing a 'chill' around welfare claims, activating transitions into employment by the shortest route, and offering minimalist, stigmatized support for those who fail its work tests. Crucially, the underlying goals of such workfare regimes are no longer focused on poverty alleviation in a straightforward sense—since the fate of many of those leaving the welfare rolls since the mid-1990s has been *working* poverty. Workfare policies are instead addressed to the problem of 'welfare dependency'—an alleged reliance on government handouts that afflicts not only particular individuals but also certain communities—the solutions to which are defined in terms of the encouragement or enforcement of work (Murray 1984).

Concretely, the term workfare is applied to programs that require welfare recipients to work—in public sector jobs, private workplaces, or in community placements—in exchange for benefits. More generally, it has become associated with a wide range of policy measures designed to improve the 'employability' and work orientations of welfare recipients, typically through job-training programs and job-search assistance. These measures are regarded as 'workfarist' when they are used in the context of compulsion or strict benefit conditionality. Beyond these literal meanings, though, workfare is now recognized as a potent symbol of US-style (or neoliberal) welfare reform.

In its most abstract sense, the term 'workfare state' denotes a virtual inversion of the principles and the practices of the welfare state, as the notion of (social) rights and entitlements gives way to a new emphasis on (personal) responsibility and obligation (see Peck 2001; Jessop 2003). Where welfare stood for the principles of needs-based entitlement and standardized treatment, workfare stands for market-based compulsion, selectivity, and local discretion. Where welfare stood for passive income support, workfare stands for active labor market inclusion. And where welfare constructed its subjects as claimants, workfare reconstitutes them as jobseekers. In its most generic form, workfare can, therefore, be defined in terms of the following three dimensions:

- individually, it is associated with *mandatory* program participation and behavioral modification, in contrast to the welfarist pattern of entitlement-based systems and voluntary program participation;
- organizationally, it involves a *systemic* orientation toward work, labor force attachment, and the deterrence of welfare claims, displacing welfarism's bureaucratic logic of eligibility-based claims processing and benefit delivery with a more insistent focus on deflecting would-be claimants into the labor market;
- functionally, it implies an ascendancy of *active* labor market inclusion over passive labor market exclusion, as workfarism seeks to push the poor into the labor market, or hold them in a persistently unstable state close to it, rather than sanctioning limited nonparticipation in wage labor in the way of welfare systems.

Table 15.2 From welfarism and workfarism

	Welfarism	Workfarism
Ideological foundations	Statist/redistributional Entitlement Aid distributed on basis of need	Market-oriented/employability-based Reciprocity and self-help Enforcement of work and work values
State strategic objectives	Reducing poverty through income transfers Responding to manifest social need	Tackling welfare dependence through the promotion of work and employability Maximizing labor market participation
Macroeconomic rationale	Maintenance of wage/employment floor Automatic stabilizer of macro-economic growth/development	Enforcement and low-wage dependence Naturalization of contingent work Normalization of income/employment insecurity
Labor regulation	Exclusion from wage labor Socially sanctioned recipient groups defined on basis of ascribed/categorical characteristics	Inclusion into wage labor Market-determined treatment groups defined on basis of job readiness/cost of intervention
Regulatory practices	Passive income support Fiscal transfers: determining entitlements of passive subjects	Active labor market integration Work activation: interventionist case management of active subjects
Discursive practices	Need and entitlement Social work/bureaucratic codes and norms	Work, personal responsibility, self-sufficiency Business/employment service codes and norms
Delivery systems	Nationally regulated systems, typically delivered through local 'outposts' Emphasis on bureaucratic evenhandedness	'Hollowing out' of national regulation Increasing emphasis on local delivery, with increased discretion for frontline workers Emphasis on responding to localized labor markets

These workfarist principles diverge significantly from those of welfarism. Table 15.2 summarizes some of the sharp contrasts between established welfare structures and emerging workfare strategies.

The reach and resonance of workfare has increased over time. In the United States, workfare has undergone a transition from a modest reform program within the welfare system through to an effective successor to that system. What began as a specific program reform within the Aid to Families with Dependent Children system during the 1970s, acquired a wider significance during the 1980s when the Reagan Administration made resources available for a range of local 'demonstration projects', with the intent of propagating workfare-style initiatives. At this time, a distinction was drawn between 'hard' and 'soft' variants of workfare: the former emphasized strict sanctions policies and a no-nonsense approach, being generally favored by conservatives; the latter were couched within a more liberal, supportive, philosophy, seeking to build the human capital of welfare recipients through education and training investments. The Family Support Act (FSA) of 1988 represented a compromise between these two approaches, while embedding the general principles of work-oriented welfare in the federal system.

The work program associated with the FSA achieved no more than mixed results, its implementation being hampered by the slowing of the economy in the early 1990s and growing political impatience on the part of state governors. This was the context for Bill Clinton's ascent to national office as a welfare-reforming governor, the tough-love stance of whom would later come to define a key strand of the accelerating workfarist drift in US welfare policy during the 1990s. With the Republican takeover of Congress in 1994, the language of welfare reform became yet more shrill, just as the attendant policy proposals became progressively more radical.

After PRWORA, the responsibility for the new system passed to the fifty states and most adopted approaches that emphasized rapid and low-cost 'labor force attachment' or 'work first' (see Brown 1997; Mendel 2002). In the context of generally buoyant job markets, unprecedented numbers of welfare recipients left the welfare rolls in the late 1990s, further bolstering the confidence of workfare advocates and adding to the allure of the 'American model' in international policy debates (see Lodemel and Trickey 2001). Various forms of workfare were being established as social policy counterparts to labor market 'flexibility' policies, both in the United States and, increasingly, in other OECD countries. At the sharp end of policy practice, Handler (2005: 15) aptly summarizes the prosaic (but increasingly generalized) realities of workfare-style programming:

> [M]any of the negative practices found in the United States are also appearing in the administration of workfare in Western Europe. In general, workfare agencies are pressed for time and to achieve 'positive' results. Rather than individually-tailored client conferences and contracts, discussions tend to be perfunctory, options are restricted, and beneficiaries agree in order to receive the assistance. There is little discussion of client needs. All programmes are selective. Agencies 'cream', that is, the 'best' clients are selected for the 'best' options (those closest to the regular, paid labor market). Clients are often selected on subjective assessments of attitudes and behavior. Programmes tend to favor clients who are younger, better educated, and with fewer social problems ... Clients complain about disrespectful attitudes. In some countries, the more marginal clients are considered to be worse off as a result of workfare—they are offered 'sink' options and further stigmatized.

In the context of a continuing trend toward short-term, unstable, 'contingent' jobs across many national economies, workfare policies propel their clients into low-paid, unstable jobs. In this sense, they exhibit a primitive logic: workfare purposefully mobilizes workers for (minimum) waged work, holding them close to the labor market in a persistently 'job-ready' state. In a sense, it provides a forced (or 'activated') supply of workers for the labor market's least desirable jobs.

Workfare at Work

The regulatory project that is workfare is not simply about replacing welfarist institutions and conventions with a parallel set of fully coherent and functioning workfarist ones. Workfare is not some deus ex machina, lowered into place spontaneously to solve the contradictions of welfarism, flexible labor markets, and urban social dislocation. Rather, workfare ideologies and strategies have emerged unevenly and iteratively, the outcome of years of institutional experimentation, policy reform, and political struggle. At the same time, what we have come to understand as workfarism remains unstable and contradictory. Nevertheless, while it may not yet be truly hegemonic, workfare certainly represents a dominating strand in international policy discourse, one of the key coordinates around which reform strategies are plotted. In more concrete terms, workfare has become the institutional codification of work-oriented welfare reform—and as such must be understood as *both* a reactive, reform strategy *and* a would-be successor to the welfare state. Part critique, part alternative, workfare's international allure is to some degree rooted in the fact that it is a policy which appears to 'fit' the current political, social, and economic climate.

In this context, workfare strategies are becoming normalized as a means of enforcing labor market participation in a climate increasingly characterized by underemployment, low pay, work insecurity, and low-grade service employment. Workfare is a creature of these political-economic circumstances, mobilizing and socializing workers for jobs at the bottom of the 'new economy'. There is consequently a real prospect of a medium-term regulatory accommodation, in the context of deepening neoliberalization, between activating forms of social policy and flexibilizing labor markets. For these two developments—which do not have a unifying, overarching, 'functional' logic in any simple sense, but exhibit distinctive origins and dynamics—may be on the way to becoming mutually reinforcing. Certainly, this logic of mutual reinforcement is evident at the level of policy development and advocacy. Workfare strategies, then, appear to make sense when the labor market is generating large numbers of contingent jobs, since these provide the 'positive outcomes' that all successful workfare programs require; it is the presence of such jobs that facilitates the deregistration of welfare recipients, which in turn means that the policy is perceived as successful. In the language of workfare, the availability of (contingent) jobs renders both feasible and legitimate the activation of the 'workless'.

Workfare is also playing a part in shaping norms of labor market socialization and participation. Where practicable, welfare is effectively removed from the option set of 'employable' individuals, rendering them effectively dependent on (low) waged employment. At the very least, the experience of welfare claiming is sufficiently destabilized so as to induce a persistent deterrent effect. In turn, the very existence of this induced labor supply is likely to further erode pay levels and working conditions at the bottom of the labor market, the mechanism that Mead (1992: 87) refers to when describing how a pool of 'willing but underemployed workers' can in effect 'create its own demand'.

Workfare strategies, therefore, contribute to the social reproduction, over a relatively short time period, of the kind of contingent labor supply which is ripe for exploitation by bottom-feeding employers. In this respect, workfare may be playing a part in the proliferation of contingent work. A perverse kind of equilibrium might be in evidence. In contrast to the welfarist dynamic, in which the establishment of a 'floor' of welfare standards effectively set (and raised) standards at the bottom of the labor market, the workfarist dynamic pulls in the opposite direction, drawing down conditions in the lowest reaches of the labor market, as decommodified shelters from wage labor are closed off and as former welfare recipients are compelled to accept whatever the market makes available to them locally.

Functionally, this is anything but a simple 'deregulation' of the labor market or a unilateral act of state withdrawal. Rather, *new forms* of state intervention are licensed. Workfarism implies extensive (if not invasive) intervention in contingent labor markets and in the moral economy of the poor. As wages have polarized, working conditions have deteriorated, and as labor market insecurity has become endemic, the socialization and integration of contingent workers has assumed the significance of a fundamental regulatory dilemma. Under welfare settlements, benefits were extended to those who found themselves between jobs, the intermittently unemployed, and those—like lone parents or the disabled—with a socially legitimate claim on a nonwage income. Under workfare regimes, the policy orientation is toward intensifying competition on a generalized basis in the low-wage labor market, rather than offering 'shelters' or protections to designated groups. So, if old modes of governmental intervention (like checking eligibility and dispensing benefit payments through bureaucratic means) are being rolled back, new ones are being rolled out. Now, state employees must actively 'case manage' program clients, sanction systems must be created to penalize noncompliance with a range of new participation rules, incentives must be reorganized around objectives like diversion, active job search, rapid exit from the rolls, and so forth. Through such means, dependence on unstable, contingent work is *administratively* reinforced as the rule, rather than the exception, for those in the bottom third or so of the labor market, whoever they are. The logic of 'employability'—in which the market determines who should be employed and how much they are worth—pervades and structures programs, which minimally socialize participants for this fate. With all kinds of entitlements under attack, those who might be considered 'job-ready' are simply turned away from welfare offices, while those that cross the threshold are subjected to a strict regime of state-administered market triage. Minimal repairs (or 'reorientations') are carried out where necessary, so that others can join the swelling ranks of the job-ready, while the 'unemployable' find themselves bumped into the recesses of an increasingly mean-spirited and grudging system of residual welfare. Appropriate 'interventions' have been designed for each of these populations, the distinguishing characteristics of which are calibrated in terms of their relative job-readiness or distance from the labor market.

The Work First Method

One way of illustrating these impacts is to consider the specific job market consequences of 'work first' programming (see Peck and Theodore 2000). This represents the cutting edge of workfarist regulatory reform in the United States, while quite clearly being the ascendant policy-of-choice at the international level. In terms of the interface between the labor market and workfare programs, work first approaches function very 'close' to the job market, aspiring to channel welfare recipients down the shortest and fastest route to employment by variously assisting, pressurizing, and accelerating employment (re)entry, exploiting the short-term turnover of vacancies to bring about exits from welfare. Both philosophically and organizationally, these programs are, as Mead (1997: 72–3) puts it, 'suffused with the work mission'. The dominant social relations, allocation systems, and dynamics of work first programs are therefore closely intertwined with the labor markets in which they operate. This represents a highly dynamic form of 'embeddedness', in which programs aspire to read and move with the market.

Organizationally, work first programs emphasize rapid labor market entry, helping clients find the shortest (and least-cost) route to employment. They rely heavily on job search preparation, to which all or most clients are exposed at the point of entry, 'using the labour market itself as the test of employability' (Brown 1997: 2). Organized around a strong 'employment message', they operationalize the philosophy that 'any job is a good job'. Work first programs seek to identify the *minimal* interventions required to reconnect clients to the labor market, anticipating that most will be able to learn (or relearn) appropriate work habits 'on the job'. They also seek to minimize both unit costs and average lengths of stay on the program (Peck and Theodore 2000).

The work first mechanism, then, is one of the principal means by which localized workfare systems are being trodden down into local labor markets, resulting in a melding of institutional and market dynamics. So, the screening, selection, allocation, and discrimination systems associated with the lower end of the labor market are, as highlighted further below, reflected in the organization of work first programs (a. k. a. 'employability'), while the operation of the programs themselves subsequently serves to restructure and reinstitutionalize channels into employment. While in some senses it is accepted as a self-evident fact that job market rules, norms, and disciplines should shape workfare programs—after all, this is central to their rationale and philosophy—it has been less clear, until recently, how workfare programs are beginning reciprocally to condition labor markets.

Several quite distinctive labor-market effects of work first programs can be identified. First, a defining characteristic of such programs is that they direct participants into low-grade, high-turnover jobs, since the methodology of work first emphasizes the achievement of job-readiness in the context of currently available vacancies. This close tracking of vacancy flows means that these programs interface with the labor market in very particular ways. On the demand side, because contingent job vacancies turn over more frequently than those in the more stable, 'primary sector' of the labor market, coupled with the fact that primary sector jobs tend to be comparatively scarce in areas of concentrated poverty and underemployment, the profile of employment opportunities available to most program participants is heavily skewed toward contingent employment. Given that constant pressure is exerted on participants to enter jobs at the first opportunity, the typical pattern for most is, therefore, to enter high-turnover, contingent jobs. On the supply side, the prevailing social and labor market characteristics of the client group tend to reinforce and even rationalize this subordinate mode of labor market entry: most former welfare recipients have personal attributes which render them 'at risk' in the labor market, being vulnerable to racial and gender discrimination, or having caring/domestic responsibilities which define them as 'marginal' workers in the eyes of employers; most will have low levels of both educational attainment and formally recognized vocational skills; and most will have discontinuous work histories, often including previous periods in low-paid, unstable work (see Eden and Lein 1997).

Second, work first methods privilege the *initial* transition into the job market. Overriding priority is placed on securing the first job after welfare, on the (optimistic) presumption that this will provide a 'stepping stone' to better-paid, more secure employment. For the most part, the experience of former welfare recipients does not square with this notion of progression. Most former welfare recipients remain trapped in low-paid, contingent employment, while many others return to the welfare rolls following job loss. A control group study of twenty welfare-to-work programs in the United States, including some of the most 'successful' ones, concluded that the earnings of program participants were only $500 per year more than for those who had made their own way, in the 'control' group (Michalopoulos and Schwartz 2000). While workfare programs may bring about increased rates of employment, marginal earnings gains often result from longer hours of work at or near the minimum wage level (Handler 2005). Yet because work first defines the initial transition into work as the decisive moment of intervention, these problems tend to lie outside the frames of reference of workfare discourse and policy evaluation. The vision of policymakers and the practical orientation of programs is instead on the first destination after welfare, the systemic logic of work first workfare being to *activate* such transitions (rather than necessarily to sustain them).

Third, work first programs tend to exacerbate, rather than counteract, 'churning' in the lower reaches of the labor market. By inducing a constant, mostly one-way, flow from welfare into entry level jobs, work first programs intensify competition for work on the supply side of the labor market, while (in the short term at least) the number of job openings is likely to remain largely fixed. This leads to endemic problems of displacement and substitution, where program participants obtain jobs at the expense of other (contingent sector) workers (Solow 1998). Employment rates are often increased (at least marginally) through this form of intervention, as work first effectively reduces access to 'stable' welfare, while concomitantly increasing the level of dependency on contingent employment. More generally, however, the aggregate effect of work first may well be to further destabilize contingent employment by increasing the substitutability of labor at the very lowest wage levels. Perversely, then, work first may achieve its short-term employment goals of raising employment rates for designated groups at the expense of long-run job security, or indeed by detaching other groups of workers from waged employment. It also represents an effective subsidy to marginal employers, who disproportionately rely on the external market for labour.

Fourth, by pressurizing rapid transitions into employment, work first programs constitute a forced labor supply for jobs in the lowest reaches of the labor market, which in turn generates a 'drag' on pay and conditions. In the medium term, some employers may expand their use of contingent workers in order to take advantage of this new labor supply. Moreover, the limited bargaining power of those currently in contingent jobs stands to be further eroded by the constant flow of former welfare recipients into the labor market, especially as these 'new' workers are compelled to accept jobs as rapidly as possible, irrespective of pay and conditions. As the work first mantra has it, '*any job* is a good job' as far as this client group is concerned. The policy-induced crowding of low-wage labor markets consequently engenders a downward pull on wages and regulatory standards.

Fifth, an important aspect of the 'market-following' methodology of work first workfare is that programs tend to work with the grain of prevailing market criteria concerning the social distribution of work. Eschewing positive actions to tackle inequality and discrimination, these programs accept as given established conventions concerning recruitment and selection, while seeking to accommodate employers' definitions of job readiness. Typically, this entails a strong emphasis on the correction of 'inappropriate' attitudes and behaviors amongst program participants, including the imposition of dress codes and training in interview etiquette (Peck 2001). Employers' definitions of 'employability' consequently permeate the internal structures of work first programs, such that most will tend to reflect and reproduce existing patterns of labor market inequality. It follows that labor market inequalities are variously anticipated, mirrored, and sometimes amplified by the internal streaming and selection procedures of such programs. The least employable—including the disabled and those requiring costly interventions to get them job ready—are filtered to the back of the queue (Handler 2005).

In summary, the dominant function of work first workfare is to compel program participants into accepting—and learning to live with—contingent jobs, in the context of prevailing conditions in local labor markets. Work first systems forcibly attach welfare recipients to the lower end of the labor market both by eroding welfare entitlements and by actively managing the transition into an initial job. In contrast to the welfarist logic of providing temporary 'shelters' *outside* the labor market for designated social groups, this workfarist logic dictates that targeted social groups are driven *into* the labor market, where they are expected to remain, notwithstanding systemic problems of underemployment, low pay, and exploitative work relations. Work first programming itself consequently plays a role in legitimating, reinforcing, and naturalizing these conditions. It is consequently associated with a perverse form of the orthodox adage that supply creates its own demand. Under workfare, an expanded and persistently insecure contingent labor supply, actively driven into employment, serves to undercut existing conditions, while creating a situation favorable to further expansion in the (relative or absolute) size of the contingent sector. So, workfarist measures do not so much raise the level of employability across the labor market as a whole as increase the rate of exploitation in its lower reaches.

Conclusion

While the number of fully fledged workfare regimes may be relatively small at the present time, the general circumstances that this postwelfarist keyword denotes—a movement away from entitlement programs, an increased reliance on market-oriented social policies, a focus on the encouragement of work and work-related values, an emphasis on mandatory job search and job placement for welfare recipients—have spread far and wide. For these reasons, Standing (1999: 314) concludes that, 'It may not be hyperbole to describe workfare as the great social experiment of the late twentieth century'. Workfare represents an incipient systemic challenge to welfare settlements. While a coherent and reproducible 'workfare state' has yet to eclipse the inherited structure of welfare states, the shift toward workfarism represents a significant and sustained political-economic tendency.

For all these signs of incipient regulatory accommodation, politics still matter in the era of workfare. Yet at the present time these politics are seriously asymmetrical: workfare advocates have the upper hand, together with favorable structural conditions; in contrast, much of the resistance to workfare has been defensive and localized. While the workfare advocacy movement has assumed an increasingly aggressive, generic, and transnational form, for the most part antiworkfare politics remain reactive, particularized, and locally specific. Indeed, explicit objectives around the weakening, division, and localization of sources of political opposition are often reflected in contemporary welfare-restructuring strategies. It seems that, once the national defenses of welfarism have been breached, the path is opened decisively to localize residual welfare and extend workfare functions.

Because workfare is prosecuted as a variegated strategy, the downloading process is heterogeneous in form and uneven in effects. Crucially, this tends to render antiworkfare politics contingent on preexisting and locally variable capacities for resistance, primarily at the urban scale. Here, resistance typically comes through some form of coalition between labor unions, antipoverty campaigners, social service advocates, and community organizations, which tend to operate in different combinations—and in pursuit of different strategic lines—in different places. For example, in New York City, where workfare is delivered through public sector placements, resistance emerged in the form of the unionization of workfare workers, drawing on the joint organizational capacities of public sector unions and community groups, and political mobilization has also occurred through the associated *Workfairness* campaign. Meanwhile in Toronto, where workfare was introduced in the form of placements in the nonprofit sector, a network of social advocacy and welfare rights groups, with the support of some of Ontario's industrial unions, established *Workfare Watch,* a lobbying and campaigning initiative, while taking steps to prevent community agencies participating in the program.

There is an important sense, then, in which local political struggles usually reflect—though are not *determined by*—the local form of workfare strategies. Where workfare slots are located in the public sector, the strategy is exposed to the possibility of unionization; where workfare relies on nonprofit sector placements, then the obvious line of resistance is to choke off the supply of places through social sector campaigning and lobbying; where workfare is oriented to wage employment in the external labor market—in many ways its tendential form—resistance is rendered difficult due to the diffuse and individualized nature of this strategy, but may take the form of boycotts, service sector unionization drives, or living wage campaigns. It would, therefore, seem that different workfare strategies call for different forms of local political response, while also being differentially vulnerable to disruption, reform, and implementation failure at the local level. However, constructing generalized and effective opposition to workfare out of a series of particularized local struggles has proved predictably difficult, though there are some early signs of cross-locality networking and some attempts to develop cross-scalar campaigns, linking local to wider struggles. While at the present time resistance to workfare tends to be sporadic and localized, it is possible that recent developments in cities like New York City and Toronto will prefigure more generalized oppositional movements (Prashad 2003).

While it is critically important, in this context, to appreciate the scale and scope of the workfare offensive, this should not be allowed to breed political fatalism. Local resistance is important symbolically and materially, but pressure must also be brought to bear on the extra-local rule systems that sustain workfarism. Certainly, simply to wait for the workfare regime to collapse under the weight of its own contradictions would be as politically complacent as it is intellectually arrogant. There has to be *engagement* with the politics and policies of workfare, both at the level of the minutiae of individual, local reform programs and at the level of ideological principle. In many ways one of the most pressing challenges facing opponents of workfare lies in the (re)connection of these levels: how to defend welfare rights without looking like apologists for a flawed status quo; how to engage in the process of policy formation without being dragged into some quasi-workfarist compromise; how to build bridges between local oppositional movements and to 'jump scale' to the national and international arenas in which workfare policy conventions are being made; how to take on transcendent neoliberal rule systems as well as concrete programs; how to turn strategies of opposition and resistance into progressive alternatives. It is both a sign of neoliberal realpolitik and a symbol of hope that these remain open questions.

References

Barbier, J. C. and Fargion, V. (2004). 'Continental Inconsistencies on the Path to Activation'. *European Societies*, 6(4): 437–60.

Brenner, N. and Theodore, N. (2002). 'Cities and the Geographies of Actually-Existing Neoliberalism', *Antipode* 33(3): 349–79.

Brown, A. (1997). *Work First: How to Implement an Employment-Focused Approach to Welfare Reform*. New York: Manpower Demonstration Research Corporation.

Edin, K. and Lein, L. (1997). *Making Ends Meet: How Single Mothers Survive Welfare and Low-Wage Work*. New York: Russell Sage.

Handler, J. (2005). *Social Citizenship and Workfare in the United States and Western Europe: The Paradox of Inclusion*. Cambridge: Cambridge University Press.

Jessop, B. (2003). 'From Thatcherism to New Labour: Neo-liberalism, Workfarism, and Labour Market Regulation', in H. Overbeek (ed.), *The Political Economy of European*

Unemployment: European Integration and the Transnationalization of the (Un)employment Question. London: Routledge.
Lodemel, I. and Trickey, H. (eds.) (2001). *An Offer You Can't Refuse: Workfare in International Perspective*. Bristol, CT: Policy Press.
Mead, L. M. (1992). *The New Politics of Poverty: The Nonworking Poor in America*. New York: Basic Books.
—— (1997). 'Welfare Employment', in L. M. Mead (ed.), *The New Paternalism*. Washington, DC: Brookings Institution Press, pp. 39–88.
Mendel, D. (2002). 'Work First, What Next?', *AdvoCasey*, 4(2): 4–13.
Michalopoulos, C. and Schwartz, C. (2000). *National Evaluation of Welfare-to-Work Strategies*. New York: Manpower Demonstration Research Corporation.
Miller, J. J. (2002). 'Eight Books that Changed America', *Philanthropy*, July/August.
Mishel, L., Bernstein, J., and Allegretto, S. (2005). *The State of Working America, 2004/2005*. Philadelphia: Temple University Press.
Murray, C. (1984). *Losing Ground: American Social Policy 1950–1980*. New York: Basic Books.
Naim, M. (2000). 'Fads and Fashion in Economic Reforms: Washington Consensus or Washington Confusion?', *Third World Quarterly*, 21: 505–28.
Peck, J. (2001). *Workfare States*. New York: Guilford.
—— (2002). 'Labour, Zapped/Growth, Restored? Three Moments of Neoliberal Restructuring in the American Labour Market', *Journal of Economic Geography*, 2(1): 179–220.
—— (2003). 'Geography and Public Policy: Mapping the Penal State', *Progress in Human Geography*, 27(2): 222–32.
—— and Theodore, N. (2000). 'Work First: Workfare and the Regulation of Contingent Labour Markets', *Cambridge Journal of Economics*, 24(1): 119–38.
—— and Tickell, A. (2002). 'Neoliberalizing Space', *Antipode*, 34(3): 380–404.
Polanyi, K. (1994). *The Great Transformation*. Boston, MA: Beacon.
Prashad, V. (2003). *Keeping up with the Dow Jones: Debt, Prison and Workfare*. Boston, MA: South End Press.
Solow, R. M. (1998). *Work and Welfare*. Princeton, NJ: Princeton University Press.
Standing, G. (1999). *Global Labour Flexibility*. London: Macmillan.
Torfing, J. (1999). 'Workfare with Welfare: Recent Reforms of the Danish Welfare State', *Journal of European Social Policy*, 9(1): 5–28.

16

Change and Continuity in Working Life

Phil James and Geoffrey Wood

Introduction

The preceding contributions have provided a host of insights into the dimensions and parameters of recent changes in the world of work, the dynamics that have been acting to shape their nature and scale, and the way in which they are impacting on working lives. In combination, the contributions have highlighted that the ways in which these lives have been, and are being, transformed do not represent complete ruptures with previously existing practices and arrangements, but rather adaptations that have varied in both scope and intensity. They have further revealed that these variations in the balance between continuity and change extend to encompass differences at several different levels including the workplace, sectoral, and national ones.

Given these last points, the first part of this concluding chapter draws on the contributions provided to make some general observations about the varying nature and extent of the changes that have been occurring in working life, and the ways in which these changes have been differentially impacting on workers. It then further draws on them to explore the dynamics underlying these variations and differential impacts and the factors that have served to shape the balance between continuity and change that they embody. Finally, the last part of the chapter goes on to consider the relationship between these analyses and the wider relevant literature.

Nature and Extent of Change

At a general level, all of the chapters in the volume have, as already noted, reinforced the widely accepted point that the world of work has been marked by important processes of change during the past few decades. They have also, at the more specific one, confirmed a number of previously identified central components and trajectories of this reform process. Thus, in combination, they have noted the international decline in trade union membership and power, the way in which the distribution of employment has moved toward the services sector, the growing reliance that has been placed on various types of 'nonstandard' employment, and on 'networked' forms of organization, the actions that employers have taken to reformulate their human resource strategies and policies, by, for example, seeking to devolve more responsibilities to frontline staff and establishing more extensive systems of performance management, and the manner in which governments have sought to change the labor market relationships of workers via the reform of welfare systems and the deregulation of employment rights.

At the same time, they have, in doing so, clearly demonstrated that while the changes taking place have often encompassed similar elements, their precise composition has varied considerably, both between and within countries. As a result, the pattern of change has been highly differentiated.

Cross-national differences in the way in which work tasks and systems have been reformed emerge clearly, for example, from Lansbury et al.'s exploration of employment relations reform in the Korean and Australian auto and banking industries. Similarly, Peck's analysis of the international trend toward the adoption by governments of workfarist welfare systems makes the point that this trend exists alongside major international differences in the degree to which countries have progressed along this path and in the way in which such policies have been formulated. Similarly again, Wood et al., in their examination of how attempts have been made internationally to enhance numerical flexibility through the reduction of job protection rights, point to major differences in the degree of such reductions, and Brewster et al., highlight, through their quantitative analysis of survey data, significant national as well as sectoral differences in the use made of certain human resource techniques.

Meanwhile, at the sectoral level, Hyman's contribution draws attention to the varying way in which worker empowerment exists in the 'old economy' and the new 'knowledge-' based one, while also noting, more generally, its limited nature, and, at the organizational one, that of Grimshaw et al. shows how considerations of trust, power, and risk can contribute to 'cross-' and 'within-' organization differences in both the use made of interorganizational contracting and its form, notably with regard to the degree to which it takes on a 'relational' character. Indeed, this last contribution also usefully further points to the way in which the use of this latter form of contracting is likely, in turn, to vary between countries as a result of differences in the extent to which their wider institutional arrangements facilitate arrangements of this type.

The Experiences of Workers

There would seem, on the basis of the provided contributions, and the wider literature on which they build, that the types of changes discussed above have, unsurprisingly, impacted on workers. Once again, however, it would seem that this impact has embodied common elements, as well as differences.

In terms of commonalities, the contributions of Hyman and James both refer to evidence which indicates that levels of work intensity have been generally rising, while levels of task discretion have been falling, with the latter's contribution highlighting the way in which these trends are having potentially important adverse implications for the propensity of workers to suffer work-related injuries and ill health. Meanwhile, the case study findings of Baldry et al. add weight to this last point by highlighting how employee health and well-being can be adversely affected by such factors as high work pressures and a lack of task control.

A number of the contributions also, albeit in different ways, highlight the way in which recent changes have been working to create more tenuous, uncertain, and insecure forms of employment relationship. This is true, for example, of Wood et al.'s discussion of government attempts to enhance numerical flexibility, Grimshaw et al.'s analysis of how interorganizational contracting is leading to job reductions, the transfer of workers between employers, the establishment of overlapping, and contradictory, patterns of line management, and adverse trends in work intensity and worker discretion, and Peck's observations concerning how workfare systems are acting not only force program participants into low-paid, insecure, contingent jobs, but, in doing so, to be simultaneously encouraging the spread of such employment and the undermining of the terms and conditions of existing workers.

Yet, as would be expected given the point made above about cross-country variations in the nature and extent of the reforms that have been occurring, it would seem that these developmental commonalities exist alongside international differences of magnitude. It would further seem that important intranational and organizational differences exist with regard to how recent changes have affected workers.

At the national level, for example, Wright and Dwyer's analysis of the quality of jobs generated in the United States from the 1960s to the 1990s shows that the long 1990s economic boom produced a pattern of asymmetrically polarized job expansion marked by a very strong expansion of jobs in the top tier of employment, strong growth at the bottom, and very limited growth in the middle. This differentiated pattern of expansion, which is noted to have been rooted in dramatic sectoral shifts in employment opportunities, is found to have resulted in the development of a much more bifurcated labor market and hence one characterized by greater degrees of inequality in terms of pay, working conditions, and job security.

A somewhat similar picture of differential impact and related inequality emerges from Grimshaw et al.'s chapter. Thus, here not only is it shown how those employed on externalized contract work frequently experience lower levels of pay and less security than those who had previously carried out the work 'in-house', but that the process of interorganizational contracting is also contributing to difficulties in identifying and eliminating sex discrimination and to the creation of new gender inequalities at work. In a somewhat similar vein, the chapter by James raises the possibility that the growth of employment in small- and medium-sized enterprises (SMEs) and the increased usage of temporary and self-employed workers is leading to growing variations in how well workplace risks are being managed, that by Baldry and his colleagues show how the impact of call center work on workers' health can vary as a result of differences in the organizational, technical, and ambient environments in which they are employed and Hyman's, as already alluded to earlier, points to the fact that the degree to which workers have been 'empowered' is likely to vary between different types of occupational group.

The Dynamics of Change

The continuities and changes in working life identified in the book's contributions, as well as the variations in them that they reveal, can be seen to be the product of a range of overlapping, and contradictory, influences operating at the national, regional, sectoral, and organizational levels. These influences can, in turn, be seen to themselves embody marked variations in terms of the direction, nature, and degree of their impacts.

Changing Market Contexts

The respective roles that the changing nature of labor, product, and financial markets have played in shaping the processes of reform that have been occurring in the past few decades loom large in the accounts of many of the preceding chapters. In short, the changes that have taken place in these markets are identified as having had a number of different implications for the external environments which face governments and employing organizations; implications which are considered, in turn, to have prompted previously extant policies to be reviewed and reformed. In particular, these changes, and associated implications, are noted to have centrally included the way in which the growing liberalization of financial markets has served to simultaneously increase the priority accorded to shareholder interests and, in part also as a result of the consequent increased attractiveness of growth by mergers and acquisitions and the greater emphasis placed on short-term business performance, engendered a need for market-based organizations to improve their efficiency and cost-effectiveness and, via the demise of trade union membership and power, facilitated government- and employer-driven reforms to external and ILMs.

In many respects these implications can clearly be viewed as being mutually reinforcing. At the same time, it would seem that care needs to be taken not to overstate the role that recent market-related developments have played in determining the precise way in which the parameters of working life have been reformulated and to correspondingly understate that played by human agency in terms of both shaping these developments and the policy responses associated with them. At the national level, for example, Wood et al.'s analysis shows clearly that governments have varied with regard to their willingness to deregulate labor markets, while that of Lansbury et al. reveals how government not only played a crucial legislative role in reconstituting the commercial markets confronting the Korean and Australian banking sectors, but also carried out this process of reconstitution in different ways and over different time periods.

Similarly, in the regional context, Hudson's exploration of the way in which industrial policy in the North-East of England has changed historically in response to shifts in government thinking, and the composition and nature of local business interests, clearly illustrates the way in which economic change is not simply an outcome of market forces. In doing so, it, therefore, further emphasizes how such change can be the result of not only economic factors but the product of related ideological and material interests.

Grimshaw et al.'s discussion of interorganizational contracting, furthermore, not only reinforces these last points by drawing attention to the way in which governments have frequently actively encouraged its usage, but also cautions against assuming that change at the organizational level is necessarily informed by a clear and immutable financial or business logic given that, in their words, 'the success of outsourcing and subcontracting depends on numerous intangible variables and outcomes that are difficult to objectify or measure'. As a result, the analysis of these authors highlights the fact that decision-making at the organization level is often likely to occur in situations of analytical uncertainty and to commonly, therefore, be the product of nonmarket, as well as market, logics, including the personal preferences of key managers and related perceptions of what constitutes 'desirable' or 'best' practice.

The Role of Institutional Contexts

Reference has already been made to a further point made by Grimshaw et al., namely that countries differ in terms of the degree to which they possess institutional frameworks conducive to the establishment of 'relational', rather than 'arm's-length', contractual relationships. This point about the way in which practices and developments at the organizational level, in part, reflect features of the wider institutional environment, however, is one that receives reinforcement, albeit, in different ways, from a number of the volume's other contributions, including those by Wood et al., Brewster et al., and James. For example, the findings reported by the second of these quoted authors identify marked differences in the employment relations practices of organizations in Britain compared with those located in a number of more coordinated European economies, while the chapter by James notes how regulatory frameworks and agencies can exert an important influence over how employers approach the management of workplace risks.

The first of these last quoted chapters further highlights the point that the actions of governments, as well as employing organizations, are institutionally constrained (or facilitated). In particular, Wood et al.'s analysis draws attention to the way in which the institutional structures, and the ideological and material compromises on which they are based, act to limit the extent to which governments in coordinated European economies are able to pursue courses of deregulatory labor market action that threaten to undermine these underlying compromises.

At the same time, a number of the chapters show that such institutional constraints and facilitators are themselves unstable and subject to change in the face of ideological and material economic and political challenges. This emerges clearly, for example, from Wood et al.'s chapter. It similarly does so from those of Hudson and Peck. Thus, in showing how changes in industrial policy in England's North East reflected shifts in the thinking of local business interests, the first of these contributions also highlights how these shifts were connected to the changing composition of these interests that stemmed from the decline in the previously dominant local coal industry. Meanwhile, Peck's analysis usefully highlights how workfarist reforms in the United States have been facilitated by a 'brutally accommodating labor market' which, by incorporating an expansion of insecure and low paid contingent jobs, has provided 'millions of "destinations" for former [welfare] recipients'.

What also emerges, however, is that the process of institutional change is often incremental and can embody a number of contradictory shifts of direction, with the result that it is frequently marked by inconsistency and incoherence. Peck's contribution also usefully highlights both of these points. In particular, he notes how neoliberal-inspired processes of reform have encompassed significant discontinuities embodying elements of both 'roll-back' and 'roll-out'.

Meanwhile, the sophisticated and rich analysis Boyer provides in his chapter concerning the role that institutional complementarities play in determining the nature, coherence, and outcomes of reform processes serves to provide valuable insights into why discontinuities of this type can be expected. For this analysis, not only highlights the differing forms of institutional and subinstitutional association that can exist within particular contexts, and the way in which these can embody both market and nonmarket relationships, but further points to how the complex nature of interinstitutional relations, and the range of combinations of mediation that may exist within them, preclude the simple replication of specific rules and practices without taking account of the entire socioeconomic context in which they were originally encountered. Consequently, it indicates that reform programs which arise from more narrowly focused forms of analysis are likely to be problematic as a result of their failure to incorporate a more holistic and well-rounded process of complementary institutional revision.

Hollingsworth's chapter, in turn, adds weight to this last interpretation, while also, more generally, noting that the complexity of the age within which we live has served to reduce our understanding of the 'social world' and thereby hinder attempts to develop more effective institutions. In particular, in his contribution Hollingsworth argues that policymaking often centers around abstract, mechanistic, and overoptimistic planning when in practice decision-making needs to accord recognition to the fact that the uncertainties which exist point to the value of experimental processes of change that are nonlinear and dynamic; a point seen to highlight the limits of currently popular benchmarking approaches aimed at promoting the dissemination of 'best practice' at the organizational level. He further and, more specifically, notes that different sets rules and practices may evolve simultaneously within national business systems which are not only dynamic but everchanging, that contradictory, rather than internally coherent, patterns of change are to be expected, and that institutional arrangements which are functional at one time may not be so at another.

Neoliberalism and its (Multilevel) Contradictions

More generally, an almost constant theme running through the book is the way in which the changes occurring in both the context and content of working life have, in large part, been driven by the rise of neoliberal policy agendas at the political level and by the adoption, at the organizational one, of practices that echo them. However, the contributions also, when taken together, make clear that the influence exerted by neoliberalism has not incorporated a clear, programmatic, logic. Rather, it has stemmed from an often experimental and ad hoc process of reform that has frequently been marked by contradictory patterns of reregulation and deregulation. Indeed, in his exploration of the implications of recent changes in financial markets for European employment relations, Grahl notes that although the opening up of these markets to external forces is very frequently part of neoliberal strategies, 'not all aspects of the global economy are welcome to neoliberals' because of the concerns they raise for key interests regarding the preservation of existing social stability and cohesion and further argues that whilst financial integration and the dissolution of existing financial structures may threaten employee interests, this does mean that existing employee rights and responsibilities will be uniformally undermined in an uncontested fashion.

Doubts also emerge as to the longer-term economic efficacy, and hence stability, of the reforms introduced. At the macro level, for example, Wood et al.'s discussion of governmental attempts to deregulate labor markets in order to facilitate greater numerical flexibility notes how they run the risk of supporting a move to low road forms of production and service delivery that can have damaging consequences for task flexibility and worker skills and development and encourage variations in levels of demand to be accommodated by job loss rather than variations in working hours. It further draws attention to evidence which simultaneously casts doubt over the economic performance of more deregulated Anglo-Saxon economies relative to that of the more regulated and coordinated economic systems found in parts of Europe. A number of the contributions, as alluded to earlier, also show that the form and depth of neoliberal-inspired reforms vary considerably across national economies, as well as between regions and organizations within them. At the organizational level, for example, Hyman's chapter on worker empowerment lends weight to this point by showing how the differing nature of work in different sectors of the economy can result in the adoption by employers of rather different systems of work organization and control. It also, at a more general level, however, reminds us of the fundamentally contradictory nature of employment relationships and how this creates inherent tensions between the desire of employers to empower workers in order to obtain their commitment and consent and the [perceived] need they have to exercise control over them in the face of short-term economic pressures.

This issue of organizational level contradictions is, perhaps, most clearly articulated in Sayer's exploration of the interrelationship between the narrowly focused instrumentalism of organizations, on the one hand, and the 'complex, mixed motivations of their members'. Thus, in this Sayer, while noting that economic organizations must in a context in which the 'priorities and quality of life are subordinate to the economy', makes the point that according recognition to workers solely on the basis of achievement can adversely impact on organizational interests by ignoring other qualities of importance to workers, including collegiality, civility, sensitivity, concern for others, and friendliness.

The Book's Contributions and the Wider Literature

The book's various contributions, when taken together, have clearly provided a range of valuable theoretical and empirical insights. In doing so, they suggest that:

- Working life has, internationally, been going through a profound period of change that, nevertheless, has been marked by a combination of continuity and change;
- The degree of this continuity has varied considerably at the national, sectoral, regional, and organizational levels;
- This variation has reflected differences in the way in which the main forces for change and continuity, labor, product, and financial markets, surrounding institutional arrangements, including the distribution of power which exists between key interest groups, and the adoption of neoliberal policy agendas, have differentially impacted on particular contexts;
- While the pursuit of neoliberal-inspired programs of reform has been a common driver of the changes occurring, the precise reforms that have been pursued and implemented as a result of them have similarly varied and typically evolved through incremental processes marked by a good deal of discontinuity, ad hocery and experimentation;
- Contradictions inherent in neoliberal agendas mean that their efficacy in terms of their capacity to engage workers and secure stable and satisfactory economic performance would seem problematic;
- This would seem particularly so given evidence to suggest that more neoliberal economies have not only seen, at the aggregate level, increasing work intensity and declining task discretion, but a growing inequality with regard to the terms and conditions under which different parts of the workforce labor; and
- It is, consequently seriously open to question whether the performance of more neoliberal Anglo-Saxon type economies is superior to that of the coordination based ones found in parts of Europe.

Perhaps unsurprisingly, these observations and conclusions receive support from important strands of the existing relevant literature. A few brief illustrations of this are provided in what follows.

In her classic study on the origins of capitalism, for example, Wood (2000) points to the protracted, uneven, and incremental nature of capitalist development, and, in doing so, notes that specific aspects of both its early regulation and practice predated the particular combination of work organization and institutions that characterizes capitalism and thereby incorporated both change and continuity. In much a similar vein, Wood (2004: 5) has observed how capitalist development has continued to be a slow and irregular process incorporating a complex web of market and nonmarket relations, as well as episodic periods of growth and crisis.

Meanwhile, De Angelis (2000: 156) has noted the way in which neoliberalism has been characterized by a strong element of opportunism, with a willingness on the part of governments and firms to depart from ideologies on the basis of expediency and other writers have observed that, even in developed liberal market economies, social and political considerations have frequently been observed to override the operations of markets (MacEwan 1999: 34) and led to the creation of institutional frameworks that embody both market and nonmarket relationships. For example, it has been observed how major exporting nations in the Far East have restricted the free movement of their currencies to promote the competitiveness of their manufactured goods (Pollin 2003) and that the agricultural sectors in most of the advanced societies continue to be heavily subsidized (MacEwan 1999). In addition, notwithstanding that neoliberal ideologies insist that labor is simply another commodity, whose trade should be unrestricted as possible, almost all neoliberal governments have been noted to remain committed to restricting the movement of peoples across national boundaries, deflecting working and lower-middle class fears of evergrowing impoverishment toward easily identifiable, and even more marginal, outsiders (MacEwan 1999: 35).

This pragmatic willingness to depart from neoliberal principles and prescriptions has, furthermore, been noted to extend from the political and ideological level to that of the workplace. Thus, while pressure to maximize shareholder value has forced 'low road' labor relations, characterized by drives to reduce wage costs, wage-related expenditures, such as pensions, and staff facilities, seeing employees as little more than short-term independent subcontractors to be used of and disposed at will (Crotty 2003: 278), it has also, in highly competitive products, prompted firms to seek the buy-in of key components of their workforces to foster innovation and functional flexibility (see also Wood et al.'s chapter). These contradictory responses have, in turn, frequently led to legislative initiatives aimed at supporting the development of dualistic internal markets that themselves engender greater 'within' country patterns of employment.

More generally, the varieties of capitalism literature has simultaneously highlighted how specific sets of practices tend to be concentrated in particular locales and regions (Whitley 1999) and the way in which broader changes at the systemic level tend to be mirrored by alterations in practice at the level of the firm. Amable (2003: 5), for example, has noted the way in which several institutional forms and associated workplace practices may, at specific times, be seen as being associated with 'good performance', while also pointing out that agents tend to adopt similar practices in line with specific institutional configurations and in conformity with cultural and social norms (Amable 2003: 6).

At the same time, it has been noted that national economies most closely associated with the liberal market ideal in the developed world, characterized as they are by a very low level of product market regulation, decentralized financial systems which allocate a prominent role to institutional investors and venture capitalists, and devolved and fragmented collective bargaining practices (Amable 2003: 16–18), allow a greater degree of room for entrepreneurial activity (Audretsch and Thurick 2001: 284). As a result, they tend to promote a considerable diversity in practice, most notably between specific high-technology industries—such as biotechnology and computer science—and 'low-tech' areas of the service economy such as fast food and customer service centers (Leborgne and Lipietz 2001); a diversity which may also be reflected at the regional level and is likely to be greater than that which exists in more cooperative varieties of capitalism (see Brewster et al.'s chapter).

Doubts, however, have been widely expressed as to the stability and efficacy of neoliberal-based reforms. Boyer (2001: 23), for example, has argued that, despite the fact that the crisis of the postwar SSA took place in the late 1960s, neoliberal economies have yet to establish a viable and sustainable regime of accumulation that overcomes the problems associated with overproduction and underconsumption (cf. Chandler 2005). More specifically, it has been observed that intense product competition has made it extremely difficult for nonfinancial firms to generate high profits on a sustained basis, while the decline of 'patient' and committed investors, as well as the rise of aggressive investors, has forced such firms to return an increasing share of their cash flow to shareholders (Crotty 2003: 270). Important consequences of these developments are seen to have been the fueling of a culture of short-termism and the, related, damaging of internal social relations as the desire to maximize shareholder value has led to an increasing downgrading of workforce interests, with all the implications that this has for 'social solidarity', and levels of both internal and external inequality with regard to income, security, and wider social benefits (Wood 2004: 80).

Against this background, it has been argued by some that, despite the global ideological dominance of neoliberalism and its hegemony in many countries, the more cooperative-based institutional frameworks which persist in a number of Western European and Far Eastern economies (Lincoln and Kalleberg 1990; Applebaum et al. 2000; Dore 2000), not only remain viable, but may, in fact, be more conducive to sustainable, longer-term, economic performance. It has, for example, been noted that, whilst commonly dismissed by their internal and external critics as unviable and uncompetitive, both Germany and Japan have retained large manufacturing sectors, and remain among the world's largest exporters. Meanwhile, apparent beacons of neoliberalism, such as the United States and the UK, remain generally uncompetitive in export markets (and, indeed, this situation has gradually worsened), other than in heavily subsidized sectors such as agriculture and arms exports, and in financial services (Mann 2003; Wood 2004).

On the other hand, it has also been noted that such economies have themselves not been immune from pressures for neoliberal reforms. In particular, against the background of the weakening position of unions and hence the basis of tripartite frameworks, cooperative models have been under threat: external competition has forced endless rounds of cost cutting, whilst financial institutions have been forced, through slow changes in ownership patterns and external investments, toward a stronger emphasis on shareholder value (Lazonick and O'Sullivan 2000). It also seems likely that such economies will continue to be the subject of neoliberal reform agendas, and it consequently remains an issue of speculation as to how far these will act to undermine key features of the social settlements on which they are based.

Conclusion

This volume set out to provide a series of contributions from leading scholars that shed light on the changing nature of working life and the dynamics that have informed the changes taking place. The pattern to emerge from them is one of significant change alongside substantial degrees of continuity, with this degree of continuity varying considerably along national, subnational, and organizational lines; a pattern that would appear to reflect the way in which a reasonably common set of factors, including the changing nature of product markets and the rise of neoliberalism, have served to both drive the process of reform, while differentially acting to facilitate and constrain it both temporally and locationally.

These observations, which have been noted to accord with important strands of the existing relevant literature, have, at one level, drawn attention to the importance of studies that provide detailed explorations of the precise way in which working life is being reformed. At another, however, they have highlighted that a rigorous and well-rounded understanding of this process of reform requires account to be taken of the manner in which it is being informed and shaped by a constellation of, inevitably, interrelated factors, operating not only within individual organizations, but also within specific labor and product markets and particular sectoral, regional, and national economies.

As a result, it is argued that the key rationale which informed the compilation of this volume, namely the desirability of bringing together the macro-orientated analyses of regulation theorists and the more micro-based, and empirically based, ones that typify much of the work of those working in the field of employment relations and the labor process tradition, has proved to have been a sound and productive one. For what the preceding contributions have highlighted, above all, is that there remains considerable scope to further our understanding of the 'why' and 'how' of working life change through the establishment of closer theoretical and empirical connections between these two strands of scholarship. For, in combination, they have reinforced the point that what happens at the workplace and organizational level is invariably related, albeit in different ways, to developments within the wider, surrounding, economic, social, and political systems. They have also further served to highlight that changes at the former levels cannot be adequately understood without detailed attention being paid to the nature of these latter developments, their causes, and the way in which they act to influence the actions of those who directly author them.

There consequently do seem good reasons to seek to establish closer theoretical and empirical links between the manner in which firms are governed and approach the social organization of work and the way in which these are shaped by changing external environmental forces arising from changes in labor consumer markets and shifts in ideology, regulatory frameworks, and macroeconomic policy. It goes without saying that future work aimed at achieving this closer linkage between workplace practices and wider societal regulatory configurations should take due account of the already rich and rigorous scholarship that exists within existing micro- and macro-orientated accounts of the changes taking place in working life and the factors that are acting to drive them.

References

Amable, B. (2003). *The Diversity of Modern Capitalism*. Oxford: Oxford University Press.

Applebaum, E., Bailey, T., Berg, P., and Kalleberg, A. (2000). *Manufacturing Advantage: Why High Performance Work Systems Pay Off*. Ithacan, NY: Cornell University Press.

Audretsch, D. and Thurik, A. (2001). 'What's New About the New economy?', *Industrial and Corporate Change*, 10(1): 267–315.

Boyer, R. (2001). 'Introduction to the English Language Edition', in B. Jessop (ed.), *The Parisian Regulation School—Regulation Theory and the Crisis of Capitalism Volume 1*. London: Edward Elgar.

Chandler, A. (2005). 'Corporate Strategy, Structure and Control Methods in the United States During the 20th Century', in G. Dosi, D. Teece, and J. Chytry (eds.), *Understanding Industrial and Corporate Change*. Oxford: Oxford University Press.

Crotty, J. (2003). 'The Neoliberal Paradox: The Impact of Destructive Product Market Competition on Nonfinancial Corporations in the Neo-Liberal Era', *Review of Radical Political Economics*, 35(3): 271–80.

De Angelis, M. (2000). *Keynesianism, Social Conflict and Political Economy*. London: Macmillan.

Dore, R. (2000). *Stock Market Capitalism: Welfare Capitalism*. Cambridge: Cambridge University Press.

Lazonick, W. and O'Sullivan, M. (2000). 'Maximizing Shareholder Value: A New Ideology for Corporate Goverance', *Economy and Society*, 29(1): 13–35.

Leborgne, D. and Lipietz, A. (2001). 'Conceptual Fallacies and Open Questions on Post-Fordism', in B. Jessop (ed.), *Regulation Theory and the Crisis of Capitalism 3—Regulationist Perspectives on Fordism and Post-Fordism*. London: Edward Elgar.

Lincoln, J. and Kalleberg, A. (1990). *Culture, Control and Commitment: A Study of Work Organization in the United States and Japan*. Cambridge: Cambridge University Press.

MacEwan, A. (1999). *Neo-Liberalism or Democracy?* London: Zed.

Mann, M. (2003). *Incoherent Empire*. London: Verso.

Pollin, R. (2003). *Contours of Descent*. London: Verso.

Whitley, R. (1999). *Divergent Capitalisms*. Oxford: Oxford University Press.

Wolfson, M. (2003). 'Neoliberalism and the Social Structure of Accumulation', *Review of Radical Political Economics*, 35(3): 255–62.

Wood, E. M. (2000). *The Origins of Capitalism*. London: Verso.

Wood, N. (2004). *Tyranny in America: Capitalism and National Decay*. London: Verso.

Notes

1. C. P. Snow was a British physicist, novelist, and administrator who became a scientific advisor to the British government in World War II. He is well known for his book about science and literature, *The Two Cultures and the Scientific Revolution* (1959). In it he argues that practitioners in each of the two fields know very little about the other and there is little communication among them. Over time, others have discussed how the increasing specialization within and between disciplines has posed serious problems in communication not only for the academic world but also for the development of effective and democratic governance (Hollingsworth 1984).
2. Harvey (1917) coined the term 'coal combine' to denote capitalist enterprises rooted in the 'coal economy' that had diversified into a wide range of activities. These vertically integrated combines were linked into oligopolistic groupings that dominated economy and politics in the region. In addition, they were connected by non-economic relationships, including those of family, friendship, and shared religion, and the informal institutions of habitual behavior and regular social interaction.
3. My thanks to Phil James for this phrase.
4. The Governor of the Bank of England seems to suggest so (King 2006).
5. See again King (2006). The last observers to register this shift are to be found in the European Commission, where they continue to insist on public sector austerity even as the financial markets relax the constraints on EU governments. If the budgetary position of member states is so fragile why are investors desperate to lend them money?
6. What are presented here are *empirical* objections to the speculation hypothesis. There is also an obvious logical objection: speculation is a zero sum game. It cannot account for the continuing massively positive net revenues of financial actors and the financial sector as a whole.
7. The Bank for International Settlements explicitly reports trade in currencies which account for at least 0.1 percent of total FX trades. If Hong Kong (1.9 percent of total trades), Singapore (1 percent), and Taiwan (0.4 percent) are treated as developed economies, then eleven developing or transitional economies are mentioned, accounting together for 3.5 percent of foreign exchange deals. These are: Mexico, South Africa, Russia, Poland, India, Brazil, the Czech Republic, Thailand, Hungary, Chile, and Malaysia. All other countries—the rest of the developing world—account for 6 percent overall. Thus, the FX market in quantitative terms concerns the OECD countries and has to be understood with reference to those countries (BIS 2005).
8. The widespread notion that 'excessive' trading in assets is a cause of price volatility is without foundation. The usual association is the opposite—the greater the turnover, the more stable the price.

9. Hedge funds, which certainly adopt speculative positions, attract attention quite out of proportion to their scale. The most important institutional investors in terms of both assets and trading are investment companies, pension funds, and insurance companies. The customer bases of these institutions are very risk averse. The European Central Bank (ECB 2006) puts total hedge fund assets at about $1 trillion in 2005. Compare the $24 trillion under the management of institutional investors in 1998 in the G-7 alone reported by Davis and Steil (2001: 10).
10. In a work which can hardly be regarded as in favor of financial liberalization, Boyer, Dehove, and Plihon (2004) recognize that one factor intensifying financial crises is a concentration of risks in the banking system—in other words underdevelopment of securities markets.
11. See, notably, the Myners Report (2001), the Sandler Report (2002), and the Report of the Treasury Select Committee (2004) of the House of Commons.
12. This statement does not apply to the attempt to stimulate institutional investment in Germany by undermining the efficient public pensions system. Personal savings are in any case high in Germany and hardly in need of this kind of manipulation.
13. For analyses, see Brenner (2002), Stiglitz (2004).
14. Compare a previous phase of Americanization—focused on production methods and managerial techniques—following the World War II. On that occasion, close imitation of US productive systems proved to be compatible with considerable *divergence* of industrial relations practices.
15. For a range of analyses, see the collection edited by Williams (2000).
16. Other conflicts were also important—especially the desire of managers to reduce risks by strategies of diversification; market-based stockholders preferred to diversify portfolios rather than corporations.
17. This was even recognized officially—see the Kok Report (2004).
18. Note, however, that reverence for US models did not extend to the rather pragmatic approach of the Americans to macroeconomics. There is here a real inconsistency in the position of EU elites: they were trying to build a unified market for bonds, especially government bonds, at the same time as they clung to the prescriptions of the Stability Pact for government borrowing. If one takes the evaluations of the bond market seriously, however, it is clear that all states in the eurozone, Germany in particular, are considered completely creditworthy.
19. To grasp the alarming scale of this one operation look back at Figure 3. The spikes in inward FDI and outward portfolio investment from the eurozone in the first quarter of 2000 result from the takeover of Mannesmann.
20. One of the most incomprehensible aspects of shareholder economics in France was labor-shedding by profitable corporations and a fortiori the closure of profitable plants.
21. The tax breaks granted to upper income groups in the 1980s were justified by the claim that they would bring down the gross salaries of senior management. Of course, the opposite of this happened.
22. Annual share trading on the Deutsche Börse grew from $509 billion in 1990 to $2.120 trillion in 2000. The crash brought this down to $1.212 trillion in 2002, when growth resumed so that trading reached $1.299 trillion in 2003. Capitalization shows the same general pattern, rising from $355 billion at end 1990 to

a maximum of $1.432 trillion at end 1999. The crash brings this down to $686 billion at the end of 2002, with a recovery to $1.079 trillion at end 2003. The number of companies quoted, however, had still not started to rise again after the crash—a maximum of 983 at end 2001 fell to 866 at end 2003 (World Federation of Exchanges).

23. The three-year research project (1999–2002) was funded by the UK Economic and Social Research Council Future of Work Program, grant number L212252038, directed by Peter Nolan. The project collected rich qualitative data through interviews with managers and workers in eight case studies of interorganizational contracting (an airport, a Private Finance Initiative, a customer service network, an IT outsourcing arrangement, post office sites, a teacher supply agency and client schools, a chemicals firm and suppliers, and a ceramics firm and suppliers). Across the eight cases, we examined issues of franchises, agencies, public–private partnerships, supply chains, TUPE, and multiemployer sites. The full research team was Mick Marchington (coordinator), Damian Grimshaw, Jill Rubery, Hugh Willmott, Marilyn Carroll, Fang Lee Cooke, Jill Earnshaw, Irena Grugulis, John Hassard, Gail Hebson, and Steven Vincent.
24. We have elaborated this argument elsewhere in order to set out the implications of applying a dynamic, integrated analysis of employment and organizational forms for the study of human resource management and employment law (Rubery et al. 2002; Rubery and Earnshaw 2005), industrial relations (Marchington, Rubery, and Cooke 2004; Rubery et al. 2003), organizational studies (Grimshaw et al. 2005), employment law (Cooke et al. 2004; Earnshaw, Rubery, and Cooke 2002), and economics (Grimshaw and Rubery 2005).
25. I should perhaps point out that it is not a Smithian analysis, first because, not surprisingly, Smith did not write much about relationships within large organizations, and second, though inspired by Smith, my application of his ideas is selective and not intended to be faithful. Neither does it endorse the Adam Smith invented by mainstream economists as a one-dimensional defender of self-interest.
26. Although it seems natural to invoke Weber here, he ironically fell prey to the modernist tendency to de-rationalize and subjectivize values and hence render practical reason and emotional reason unintelligible.
27. This is an implicit challenge to Marxism's valuation of labor as an end in itself (see O'Neill 1998).
28. As Smith well understood, people need others—he wrote of the 'horrors of solitude'—for their sociability and for recognition and approval, and are capable of appreciating others for their own sake and respecting them.
29. This tendency is probably gendered and classed, and perhaps ethnically variable, being more common amongst men and those who do not have inherited advantages.
30. Here, I am stretching the concept of internal goods beyond MacIntyre's formulation, so as to include not only elite activities, such as architecture or medicine, but more basic ones.
31. While their analysis of the economy of esteem is valuable, I think Brennan and Pettit underplay the importance that people attach to internal goods and 'praiseworthy acts' and to the welfare of others, even if it fails to bring

recognition or praise. There is satisfaction to be had in the successful completion of the task in itself, even if no one else notices it. I think it is also a mistake to represent the nature of relations of esteem primarily through the metaphor of economy, when it should be taken as a matter of justice and morality.

32. There are parallels here with Smith's 'impartial spectator', though the latter's scope goes beyond judgments of esteem to all moral evaluation.
33. This is underestimated in Brennan and Pettit's account: they tend to see esteem as a competitive zero sum affair, so that if all succeed, esteem and self-esteem are neutralized. For many tasks there are absolute criteria of quality or adequacy of performance, and especially if there is some cooperation among the workers, then even in a group where everyone achieves them, their satisfaction is a source of self-esteem.
34. 'In the realm of ends everything has either a *price* or a *dignity*. Whatever has a price can be replaced by something else as its equivalent; on the other hand, whatever is above all price, and therefore admits of no equivalence, has a dignity.' (Kant).
35. This insight is due to Hegel's celebrated analysis of the master–slave dialectic.
36. A distinction might be drawn here, following Charles Taylor (1994), between unconditional recognition for people simply as human beings, and conditional recognition, which depends on behavior and character. Esteem is a conditional form of recognition. While it might appear that unequal conditional recognition is compatible with unconditional equal recognition for personhood, in a society structured by class, gender, 'race' and other key inequalities, which have little or nothing to do with merit, access of individuals to practices and situations in which they can earn esteem is highly unequal (Sayer 2005).
37. This focus of attention on the position in Britain and other developed economies means that the chapter does not examine the issue of how recent political and economic developments, including those arising from globalization and the activities of multinationals, are impacting on health and safety standards in other, emerging, ones. For a discussion which highlights the importance of this issue see Nichols (1997).
38. Throughout this Chapter we use the expressions 'job expansion' or 'job growth' to mean *net* job expansion (i.e. the net result of job creation and job destruction).
39. The criterion in the Stiglitz study is the median earnings in the *median cell*, not the median earnings of the labor force as such. In principle, these could be quite different.
40. While it is the case, of course, that the estimates of median earnings will be highly unstable for cells in which there are few cases, these cells also contribute virtually nothing to the patterns of job growth and thus these measurement problems cannot affect the overall results. The patterns are unchanged if small cells are dropped.
41. For details of the categories used for both the earlier and later periods see Wright and Dweyer (2003: Appendix A). The basic patterns of results in the 1980s and 1990s data were substantively the same when we used the simpler classification scheme used in the 1960s, so this shift in categories does not significantly affect our conclusion.

42. A comparison of patterns of job expansion in the 1990s using earnings as the basis for indexing jobs and a number of other indicators—SEI, education, and unemployment rates—is presented in Wright and Dweyer (2003: Appendix B).
43. This will be especially the case where there are relatively steep seniority wage trajectories in a job, since in such cases newly hired younger people in a period of rapid job growth are likely to have lower earnings than the median person already in the job.
44. It is important *not* to interpret the results from the study of patterns of job expansion as bearing directly on the question of changes in income distribution. In principle one could have absolutely even growth of jobs across the distribution of job types and still have rapidly increasing income inequality—either because the spread of income across job types was increasing or because earnings inequality within job types was increasing.
45. A detailed discussion of the data is available in Wright and Dwyer (2003: Appendix A).
46. Contrary to much popular opinion, part-time employment did not increase as a proportion of the labor force in recent years and in fact declined in the course of the 1990s expansion from 18.1 percent of employment in 1992 to 16.2 percent in 2000 (Bureau of Labor Statistics data). For a discussion of trends in part-time work, see Levenson (1996).
47. There is a certain arbitrariness in any effort at disaggregating broad occupational categories into more homogeneous components. We did not adopt a mechanical decision rule, since we needed to balance pragmatic considerations about generating reasonably large categories, conceptual issues of the homogeneity of the content of different occupations, and empirical issues of their homogeneity with respect to the criterion of median earnings. In order to see if our specific disaggregation choices affected the results we examined the general patterns of job growth under a number of different occupational breakdowns, and in no case were the basic patterns substantially affected.
48. For the full list of occupational codes for each period, see Wright and Dwyer (2003: Appendix A2).
49. See Wright and Dwyer (2003: Appendix A2) for details of the sector coding.
50. For details of measurement issues connected to the earnings variable, see Wright and Dwyer (2003: Appendix A3).
51. Since jobs come in lumpy units, it is not possible to aggregate the rank ordered jobs into groups each containing exactly 20 percent of employment. Thus, for example, of the five quintiles in 1992, one (the 4th quintile) contained 21.3 percent of employment and one (the highest quintile) 18.7 percent. None of the patterns we will be examining are significantly affected by these deviations from equal quintile categories.
52. Job growth was especially marked in the top *decile*, which accounted for 3.2 million of the nearly 5.5 million job expansion in the top quintile. The bottom decile also showed relatively strong growth: 1.75 million jobs of the 3 million in the bottom quintile occurred in the bottom decile.
53. It might be objected that these results are affected by (a) the exclusion of part-time work, and (b) by the growth of the kinds of jobs filled by young workers rather than

the core adult part of the labor force. In analyses not shown here, neither of these factors account for the patterns observed. For details, see Wright and Dwyer (2003: Appendix C).

54. As explained in detail in Wright and Dwyer (2003: Appendix A1), there are a number of gaps in this time series: (1). The data were unreliable for the early 1960s, so we had to begin the 1960s expansion in 1963 rather than 1961; (2) There were also data problems in the early 1970s—there was a short contraction and short expansion in this period—so we begin the 1970s data with the 1973–4 contraction; and (3) The occupational categories changed in 1983, so we begin the 1980s expansion in 1983 rather than 1982. The time series ends in 2002 because in 2003 the CPS adopted the radically new occupational classification scheme used by the US Census in 2000.
55. As noted earlier, increasing income inequality is in principle consistent with a completely flat pattern of job growth across job-quality quintiles because (a) the income spread between the best and worst job-types could be increasing even if both types of jobs are growing at the same rate, and (b) increasing earnings inequality can occur within job-types.
56. It is important to remember that in the 1960s data we could not differentiate Hispanic whites from non-Hispanic, so the categories are not strictly comparable in the two periods. In any case, the percent of blacks in the job expansion in the top quintile increased from 4.5 percent in the 1960s to 13.3 percent in the 1990s.
57. Immigration data were available in the CPS only beginning in 1994. 'Immigrants' are here defined as 'foreign born'. There is no implication that these jobs were filled by people who immigrated in this period, but simply that they were foreign born.
58. The contrast between the 1980s and 1990s is especially sharp for services involving high human capital: business services, FIRE, public administration, miscellaneous professional services, medical services and educational services. The middle quintile of these sectors combined contributed just under 10 percent to total job expansion in the 1980s, but −1 percent in the 1990s.
59. The Immigration and Naturalization Service (2001) estimated that 'About 5.0 million illegal undocumented immigrants were residing in the United States in October 1996 with a range of about 4.6 to 5.4 million.... The population was estimated to be growing by about 275,000 each year.' Many—perhaps most—of these undocumented immigrants would be missing from both the census population estimates used to generate sample weights and in the CPS surveys themselves. For a discussion of undercounts of low-income populations in surveys using weights derived from the census, see Juhn and Potter (1999) and Anderson and Fienberg (1999).
60. If we look at the bottom *decile* of jobs, then retail and personal services make up 86 percent of the job growth (1.5 million jobs) in the 1990s, i.e. most of the growth in these two sectors in the bottom quintile actually occurs in the bottom decile of the job structure.
61. As indicated earlier, the contribution of the bottom quintile of jobs to total job expansion increased from 10 percent in the 1960s to 15 percent in the 1970s and 20 percent in the 1980s and 1990s. This trend is consistent with the trend in the erosion of the minimum wage: it was at a peak in the late 1960s, eroded slowly in the 1970s and more rapidly in the 1980s.

62. Details are presented in Wright and Dwyer (2003: Appendix A2). Our classification of high-tech sectors is based on work by Benner (1998) supplemented by personal communications with Benner.
63. It is possible, of course, depending upon patterns of cohabitation and family size, that people working in jobs in the bottom quintile of the employment structure may not actually have standards of living that fall below the poverty line. A two-earner household in which each working spouse worked full time at the minimum wage would have a household income just above the official poverty line. Nevertheless, the expansion of poorly paid employment is one of the factors that increases the weight of the working poor in the American structure of inequality.
64. The Earned Income Tax Credit is a move in the direction of partially delinking income and job-earnings, thus softening the impact on people's lives of increasing polarization in the job structure. A more radical extension of this delinking would be a full-blown negative income tax or an unconditional basic income (Van Parijs et al. 2001).
65. For a discussion of the implications for mobility prospects of immigrants of a structure of economic opportunity increasingly being marked by a polarized structure of menial jobs at the bottom and high-wage jobs requiring a college degree at the top, with little in the middle, see Portes and Zhou (1993).

Index

Lightning Source UK Ltd.
Milton Keynes UK
UKHW010642130223
416869UK00003B/200

9 780199 291779